The Holocaust and North Africa

The Holocaust and North Africa

Edited by

Aomar Boum and

Sarah Abrevaya Stein

Stanford University Press

Stanford, California

Stanford University Press
Stanford, California

Published in association with the United States Holocaust Memorial Museum.

Library of Congress Cataloging-in-Publication Data

Boum, Aomar, editor. | Stein, Sarah Abrevaya, editor.
The Holocaust and North Africa / edited by Aomar Boum and Sarah Abrevaya Stein.
Stanford, California : Stanford University Press, 2018. | Includes bibliographical references and index.
Identifiers: LCCN 2018004661 (print) | LCCN 2018021135 (ebook) |
    ISBN 9781503607064 (e-book) | ISBN 9781503605435(cloth) |
    ISBN 9781503607057(paperback)
Subjects: LCSH: Holocaust, Jewish (1939–1945)—Africa, North. |
    Jews—Persecutions—Africa, North—History. | Antisemitism—
    Africa, North—History. | World War, 1939–1945—Africa, North. |
    Collective memory—Africa, North.
Classification: LCC DS135.A25 (ebook) | LCC DS135.A25 H65 2018 (print) | DDC
    940.53/180961—dc23
LC record available at https://lccn.loc.gov/2018004661

Cover designer: Rob Ehle

Cover photograph: Sidi Mahrez Mosque, Tunis, early 1943. Bundesarchiv.

Typeset by Bruce Lundquist in 11/13.5 Adobe Garamond Pro

Contents

The Holocaust and North Africa

Introduction

Aomar Boum and Sarah Abrevaya Stein

"**WHAT WOULD I HAVE DONE** if I had been a German Jew on his way, with all his family, to the gas chambers, or, worse, condemned to become a slave member of these unimaginable Sonderkommandos, expected to throw his own co-religionists in the flames of ovens, before being thrown there in his turn?" This question motivated Algerian writer Anouar Benmalek to craft *Fils de Shéol* (Son of Shéol), a new work of fiction that reflects the burgeoning interest in the Holocaust among francophone Algerian novelists.[1] *Fils de Shéol* intertwines the stories of three generations of a single family tarred by multiple genocides: a German teenager, Karl, on his way to the Nazi gas chambers of Poland; his father, Manfred, a *Kapo*; his mother Elisa, an Algerian Jewish woman marked by French colonialism; and his grandfather, Ludwig, who served the German army in colonial southwest Africa (present-day Namibia), where he witnessed the genocide of the Herero. As Benmalek argues in a series of interviews prompted by the book, *Fils de Shéol* is also motivated by the sense that it is time for Africa to reclaim its own histories of genocide, beginning with the case of the Herero.[2] So it is that Benmalek, a Moroccan-born Algerian Muslim author, co-founder of the Algerian Committee Against Torture, has written a work that fictively integrates the history of the Holocaust, North Africa, colonial acts of genocide in Africa, Muslims, Jews, and their complexly intertwined—and sometimes conflictual—forms of collective memory.

It is striking that *Fils de Shéol*, a gripping and haunting novel, triangulates North African history with the Holocaust by way of Namibia and a German teenager. The historical connections between the Holocaust and colonial violence have been amply explored, to be sure, enumerated by theoreticians of colonialism since the 1940s (including W. E. B. Dubois, Aimé Césaire, Frantz Fanon, Hannah Arendt, and Jean-Paul Sartre).[3] Yet a shorter, more direct vector links the Maghreb and the Holocaust more than even these writers recognized. The Holocaust, after all, has a North African dimension of its own, albeit one that has been hitherto unexplored. It is the aim of this pioneering volume to flesh out our understanding of the ways the Holocaust unfolded in North Africa, a region considered marginal, if not to World War II (which was fought in part on North African soil), then to the racial and genocidal policies of the Nazis and their allies.

In this introduction we begin by offering a short historical survey of the Holocaust's manifestations in German-, French-, and Italian-occupied North Africa. In addition, though with considerably more brevity, we describe the circumstances that faced Jews from North Africa who found themselves in Europe over the course of World War II. A second, somewhat more meditative section returns us to the probing questions raised by Benmalek's *Fils de Shéol*: Why has North Africa been written out of Holocaust history and memory, and, conversely, why has the Holocaust been excised from so many narratives about North Africa? Finally, a last section introduces the reader to the essays that follow. Here, we suggest—as do the essayists themselves—that alongside a penetrating silence about the Holocaust and North Africa there exists a rich body of texts, voices, and archives that await our attention.

Jews, Muslims, and the Holocaust in North Africa: A Historical Overview

On the eve of World War II, the Maghreb was home to one of the largest and socially vibrant Jewish populations in the Islamic world. Most of these Jews were indigenous to the region, with a history that dated to the pre-Islamic period. Others immigrated to North Africa during the Spanish Inquisition or after their exile from Iberia, settling in northern urban centers such as Tétouan and Oran. By the modern period, Jews constituted an overall minority in North Africa, with Muslims (Arab and Amazigh, or "Berber") the dominant population. Still, in certain cities and towns, Jews made up a significant percentage (and/or highly visible portion) of the whole, with many playing influential roles as artisans and merchants.

The total population of North African Jewry hovered at half a million before the outbreak of the second global conflict of the twentieth century. In 1941 a census by the French wartime government based in Vichy put the number of Algerian Jews at nearly 110,000 and counted an additional small population of foreign Jews. Neighboring Tunisia claimed 80,000 Jews and Morocco 240,000. Forty thousand Jews lived in Libya during its protracted Italian colonization, concentrated primarily in Tripoli and Benghazi. All told, Jews in interwar North Africa lived under different legal regimes, spoke a variety of languages, hewed to different *minhagim* (religious rituals), and could claim diverse ancestries. They were less a single, discrete population than an internally diverse one.

Most of the Jews in interwar Algeria were citizens of France, according to the 1870 Crémieux Decree.[4] In Morocco and Tunisia the Jews (like their Muslim neighbors) were colonial subjects rather than citizens, but their legal and social rights were generally protected and a significant number of Tunisian Jews became French citizens in 1926, according to the Morinaud Law.[5] Although it is difficult to generalize, one could argue that Jews were perceived as "native" by most Muslims, but many Jews nonetheless lived in separate neighborhoods (known in Morocco as a *mellah* and in Tunisia as a *hara*) and followed a traditional way of life influenced by rabbinic authority.[6] At the same time, North African Jews' exposure to French, Spanish, and Italian culture (especially to the Alliance Israélite Universelle, the Franco-Jewish philanthropy and educational organization) since at least the nineteenth century prompted waves of modernization and embourgoisement, leading Jews to become vehicles of social and cultural change not only for their communities but for the Maghreb as a whole.

These populations experienced different legal and political regimes before the war and thus experienced World War II in different ways as colonial rule was complexly overlaid with fascism. As in Europe, in North Africa the Holocaust was not a single affair, nor did it hew to a single chronology.

When Germany occupied France in May 1940, the terms of the armistice divided the country in two. Germany assumed control over northern occupied France; the southern third of France and its North African colonies (their colonial bureaucracy still largely intact) was led from the city of Vichy, under the oversight of Marshal Henri Philippe Pétain. Vichy policy would differ across Morocco, Algeria, and Tunisia, much as Nazi policy differed across Ukraine, Belarus, and the Baltic states. Daniel Schroeter's and Ruth Ginio's contributions to this volume (Chapters 1 and 3, respectively) help parse the complexity of Vichy law (as does Jens Hoppe's contribution [Chapter 2], which looks at the nuances of Italian fascist law in colonial Libya). We therefore summarize this history only tersely here.

The Vichy regime adopted its first anti-Jewish statute in October 1940, determining that Jews in mainland France and Algeria were to be defined by race—that is, based on the religion of their grandparents. These Jews found themselves barred from public office, including governmental work, the military, and classroom instruction in all but Jewish schools. The same month, the Vichy regime overturned the Crémieux Decree, which had granted French citizenship to most Algerian Jews in 1870. With this ruling, Algerian Jews became stateless overnight. In neighboring Morocco and Tunisia (as discussed by Susan Gilson Miller and Daniel Lee in Chapters 12 and 6, respectively), where most Jews were, legally speaking, colonial subjects rather than citizens, Vichy law defined Jews differently, as part of a religious community and not a racial group. The distinction allowed the Jewish communities in question to maintain a degree of autonomy throughout the war, even during the short occupation of Tunisia by German authorities (November 1942–May 1943).

Although Morocco and Algeria never fell under direct German control, Vichy authorities were all too willing to remain impassive when anti-Semitic settlers attacked Jews (and sometimes native Muslims) and targeted their property and businesses for spoliation after the introduction of the anti-Jewish laws. North African Jews who fell under the rule of Vichy, like the Jews of France, were barred from most sectors of the economy, with quotas (*numeri clausi*) limiting the number of Jews who could operate as teachers, lawyers, doctors, journalists, students in public schools and universities, and so on. The existential repercussions of this restriction were particularly heady for Algerian Jews, because they (in counterdistinction to Algerian Muslims) had long served the French bureaucracy and its political and legal institutions.[7] Jewish property was subsequently Aryanized by Vichy decree (the process was stalled in Tunisia because of the intervention of the bey), and Jews in Moroccan cities were forced to move from outlying neighborhoods into the *mellah*. The extent to which Moroccan Jews did (and did not) feel the sting of these measures is a question at the heart of the essays included here by Susan Gilson Miller, Alma Heckman, and Aomar Boum and Mohammed Hatimi (Chapters 12, 9, 5, respectively).

Beginning in 1940, the Vichy authorities established ribbons of penal, labor, and internment camps across the Maghreb and Sahara and repurposed existing camps to serve as wartime sites of internment.[8] In Italian-ruled Libya, as Jens Hoppe shows us in Chapter 2, these patterns were echoed but not duplicated. Meanwhile, hundreds of Jews of North African origin living in Paris and its environs were sent to the Drancy internment camp and, from there, to concentration and death camps in Eastern Europe.[9]

In the Maghreb and Sahara the inmate population included North African Jews (including some who held foreign passports), Allied prisoners of war, and an international population of men who participated in the Spanish Civil War on the side of the International Brigade. These camps, and the day-to-day experiences and subsequent literary constructions of their internees, are the subject of several essays in the present volume, including those by Aomar Boum, Lia Brozgal, and Susan Slyomovics (Chapters 7, 8, and 4, respectively). Together, the contributors explore virtually unexplored dimensions of the Holocaust, bringing the North African story of World War II ever more closely aligned and integrated with the European one.

In their co-authored essay, Hatimi and Boum revisit the effect of Vichy policies on the Jews of southern rural Morocco—and their implications for Jewish-Muslim relations in the region (Chapter 5). Although French authorities refrained from enforcing anti-Jewish laws and regulations

FIGURE 1: Jewish men in Tunis on their way to forced labor. Source: Bundesarchiv, Bild 183-J20382; photo: Lüken, December 1942. Reprinted with permission.

FIGURE 2: An unidentified worker walks by the railroad tracks at the Im Fout labor camp in Morocco, 1941–1942. Source: United States Holocaust Memorial Museum Archives, Washington, D.C., Photograph 50720, courtesy of Sami Dorra. Reprinted with permission.

in Morocco's south, war and drought had a deleterious (if indirect) effect on the businesses of local Jewish peddlers and merchants. At the same time, the economic crisis spawned by the war influenced legal and social customary relations between communities. For example, Muslim litigants (at times encouraged by French military officers) refused to repay loans to Jewish creditors or repossessed land sold to Jewish merchants before the war. Despite this turbulence, relations between the communities were in general positive, notwithstanding the fact that many local Jews were forced by economic circumstance to emigrate from their rural homes to the cities of Marrakesh, Essaouira, Casablanca, Taroudannt, and Agadir (even before so many left for destinations abroad).

Thus the Holocaust was experienced by Jews in North Africa through the implementation of French and Italian racial laws, the expropriation of property and economic disenfranchisement, and internment and forced labor. Some Maghrebi Jews were deported to death camps from North Africa; North African Jews living in France were deported from Western Europe. These events unfolded against a backdrop of war and what might be understood as a double occupation, by which French and Italian colonialism overlaid and interacted complexly with fascism.

Perhaps there is something in this history that dictates why the history of the Holocaust and North Africa has fallen between stools; is it, after all, because it sits comfortably on more than one? This, after all, is at once a European and a North African story—a story of the encounter between imperialism and fascism, colony and continent. In this, it finds singular peer with the island of Rhodes, the only colony other than Tunisia from which Jews were deported by the Nazis during World War II.

These ruminations return us to the foundational questions raised by Benmalek, with whom this Introduction began. What is at stake in studying the Holocaust and North Africa? Why has silence swirled around this topic, and when have voices filled the void? To address these questions, we move from the realm of history to the interactive realms of scholarship, literature, and memory.

Pushing the Boundaries of the Holocaust

Scholars' understanding of the geographic reach of the Holocaust has been expanding ever since scholarship on the topic first took shape. Germany, as a site of organized perpetration, was the spatial pivot of the earliest generation of Holocaust scholars. But the field has not been so limited for a long time. Today, scholars scrutinize the Holocaust through a dizzying variety of places and spaces, reimagining its geography (and chronology) with reference to overlooked diaries of Jews from Alsace to Warsaw, pilloried furniture of Paris, frozen bank accounts in Switzerland, the dismantled cemetery of Thessaloniki, the intricacies of Nazi policies in Ukraine, and German historical memory.[10] This geographically prismatic approach is mirrored in scholarship (and, as we have seen in Benmalek's case, fiction) that stretches the timeline of the Holocaust to encompass genocides before and after it and that interpolates the Holocaust through the history of decolonization and today's refugee crises (among other phenomena).[11] Literature on the subject seems continually to seek an ever wider array of voices and perspectives on the Holocaust and its victims and perpetrators. Given this spectrum of activity, the field of Holocaust studies has become dense and also fractured, and the question for a current generation of Holocaust scholars is not so much whether the study of the Holocaust has "limits" (in the formulation of Saul Friedländer's 1999 classic edited volume) but whether Holocaust historiography and Holocaust memory have (or should have) an "ethics" of its own.[12]

Yet it is a striking quality of the diverse field of Holocaust studies that, even as our information becomes ever more detailed—accommodating even the most fine-grained digital mappings of Nazi concentration camps[13]—entire geographic realms of Holocaust history remain opaque.[14] Our aim with this volume is to shed light on one such murky zone, North Africa, as part of an ongoing (and still incomplete) effort to flesh out the details and push the boundaries of Holocaust history.[15]

The opacity of this history is not accidental—or, better put, it has many causes. European-centered Holocaust studies have played a role in marginalizing the North African story, and the politicization of the Holocaust in Israel and the states of North Africa has rendered the topic historical taboo. In these contexts many scholars have been repulsed from exploring the impact of Nazi and Vichy-era anti-Jewish laws in North Africa during World War II (whether consciously or unconsciously)—or from unraveling the complex legacy of the war on the decades and diasporas that followed in its wake.

The essays in this volume consider a range of reasons for these omissions. Here, we highlight two. First, some scholars prefer to see the Holocaust as a continental affair. This argument tends to be formulated not so much de jure as de facto. We can see the rational at work in the finite European-bound geographic reach of many otherwise sophisticated historical surveys or documentary collections, even if few scholars would make the point with affirmative conviction. In her research on the myriad German women who participated in Nazi genocidal warfare, Wendy Lower writes that the Holocaust "was unfolding in different forms and at different stages across Europe; it was neither a foregone conclusion nor the comprehensive event that we perceive it as today."[16] This is a sober conclusion, but one that forestalls the current approach, imposing as it does implicit limits on the geographic reach of the Holocaust, even as multiply configured. The Shoah, the implication stands, was demarcated by the waters and political boundaries that bound Europe together: Whatever its complexities, geography defines it.

This position finds echoes in contemporary Israel, where the Holocaust has long been claimed as a European Jewish trauma and, at the same time, a generalizably Israeli one.[17] The results are contradictory. On the one hand, Israeli Jewish youth of North African and Middle Eastern heritage (along with Muslim citizens of the state) are expected to be swept up, along with all other Israelis, in the public witnessing and commemoration of European Holocaust history, a component even of kindergarten education in Israel.[18] On the other hand, Middle Eastern and North African Jewish histories—including the Holocaust chapter of the North African Jewish story—are terribly underrepresented in curricula and textbooks, constituting, in the visual vocabulary of the Mizrahi artist and activist Meir Gal, only "9 out of 400" pages of the typical Israeli textbook.[19]

Taking the view from the Maghreb, we become attuned to a second and converse point. For some scholars of North Africa the Holocaust chapter is a distraction from a larger history and point. The spotlight is shifted away from the long history of colonial violence against Muslims and toward a history of Jewish persecution. Other scholars of North Africa and the Arab world raise questions about the scholarly attention afforded the Nazi death machine. They argue that there are too many publications about the Holocaust and therefore no need for further inquiry. Whether for these reasons or others, we can find, among surveys and documentary histories on North Africa, an uncanny, inverse parallel to the previous trend: the topical elision of World War II.

There are exceptions to these trends. Michel Abitbol authored a pioneering work in 1983, and a variety of publications in French, Hebrew,

German, and English followed.[20] This oeuvre includes encyclopedic work produced by Yad Vashem: The World Holocaust Remembrance Center and a number of memory books generated by communities of North African descent in Israel.[21] In Washington, D.C., the United States Holocaust Memorial Museum is gathering archival material on Vichy France and its policies in North Africa and is nurturing scholarship on the period. More recently, a 2016 special issue of *Revue d'Histoire de la Shoah* is a collaboration between Paris's Mémorial de la Shoah: Musée et Centre de Documentation and Jerusalem's Ben-Zvi Institute for the Study of Jewish Communities in the East. This special issue, titled "The Jews of the Middle East Confront Nazism and the Shoah (1930–1945)," translates for readers of French recent trends in Hebrew scholarship on the topic.[22] Edited by Haim Saadoun (also a contributor to the present volume) and Georges Bensoussan, the contributors to the journal issue argue that the Holocaust had a powerful and hitherto underestimated reach into North Africa and the eastern Arab world, where (Bensoussan argues in a forceful editorial) Muslim indifference to Jewish suffering laid the foundation for Jews' subsequent embrace of Zionism and emigration.[23] Although this position finds echo in contributions to the current volume, our editorial emphasis is on filling in neglected historical details rather than advancing a position as self-consciously opinionated as Bensoussan's.

In nonacademic circles in Israel too, scholars are beginning to attend to Mizrahi and Maghrebi Jewish history after a long period of silence and sometimes deliberate marginalization.[24] As early as the late 1960s, the Israeli government became alarmed that Sephardi and Mizrahi Jews in Israel perceived the Holocaust as a European Jewish story.[25] Over time, this realization led to the development of educational and political programs that sought to transform the Holocaust into a unifying Jewish and Israeli narrative, one accepted by Mizrahi and Sephardi Israelis as well as by Ashkenazi Israelis. This shift required activism and governmental incentive; Mizrahi activists pushed for education on and public awareness of North African and Middle Eastern Jewish history and culture, including the periods of French, Spanish, Italian, and German colonialism and the Holocaust.[26] The partial success of these efforts is reflected in a recent Israeli Ministry of Education mandate to teach Mizrahi history in public schools.[27]

Writers of fiction have also helped to bring Holocaust-era North Africa to light. Yossi Sucary, an Israeli author of Libyan background, has joined the tide of those critical of the Ashkenazi hegemonic discourse that continues to prevail in Israel.[28] Sucary's 2016 novel *From Benghazi to Bergen-Belsen*, inspired by the author's mother's history, presents the story of Silvana, a young woman whose family lived a comfortable life in Benghazi until they were deported by Nazi officers to the German concentration camp of Bergen-Belsen. In Bergen-Belsen they experienced the hardships of internment, weathering snow and bitter cold as well as the degradation endemic to Nazi camps.[29] *From Benghazi to Bergen-Belsen* has become an integral part of the educational curriculum in Israel. Still, Sucary remains a critic of what he understands to be Israel's historical erasure of a portion of its citizenry. Sucary has dwelled on this erasure with stark cynicism.

I wanted to believe that the Nazis' bullets, which struck the heads of my mother's 12- and 13-year-old cousins with frightening precision, accidently missed the history books of the State of Israel. . . . I wanted to believe that when Nachum Goldman, the President of the World Zionist Organization, rejected my aunt Saloma, who asked to receive reparations after her young son was shot at point-blank range by the Germans, he did so because he truly believed his own words: "You have never seen a German in your life, you have an Oriental Imagination."[30]

Haunted by a history unwritten and ignored, Sucary nonetheless acknowledges the slow but steady transformation in Israeli attitudes and policies toward North African cultures, histories, and memories. "And now, without a shred of cynicism, I want to believe that despite not having even an ounce of bitterness over these historical distortions, I am very happy that things have changed over the past few years, that justice has been served. That is enough for me."[31]

Moving from Israel to the Maghreb, we find that North African writers are also beginning to fill a deep void of silence, sometimes despite a degree of personal risk. After all, the embrace of research on Jewish and Holocaust history in the Maghrebi and Middle Eastern contexts is associated with a degree of public stigma. Anouar Benmalek has even incurred death threats for his validation of the Holocaust.[32]

In Germany the historians of the Claims Conference and the process of German *Wiedergutmachung* (granting of reparations) have uncovered North African Jewish histories of the Holocaust that were buried in the archives. Propelled by the need to indemnify and constantly rethink categories of reparations set in the 1950s, these scholars—including Jens Hoppe, who is represented in this volume—have been indefatigable in documenting the unfolding of the Shoah in North Africa and in paving the way for survivors of certain Algerian war camps to receive reparations.[33]

Despite these considerable strides in attending to the history of the Holocaust and North Africa, from the perspective of scholarship, justice has not been served. The existing landmark work on the history of the Holocaust in North Africa demands to be expanded, updated. This becomes all the more true as even more original documentation about the Holocaust in North Africa is collected, cataloged, and made available to researchers. Today, original, largely unexplored documentation pertaining to the Holocaust in North Africa abounds in archives (and private hands) in North Africa, France, Israel, the United States, and beyond. What's more, there is a wealth of published (or otherwise available) memoiristic and *lieu de mémoire* literature, some of which is explored in this volume. Rich sources surround us, and it is time for scholars of North Africa, Europe, and the Holocaust to attend to the stories they tell.

The Holocaust and North Africa: About this Book

This book offers a series of North African histories of the Holocaust— the emphasis being on the Holocaust *and* North Africa, because we cannot offer a complete account of the Holocaust *in* North Africa and because our focus encompasses not only the years of trauma but also the impact of the Holocaust on North African Jews and Muslims in the postwar period and its ongoing reverberations through memoir, memory, literature, and politics.

The essays that constitute this book seek not only to flesh out our skeletal understanding of the history of the Holocaust in North Africa but also to hone in on the sometimes dramatic and sometimes subtle manifestations of this history, country by country and region by region. Significantly, our gaze is not just on coastal cities, which tend to receive the most scholarly attention; we also look at rural sites and communities, including the Moroccan *bled* (the pre-Saharan region of rural Morocco) and the Sahara, where the Vichy regime built so many wartime labor and concentration camps. Libya and French West Africa, other neglected zones of the Holocaust, also receive attention here, allowing us to broaden and deepen the overall historical landscape. Finally, the essays in this volume meditate on the question of how central the Maghrebi story is to the holistic Holocaust narrative. This approach generates novel observations on North Africa and World War II based on new historical and ethnographic sources.

The contributors to Part I, Daniel Schroeter, Jens Hoppe, and Ruth Ginio, explore the intersecting and overlapping political contexts that provided the political bedrock for World War II in Morocco, Tunisia, Algeria, Libya, and French West Africa, considering the nuanced unfolding of policy "where colonialism and fascism meet." The contributors in Part II, Susan Slyomovics, Aomar Boum and Mohammed Hatimi, and Daniel Lee, shed light on individuated stories of occupation, internment, and race laws in Vichy North Africa. In Part III contributors Aomar Boum, Lia Brozgal, and Alma Heckman explore the ways in which the Holocaust and war reverberated across North Africa, producing novel narratives and influencing the course of politicized Jews.

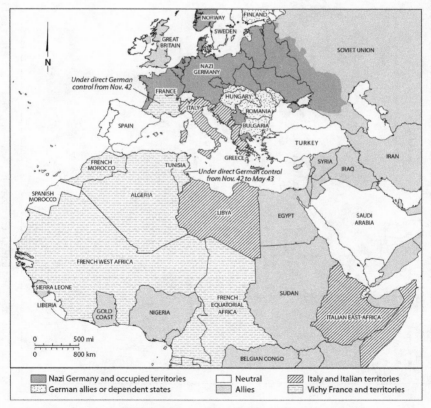

MAP 1: French-occupied North Africa and French West Africa, c. 1942

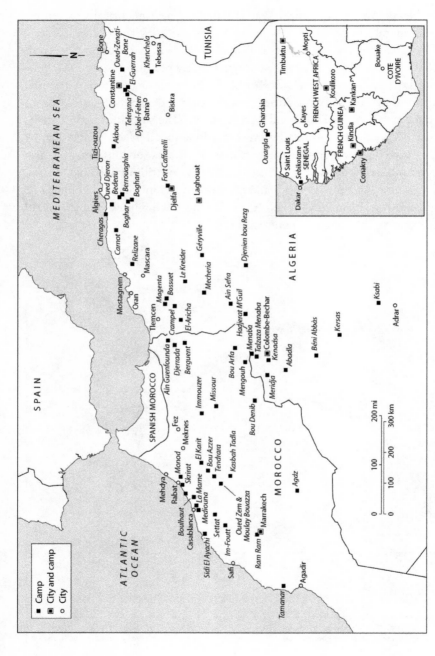

MAP 2: Penal, labor, and internment camps in French-occupied North Africa and French West Africa.

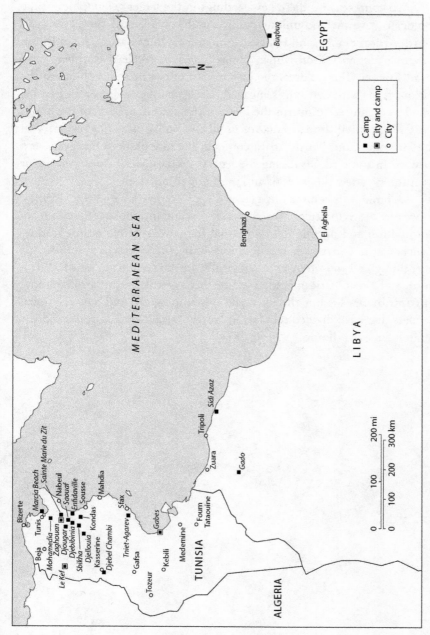

MAP 3: Penal, labor, and internment Camps in German-occupied Tunisia and Italian-occupied Libya

To contextualize these new readings in the larger geographies of the Holocaust, we include unique comments by scholars of the Holocaust, North Africa, France, and Holocaust memory: Omer Bartov, Susan Rubin Suleiman, Susan Gilson Miller, Haim Saadoun, Michael Rothberg, and Todd Presner. They address the importance of the present volume to the various fields with which it is engaged. These comments appear in Part IV, which is organized to mirror the focus of the preceding parts of the book.

Readers will find circularity in all the book's parts, as the story of the Holocaust and North Africa compels one to look both backward and forward in time, reconsidering the legacy of colonialism, for example, or questioning anew the roots of anti- and postcolonialism.

All told, this volume fills a layered void. It unveils forgotten histories, showcases hitherto neglected archival stories, and interpolates them—from both within and outside the traditional framework of Holocaust studies. Crucially, the essays gathered here weave together a conversation carried out, though all too often nondialogically, in the American, Israeli, European, and North African academy. Together, our diverse and brilliant pool of contributors disrupt the regional, epistemological, and conversational borders that have divided scholars in North Arica, Israel, Europe, and the United States until now.

Part I   Where Fascism and Colonialism Meet

1

Between Metropole and French North Africa
Vichy's Anti-Semitic Legislation and Colonialism's Racial Hierarchies

Daniel J. Schroeter

ON MARCH 14, 1943, the French high commissioner in North Africa, General Henri Giraud, abrogated the Crémieux Decree, the 1870 law that had granted French citizenship to Algerian Jews. Since Operation Torch, the Allied invasion of North Africa beginning on November 8, 1942, and the rapid takeover of Morocco and Algeria, Jewish leaders in Algeria were demanding the restitution of their rights, which had been stripped from them by the Vichy government. However, the anti-Semitic laws of the Vichy regime were not to be quickly rescinded: The Americans had struck a deal with the French to cease the hostilities and to induce them to join the Allied side. Consequently, much of the administration that had previously served the Vichy government remained intact in the North African colonies. Admiral François Darlan, who had commanded the French forces for the Vichy government, continued his command in cooperation with the Allies until his assassination on Christmas eve, and a few days later, in the last days of 1942, General Giraud assumed his position.[1]

Giraud's decree on March 14 came amid public pressure to rescind the anti-Semitic legislation that had been implemented across French North Africa by the Vichy government. Jewish organizations and government officials and leaders in Britain and the United States, including President Roosevelt, had campaigned for the repeal of the racial laws. But Giraud and many of the French authorities in Algeria who had previously served the Vichy administration, including Marcel Peyrouton, who was appointed governor-general in January and who had been a prominent figure in the Vichy regime, were opposed to lifting the discriminatory laws, claiming that it might inflame Muslim opinion against the government and that this would be dangerous during wartime. Allied forces were then engaged in fierce battles to recover Tunisia, which was occupied by German and Italian forces from the time of Operation Torch in November 1942, and many American officials supported the position advocated by French officials.[2] But on March 14, 1943, General Giraud succumbed to pressures and reluctantly repealed Vichy's racial laws, yet at the same time he abrogated the Crémieux Decree. Girard justified the latter action in a speech in which he declared that "the suppression of these laws or decrees reestablished the French tradition of human liberty and the return to equality for all before the law. . . . With the desire to eliminate all racial discrimination, the Crémieux Decree, which in 1870 established a difference between Muslims and Jews, is abrogated."[3]

Jewish leaders and organizations and some American and British journalists expressed outrage at this discriminatory measure, which deprived Jews of their citizenship, claiming that it was intended to appease the Muslim population. The American Jewish Committee enlisted Hannah Arendt in its campaign, publishing and disseminating her article "Why the Crémieux Decree Was Abrogated." In an incisive analysis of the history of anti-Semitism in Algeria, Arendt indicts the colonial administration, "that is even more anti-Jewish than anti-native," for its repeal of the decree that would effectively place Jews in a worse position than the Muslims. In Arendt's interpretive framework, imperialism and anti-Semitism were closely linked. It was, according to Arendt, the "French colonials" who implemented the measure, because they were no longer controlled by metropolitan France. Arendt proposes that Giraud "acted as an agent of those French colonials who always wanted to bring under their 'dictatorship' the only part of the Algerian population that so far had escaped their arbitrary and selfish rule" (namely, the Jews). Arendt continues, "The French colonials, in other words, took advantage of France's defeat and of their freedom from the control of the mother country in order to introduce into Algeria a measure which they would never have been able to obtain through legal channels."[4] Arendt distinguishes between the metropolitan efforts through governors appointed in Paris to assimilate and naturalize Algerian Muslims, and the French colonials who were intent on maintaining the natives in an inferior status to better exploit their cheap labor. In Arendt's view, metropolitan France had a mitigating effect on Algeria, but with France under Nazi occupation, there was nothing to prevent the violation of the rule of law.

Curiously, Arendt does not devote attention in her article to the anti-Semitic Statut des Juifs (Statute for the Jews) of October 3, 1940 (revised in 1941), and does not even mention its repeal in March 1943 on the very same day that the Crémieux Decree was abrogated. Even more surprisingly, Arendt makes no reference to the fact that the Crémieux Decree of 1870 was first abrogated in October 1940 a few days after the Statut des Juifs was enacted. Jews had therefore already been stripped of their citizenship rights by the Vichy government, and the decree's second repeal by Giraud was therefore considered particularly egregious. The technical reason that Giraud deemed it necessary to re-abrogate the Crémieux Decree was that the decree would have been reinstated, because all the laws and statutes since the installation of the Vichy government had been declared null and void. Giraud's declaration that the measure was needed to eliminate racial discrimination was a pretext to do just the opposite. As I argue, the overriding concern was that the restoration of Jewish political rights would spur Muslim demands for political rights, which would challenge French colonial rule and the racial hierarchy on which it was based.

Ironically, the annulment of the Crémieux Decree in 1940 was the first explicitly anti-Jewish measure implemented by the Vichy government in French North Africa.[5] In retrospect, it is unknown whether Hannah Arendt willfully omitted this essential fact—that this was the second abrogation of the Crémieux Decree—and amid the turbulence of the war, it is unclear how much of the details of Vichy rule in Algeria were known. The abrogation of the Crémieux Decree in 1940, however, did come at the behest of the metropolitan authorities and was not a separate measure by the colonial administrators of Algeria, who were still considered an integral part of France under the Vichy government.

If Arendt was unaware of the previous abrogation of the Crémieux Decree in 1940, as implied in her article, she was certainly aware of the repeal of the racial legislation of the Vichy government, which was broadcast internationally, as the editors of the American Jewish Committee's journal remarked in the preface to Arendt's article. Arendt's omission of the repeal of the anti-Semitic legislation does raise a fundamental question about how to interpret the relationship of the French empire to the Holocaust. After all, it was the abrogation of the Crémieux Decree, the focus of Arendt's article, that most clearly revealed the close connection between imperialism and anti-Semitism, and it was the Statut des Juifs, based on the Nuremberg racial laws, that explicitly showed the relationship of National Socialism to colonial North Africa. Arendt's focus on the Crémieux Decree and its abrogation rather than the anti-Jewish statute draws our attention to the history of colonial anti-Semitism in Algeria, which, as noted in her article, was part and parcel of an ideology of exploitation of the Muslim population.

Yet can we disentangle the abrogation of the Crémieux Decree, for which many French settlers advocated, from the radical anti-Semitic legislation of the Nazis, implemented by the Vichy government with few modifications in France and the colonies? If we accept the argument that the Holocaust was rooted in European imperialism, as Arendt later argues in *The Origins of Totalitarianism* (1951), can we then infer that National Socialism, expressed through the anti-Semitic legislation, was also integral to the history of colonialism? By leaving out of her analysis the connection between the abrogation of the Crémieux Decree and the Nazi-influenced Statut des Juifs, Arendt seems to suggest otherwise.[6]

The Holocaust *and* or *in* North Africa?

The anti-Semitic legislation of the Vichy government in the colonies revealed that "the long reach" of the Holocaust extended to Europe's southern Mediterranean shores,[7] even if the consequences were much less lethal than in Europe. The Jews of North Africa were spared the horrors of the European extermination camps and thus have been largely excluded from histories of the Holocaust that focus on the destruction of European Jewry.

Although the Maghreb remains very much on the margins of the larger field of Holocaust studies, since the 1970s scholars have produced a body of literature on the effects of the Vichy regime and Germany on the Jews in North Africa during World War II. The impetus for these studies, largely produced in Israel, is to integrate North African Jews into the World War II and Holocaust narrative and to include the testimonies of Jews from Arab lands.[8] Since the foundation of the State of Israel, the Holocaust has been a fundamental part of Israel's national identity. But the Holocaust narrative has been all about the destruction of European Jewry, and the Mizrahim (as Jews from Asia and Africa are called) in Israel have not been seen as part of that story.

After the mass immigration from Middle Eastern and North African countries to Israel in the 1950s, it became all the more imperative for the European Zionist leadership to educate the population as a whole on the Holocaust as being central to Israeli national identity, including those populations whose origins were from countries distant from the European death camps. Holocaust education as a way to unify the nation was a prime objective of Israel's official Holocaust institution, Yad Vashem (The Holocaust Martyrs' and Heroes' Remembrance Authority). The Eichmann trial (1961–1962) also had a crucial didactic purpose: to unify the country through survivor testimonies, which then shaped Israel's collective memory of the Holocaust. Mizrahim were to identify with the Holocaust narrative, not as *their* story but as part of the more general experience of the Jewish people. However, this only served to reinforce the sense of exclusion and discrimination that they felt in Israel.

The mobilization of ethnic politics, especially since the defeat of the Labor Party in 1977, caused a shift in discourse regarding Mizrahim and the Holocaust. Rather than rejecting the Holocaust as a story of Ashkenazim, Mizrahim and especially some North African Jews sought to inscribe themselves in the Holocaust narrative from which they had been excluded, and scholarship followed suit. Studies on the impact of the Vichy regime and Germany on the Jews in North Africa have thus been shaped by political questions pertaining to the exclusion or inclusion of Mizrahim in the larger history of the Holocaust.[9]

The inclusion of the Jews of the Maghreb as victims of the Holocaust had legal implications in the twenty-first century, when Germany agreed to recognize North African Jews as Holocaust survivors, thus entitling them to receive compensation.[10] Reparations to Holocaust victims in Vichy-controlled North Africa were the latest and probably the last cause of the Claims Conference for Jewish victims of the Holocaust, the organization founded in 1951 that negotiated with the German government for reparations. Germany had already accepted the principle of compensation for Jews who suffered under European collaborationist regimes. Not surprisingly, compensation was all the more complicated when it involved colonies of collaborationist regimes, which was the case for French North Africa. In 2011 Germany agreed to reparations that included one-time payments to victims in Morocco, on the principle that they were subject to regulations restricting freedom of movement.[11]

Although the initiative to recognize North African and especially Moroccan Jews came from political leaders in Israel and was driven by ethnic identity politics, lawyers for the Holocaust Survivors Rights Authority at the Finance Ministry of the State of Israel, gatekeepers to the funds, have sparred with lawyers representing Moroccan and Algerian Jews[12] about the degree to which Jews suffered as a result of direct or indirect actions of Nazi Germany through the anti-Jewish laws and measures. The extent of the impact of Vichy rule in North Africa is also disputed by historians who have been consulted by lawyers on both sides to offer their expert opinions. What is at stake in these (mis)representations of the history of the Holocaust are the lives of thousands of mainly elderly North African Jews, most of whom are poor and some of whom are in dire straits, who stand to receive regular stipends that could help ameliorate their condition.[13] Scholarship and historical interpretation is thus mired in the contested terrain of identity politics and national narratives and the agenda to redress the discrimination against North African Jews in Israel.

Although the degree to which Jews in French North Africa suffered during Vichy rule or during the six-month German and Italian occupation of Tunisia in 1943 is a subject of debate, historians would all agree on the impossibility of disentangling the prior history of colonialism from Vichy's anti-Semitic policy. However, the German reparations are predicated on the idea of a unique debt that Germany owes to the Jews; colonialism and colonial violence, of which Muslims were also the victims, is not a criterion. Investigating the entanglement of colonialism with Vichy's racist laws might therefore diminish the claim of German responsibility for the anti-Semitic measures that adversely affected the Jews in North Africa. Determining whether North African Jews are "Holocaust survivors," therefore, is a question that occludes the relationship of colonialism to Muslims, who were victims of some of the same processes of modernity and racism—the rivalries of nation building and empires, of creating racial homogeneity, and international racial struggle—that arguably culminated in the Holocaust.[14]

I propose that in interpreting the significance of the Holocaust on Europe's peripheries, we cannot disassociate the long history of colonialism from Vichy's racial policies and anti-Semitic laws. Nor can we separate, in the colonial setting, the anti-Semitic legislation from colonial policy that during the Vichy era sought to solidify the hierarchical relationship between Muslims, Jews, and the European settler community. The abrogation of the Crémieux Decree—"the end of a seventy-year-old scandal," as noted by Charles Maurras, leader of the extreme right-wing and anti-Semitic Action Française[15]—first by the Vichy government and then by General Giraud, had repercussions across the Mediterranean and North

Africa; it exposed the close connection between colonialism and radical anti-Semitism that reverberated on both shores of the Mediterranean, between the metropole and French North Africa.

The Vichy Government in North Africa

Following the fall of France and the establishment of the Vichy government in June 1940, French North Africa and other parts of the French empire became de facto parts of the French collaborationist government, and most of the colonial officials continued to occupy the same positions in the administration; some were even enthusiastic supporters of the Vichy government's fascist ideology, the "National Revolution." Because Algeria was considered an integral part of France, the Vichy laws were directly applied, without the intermediate step required in the North African protectorates, where all laws were adopted as decrees of the sultan in Morocco and the bey in Tunisia. The abrogation of the Crémieux Decree in 1940 was therefore not independent of metropolitan France.

The Statut des Juifs was commonly known as the Alibert Law, named after Vichy's minister of justice, Raphaël Alibert, an anti-Semitic extremist and disciple of Charles Maurras, who believed that French Jews should be denaturalized. The law was promulgated by Marcel Peyrouton, who became minister of the interior of Vichy in September 1940. Peyrouton had a long career in colonial North Africa and was well known for his antisocialist, anti-Semitic, and rightist views. He was resident-general in Algeria (1931–1933) and then in Tunisia (1933–1936) and then took the same position in Morocco in 1936. His tenure as resident-general in Morocco lasted only a few months; he was dismissed by Léon Blum and the new Popular Front government, which appointed Charles Noguès in his place. It is therefore not surprising that Peyrouton, as Vichy's minister of interior, was responsible for abrogating the Crémieux Decree.[16]

Alibert was to claim in the 1950s that Peyrouton was the true creator of the Statut des Juifs.[17] Peyrouton defended his role in his apologetic account of the Vichy regime and was critical of his accusers for having presented him as the initiator of the anti-Semitic statute, and he also suggested that the Nuremberg laws were imposed on them by the Germans. Had they not promulgated the decree, Marshal Pétain would have been "swept away and replaced by the racist accomplices of France." Peyrouton exonerated himself by saying that between September and October 1940, some fifty ships left the metropole for Morocco with thousands of passengers, mainly Jews of varying nationalities, and this could not have happened had not functionaries of the Ministry of Interior helped or turned a blind eye.[18] Nowhere in Peyrouton's memoirs does he mention the abrogation of the Crémieux Decree, but then again, it is doubtful that Peyrouton ever thought that his action needed any justification or that it had anything to do with the Vichy racial laws.

Between 1940 and 1942 the colonial government in Algeria and the French protectorate administrations in Tunisia and Morocco implemented the Nazi-inspired anti-Semitic Statut des Juifs and other anti-Jewish discriminatory laws that had been enacted by the Vichy authorities in metropolitan France. Jews were excluded from public office and a wide range of occupations and were subjected to the *numeri clausi* that severely restricted the number of Jews in public schools and greatly reduced those allowed in the liberal professions. A census was ordered to compel Jews to provide detailed information on their professions and property, in preparation for the expropriation Jewish-owned businesses and enterprises with the aim to "Aryanize" the Jewish economy.[19] Maxime Weygand, Vichy's delegate general and commander-in-chief in Africa, endeavored to implement the anti-Jewish legislation rigorously in North Africa, especially in Algeria, sometimes exceeding the severity of the laws in metropolitan France.[20]

Olivier Le Cour Grandmaison has argued that the Statut des Juifs, revised in 1941, was embedded in a long colonial history of juridically sanctioned racial discrimination of the state, and it was this legal precedent and reasoning that helped formulate Vichy's anti-Jewish legislation. To support his argument, he focuses on the role played by Peyrouton, known in the metropole for his colonial expertise on North Africa, and Joseph Barthélemy, a well-known jurist and legal scholar who succeeded Alibert as minister of justice in the Vichy government, a post he held from January 1941 to March 1943.[21] Barthèlemy had been critical of the Crémieux Decree and theorized about how the imperial system needed to be based on the inequality of races. The idea that Vichy's anti-Semitic laws can be traced to the colonies is countered by Emmanuelle Saada, who contends that juridical experts in Vichy made no reference to the colonies but referred instead to German law and saw the anti-Jewish legislation as an innovation.[22]

In a sense, both Le Cour Grandmaison's and Saada's arguments are complementary. The evidence supports the idea that German influence and pressure shaped the anti-Jewish legislation in Vichy, but the juridical ideas excluding Jews, of "denaturalizing" them of their citizenship, were an integral part of anti-Semitic and racial thinking in both the metropole and the colonies before the Nazi era. The Nazi laws brought anti-Semitism to a new extreme in France, which had few precedents in the French legal system (hence recourse to Nazi law), but the concept of exclusion based on race was compatible with French empire. The willing, if not enthusiastic, participation of the Vichy government and French jurists on both sides of the Mediterranean shows the extent to which North Africa and the metropole, colonial racism and Nazi anti-Semitism, overlapped. Even if Vichy's anti-Semitic Statut des Juifs and other anti-Jewish legislation did not originate in the colonies, colonialism's racialized logic facilitated the ready reception and implementation of racial legislation during the Vichy period.

This racialized logic, rooted in colonial Algeria, was reflected in the abrogation of the Crémieux Decree, an act that had been advocated by many French settlers, who had been demanding its repeal ever since it was enacted in 1870. The repeal of the Crémieux Decree stripped the Jews of Algeria of their political rights as citizens. They became classified as "indigenous," as was the majority Muslim population. Thousands of Jews outside Algeria—in Morocco, Tunisia, and France—who had been naturalized in Algeria by virtue of the Crémieux Decree also faced the loss of their French citizenship.

It should be noted that the few French Jews who were able to retain their citizenship were not shielded from the anti-Semitic laws of exclusion, except for a small number who had been highly decorated for their military service. A well-known French jurist and judge in Rabat, Morocco, during the Vichy period, remarked:

The Jew who remained a citizen does not have a noticeably better status than the Jew who reverted back to being a subject and conversely, the subject Jew does not have an inferior status to that of the citizen Jew. Even if the Crémieux Decree had not been abolished, it would not in fact, following the law of October 3, 1940 [the Statut des Juifs], have had any effect. The situation of Jews remaining citizens is almost the same as those who became subjects again. The disabilities attached to the condition of being a Jew are in effect more numerous and burdensome than those attached to the status of subject. The advantage of being a citizen is annulled by the disadvantage of being a Jew.[23]

The fact that both Jews who were stripped of their citizenship and Jews who retained it were subject to the anti-Semitic laws of exclusion (which were equally applied to Jews with foreign nationality) provided little solace to those who were "de-citizenized."[24]

In Algeria the abrogation of the Crémieux Decree and the anti-Jewish laws were intertwined, causing much confusion among colonial administrators and the legal establishment.[25] Even Jews who retained their French citizenship, apart from a few who qualified for exemptions from some of the exclusionary laws, were subject to the same anti-Semitic legislation. It was the loss of citizenship that caused even greater trauma for Algerian Jews than the Statut des Juifs.[26] The abrogation of the Crémieux Decree, long sought by many of the *colons*, remained a painful memory among many Jews of Algerian origin.[27]

Although the Statut des Juifs was intended to both satisfy Vichy's Nazi allies and garner the support of anti-Semitic fascists in the metropole, combined with the repeal of the Crémieux Decree, it also had its specificity in the colonial system, which was closely connected to colonial policy. Not only were these laws intended to satisfy the European settlers, who were for the most part more enthusiastic for Vichy's National Revolution than was the population on the French mainland, but they were also meant to appease the Muslim population, by exploiting their perceived resentment toward the Jews' advancement in and association with the colonial power. The laws of exclusion, the removal of Jews from public positions, and the effort to reduce Jews' economic and social standing in society were based on the assumption that the advancement of the Jews was what caused resentment and hostility to French rule. The abrogation of the Crémieux Decree was justified by "redressing an injustice with regard to indigenous Muslims."[28] The French hoped that demoting the Jews' status would stem the growth of those anticolonial nationalists across North Africa who had, since the beginning of the Third Reich, turned increasingly to Germany for support and who denounced Jews for having too much power and for their complicity with the French colonial rulers.

The Algerian branch of the Croix de Feu, the fascist movement whose numbers grew exponentially in the 1930s, opened its doors sporadically to Muslims in order to increase its numbers, exploiting anti-Semitism and offering greater equality to draw Muslims to its cause. The Croix de Feu blamed the Crémieux Decree for the Muslim-Jewish violence in Constantine in 1934 and used its opposition to Jews and the rejection of the Crémieux Decree to appeal to Muslims. Some Muslims adhered to the anti-Semitic ideologies and supported anti-Jewish boycotts. Some Muslim intellectuals saw an alliance against Jewish influence, but the transparent racism of the Croix de Feu and its opposition to extending rights to Muslims militated against its success. The effort to recruit Muslims was short-lived, and by mid-1936, as increasing numbers of Algerians were turning more to nationalist causes, the Croix de Feu espoused the doctrine of European racial supremacy.[29]

Some Muslims subsequently welcomed the anti-Jewish laws implemented by the Vichy government, expecting that their position would improve at the expense of lowering the status of Jews, but this was by no means a unanimous position.[30] The leading Muslim political leaders understood that the demotion of the Jews' status would not be accompanied by the advancement of Muslim political rights. Cheikh Tayeb El Okbi (cofounder of the Association des Oulémas), Messali Hadj (of the Parti du peuple algérien [PPA]), Ahmed Boumendjel (another leading PPA figure), and Ferhat Abbas (of the Fédération des Élus)—all condemned the anti-Semitism of the Vichy regime. For both Hadj and Abbas—the two leading nationalist figures in the 1930s—the supposed equality between Muslims and Jews to be gained by abolishing the Crémieux Decree was an "equality at the bottom end" and meant no progress for Algerians. To the contrary, the abrogation of the Crémieux Decree demonstrated the precariousness of French citizenship and revealed that the regime could not be reformed. This only further spurred Muslim political leaders to seek full rights as citizens and further radicalized the nationalists.[31]

The abrogation of the Crémieux Decree was therefore intended not only to demote the status of Jews but also to further block the political rights of Muslims and to redefine the meaning of "indigenous" imperial subjects of France in an effort to maintain the French empire and the privileged position of the European (Christian) settlers. The repeal of the Crémieux Decree together with Vichy anti-Semitic legislation in North Africa was thus integral to the colonial racist thinking that took shape long before World War II.

The Crémieux Decree and the Racialized Order

The Crémieux Decree of 1870 granted the "indigenous Jews of the Departments of Algeria"[32] French citizenship en masse, with the exception of the Jews of the Mzab, which was not annexed to the Algerian colony until 1882.[33] Before 1870 the route to citizenship was the same for Jews and

Muslims: According to the *sénatus-consulte* of 1865, as a prerequisite of individual naturalization, indigenous Muslims and Jews had to relinquish their personal status (defined by religious law). The *sénatus-consulte*, which defined Muslims and Jews as "indigenous" (*indigène*) subjects of France, thus made a distinction between the quality of being French nationals and French citizens, a concept unique to colonial Algeria and distinct from metropolitan France, where the difference between nationality and citizenship was often blurred.

In effect, the process to become naturalized as citizens was not really "naturalization," insofar as Muslims and Jews were already defined as French nationals, albeit without civil rights. But jurists subsequently defined the process as "naturalization," because this was an essential prerogative of the state, which monopolized who could be considered worthy of acceptance in the French nation. Colonial authorities were subsequently opposed to the Crémieux Decree, precisely because it raised the specter of "collective naturalization" of the Algerian Muslim population and because it could be used by the colonial Algerian administration and the Ministry of Justice to disqualify any proposal of political reform.[34] The Crémieux Decree also had repercussions throughout the expanding French empire because it raised questions about the definition of natives and their distinction from citizens.[35]

The European community in Algeria immediately mounted an angry campaign against the Crémieux Decree. The *pieds noirs* were particularly incensed about the electoral issue and the large number of Jews who would vote against settler interests. A result of the protests was the Lambrecht Decree of October 1871, which further defined "indigenous Jews," stipulating that only Jews born in Algeria before the conquest or those born of parents established in Algeria at the time of conquest would be considered indigenous and thus entitled to remain on the electoral lists, that is, to be entitled to political rights that resulted from the Crémieux Decree.[36] However, the Lambrecht Decree had little effect on Moroccan and Tunisian Jews; the second generation was able to acquire French nationality on reaching the age of majority.[37]

The French conquest of the Mzab in 1882, which occurred shortly after the conquest of Tunisia, produced a long-lasting debate over whether Mzabi Jews should be considered citizens by dint of the Crémieux Decree, but the argument that they fell outside the departments of Algeria prevailed, and their indigenous status was maintained based on the argument that they had not reached a high enough level of civilization.[38] The question of the Mzabi Jews brought into sharp relief the deep anxieties that the Crémieux Decree produced for the French over the preservation of racial hierarchies across North Africa.[39]

The Crémieux Decree and the debates about the mass enfranchisement of the Jews caused further legal deliberations on the status of Muslims and Europeans in Algeria. The naturalization law of 1889, which legislators and jurists from Algeria helped to enact, transformed children of immigrants born on French soil into citizens, based on the principle of *jus soli* (right of the soil).[40] The law applied to Algeria, because it was considered a part of France, and automatically naturalized as French citizens a mass of non-French Europeans: Spaniards, Maltese, Sardinians, Corsicans, and Italians. The extension of citizenship to second-generation immigrants, advocated by Algerian representatives in the Chamber of Deputies, was motivated by both concerns of large concentrations of foreigners along France's borders and the desire to conscript children of immigrants into the military. For Algeria it also served the purpose of maintaining the predominance of Europeans in the colony[41] and increasing the number of Christian Europeans to the electorate, motivated in large part as a counterbalance to the Crémieux Decree and the enfranchisement of the Jews. It also resulted in the intensification of anti-Semitism, as the European Christians from the Mediterranean, to demonstrate their worthiness as "French," exploited antipathy toward the Jews, whose assimilability was even more questionable than their own.[42]

The 1889 naturalization law also further defined the status of indigenous noncitizen Muslims by stating that Muslims residing in Algeria (which would include foreign Muslims) would be subject to Muslim personal status law. But jurists determined that children of Muslim Moroccans or Tunisians, born in Algerian territory and residing in Algeria when they reached the age of majority, would become French citizens in much the same manner as European Christians were naturalized; the law stipulated that children born to a non-French father, himself born on French soil, or children born in Algeria to a father who was not born on French soil would be considered French citizens. The inclusion of non-Algerian Muslims provoked vociferous opposition in Algeria that continued until the Vichy period and was based on the same racist discourse used against Algerian Muslims and Jews: that Muslims were not civilized enough to allow them to exercise their rights as citizens.[43]

In the years that followed, the European settler community, including elected French officials, continued their protests against the Jews and their political rights, and a new campaign to abrogate the Crémieux Decree gained momentum. The influence of Jews in elections and competition for power and influence in municipal government in Algeria were the catalysts for the anti-Semitic campaign and the repeated efforts to eliminate Jews from the electoral lists.[44] Algeria was the site of some of the worst manifestations of anti-Semitism, especially during the height of the Dreyfus affair.[45] Although Jews came to embrace the ideals of France and adopted French language and culture, many of the European settlers (*pieds noirs*) continued to regard the Jews of Algeria as unassimilable and foreign, despite their naturalization as French citizens.[46] The particular intensity of settler anti-Semitism was shaped by an ideology that Algerian Europeans constituted a unique racial fusion of "Latins" that was separate from the metropole. Many joined local parties, leagues, and movements of the extreme right or local branches of metropolitan political parties and leagues, which regarded the Jew as a racial enemy.

The abrogation of the Crémieux Decree remained a cause of politicians and European settlers. Throughout the history of colonial Algeria, it resurfaced during times of crisis, such as during the Dreyfus affair and in the 1930s, especially when questions were being raised about expanding political rights to Muslims. From the time of its enactment in 1870, the Crémieux Decree therefore remained a festering wound among the *pieds noirs*. It was blamed for Muslim discontent against colonial rule, was considered a threat to the racial dominance of Europeans over Muslims and Jews, and was held as a symbol of resentment toward the metropole and the Third Republic.

The Crémieux Decree Beyond Algeria's Borders

Whatever the original motivations for the Crémieux Decree in metropolitan France—the influence of French Jews advocating for the emancipation of their Algerian coreligionists or the desire of metropolitan France to increase the number of loyal French citizens—many in the colonial lobby had misgivings about the decree and regarded it as a miscalculation or, worse, a grave error. Although opponents were unsuccessful in repealing the decree before the Vichy regime came to power, because Algeria was regarded as an integral part of France and revoking the rights of French

Jewish citizens would have caused insurmountable legal complications in the metropole, opposition to the Crémieux Decree shaped policy in the French protectorates of Tunisia (established in 1881) and Morocco (established in 1912). Opposition to the collective naturalization of the Jews was an integral part of the logic, if not one of the motives, for maintaining the fictive sovereignty of Tunisia and Morocco as "protectorates," where Jews remained "indigenous" subjects of the bey and the sultan, respectively. In the colonial logic, maintaining Jews in their place in the social hierarchy and, at the same time, keeping the symbols of sovereignty would help gain Muslim acquiescence to colonial rule. This would reinforce the privileges of the European settlers, unfettered by Jewish competition, which, it was believed, had been produced by the enfranchisement of the Jews in Algeria and which had caused both the hostility of the *colons* toward the metropole and the hostility of the Muslim population. The Crémieux Decree was thus a negative model, a referent used repeatedly against any efforts to "emancipate" the Jews.

A constant motif in the criticism of the Crémieux Decree, from the time of its enactment in the nineteenth century, was that it would inflame Muslim opinion against French rule. The Kabyle revolt, which engulfed Algeria in 1871, was blamed on the Crémieux Decree by some of the *pieds noirs*, despite the fact that the leader of the revolt did not object to the naturalization of the Jews.[47] But as far as can be gauged, the opposition of the Muslim population to the Crémieux Decree was negligible in 1870 and in the years after, and some Muslim leaders even expressed their approval.[48] Despite the indifference or muted opposition of Muslims, the risk of inflaming Muslim resentment of colonial rule as a result of privileging native Jews over Muslims became the principal justification for not granting collective French citizenship to Jews in the French protectorates.

Concerted efforts for a Crémieux type of decree in Morocco by the Westernized elites and the Alliance Israélite Universelle, the most important Franco-Jewish organization with its network of schools across the Mediterranean basin, were to no avail. Furthermore, the existence of Algerian Jews or Jews who had acquired French nationality in Algeria greatly vexed the French authorities in the protectorates. Jurists in Tunisia sought ways to limit the number of Jews registered as French nationals and ways to consider them subjects of the bey.[49] The mass enfranchisement of indigenous Jews was thus seen as a challenge to the racializing logic of the protectorates and a threat to settler privilege. It was deemed sufficient to allow a restricted number of Jews access to the modern colonial sector to serve as intermediaries while blocking the vast majority of indigenous Jews from European society.

Nevertheless, Jewish ascendancy for many of the *colons* had still gone too far in Tunisia and Morocco. In Tunisia, Italian citizens, including indigenous Jewish residents with Italian nationality, outnumbered French citizens until 1936.[50] This demographic fact was one of the main reasons the Tunisian protectorate authorities implemented in 1923 a law to ease restrictions on acquiring French nationality for nationals of Western powers and for Tunisian Muslims and Jews. By making the conditions for naturalization less restrictive, the 1923 law sought to offset the number of non-French "Italians."[51] To avoid any concern that too many Jews and Muslims would become French citizens, the resident-general, Lucien Saint, was quick to distinguish between the Tunisian law and the "very reckless" Crémieux Decree, asserting that there was no intention to naturalize Muslims and Jews en masse. Nevertheless, the 1923 law, which likely sought to create a Tunisian elite who would be loyal to France, became a major target of the Tunisian nationalist movement.[52]

Morocco was even more restrictive than Tunisia about expanding eligibility of citizenship to indigenous Jews. Morocco did not have the problem of competing Italian interests. It was more concerned about Spain, whose imperial ambitions were constantly frustrated by their subordinate status to the French in the Moroccan protectorate.[53] Some Spaniards contemplated granting citizenship to Sephardi Jews as an instrument of expanding their influence in Morocco, pointing to the Crémieux Decree as having greatly facilitated French imperial interests in North Africa.[54]

The idea of offering Sephardim the opportunity for naturalization did not originate with the most recent Spanish legislation of 2015, which allows descendants of Jews expelled from Spain in 1492 to apply for citizenship. A similar law was first enacted in 1924 and was aimed mainly at former Ottoman citizens for the purpose of attracting Jewish capital rather than Jews.[55] But even if this legislation was intended to help Spain increase its influence at the expense of the French, the Spanish were also not particularly interested in promoting Jewish ascendancy in Morocco. The idea was revived only during the Vichy period, when the Spanish renewed their offer to naturalize Sephardim, with the claim that they were protecting their protégés in the French zone from the anti-Semitic laws but with the intention of undermining French interests and attracting Jewish capital. Well aware of Spain's aims, the French blocked the issuing of Spanish papers in their zone.[56]

The number of indigenous Moroccan Jews acquiring French citizenship during the protectorate remained small and restricted,[57] but Jews' access to the modern European sector was accelerating and their numbers were disproportionate and far greater than the Muslim population. They were especially facilitated by the modern education provided by the Alliance Israélite Universelle, which had become the quasi-official national educational system for Jews in Morocco. For Jews with means, especially those involved in foreign trade, Morocco also was a marketplace for foreign nationalities.[58] Furthermore, about 10,000 "Algerian" Jews in Morocco held French citizenship;[59] some of them were of Moroccan origin but had ancestors who had settled in Algeria, where they acquired French nationality. Indeed, Moroccan and Algerian identities were porous, especially for Jews living in the bordering regions of western Algeria and eastern Morocco, where Jews often migrated back and forth between the Oujda region and the province of Oran.[60] Therefore, when the Crémieux Decree was abrogated in 1940, it reverberated across French North Africa.

Muslims, Jews, and Citizenship Questions in the 1930s

The changing circumstances in the 1930s challenged the supposed stability of colonialism's racial hierarchies in North Africa and increased tensions between Muslims, Jews, and the settler population. The convergence of pan-Islamic or pan-Arab nationalism with the rise of the Nazi Third Reich, fascist regimes in Spain and Italy, conflict in Palestine, and growing anti-Semitism heightened tensions across the Maghreb.

Muslim elites in Algeria were pressing for and had already obtained expanded political rights, if ever so minimal, yet most Muslims remained, unlike Jews, indigenous subjects rather than full citizens of France. It was the Crémieux Decree, presented as the example of the doctrine of "collective naturalization" that was used as a counter model to rebuff any proposal to extend citizenship to indigenous Muslims. Thus the rapporteurs of the 1919 Jonnart Law, which expanded political rights to eligible Muslims, a concession made because of the thousands of Algerians who had served in the French military during World War I, emphasized its difference from the Crémieux Decree.[61] The 1919 law did not replace the *sénatus-consulte* of 1865, the law that required individuals to relinquish their personal status to become French citizens, and it excluded indigenous Muslim and Jews (the latter still denied French citizenship) in the military territories and the districts of the south. The obstacles imposed in the process of naturalization and the requirement to relinquish personal status precluded all but a few Muslims from obtaining French citizenship. Another 1919 law to "extend political rights to the *indigène*" did allow for eligible Muslims to be included in the local electoral college (a kind of intermediary stage between French citizens and subjects, or "half-naturalized" citizens, as Charles-Robert Ageron called it) for those Muslims who refused to give up their traditional Muslim status but were deemed worthy of limited political rights.[62]

Politicians in metropolitan France debated the question of whether Muslims might be made French citizens with political rights, a kind of extension of the Crémieux Decree to all Algerian subjects. Some younger Algerian Jewish leaders also questioned why the Crémieux Decree was not also applied to Muslims.[63] But European settlers and the colonial administration in Algeria were adamant in their opposition to any such proposal and effectively blocked most bills that would have increased the political rights of Algerian Muslims. They especially railed against the Blum-Viollette bill of 1936, which would have extended political rights to 21,000 Algerians among the educated elite.[64] In particular, extreme right-wing and fascist parties, which were attracting a growing number of European settlers to their ranks, rallied against the bill. The settlers feared that it would spell the end of European privilege and hegemony, and the grand rabbi of Algiers warned Blum of the potential dangers for the Jewish community.[65]

The extension of full citizenship rights by the Crémieux Decree was originally met with the opposition of some Jews, because it meant giving up a large degree of their religious autonomy and control over personal status.[66] By the 1930s, however, despite, or rather because of, the rising tide of settler anti-Semitism, few Jews would consider relinquishing their privileges as Frenchmen, which had come about as a result of the exclusion of Muslims. If Muslims were relatively indifferent to the Crémieux Decree in the nineteenth century, in part for the same reasons that Jews were ambivalent—that is, they were not willing to accept giving up jurisdiction of their personal status—the various proposals and negotiations over Muslim citizenship in the 1930s raised the specter of the Crémieux Decree and the inferior status of Muslims over native Jews that the decree had come to represent. The abrogation of the Crémieux decree by the Vichy government in 1940 was therefore as much about preventing any further justification for the expansion of political rights to Muslims as it was about demoting the status of the Jews of Algeria.

Vichy's Colonial Jewish Policy Across North Africa and the Mediterranean

The question of rescinding the citizenship of French Jews was not unique to Algeria; it was part of Vichy policy for metropolitan France. Already by July 1940, 15,154 Jews had lost their citizenship as the result of a law, modeled on the Nazi racial legislation of 1933, that was designed to strip French nationality from those who had been naturalized since 1927, which especially targeted Jews.[67] But the stripping of citizenship rights of Jews in Algeria went much further, reflecting the extent to which the anti-Jewish laws there were, in part, the result of pressure from the colonies that predated Vichy's National Revolution. It also demonstrates the extent to which colonialism and National Socialism were ideologically cut from the same cloth.

The abrogation of the Crémieux Decree had repercussions beyond Algeria. The effects were also felt in France and other French colonies. In 1941, 26.4% of Jews in Marseilles were natives of Algeria, and with the abrogation of the Crémieux Decree, those who had been naturalized as a result of the decree were stripped of their citizenship. Some petitioned to keep their citizenship in accordance with the stipulation that allowed exemptions for those who were honored for their decorated military service to France. But only 1.5% were able to keep their status as French citizens, either because they had acquired their citizenship before 1870 or because their military service was recognized as sufficiently meritorious (after 1870).[68]

The abrogation was particularly felt in Morocco, not only because of its effect on the thousands of "Algerian" Jews who stood to lose their French citizenship but also because it raised questions about the racial hierarchy of the protectorate. The problem of how the abrogation affected the numerous French Jewish citizens in Morocco, many of whom were of Moroccan ancestry, was a particularly vexing issue for the French authorities. Many of these "Moroccan" Jews, who had resided in Algeria, were naturalized by the Crémieux Decree, whereas others became French citizens by individual naturalization either before or after the decree. The French authorities and European settlers in Morocco were obsessed with how the abrogation of the Crémieux Decree affected French citizens of Moroccan origin and what that would mean in terms of the application of the Statut des Juifs in Morocco.[69]

As a protectorate, Morocco was in theory a sovereign country, and all legislation was promulgated as royal decrees (*dahirs*) by the sharifian monarch. In reality, the legislation was drafted by the French authorities, translated into Arabic, and rubber-stamped by the sultan of the 'Alawid dynasty. The discriminatory *dahirs* replicated in most respects and enacted the metropolitan Statut des Juifs in Morocco and were applied to both Moroccan and non-Moroccan Jews. No differentiation was made between French Jewish citizens and foreign Jews in Morocco. There were, however, a few distinctions between Moroccan and non-Moroccan Jews. In the *dahir* of October 1940, based on the metropolitan Alibert Law, non-Moroccan Jews residing in the protectorate were given the same racial definition as in France—"every non-Moroccan . . . with three grandparents of the Jewish race or two grandparents of the same race if his/her spouse is also Jewish"—whereas Moroccan Jews continued to be defined by their religion.[70] The same distinction was also made in the French protectorate of Tunisia. The metropolitan Vichy administration opposed this distinction, but the local colonial authorities were able to prevail. There was a certain logic for maintaining this distinction in the protectorate. If Moroccan Jews were to be defined by race in the same category as non-Moroccans, then it would challenge their indigenous status and the colonial hierarchies on which the protectorate system rested.[71] There was therefore a *racist* logic for rejecting the *racial* definition of Jews.

A racial definition of Jews would have meant that Muslim descendants of Jewish converts to Islam would have been defined as Jews, and this was a direct challenge to the sultan, Mohammed ben Youssef, because it questioned his sovereignty as Islamic ruler. This was also problematic for the French authorities, because the protectorate was also based on and legitimized by the preservation of the dynasty and its Islamic ruler with his Muslim and Jewish subjects. However, the 1941 *dahir* that followed the metropolitan Statut des Juifs, which came with the intensification of pressures from the Vichy government after the creation of the Commissariat Général aux Questions Juives (CGQJ), headed by Xavier Vallat, eliminated this distinction between Moroccan and non-Moroccan Jews and applied the same racial definition to both.[72] Vallat endeavored to see that the anti-Jewish laws were strictly applied in the colonies and traveled to North Africa for that purpose. During his two-day visit to Morocco, he met with Resident-General Noguès, French military and civilian leaders, and Sultan Mohammed ben Youssef to ensure compliance with his more draconian directives, and then he proceeded to Fez, where he went with an official entourage of the local authorities into the *mellah* to intimidate the Jewish community and its leaders.[73]

Although all Jews were now defined by race, the *dahir* of 1941 did make one important distinction between Moroccan and non-Moroccan Jews. Moroccans were permitted to continue practicing traditional artisanal activities and the retail trades, out of concern that banning Jews from these professions would destabilize the economy and thus undermine the strength of colonial rule. Therefore, being an indigenous Moroccan subject of the sultan could be more advantageous than being non-Moroccan.[74]

What the abrogation of the Crémieux Decree implied for French Jewish citizens in Morocco, especially for the Algerians of Moroccan origin, was far from clear, either for the French administrators, jurists, or the Jews. In Algeria, it implied that the Jews would be regarded as indigenous and, in theory, assimilated into the indigenous Algerian Muslim population. Yet in one important respect the Jews were not simply reverting back to their pre-1870 status, as it might appear and as it has often been described. The abrogation of the Crémieux Decree stipulated that French civil law regarding personal status would still apply. Indeed, in the 1890s the idea of removing citizenship and political rights while still applying French civil law had been part of the anti-Semitic campaign to repeal the Crémieux Decree. In this sense, Jewish status after October 1940 remained distinct from indigenous Muslims, whose status as indigenous subjects of France was based on retaining their personal law and on rejecting their Muslim personal status, the criterion for individual naturalization as citizens. This legal distinction, revealed by the abrogation of the Crémieux Decree, was again to raise the question of racial hierarchies for Vichy, impelling them to simultaneously redefine the category of "indigenous" for *both* Muslims and Jews. As a consequence of these legal problems across North Africa, the abrogation decree was revised and again enacted in February 1942, as I discuss in what follows.[75]

As we have seen, in the racial hierarchies established in colonial Algeria, a distinction was invented between French citizens and nationals, the latter category reserved for non-European subjects of France. The same logic applied to other French colonies, but in Morocco Jews were already indigenous subjects, like the Muslims, not of France but of the sultan, and both kept their personal status. This meant that native Jews even had a lower status than Muslims, a situation that the French colonial authorities preferred. Although no longer subject to discriminatory stipulations of *dhimmi* status, they did relinquish part of their judicial autonomy to the Makhzan courts, because the powers of the rabbinic courts were reduced to matters of personal status.

The Makhzan courts, recreated by the colonial administration, assumed control of many of the prerogatives formerly held by the Sharia courts, whose power was also greatly reduced. Jewish leaders regarded the Makhzan courts as prejudicial, and the injustices and arbitrariness of the Makhzan courts was one of the major grievances of Jewish leadership, an argument for allowing Jews to be judged by French courts and thus according Jews French citizenship.[76] The abrogation of the Crémieux Decree was therefore a major blow to the many Moroccan Jewish leaders who had long advocated for the extension of French citizenship to the Jews of the protectorate.

What the abrogation of the Crémieux Decree and redefinition of indigenous status in Algeria meant for the offspring of Moroccan immigrants naturalized in Algeria but resident in Morocco was a subject of debate and concern not only for the Jews but also for the colonial authorities and the anti-Semitic *colons*. Would the loss of their French citizenship imply that French Jewish citizens in Morocco would become native subjects of France, for which there was no provision in the Moroccan protectorate? Would Algerian Jews of Moroccan descent, with the loss of their French citizenship, become Moroccan citizens and subjects of the sultan, which would be one way that Moroccan law could be interpreted?

Significantly, the origins of Moroccan citizenship were connected to problems arising from Jews obtaining foreign nationality abroad and returning to Morocco with newly acquired rights as foreign nationals. An article in the 1880 Madrid Convention, a meeting between the European powers and Morocco to curb the abuse of the system of consular protection, sought to limit the proliferation of Moroccans returning with foreign nationality. Moroccans naturalized abroad who returned to Morocco "after a period of residence equal in time to that which was legally necessary to obtain naturalization" would again be subject to Moroccan law.[77]

Although not intended as a nationality law, the article did establish the principle of "perpetual allegiance" to the sultan, which became the basis of the legal concept of citizenship during the protectorate.[78] Indeed, it became the legal justification for excluding Jews from acquiring French citizenship and for maintaining the vast majority of Jews as indigenous subjects of the sultan.

In principle, then, French Jewish citizens of Moroccan descent in the protectorate could be considered Moroccan, but it seems that most remained French citizens based on the laws of nationality that applied to the French empire. Before the war the French had little interest in challenging this, because having a relatively small and controlled cadre of Jews in the colonial sector who could serve as intermediaries was in their interest. But with the revocation of French citizenship by the colonial Vichy regime and with the reversion of Jews to indigenous status, the French sought to rectify the problem of loopholes to ensure that Jews of Moroccan descent could no longer be considered French nationals, basically meaning that they would revert to being Moroccan nationals.

In hindsight, there were few benefits—and a few disadvantages—to having French over Moroccan citizenship during Vichy rule. The sultan may have exercised his sovereign powers by intervening in favor of Jews from Algeria, whom he considered his subjects because of their Moroccan origin.[79] But Algerian Jews in Morocco fought vigorously to preserve their French nationality and to claim the rights to which they felt entitled.[80] Jews with political rights as French citizens meant not only a status above Muslims but also a status above indigenous Jews. Loss of citizenship was probably perceived as worse than becoming indigenous, for in the long run it could only have been believed that the anti-Semitic Vichy regime was ephemeral and that the principles of the French Republic would be restored.

Some Jews petitioned for their status as French citizens to be recognized on the basis that they were Moroccans naturalized in Algeria after the Crémieux Decree was promulgated, implying that its abrogation on October 7, 1940, would not affect them.[81] In Algeria there were also about 1,300 Jews who did not lose their French citizenship when the decree was abrogated in 1940, mostly because they had been naturalized individually before or after the decree. This loophole was unsettling for the French authorities and jurists across North Africa. In Morocco the European settlers put pressure on the central administration of the resident-general (the

Residency) to work toward remedying the situation. Despite the fact that French Jews were subject to virtually the same discriminatory laws as all other Jews, the president of the North African branch of the Légion Française des Combattants, the veterans' organization, which served as a spearhead for Vichy's National Revolution, complained to the CGQJ about this "anomaly" of Algerian-born Jews of Moroccan origin who had the same status as foreigners born in French territory and thus enjoying the political rights of French citizens.[82]

The resident-general in Morocco, Noguès, was also anxious to remedy this situation and informed Vallat of the numerous Algerian Jews claiming to be entitled to remain French citizens because of their Moroccan descent. According to the laws of 1889 and 1927, those born in France or Algeria of foreign parents were regarded as French. Others were circumventing the abrogation of the Crémieux Decree by invoking their status as indigenous subjects of the sultan, based on the law of perpetual allegiance, and thus evading the law that would have made them indigenous subjects.[83]

A further problem was the Jews of Moroccan descent who were foreign nationals of other countries but living in Morocco. This situation was a source of much conflict between the protectorate authorities and foreign diplomatic representatives, who sometimes endeavored to protect their citizens who were subject to the anti-Jewish legislation. Noguès proposed changing the law so that "nationals of a country under the Protectorate of France should not be regarded as aliens under the laws of nationality, not having ever lost their original nationality."[84] Such a provision, which would be applied retroactively, would allow for the review of the situation of many Jews who had been able to receive French citizenship by making false statements, as it was argued. The "anomaly" of those Jews of Moroccan and Tunisian origin who retained their French citizenship, unaffected by the abrogation of the Crémieux Decree, was taken up by jurists in the Ministry of Justice soon after the creation of the CGQJ, with proposals to revise the law of October 7, 1940.[85]

The numerous legal questions and problems created by the abrogation of the Crémieux Decree across North Africa caused the Vichy authorities in Algeria to redefine "indigenous" as a racial category for both Muslims and Jews and to further specify the legal meaning of the abrogation of the decree.[86] Although the law of February 18, 1942, that replaced the original 1940 law abrogating the Crémieux Decree was in most respects the same, subtle yet significant differences between the two laws exist. The law of October 7, 1940, refers to the Jews of the departments of Algeria who would remain under French law, but this meant that the Mzabi Jews were not included, a point specifically discussed by Vichy jurists. This might not seem that relevant, because the Mzabi Jews had not been beneficiaries of the Crémieux Decree in the first place and were still classified as indigenous and thus not subject to French civil law as it pertained to personal status. But symbolically the original exclusion and now the inclusion of the Mzabi Jews was essential to Vichy's definition and racialization of the category of "indigenous."

The revised law of February 18, 1942, subtly changed the language to read the "indigenous Jews of Algeria" rather than the "departments of Algeria"; and rather than referring to Jews *remaining* under the jurisdiction of French law, it simply refers to Jews ruled by French law, thus applying the law to all Jews. This created a new kind of "French subject" in which French personal status law applied without any political rights as citizens, precisely what anti-Semites had attempted but failed to legislate in the 1890s. This was in contrast to the *sénatus-consulte* of 1865, in which Jews together with Muslims retained their personal status according to their religion.

The abrogation of the Crémieux Decree also raised questions about the indigenous status of Muslims. The law of February 18, 1942, was in conjunction with and preceded by a law that redefined and revamped the legal definition of nationality for Muslims, which was issued the previous day, on February 17. As in the case of the Jews, the authorities across North Africa were concerned about the "anomaly" of indigenous French protégés and immigrants: Muslim children of Tunisian and Moroccan immigrants in Algeria who had become French and thus enjoyed a higher status than European foreign nationals. The racist law of February 17 transformed French citizens of Muslim origin into indigenous Muslim subjects, with the purpose of doing for Muslims what the Crémieux Decree's abrogation did for Jews. Likewise, in redefining the indigenous status of Jews, the law of February 18 stipulated that Moroccan or Tunisian Jews who acquired French nationality as a result of their birth or residence in Algeria were henceforth to be subject to the same status as Algerian Jews, effectively removing their French citizenship. These laws thus created a concept of "subjects of empire," now unquestionably connected to racial criteria.[87]

The French hoped that the leveling of the playing field between Muslims and Jews, by transforming their legal status, would curry favor with the Muslim population, despite their not very well concealed aim of ensuring that Muslims would remain indigenous and without political rights. The abrogation of the Crémieux Decree and the revised stipulations of 1942 actually gave Jews an inferior status. The law pronounced that Jews could become naturalized French citizens through the *sénatus-consulte* of 1865, which had allowed Muslims and Jews to become naturalized French citizens if they agreed to give up their personal status and be governed by French civil law. But the laws that abrogated the Crémieux Decree stripped the Jews of citizenship while maintaining—or applying in the case of Mzabi Jews—the jurisdiction of French civil law. Although the abrogation of the Crémieux Decree stated that the Jews' political rights were to be regulated by the stipulations establishing the political rights of indigenous Algerian Muslims, unlike indigenous Muslims, Jewish personal status was not applied to them. So if the basis for acquiring political rights was relinquishing personal status, according to the *sénatus-consulte* of 1865, did this not mean effectively that Jews had no grounds for applying for naturalization? That question is not explicitly addressed by the law, which would have been complicated by the contradiction of restoring the indigenous status of the Jews while retaining their French personal status.

Already by 1940 the French were concerned that Jews might find a way to regain some of their rights, and just a few days after the 1940 abrogation decree a second law was promulgated that made Jews ineligible for naturalization by the process stipulated by the Jonnart Law of 1919, which set conditions for allowing *indigènes* to become French citizens. The addendum to the abrogation of the Crémieux Decree was probably deemed necessary, because most Jews, unlike Muslims, would have met the criteria stipulated in the Jonnart Law for individual naturalization, which they would have fulfilled as former French citizens.[88]

In redefining indigenous status in Algeria, which implicitly created "imperial subjects," the Vichy authorities were clearly also looking at the racial hierarchies in Morocco. What the implications were for the many Jews from Algeria in Morocco, formerly French citizens—now indigenous subjects of France—is unclear. At the end of the day, during the Vichy period it probably made little difference for the Jews' actual situation because, either as Jewish French citizens or indigenous subjects of France, they would still be subject to the same laws of exclusion that affected other Jews. Only those French Jews who had been honored as decorated soldiers could retain or apply for citizenship and not be subject to the anti-Jewish laws. And the pages of petitions submitted to the French colonial authorities show that few petitions were accepted.

Of even greater concern for the French authorities across North Africa than the numerous legal complications and loopholes that emerged from annulling the Crémieux Decree, was how its abrogation might affect the Muslim population and the anti-French nationalist intelligentsia. French authorities made occasional references that the abrogation might cause Jews and Muslims to unite against colonial rule, but more often they thought that it would garner support for the colonial government. So obsessed were the French with thinking that the Crémieux Decree was the source of all problems that many believed it united Muslims against colonial rule across North Africa. Even in Morocco, where the decree should have been much less of a concern, the authorities were worried about the growth of anti-French nationalists and thought that the abrogation of the Crémieux Decree might win support of the Moroccan intelligentsia.

From the beginning of the Third Reich the French had been particularly anxious about the growth of the nationalist anticolonial movement and Nazi support and funding of anti-French activities. Nazi anti-Semitic propaganda, which was being disseminated in Morocco, partly through nationalist channels, often emphasized France and the Jews as part and parcel of the same enemy. The French monitored anti-Semitic influence among the Muslims not as a matter of principled opposition but to determine how it was being instrumentalized by the Nazis in their anti-French campaign. The northern Spanish Zone in Morocco, especially Tetuán, was the hub of anti-French nationalist activities, supported by Germany and encouraged by the Spanish authorities. A number of nationalist leaders took refuge in the Spanish protectorate after the wave of arrests and suppression of the movement under Noguès in 1936–1937. The Spanish nationalist uprising in Morocco that led to the civil war and Hitler and Mussolini's support of Franco further encouraged the spread of both Nazi propaganda and anti-French nationalist activities through the Spanish protectorate. Spain, the weaker colonial power in Morocco and overshadowed by the French protectorate, had long coveted expanding its dominion over the French Zone in Morocco, and the fall of France presented it with an opportunity. However, the Nazi-Vichy alliance precluded the possibility that Spain would take control of the French protectorate.[89]

For the Vichy government the anti-Semitic laws were also seen as an opportunity to regain the initiative and to placate nationalists, who were increasingly merging anti-French protests with anti-Semitism, encouraged by the Nazis. The armistice with Germany and the German-Vichy alliance were intended to contain German influence in North Africa and to preserve the independence of the French empire. For this reason the abrogation of the Crémieux Decree might also have served the purpose of regaining Muslim support or at least acquiescence to French rule.

In 1940 a circular was sent around to various *contrôleurs civils*, police, and military authorities throughout Morocco to elicit reactions from the population, especially the Muslim educated elite, on the abrogation of the Crémieux Decree. The French authorities reported that Muslims, especially Algerians living in Morocco, welcomed its abrogation, because it was a blow to Jewish ascendancy, especially in educated and nationalist circles.[90] Yet in reading the various reports sent to officials of the Residency in Rabat, the local authorities seem to be following a template, as though they were supplying answers that the Residency wanted to hear. One wonders, moreover, how the various regional authorities would have had access to public opinion or how reliable their sources could have been, considering how closely the French controlled and censored information.

It is therefore difficult to assess how much the denigration of the Jews by the abrogation of the Crémieux Decree was applauded by the Muslim educated elite in Morocco. If in Algeria some educated Muslims had understood that revoking the rights of Algerian Jews hardly bode well for improving their own status, as we have seen, then in Morocco, where Jews were already indigenous and in some respects subordinate to Muslims, it could hardly be expected that the abrogation would curry much favor among the Muslim population. Overall, it is unlikely that the Crémieux Decree and its abrogation elicited much response from the Moroccan Muslim population as a whole. In Morocco as well as in Algeria it was an illusion to think that, by demoting the Jews' status, Muslims nationalists would relinquish their claims for greater political rights, which they had sought with increasing intensity since the 1930s. Yet the French authorities were concerned enough to systematically investigate Muslim reactions in Morocco to the abrogation of the Crémieux decree, so much was it a symbol of the racial hierarchies in colonial North Africa.

Across North Africa France's Jewish policy during World War II was significant in determining France's relationship to the Muslim population and its perceived ability to maintain the French empire as nationalist movements grew in the later part of the war and after. But the main concern of the French in connection with the question of Jewish rights was more about Muslims and the rising tide of nationalism than about Jews. The French administration claimed that restoring the Crémieux Decree in wartime would incite the Muslim masses and bring to the forefront the demands of Muslims across North Africa, with negative consequence for the French empire. Muslim nationalists, at least in part, must have realized that the abrogation of the Crémieux Decree, with its ostensive goal of leveling the playing field, brought no improvement in the status of Muslims, making them only more aware of their inferior rank in the social hierarchy.

The question of restoring Jews' rights after the Allied landing could at least be used as leverage for trying to improve the status of Muslims, and thus the restitution of the Crémieux Decree, without according the same rights to Muslims, could unleash Muslim anger toward the Jews. For their part, some Jewish leaders sought to gain the support of Muslims for the restoration of their rights and to demonstrate that the argument of Muslim hostility carried little weight.[91] After the Allied landings in November 1942, some leading Jewish figures in Algeria wanted to see equal rights granted to Muslims with the restoration of the Jews' political rights.[92] Jewish leaders generally were divided on the question of how much political rights should be extended to Muslims, but all were agreed that the Crémieux Decree should be restored.

One of the key players leading the cause for restoring French citizenship to the Jews of Algeria was the French Jewish jurist and human rights advocate René Cassin, who was a leading figure in the Free French resistance led by Charles de Gaulle. In his capacity as commissioner of justice and public instruction, Cassin denounced the re-abrogation of the Crémieux Decree as a "racist law" with its pretext of establishing racial equality. He justified his position for restoring the decree with the argument that only a small number of Muslims had become French citizens, not wanting to give up their personal status, a point also made by Hannah Arendt.[93] Cassin nevertheless did see the link between restoring Jewish rights and improving the status of Muslims and advocated for expanding rights and citizenship to a much larger number of Muslims, but he also saw the benefits of French empire for promoting liberal internationalism.[94]

It was not until October 20, 1943, after the Free French government, the Comité français de Libération nationale, was in control, that the Crémieux Decree was reinstated.[95] But as legal historian Yerri Urban remarks, none of Giraud's ordinances abolished the law of February 17, 1942, on Muslim *indigènes*,[96] which was a part of the legacy of Vichy's racial legislation and inextricably connected to the long history of the Crémieux Decree and its abrogation.

The colonial administration in North Africa, even after the Comité français de Libération nationale was in control, continued to maintain the idea that the abrogation of the decree had corrected a serious error of the past; its restitution might have grave consequences for their continued control of their North African colonies. They were concerned about Muslim reactions to the restitution of the decree not only in Algeria but also in Morocco, and a survey was sent out again to colonial administrators in both Algeria and Morocco, just weeks after the Crémieux Decree was restored. The same questions and scripted response came from the local and regional French authorities, as had been the case with the abrogation of the Crémieux Decree in 1940: All concurred that many Muslims were opposed to the restitution of the decree, mainly because it would show favoritism to Jews and disregard Muslims, who were hoping for an improvement in their civil status.[97]

The Jews, however, welcomed the liberation of North Africa, and for many, faith in the French Republic was restored. The Jewish leadership across North Africa was quick to reassert the place of Jews in the French empire even before the end of World War II, attributing the Vichy anti-Semitic laws to the influence of Nazi Germany and declaring their allegiance to "the good France" as opposed to the Vichy regime.[98] In retrospect, this was understandable, because few were to predict that in just a few years after the end of World War II, the State of Israel would be formed and the French empire would crumble.

Conclusion

Vichy's anti-Semitic laws replicated in many details Nazi anti-Semitic legislation, connecting in documentable ways France's colonies to the Holocaust. But as implemented in North Africa, Vichy's Jewish policy is legible only in the colonial context. Seen on a longer continuum, Vichy's anti-Semitic legislation was integral to French colonialism, embedded in the racial policy toward both Muslims and Jews across North Africa that both predated and followed the war. The abrogation of the Crémieux Decree, both by the Vichy government and again after the liberation of North

Africa, brings into sharp relief how the Holocaust and colonialism coincided on Europe's margins. More than just an anti-Semitic act, the abrogation of the decree demonstrates how the French preferred the indigenous status of Jews in the Moroccan and Tunisian protectorates over the Algerian model. The re-abrogation of the Crémieux Decree after North Africa was liberated by the Allied forces at the very same time that the discriminatory laws of the anti-Jewish Statut des Juifs and *dahirs* were annulled was a mask for denying the Muslim population rights under the guise of creating equality between Muslims and Jews. The attempt to maintain the racial supremacy of Europeans through a policy of divide and rule served only to exacerbate Muslim-Jewish tensions, the consequences of which reverberate to this day in relations between the two communities.

2

The Persecution of Jews in Libya Between 1938 and 1945
An Italian Affair?

Jens Hoppe

AFTER ITALY declared war on Turkey on September 29, 1911, Libya, or rather the provinces of Tripolitania and Cyrenaica, came under Italian suzerainty with the Treaty of Ouchy of October 18, 1912. Because of significant armed resistance to Italian rule, the Italian army did not gain control of all of Libyan national territory until the early 1930s. This resistance was finally broken by the most brutal means,[1] which included using poison gas against the civilian population; according to conservative estimates, the Italians killed at least 70,000 civilians.[2] Nevertheless, Libya was regarded as an exemplary fascist colony where new town planning measures were implemented and the "new fascist man" was to be created.[3]

The 1931 census recorded 25,103 Jews living in Libya, representing 3.57% of the population.[4] Consequently, the proportion of Jews in the total population was significantly larger in Libya than in Italy, where the country's 39,112 Jews constituted only 0.09% of the Italian population. Apart from Jews with Italian citizenship, other Jews living in Libya at the time held citizenship of another nation, mainly France or Britain. The largest and most important Jewish community was in the capital, Tripoli, and numbered 15,637 in 1931. The second largest community was in Benghazi with 2,767.[5]

Here, I do not examine the attacks on and persecution of Arabs and Berbers carried out by the Italian institutions, although these followed a powerful tradition of lengthy and bloody disputes. I focus instead on the measures against Jews, particularly those passed between 1938 (when the so-called racial laws were introduced in Libya) and 1943 (when the British

Eighth Army occupied the country and ended Italian rule). In doing so, I closely examine the internment of Jews in special camps and the deportation of foreign Jews to Tunisia or Italy in 1942. To put these findings in context, I include background history since the 1920s and extend to the period after 1943, especially the pogroms of November 1945, before finally assessing the Libyan situation.

The main question to be answered is, Who is responsible for anti-Jewish violence in Libya? To answer this question, we have to look at three things: (1) what the Italians did, (2) how the policies against the Jews in Libya changed during World War II as a result of the presence of the German Wehrmacht and the fighting between the Axis troops and the British Eighth Army between 1941 and 1943, and (3) what happened under the British Military Administration (BMA) of Libya after January 1943.

The persecution of Jews in Libya cannot be traced back to a German diktat, nor did it arise only because of German diplomatic pressure. And the Italians did not need to adjust to the German approach, because in 1938, when the Italian racial laws came into effect, the Germans were not yet interested in persecuting the Jews in Libya. The development, instead, was based on an independent "maturing process" of fascist anti-Semitism, which Michele Sarfatti regards as decisive for Italy in general.[6] But at the same time we must not forget that since 1933 the anti-Semitic politics in the German Reich had been well noted by the fascists. It remained present, in other words, as a positive or negative example. Thus, based on different players in that area, the persecution of the Jews in Libya was neither purely an Italian nor solely a German-Italian affair but also a Libyan affair.

Geography plays a special role in this story, because the experience Italy gained in East Africa, and above all in Abyssinia, resulted in the strict segregation of the races, prompted by fears of "commingling" and thus the feared end of the (utopian) "new fascist Italian."[7] The Italians in (East) Africa developed racial segregation, later taking it to Italy and from there reimporting it to (North) Africa. At the end, the European, African, and Muslim worlds clashed in Libya, and this shaped the persecution of the Jews in a particular way.

So far, other historians have rarely focused on the question of responsibility. Jeffrey Herf mentions in his important work about Nazi propaganda for the Arab world that an adequate examination of the impact, reception, and aftereffects of this propaganda is beyond his work.[8] Libya itself played only a minor role for him. The same is true for David Motadel's book about Islam and Nazi Germany's war, because this work also is not an account of the Muslim response to Nazi Germany.[9] Klaus-Michael Mallmann and Martin Cüppers took almost no notice of the Italian policy against Libyan Jews and focused on German strategy in particular for the time after a possible victory over the British army in Egypt.[10]

It is interesting that West German indemnification laws, above all the Bundesentschädigungsgesetz (Federal Compensation Law; BEG), resulted in raising the question of specific Nazi injustice for the persecution of Libyan Jews in the 1950s and afterward. Because under the BEG one of the basic requirements for indemnification is German instigation for persecution by a foreign country, the indemnification offices and/or judges must clarify whether the German Reich influenced the persecution of Jews in Libya. This, in turn, requires an answer to the question of whether Italy was subject to German influence.

Legally, as defined by the BEG, instigation does not mean exerting force or incitement to conduct a certain act of persecution; a general encouragement is sufficient. Therefore the indemnification law requires only that an anti-Jewish measure of a country should simply have lain in the general direction of the German demand for the persecution of the country's Jews. The fact that the German government caused a foreign country to take general anti-Jewish measures was thus solely decisive.[11]

In the framework of West German compensation, the imprisonment of the Jews deported from Libya in three Tunisian internment camps (see the section "Internment in Camps and Deportation") was compensated as "deprivation of liberty." Thus in Germany this dimension of the persecution of Libyan Jews was recognized as Nazi injustice. This assessment was based on the actions of the French Vichy authorities in the Tunisian protectorate. That is, *imprisonment* in the camps constituted the actual grounds for compensation, not *deportation* by the Italian authorities. Thus, as a result of instigation, the Vichy government was regarded as subject to German influence.

The assessment of anti-Jewish measures in Italy itself—above all the deprivation of liberty because of internment in camps—has been contradictory. In 1958 the Oberlandesgericht (Higher Regional Court; OLG) in Frankfurt am Main ruled that the imprisonment of Jews in Italy is compensable because, in the legal sense, the measures of the Italian government must count as having been German-instigated.[12] This point of view was supported two years later by a decision of the Bundesgerichtshof (Federal Supreme Court; BGH).[13] By contrast, in January 1967 the Koblenz OLG (and in December 1971 and March 1972 the Zweibrücken OLG) insisted that deprivation of liberty by Italy was not instigated by the German Reich and was consequently not compensable.[14]

Nevertheless, Jews who were interned in Italy in the Ferramonti di Tarsia camp received compensation for their deprivation of liberty there. No compensation has been paid to Jews held captive in other Italian internment camps before the surrender of Italy in September 1943. This was because internment in these camps was considered an independent measure taken by Italy without German instigation.[15] Exceptions were made solely for Jews who were denied the protection of the Reich, that is, German Jewish citizens who were interned in Italy before September 1943.

Because Libyan Jews also applied for compensation for imprisonment in the camps in Libya in the framework of the BEG, this matter also had to be adjudicated. The result was that more than 2,000 Jews received compensation for deprivation of liberty.[16] Thus one can say that the West German side recognized the persecution of the Jews in Libya in the form of camp imprisonment as an injustice based on German instigation for Italian actions. However, in March 1978 the Koblenz OLG determined that imprisonment in the Giado camp (also spelled Jadu or Gado) was not German-instigated; rather, the military points of view had caused the Italian authorities to deport the Jews from Benghazi.[17] This standpoint was based above all on the denial of all anti-Jewish racial persecution in Libya, because it was assumed that there had been no racial persecution. The Koblenz OLG built their finding on a false definition of instigation: Although the BGH considered that merely a suggestion was necessary to recognize German instigation, the Koblenz OLG required direct *and* successful influence. The court admitted that Germany had exercised pressure on Italy to persecute the Jews but determined that it had not been successful and therefore that no compensation ought to be paid. This is a completely wrongful conviction, because, in accordance with the decision of the BGH, the only legal condition on the pursuit of compensation is that persecution was in line with the German demand—which, of course, applied to every kind of internment of Jews!

Jews from Libya who were deported to Europe and finally interned in the Bergen-Belsen concentration camp also received compensation from the United Kingdom in 1965 and later as a result of the global agreement reached between the Federal Republic of Germany and Great Britain.[18] For Great Britain, however, it was solely the fact of imprisonment in the

Bergen-Belsen camp that was relevant, not the imprisonment in Libya or the deportation to Italy and internment there. Thus ultimately compensation was paid to Libyan Jews with British citizenship for their experience of German but not Italian persecution. Does that imply that only Germany was responsible for the persecution of Libyan Jews? The following pages will tell us what happened and who was the culprit.

Anti-Jewish Actions Against Libyan Jews from the Beginning of Fascist Rule

The fundament for the persecution of the Jews in Libya was built by the Italian fascists. To understand how they treated the Jewish minority, we need to go back to the early 1920s. In this section I also make clear that the "first" responsibility for anti-Jewish violence in chronological order goes to the Italians.

Soon after fascist rule began in Italy at the end of October 1922, skirmishes broke out between Italians and local Jews in Libya, a colony that would to a certain degree be in a state of war until 1931. Thus in August 1923 Italian soldiers and fascists in Tripoli's Jewish quarter, the *hara*, violently attacked the Jews, who defended themselves; some of the attackers also suffered injuries. In October 1923 an Italian soldier eventually died from the injuries he had suffered in the *hara*.[19] Michele Sarfatti points out that the Italian protagonists acted without orders from the government in Rome and represented an extreme trend in the fascist movement. They were, nevertheless, part of the fascist movement, intentionally acting as fascists and specifically attacking Jews.[20] Similar sporadic attacks also occurred in Italian towns, for example, Livorno and Trieste in 1923, Florence in 1925, and Padua in 1926. In Italy the target was Jews (or Jewish facilities, which were also attacked)—and other anti-fascists—who were considered opponents of the fascist system. In this way, the specific anti-Jewish line of attack conjoined with the direction of national politics.[21]

Apart from the early attacks (which were attributed to the fascists and took place following the seizure of power and the period in which Italian authority was being secured), further anti-Semitic actions were also carried out in Libya. For example, in 1932 fascists made several attacks on Jews in Tripoli. At the end of 1936 a decree that forced shops to open on Saturdays resulted in the whipping of two Jewish proprietors who kept their shops closed on Sabbath to observe the prohibition of labor on that weekly Jewish holiday.[22] Renzo de Felice argues that this was not an anti-Semitic action because Muslim inhabitants were also whipped in Libya as punishment for violating Italian orders.[23] In so arguing, however, de Felice completely overlooks the fact that the requirement to open on Saturdays put only the Jews in a difficult situation and was in fact aimed directly at them. The Jewish side certainly perceived the various attacks by fascists as anti-Semitic, as Sarfatti can prove of the earliest incidents in Tripoli (with reference to a letter written in 1923).[24] Referring to the Libyan events, Thomas Schlemmer and Hans Woller also share this point of view that under certain circumstances the potential violence of Italian fascism was directed at Jews, who were explicitly attacked *as* Jews.[25]

The first phase of the anti-Jewish actions in Italy and the Italian colonies was characterized by occasional violent attacks and by rare anti-Jewish propaganda, which was spread from the start and gradually increased with time. As Schlemmer and Woller note, an anti-Semitic fever rose steadily after the fascists came to power.[26]

In addition to the Italian-Jewish conflicts in Libya, Arabs carried out targeted attacks on Jews. These attacks were partly connected to events in Palestine[27] and were connected to the pre-1912 era of Ottoman rule, when Muslims in Tripolitania often attacked Jewish peddlers and/or stole their wares.[28] In the Italian era these attacks occurred significantly less frequently, but they did not disappear completely. Harvey E. Goldberg writes, "In spite of relative stability imposed by the Italians tensions between Muslims and Jews continued to be present, and at times the religious aspect of these tensions was apparent."[29] Goldberg refers, for example, to a serious incident in 1927 when, on the eve of Mawlid (celebration of the birth of the prophet), Jews were attacked by Muslims.[30]

The appointment of Italo Balbo as governor of Libya in January 1934 led to disputes with the Jewish community in Tripoli, because Balbo did not take into consideration the Jewish tradition of the region at all. Overall, the situation of the Jews in Libya deteriorated. The turn of the year 1935/1936 is considered a decisive milestone in this process, because it was probably then that Mussolini decided to introduce binding legislation directed at Jews, whereas previously Jews were being ousted from important positions only gradually and not by decree.[31] The background to this change was the war against Abyssinia, which began in 1935. This war was regarded as the motor for national regeneration, from which a new Italian people competent to rule was to emerge. At the same time, racial policies developed in Italian East Africa, encompassing Abyssinia, Eritrea, and Italian Somaliland, stipulated a clear segregation between the indigenous black population and the Italians and became a catalyst for anti-Semitic legislation.[32] Enzo Collotti explains that the contact with black Africans in 1935 and later encouraged the idea of a possible "contamination" of the imagined *"Razza Italiana"*; this notion spread in Italy and proved the basis for the issuing of racial laws.[33] This form of racism (based on racial laws) could then be directed against ethnic white minorities (such as Croatians and Slovenes) as well as against Jews in the Italian mother country and indeed also in the colonies.[34]

The Leggi per la Difesa della Razza of 1938 and Their Effects on Libyan Jews

In this section about the Italian racial laws (Leggi per la Difesa della Razza) I show the big step from single actions to organized persecution by law. Michele Sarfatti has described in great detail the evolution of the fascist government from 1936, which led to the legal exclusion and persecution of the Jews.[35] Various laws issued in 1938 were of key significance, in particular, Law 1381/1938, which outlined the expulsion of foreign Jews compelled to leave Italy, the Dodecanese, and Libya by a certain date; Laws 1390/1938 and 1630/1938, which regulated the removal of all Jewish children from state schools; and Law 1728/1938, which defined who counted as Jewish, forbade marriage between "Aryan" Italians and members of other races, excluded Jews from the army, and banned Jews from holding various administrative and party offices and positions.

I turn now only to the question of who was persecuted as a Jew, because it is thus possible to show the breadth of the group of people with Jewish background who were subject to anti-Semitic persecution by fascist Italy. The definition of Law 1728/1938 was supplemented by ministerial regulations.[36] Who was regarded as a Jew in the fascist sphere of control? The definition included six metrics:

1. A person with two Jewish parents, even if this person was not practicing Judaism

2. A person with a Jewish mother, if the father was unknown

3. A person with a Jewish Italian parent and a foreign parent, even if the foreign parent was not Jewish

4. A person with one Jewish parent, if this person was married to a Jewess or a Jew

5. A person with a non-Jewish Italian parent and a foreign Jewish parent, if the Jewish parent did not officially belong to a non-Jewish religion before October 1, 1938[37]

6. A person with more than two Jewish grandparents[38]

The Italian census of August 1938 was the first to use racial criteria to determine who was a Jew. Apart from 46,656 Jews who registered as members of Jewish communities or as foreign Jews, more than 4,400 people counted as members of the *Razza Ebraica*, the Hebrew race, and thus were deemed quasi-Jews by the fascists. There are also figures for Libya based on the listed racial definition. Accordingly, in June 1939, the total number of Jews was 30,873; broken down into the new provinces established by the Italians, their numbers are 22,984 in the province of Tripoli, 3,653 in the province of Benghazi, 3,369 in the province of Misurata, 863 in the province of Derna, and 4 in Fezzan.[39]

With the issue of the various anti-Jewish laws in 1938, the situation of Libyan Jews changed significantly. As Patrick Bernhard points out in reference to a letter to the Italian Colonial Ministry dated December 13, 1938, although the Leggi per la Difesa della Razza were not introduced in Abyssinia, they were introduced in part in Libya.[40] These laws affected 5,770 people more than the 25,103 designated Jews of 1931, who, as a result of being classified as belonging to the *Razza Ebraica*, were subject to fascist persecution. Consequently, all Jewish teachers had to leave the state schools in Libya, and all officials and employees of the municipalities, banks, and public institutions lost their jobs. Subsequently, in 1938 a Jewish secondary school was founded. Jewish teachers from Italy who had been forced to leave the state schools there taught at this school.[41]

As a result of this new legislation, Jews had to register their property with the PAI (Polizia dell'Africa italiana). Jewish businesses were no longer given public contracts and were later no longer allowed to supply the army, police, or government facilities. Even the Italian colonial police no longer carried out their general duties when Jews were concerned. With regard to the possibility of becoming an Italian citizen, differences were made between Arabs and Jews: Law 70/1939 of January 9, 1939, availed to Muslims a special Italian citizenship in the colony. Jews, by contrast, were expressly denied the possibility of obtaining Italian citizenship.[42] Until 1939 no German exertion of influence with regard to the persecution in Libya can be found. The Italians have to take responsibility for these legal measures.

The laws introduced thus far exacted their toll. Numerous Jewish families became impoverished, having lost their economic foundation. Business transactions were difficult and to a great extent impossible. The tensions between Jews and Arabs also increased, because the laws permitted Italians and Arabs to regard Jews as inferior and to treat them accordingly. An essential effect of these laws was, as Maurice M. Roumani notes, that they "caused the greatest damage to the social life in the country as it strengthened the distinction between Italians, Jews, and Arabs in Libya."[43] With the beginning of military fighting in North Africa in September 1940, the situation for Libyan Jews worsened again.

The Increasingly Radical Persecution of the Jews After September 1940

With the fighting in North Africa new players entered the stage: the Germans and the British. Both had a strong impact on the persecution of the Jews. The "second" responsibility for the persecution of the Jews in Libya goes to the Germans, because they were spatially seen there when the Italians tightened their anti-Jewish measures. The attack on Egypt by Italian troops not only met resistance from the British (which led, after December 1940, to the temporary loss of Cyrenaica, including Benghazi) but also led to a rebellion by Arab and Berber tribes in the eastern part of Libya. The Italians consequently faced a double front: They had to quell a rebellion and at the same time drive back the British army. The latter was accomplished only after some British units withdrew to Greece and German troops under Erwin Rommel were deployed in Africa, at the end of March 1941. As a result of these events, large parts of Cyrenaica were recaptured by the Axis powers. The Italian authorities reacted to the military development with attacks against Jews, whom they automatically suspected of collaborating with the British, that is, of supporting Italy's enemy. Individual Jews who were accused of treason were given long prison sentences.[44]

Since the beginning of the war, diverse anti-Jewish preconceptions of the local Italian population had also been coming to light. Victor Magiar, a Libyan Jew, described the Italian accusations in his essential book *E venne la notte* as follows: "The Jews soon were accused of speculation and of profiting from the war, of buying and selling all the time by chance to get a permanent increase in value, of concealing food supplies for sale [later] on the black market, of leading Allied air raids by sending light signals."[45] The grounds for these anti-Semitic views of the local Jews were built up by Italian fascist propaganda, not by the Germans. The Germans did not want to undermine their ally's imperial ambitions in North Africa, in particular with regard to Libya, and therefore focused their propaganda on Egypt and the Middle East.[46] Because they had suffered so much under Italian subjugation, most Libyan Muslims were opposed to the Italians and the allied Germans.[47] The Germans were fully aware of this situation: German diplomats were reporting that in the aftermath of the occupation of Libya and the war in Abyssinia, the Arabs preferred the British to the Italians.[48]

The anti-Jewish preconceptions expressed by Italians living in Libya were based on the same images as in European regions. For example, after German and Romanian troops attacked the Soviet Union in June 1941, the Jewish population in Romania, particularly in the eastern part of the country, was accused of almost the same things that Magiar noted—war profiteering, selling food on the black market, and aiding the Allies. What we can see here is a world of anti-Semitic preconceptions that spread throughout Europe and the European colonial population in North Africa and was readily supported by Italian anti-Jewish propaganda.

At the beginning of April 1941, two Jews were killed in Benghazi when Italian fascists plundered Jewish businesses and apartments after the first withdrawal of British troops.[49] Also in April 1941 numerous incidents occurred in the Libyan capital, among other places. Thus, for example, between April 7 and 12, 1941, two Jews were beaten up by several attackers in Tripoli and others were mishandled by Italian officers in Suq al-Turq.[50] After the Allied bomb attacks of April 20–21, 1941, fascists, soldiers, and Italian civilians attacked individual Jews.[51] In May 1941 the Italian authorities set up a special tribunal in Benghazi for proceedings concerning Jewish individuals' ostensible support for the British. On September 19 this tribunal sentenced a Jew to death, but British troops were able to free him when they occupied Benghazi for the second time. Other Jews received lengthy prison sentences.[52] These incidents show that Italian anti-Jewish propaganda was not unsuccessful, in particular after 1936, because Jews were targeted and attacked as Jews and served as scapegoats for negative developments in Libya. This logic also applied to the Muslim population: "Otherwise, apart from old hostilities, the Arabs also put a large part of the blame for the difficult economic situation on the Jews."[53]

In September 1941 Ettore Bastico, the new governor of Libya, demanded that all foreigners be removed from Libya. He included in his list of potential deportees some 1,900 "Anglo-Maltese," 1,600 French Jewish subjects and members of the protectorate (i.e., Jews with French and Tunisian citizenship), 870 British Jewish subjects, 715 French Muslim subjects and members of the protectorate, 155 other Muslim foreigners, 225 Greeks, and smaller groups of subjects with citizenship of other countries.[54] Because of the development of the war, this plan was not implemented: In November 1941 British troops led a second attack and were able to conquer Cyrenaica, including Benghazi, again. In the first half of 1942, Rommel, with German and Italian units, succeeded once more in expelling (this time completely) British troops from Libya and advanced as far as El Alamein in Egypt. The persecution of Jews thus became radicalized, as the Axis defeat of the British army opened the door. After the loss of Italian East Africa, Mussolini decided to carry out in his last remaining colony the policy of *sfollamento*, which can be translated as "removal," thereby realizing, at least in part, Ettore Bastico's plan.

The Italian authorities also worsened the Jews' everyday life. For example, Jews were at a disadvantage as regards the provision of food; they simply received less than Italians and Arabs.[55] Numerous Jewish schools (such as the Alliance Israélite Universelle school) and also Jewish associations (such as the Makkabi Sports Club and the Zionistic cultural organization Ben Yehuda) were closed, limiting communal life.[56]

However, it was only with Law 1420/1942 of October 1942 that all Italian anti-Jewish laws were introduced in Libya—that is, only shortly before the end of Italian rule over this North African colony but before the final Axis setback at El Alamein in November 1942.[57] The special situation in Libya can be recognized by the fact that, according to Law 1420/1942, Muslim faith also played a part in defining who is a "Jew" (in contrast to the definition of the *Razza Ebraica* introduced in Italy). The new law regarded a person a non-Jew if their father was born a Jew but had become a Muslim before January 1, 1942, or if they had an unknown father and their mother had become a Muslim before January 1, 1942. This law also mandated that there no longer be any acknowledged difference between Italian, Libyan, and foreign Jews.[58]

Why did the last and comprehensive step come only in October 1942? The most important part of the answer is that in the Italian motherland the persecution of Jews intensified in 1942. This happened against the backdrop of military developments in Europe and North Africa. After the second British retreat in spring 1942, the Italian authorities expected a military victory on the one hand and, on the other, wanted to clear the Libyan area of "the enemy's friend," as the Jews were seen. But they needed time to move the persecution of the Libyan Jews to this state.

Internment in Camps and Deportation of Foreign Jewish Citizens

We turn now to whether the treatment of the Jews in 1942 was a special case. To put it differently, Was the incarceration or the deportation of Jews living in Libya something new to the Italians in North Africa? Here we can see that the British military shortcomings made severe persecution of the Jews possible. The fate of the incarcerated or deported Jews has to be described in detail, because it shows clearly who was responsible for what. So, in this section I include depictions of the living conditions in some of the internment camps.

The recapture in 1942 of Libyan territories (which had briefly fallen under British rule for a second time) created a special situation. On February 7, 1942, Attilio Teruzzi, from the Ministry for Italian Africa, informed the Libyan governor-general, Ettore Bastico, and the chief of General Staff of the Italian Forces, Count Ugo Cavallero, that Mussolini had ruled that all Jews were to be interned in a concentration camp in the hinterland of Tripolitania.[59] In addition, foreign Jews were to be deported from Libya. In fact, up to 870 British Jews were taken to Italy,[60] 300 alone from Tripoli to Naples between January and March 1942, followed by 120 more. After the recapture of Cyrenaica, British Jews were also deported by ship from Benghazi to Italy, after which they were taken to Bologna. All the deportees had to live in Italian camps. When Italy capitulated in September 1943, these Jews fell into German hands, and in 1944 they were deported either to the Bergen-Belsen concentration camp or the German internment camp of Vittel in France.[61] Although the Libyan Jews interned in Vittel were able to return to their country in November 1944, those liberated in Germany did not manage this until September 1945.[62]

French Jews residing in Libya were taken overland to Tunisia by the Italian authorities. According to a report by the PAI, 1,861 Jews along with some Muslims had been deported to the French protectorate by August 1942.[63] The Vichy authorities there placed only the Jews in three different

FIGURE 3: Libyan Jewish survivors of Bergen-Belsen returning to Tripoli, August–September 1945. These Jews were deported from Italian-controlled Libya in 1942 because they held British passports. Interned first in concentration camps in Italy, they were deported to Bergen-Belsen after Italy was occupied by Germany. The prisoners remained in Bergen-Belsen for six months before being liberated by Allied troops. Source: Yad Vashem Photo Archive, Jerusalem, 1495/9. Reprinted with permission.

camps, namely, La Marsa (or Marcia Plage) near Tunis, Agareb (or Tniet-Agarev) near Sfax, and Gabes. With the German-Italian occupation of Tunisia in November 1942, these internment camps came under German control. The inmates remained incarcerated in the three camps until their liberation by the Allies in April or May 1943. During the Allied bombing of La Marsa, more than fifty internees were killed.[64]

Statements by witnesses in the early 1970s describe the Gabes camp (which was similar to the two other camps) as incarcerating only Jews, especially those with Tunisian citizenship. The camp was fenced and strictly guarded, internees were strictly forbidden to leave the camp on their own.

The Libyan refugees [i.e., the Jews deported from Libya] were housed very poorly, suffered from hunger and thirst. Hygiene and medical care were extremely poor so that many camp inmates fell ill. Even if individual inmates were occasionally allowed to leave the camp to go shopping, with a special permit and an escort [of security guards], the majority of the Libyan refugees remained imprisoned for months in the Gabes camp and were not able to leave it.[65]

According to Pinkas Hakehillot, there was no running water in the Agareb camp, holes in the ground served as toilets, and medical care was provided only by the Sfax Jewish community. Until November 1942 the camp guards were French gendarmes; subsequently they were Germans and Italians.[66] Thus three different European persecutor groups (i.e., Vichy-oriented French policemen, Nazi German soldiers, and Italian soldiers) of the Jews deported from Libya to neighboring Tunisia between the summer of 1942 and the spring of 1943 illustrate the links between different anti-Jewish policies during World War II, and the war developments played a major role in what happened to the Jews.

Between February and June 1942, the Italian PAI transported Jews with Libyan and Italian citizenship from Benghazi, Barce, Derna, Susa, Tobruk, and other places in Cyrenaica by truck to the Giado camp in Tripolitania. In the summer of 1942, 2,537 internees were held at Giado;[67] these families had been deported at two-week intervals from their homes following a summons in the synagogue. Three hundred eighty Jews followed later, until only around 120 remained in Cyrenaica.[68] Some Jewish families were not placed in Giado but in the Yefren (or Yafran) camp.[69] According to other sources, Jews were also interned in camps in Gharyan (or Garian, about 50 kilometers east of Yefren) and Tigrinna (or Tegrena, some 5 kilometers south of Gharyan).[70]

Because of the program of internment, from the point of view of the Italian authorities the imagined "danger" posed by Jews in eastern Libya had been to a large degree averted. The living conditions in Giado were extremely bad, because there was neither adequate room for the internees nor sufficient food. "The daily rations in the camp were very poor and included no more than a few grams of rice, oil, sugar and coffee made out of barley seeds."[71] Because medical care was also completely inadequate, between February 1942 and January 1943 at least 562 inmates died, most of them succumbing to a typhus epidemic.[72]

The Jewish families in Giado organized their own camp council, presided over by Camus Suarez. The council consisted of a *capo*[73] elected from each barrack. In negotiation with the Italian head of camp, Major Guerriero Modestino, Suarez secured permission to leave the camp occasionally to organize food supplies.[74] Otherwise, PAI police guarded the inmates and ensured that nobody left the camp. Some Arabs were among the guards, though, according to witnesses, and Germans regularly came to control the internment of the Jews.[75] In Giado the Jewish *capos* organized daily life, distributing firewood and food, which was sometimes sent by the Jewish community in Tripoli. They also converted a camp building into a synagogue so that the internees could practice their Judaism under the extreme conditions of detention. Because the Italian camp leaders allowed Arab traders to sell food to interned Jews, better-off families were able to buy small extra amounts of food. This also meant that the Arab population in the surrounding areas was aware of the inhumane conditions of the imprisoned.

Only when the British managed to stop typhus from spreading and treated the survivors, so that they were able to live a normal life again at home, were the interned once again taken back to Cyrenaica family by family, at two-week intervals. After the liberation of the camp on January 24, 1943, the American Jewish Joint Distribution Committee financially supported this process.[76]

Although in Italy forced labor for Jews between 18 to 45 years of age was introduced on May 30, 1942, this did not occur in Libya until an ordinance was issued on June 28. Subsequently, the Italian authorities took some 3,000 Jews from Tripolitania to the Sidi Azaz camp (near the town of Homs), 1,000 alone from the town of Tripoli. The men were to be deployed as forced laborers in infrastructure projects, but many of them were assessed as physically unsuitable and were able to return home. Only a third remained in the camp.

Unlike in Giado, as far as is known, only three inmates were killed in Sidi Azaz: one by an Italian guard, one in an accident involving a truck, and one by an Arab.[77] The inmates in Sidi Azaz also established a synagogue, in a tent. They managed to persuade the Italian camp leadership to allow the Sabbath to be a work-free day. The Jewish *capos* in Sidi Azaz were able to travel to Homs occasionally to buy food for the forced laborers. The Jewish community in Tripoli also provided food for the poorest camp inmates so that they did not starve.

About 350 Jewish men were taken from Sidi Azaz to Buk Buk (or Buqbuq) at the end of August 1942, where they were deployed in constructing roads that would connect Libya to Egypt. In October 1942 the British bombed the camp, and finally, in the course of the retreat of the German-Italian troops from Egypt, it was abandoned in November.[78] The extremely poor living conditions in Buk Buk made many Jewish forced laborers ill; these individuals were released from camp imprisonment by an Italian doctor and able to return to Tripoli. As a result, the number of inmates had fallen to roughly 200 by the end of October.[79]

FIGURE 4: Bilingual signboard at the entrance to Buk Buk labor camp, 1942. The Hebrew reads "Shadday" (God Almighty); the Italian reads "First Jewish Corps" (top) and "Labor Camp for Jewish Workers" (bottom). The name Mose/Moshe Hadad refers to the camp Kapo, the prisoner assigned to serve as camp overseer. Source: Heritage Center of Libyan Jewry, Or Yehuda. Reprinted with permission.

Apart from this widespread persecution in the form of internment of Jewish families and the imprisonment of Jewish men as forced laborers, in the summer of 1942 local incidents targeted individual Jews. In March 1942 a Jewish woman was sentenced to 24 years' imprisonment because she had waved at the advancing British troops.[80] The fact that the fascists stopped at nothing, including judicial murder, is shown by the sentencing to death of three young Jews accused of plundering. The three were hanged in July 1942. Patrick Bernhard assumes that the Italian authorities intended this act to be a warning to the Jewish community.[81]

Was the internment of civilians or their deportation abroad, as carried out with Jews in 1942 in Libya, a unique form of persecution conducted by the Italians in comparison with Italy's actions in Africa during the fascists' time? In Libya itself, during the phases of the recapture of the country by the Italians in the 1920s and early 1930s, tens of thousands of civilians were imprisoned in concentration camps in the Libyan desert in order to break the resistance movement headed by the Sanussi movement in Cyrenaica.[82] But there were also examples of deportation to neighboring countries; in the course of conquering Abyssinia, the Italian authorities deported a portion of the intelligentsia to neighboring Italian Somaliland.[83] These examples show that the measures taken in Libya were not out of the ordinary. On the contrary, the Italian authorities walked on familiar ground. What was different, however, was the targeting of Jews, who were persecuted by dint of being Jews, without consideration of individual guilt. This qualitative difference is at the heart of the radicalization of 1942, which highlights the anti-Semitic attitude of the Italian leadership in Rome and in Tripoli. In Libya there was the added element of virulent anti-Semitism that came from the bottom up, so to speak, being widespread not only among the local fascists and Italian soldiers but also among Italian colonists.[84]

Were Jews Persecuted Under the British Administration?

The complete occupation of Libya by the British Eighth Army in January 1943 ended Italian suzerainty. But did this also mean the end of anti-Jewish persecution? The Italians and the Germans left the stage, and another major player entered it: the Libyan Muslim population looking for independence. Under Italian domination, Libyan Muslims were not engaged in anti-Jewish riots.[85] This only happened under British rule.

Maurice Roumani describes the situation of Libyan Jews in 1943 in clear terms: "The demeaning effects of the Italian racial laws, war and concentration camps took a heavy toll on the Jewish community. Those repatriated from the Giado concentration camp and from other camps returned to find their homes ransacked and destroyed, their shops bombarded and in ruins, and hardly any aspect of community life left."[86] Jewish soldiers of the Eighth Army supported the Jewish communities in Libya, in particular in rebuilding community life and establishing Jewish schools. Alongside this, it was above all the psychological support that was significant, because it gave the Libyan Jews renewed self-confidence and a positive Jewish identity.

Until 1951, when the British administration ended, there had been no kind of persecution of Jews under the British Military Administration (BMA). Consequently, the answer to the question of whether the BMA perpetuated anti-Jewish activities is a clear negative. The relationship between the BMA and the Jewish communities was, however, not without conflict. There were significant differences with respect to education, with the Jewish side expressing the wish for separate schools for Jews and Arabs, wanting lessons to be taught in Hebrew instead of Arabic, and wanting Jewish girls to attend school. The BMA rejected the Jewish demands outright, although even the Board of Deputies of British Jews supported the Libyan Jews in 1944.[87]

Apart from the tension with the British administration, there were disputes with the local Muslim population. The years after 1943 found Libya in an economic crisis against which the BMA took no long-term measures. At the same time, Arab nationalism, supported partly by Libyans returning from Egypt who belonged to the Sanussi movement, resulted in Jews being ostracized. This time the violence against Jews was not official but came instead from the bottom up. In 1944, for instance, the *qadi* (Sharia court magistrate) of Homs gave anti-Jewish addresses in a mosque, and only three months later the rumor was spread that Jews had murdered an Arab girl.[88]

When, at the beginning of November 1945, the anti-Jewish riots in Cairo, Alexandria, Suez, and Port Said that caused several deaths became known in Libya, pogroms quickly followed in Libyan towns: On November 4, 1945, synagogues and apartments of Jewish families were ransacked and Jewish-owned shops were plundered. It is interesting that outside the *hara* signs were painted on houses allowing the protagonists to differentiate between Jews on the one hand and Italians and Muslims on the other.[89]

Similar violent attacks against Jews were started by individuals or small groups of Arabs, for instance members of the Hizb al-Watàni nationalist party in Amrus, Kussabat (part of Homs), Tajura, Zanzur, and Zawia; in these places the aggressors used, among other things, sticks, iron rods, knives, cudgels, and hand grenades against their victims. A report dated November 14, 1945, from Tripoli describes the vicious persecution of Jews in the Libyan capital, which had served as a place of refuge for Jews: "bodies being quartered, children killed by bashing them against stone walls, old men pushed from windows and roofs and a hand grenade tossed into a synagogue,"[90] and it is clear here that the deaths of the Jews was intended. This episode shows that alongside the devastation of synagogues, the very center of the Jewish communities was the specific target. Witnesses later described individual murders, such as that of a young Jew who was fleeing and simply stabbed to death by an Arab. The Jewish quarters of Tajura and Suk al-Juma (now part of the town of Tripoli) were plundered and burned, and thirty-four Jews were murdered in Suk al-Juma alone.

In all these places, three days of brutal violence left 129 Jews dead and 450 wounded. A Jew later died from the injuries he suffered; for this reason, the number of victims is regularly given as 130. However, Harvey E. Goldberg reaches a higher number: 40 Jews murdered in Amrus; 38 in Tripoli, which was much larger; 34 deaths in Zanzur; 13 in Zawia; 7 in Tajura; and 3 in Kussabat.[91] Based on these data, we can conclude that 135 Jews were murdered in the Libyan pogroms of November 1945. Not all Muslims took part in the pogroms; in contrast, individual Arabs saved Jews by taking them into their houses temporarily.[92]

According to Roumani, in Zanzur 30 (rather than the 34 quoted by Goldberg) of only 120 Jews who lived in this town were murdered in a single pogrom. The death toll included six children. A synagogue there, as well as apartments and shops belonging to Jews, were plundered and burned down. In Kussabat Jewish girls and women were raped, and there were forced conversions to Islam; two Jewish men in the surroundings were murdered. In Amrus Jews who had been killed or fatally injured were soaked in petrol, which was then set alight so that some of them were burned alive.[93] In contrast to the war years, the postwar violence toward Jews was restricted to Tripolitania, whereas things generally stayed calm in Cyrenaica.

Let us return to reflect on the role of the BMA in stoking or sanctioning this violence. What we can conclude is that, even if the persecution of Jews was not initiated by the BMA or British administrative bodies, the BMA did nothing to prevent it and on the contrary at first underestimated the pogroms and consequently did not do enough for Jews at risk, even when it had indications of impending violence.[94] It is true that British soldiers evacuated eighty-four Jewish residents of Benu Ulid and the survivors of the Zanzur pogrom.[95] Having said that, the BMA made it impossible for Jewish soldiers in Tripoli to take active measures to protect those affected, because they had to remain in the barracks. The Jewish soldiers in question considered this discrimination, because of their being Jewish.[96]

The pogroms again significantly exacerbated the relationship between the Jewish and Muslim populations in Libya. Furthermore, more than 5,000 Jews in Tripolitania were dependent on the assistance of Jewish communities, 2,000 were in displaced persons camps because they no longer had a home, and a further 1,000 individual Jews from Zanzur and Tripoli were in repatriation camps on the outskirts of the capital.[97] Even if it were possible to accommodate most of these women, men, and children in normal living conditions within a reasonable period, the Jewish community was left with a feeling of insecurity and alienation—in addition to the bitter disappointment they felt toward the British authorities they had welcomed as liberators in 1943.[98]

In fact, it was only two years later, in June 1948, that violence toward Jews broke out again in Libya. Bernard A. Facteau, an American lieutenant commander working in Naval Intelligence, wrote in November 1945 that, in view of what happened in Egypt and the Middle East, the riots were precipitated by Arab fear and hatred of Jewish encroachment in Palestine and were part of a general pattern of Muslim antiforeign sentiment, which was fundamentally based on religious principles.[99] This is also true for Libya, because the Jews there were strongly linked to the British, that is, a non-Muslim foreign authority. Harvey E. Goldberg mentions that for Libyan Muslims the pogroms were a sign that everything foreign (which Jews had been made by recourse to their religious otherness and historical social subordination as *dhimmi*) was to be "eliminated" in order to gain an independent, Muslim Libya.[100] The riots were a signal to both Jews (that they should leave the country) and Muslims (that they should act together and put pressure on all foreigners—real and imagined—to leave the country too).

Conclusion

From 1938 to 1943 the Italians (or from 1941 to 1943 the Italians and the Germans) were accountable for the persecution of Jews as part of a fascist racial policy that first developed in Italian-ruled areas of Africa and later spread to include the Jews. But Jewish persecution did not end completely after the total military defeat in Africa in May 1943. It shifted to Arab and Berber groups of the population, whose outlook was anti-Jewish, despite, or perhaps precisely because of, the British occupying administration.

What was specific to Libya in this story of anti-Jewish persecution? Or, to put it differently, which influencing factors shaped the persecution of Libyan Jews? And who was responsible for that? These questions cannot be answered by naming a single factor or a single group of perpetrators. So in this section I describe many factors of influence, including a look at Italy, Africa, and legal bearings.

A fundamental factor was the fascists' view of Libya as a model colony. After introducing racial policies in 1938, the legal differentiation was not just between the *Razza Italiana* and the *Razza Ebraica* (as in the Italian mother country); there was an additional racial delimitation of the Muslim population. Consequently, the Jews were doubly disadvantaged: first in relation to the Italians as chief masters and second in relation to the Muslims, who occupied the quasi-hierarchic second tier of three. Beginning in January 1939 Libyan Jews alone were completely debarred from "Italian" citizenship.

Although the Italian colonists who came to Libya were, from 1922 on, apparently fascist orientated above all, a substantial part of the Italian population in Libya held an attitude that was more anti-Jewish than what was found in Italy. Renzo de Felice describes the fascism of the Italian colonial society as bigoted and fanatic.[101] This attitude encouraged local attacks on Jews as early as the 1920s. And we can understand why the persecution of the Jews in Libya was more severe than in Italy: More Italians were willing to persecute Jews.

In addition, Africa offered the Italians a specific scope of experience—the persecution of demographic groups—that could be transferred to the persecution of the Jews in Libya: interning civilians in camps intended to combat opposition to Italian rule in Libya. Deportations were also practiced in Abyssinia, though there the target was the intelligentsia and not a specific "racial" group. Nevertheless, the Italian colonial administration was able to make use of the experience gained in Libya and Abyssinia. For Thomas Schlemmer and Hans Woller this scope of violence is characterized by the fact

that fascist Italy was conducting war from the start and using means, first in Libya and then in Abyssinia, which are without parallel in the history of colonialism and which in many ways already anticipate the war and extermination practices that came to full fruition in the Second World War: mass relocation, killings as reprisal, concentration camps, the calculated use of starvation as an instrument of warfare and the targeted elimination of political-cultural elites, not to mention the use of poison gas.[102]

Added to this was Italy's own experience with incarceration of Jews. As of the summer of 1940, in Ferramonti di Tarsia there was an internment camp for Jews (and a few non-Jews, such as Chinese seamen) where mainly foreigners were imprisoned. This camp existed until Italy capitulated in September 1943 and was under fascist administration and guard.[103] This means that a role model already existed in the mother country before the incarceration of the colony Jews started in 1942 and that the Italian administrative bodies had by this time practical experience with the incarceration of Jews on which they could rely in Libya.

This also points to a further detail: The persecution of the Jews in Libya between September 1940 and January 1943 took place in a country that was conducting war with Italy, or, from 1941, the Axis powers, on the one side, and Great Britain on the other. As described earlier, the course of the war in North Africa played a significant part in the persecution of Jews in Libya. This is quite apparent from a counterfactual consideration of World War II on the African continent: If in autumn 1940 the Italian army had been able to advance as far as the Suez Canal and defeat the British troops in Egypt, the persecution of the Jews would have taken a different course. There would have been no radicalization, as in 1942, because the Jews would not have entered the stage as supporters of the British— and consequently the fascists would not have had to find a drastic solution (such as the internment of Jewish families in Giado or deportation abroad). It is more likely that Jews in influential positions would have been ousted from their positions and that subsequently all Jews would have been gradually banished from the workforce.[104] Whether Mussolini's plan to settle Jews from Europe in Abyssinia[105] could also have been applied to Libyan Jews, thus virtually displacing them from one Italian colonial arena in North Africa to another in East Africa, did not, however, depend on the course of war in North Africa. Rather, it was the plans of the Nazi leaders in the German Reich that were decisive. Only if Hitler had agreed to such a solution—for example, by analogy, as Germany did relative to the intermittently conceived Madagascar (an island off the coast of southeast Africa!) solution—could there have been forced relocation to Abyssinia.

Another factor that affected the situation of Libyan Jews is relevant: the German Reich. Patrick Bernhard has already referred to the special cooperation between Germany and Italy on colonial issues.[106] This included the cooperation between the PAI and the Security Police or the SS. Some of the German SS officers trained by the Italian side went to Libya in 1941.

Survivors of the camps also reported repeatedly that Germans appeared to control internment. It cannot be said with certainty whether the master (the PAI) was showing the trainee (the SS) how to handle internment of indigenous Jews or whether it was the other way around. Because the situation in 1942 was different from that of the year before (and in addition the success of Erwin Rommel in spring 1942 also increased the scope and the position of power of the SS), it is certainly plausible that the German SS was the master of the Italian PAI. Ultimately, in retrospect, it is clear that the interned Jews saw themselves as controlled by the Germans.[107]

This raises the question of whether the Germans exerted influence in Libya. As has been proven, Rommel ordered the Italian authorities to do everything necessary to ensure that he had calm behind the front and to stop spying.[108] This scope of influence extended to the issuing of anti-Jewish measures, which meant that the PAI was able to assume that the Germans would approve all such measures. In the summer of 1942 the Germans also pressured the Italians to deport all Jews to Europe—but this demand came to nothing because of the course of the war.[109] However, taken in isolation, the presence of German troops resulted in the intensified persecution of the Jews by the Italian authorities.[110] De Felice calls this "the ever-growing German influence and pressure."[111]

With the PAI, Libya had an instrument created in 1936 as an elite corps of the fascist regime. Many Italians who served in the colonial police force had previously taken part in the Spanish Civil War on the side of the putschists. Among them were many who supported the use of force against civilians.[112] However, this violence was directed not only at Jews but also at Muslim Arabs and Berbers. When the British troops ousted the Italian army from Cyrenaica at the end of 1940, there were outbreaks of violence by the local population against the Italian citizens and colonists in which some 100 Italians were murdered.[113] The Italian troops, the fascist militia, the PAI, and simple colonials countered this violence with more violence when the two recaptures of Cyrenaica gave them the chance. At this point, Arabs were shot or arrested by the PAI on a grand scale. In Barce and Tripoli numerous Arabs were hanged. The persecution of Jews in Libya was thus being conducted at a level of violence that exceeded the limits of a civil system. This made the situation in Libya quite different from that of Italy before September 1943.

With the occupation of further parts of the Italian mainland by the German Wehrmacht and the subsequent combat actions up to May 1945, the violence of Italian fascists against Jews also increased dramatically. Then, in Italy, Jews were repeatedly arrested by Christian Italians; in Rome they were also specifically sought out in the underground and handed over to the German occupying bodies; however, the deportation of those arrested was taken over by the Germans and not the Italians, as in Libya.[114] Part of what happened in Italy after September 1943 came first in Libya in 1942. So, with regard to the persecution of the Jews, the periphery reached life-threatening persecution faster than the center.

The Germans conducted anti-Jewish propaganda in the Middle East and North Africa through radio broadcasting and leaflets dropped by airplanes. The propaganda included recitation of Quran suras with anti-Jewish statements, such as 5.82: You will surely find the worst enemies of the Muslims to be the Jews and Polytheists.[115] But the German foreign minister, Joachim von Ribbentrop, decided in February 1942 that in Libya German propaganda should not include any appeals to nationalism and that there should not be any general Islamic propaganda on religious grounds, because Mussolini intended to keep the colony under Italian control.[116] This for sure limited the German influence on Libyan Muslims. What is more, "Overall, German propaganda failed."[117] The vast majority of the Muslim population in the whole region showed no reaction to German calls for religious violence, and the Islamic slogans of Germany's propaganda had little resonance in religious circles and among leading 'ulama.[118]

This leads to the main question of this chapter that finally has to be answered: Was the persecution of Libyan Jews an Italian affair? As we have seen, until the beginning of 1943 the most important decisions affecting the persecution of Jews in Libya were made in Rome. The Germans did not exercise direct influence. But there was political cooperation at the highest level, joint warfare in North Africa, headed by Rommel, close cooperation between the PAI and the SS, and German control of the Giado camp. Because Italy had been aware of the German point of view on the violent persecution of Jews (i.e., organized mass murder) since the end of 1941 or the beginning of 1942 at the latest, Germany's mass killing policy could serve as a negative or positive pattern. In this sense, the persecution of Libyan Jews was not a purely Italian affair.

By the end of 1942 Libyan Jews had suffered economic damage and were socially isolated by the Leggi per la Difesa della Razza. Fascism positioned them as inferior in the 1930s. But many Arabs also felt a distance between Jew and Muslim. Although Jews had been settling in the Libyan region since ancient times, in the era of Italian fascism (and directly after this) they were made strangers who could serve as scapegoats for all negative developments, not only in the eyes of the Italians but also subsequently by Arabs.[119] This newly created distance provided a basis for the murderous violence against Jews that broke out in Tripolitania in November 1945 under the eyes of the BMA.

Therefore there is also a Muslim perspective, which was evident not just in the pogroms of November 1945. When in December 1936 two Jewish businessmen who kept their shops closed on the Sabbath, despite the order to open them, were publicly whipped in Tripoli, the crowd of Muslims watching showed approval and made derogatory comments.[120] Victor Magiar also refers to the anti-Jewish views of the Hizb al-Watàni party, which was represented by the exiles of the Italian era who were active in Libya.[121] Alongside friendly relationships between Jews and Muslims, religious and political tension between these populations existed, and this explains repeated eruptions of violence from the Muslim side. Jeffrey Herf points to Muslim antipathy toward the Jews, which had been a longstanding component of Islam traditions.[122]

To conclude, we see diverse players active at different times. It is clear that the persecution of Libyan Jews inside and outside the country was shaped by different points. The responsibility for the persecution goes to all players to different degrees at certain times: The first phase of the persecution started with the fascist power grab and ended with the landing of German Wehrmacht forces under General Erwin Rommel in 1941. During these years, the Italians were responsible for the persecution of the Jews. At this time the persecution was not life-threatening.

The second phase lasted from 1941 until the beginning of 1943, when the British army evicted the Axis troops from Libya. In this phase Germans and Italians were responsible for the persecution, which became life-threatening, in particular for the Jews in the Giado camp. Who was the key player at this time? All decisions regarding the implementation of anti-Jewish laws, the deportation of foreigners, the incarceration of Libyan Jews, the forced labor of male Jews, and so on were made in Rome or Tripoli. So, the answer is, Italy! But behind the scenes the Germans were heavily involved, notably Rommel (and the Wehrmacht), the SS, and the German Foreign Ministry. That was the reason for the positive BEG court decisions mentioned in the introduction. And finally, regarding the Jews deported by Italian authorities to Tunisia, the French Vichy-oriented administration persecuted these Jews according to their own Vichy policies. So, for this group of Jews, a third party was responsible for their persecution: France. But France's responsibility ended in November 1942, when it shifted to the Germans, after they occupied large parts of Tunisia.

The last phase spans the time from January 1943 until 1951, when Libya was controlled by the British Military Administration. This time Muslim groups, such as the Sanussi movement, actively acted against the local Jews, reaching the first culmination in the November 1945 pogroms. Motadel describes the basis for this as follows:

One of the most persistent and socially widespread forces of anti-imperial mobilization was religious. Anticolonialism and Islam were in fact often closely intertwined, with religious authorities leading anti-imperial movements and employing Islamic rhetoric to unite Muslims—a phenomenon that could be observed particularly well in North Africa.[123]

In Egypt, after the anti-Jewish riots in November 1945, anti-British riots took place in the spring of 1946. This also indicates that the Jews (deemed foreigners) were closely linked to the British, and therefore the Arabs and Berbers persecuted them as Jews and as foreign non-Muslims, with the result that they were responsible for what happened in the third phase. And the British? They were not responsible for these anti-Jewish actions but for what they did not do: protect the Jews from murderous violence. The main reason for the reluctance was the British effort to gain Muslim support in the Cold War, and for this they did not want to offend Arabs and Muslims by protecting local Jews extensively.[124]

3

The Implementation of Anti-Jewish Laws in French West Africa
A Reflection of Vichy Anti-Semitic Obsession

Ruth Ginio

HISTORIANS OF AFRICA have long perceived World War II as a major watershed in the history of the continent. It is only recently, though, that historians of World War II have begun to see the importance of integrating Africa into the history of the war and that of the Holocaust. This volume is part of the academic attempt to examine the effects of this world conflict beyond the regions that were at the center of the events.

Despite the recognition of the importance of World War II to the history of Africa and especially its impact on colonial rule and the growth of resistance to it in various African colonies, not much had been written on the actual events of the war in Africa until the mid-1990s. Most scholars studying the importance of World War II to the decolonization process in French West Africa set their starting point in the Brazzaville Conference of 1944 and have not examined how exactly the war triggered the political, social, and economic transformations in the late 1940s and 1950s.[1]

Since the mid-1990s this lacuna has been gradually filled, and much more is known today about the various ways the war influenced African lives.[2] Still, more research is needed to integrate the events of the war in Africa into the global history of World War II.

In this chapter I look beyond the territory of North Africa to examine the Vichy period in French West Africa (FWA) and to reconstruct the implementation of the ideology of the National Revolution—and, more specifically, anti-Jewish legislation—across the empire. Following recent historiographic trends, I examine Vichy colonial policy toward the Jews within the context of colonial history, placing it in the more general

Vichy colonial ideology and tracing the importance of FWA to the Vichy regime in France.[3]

To frame this discussion of Jews in the colonial context, I first present the background for understanding the context of FWA on the eve of the war. I then discuss the situation in the French empire following the fall of France in June 1940 and the establishment of the Vichy regime. Next I examine the magnitude of the French empire to the Vichy regime and consider that regime's efforts to extend the ideology of the National Revolution to its West African colonies. Finally, I examine in detail the implementation of one aspect of Vichy ideology in the region of FWA: the persecution of the tiny number of Jews in the federation as part of the implementation of Vichy laws.

Throughout this essay I maintain that, even though FWA was never a center of Jewish life and the number of Jews was insignificant there, the region can serve as an excellent case study to demonstrate the major effects of the persecution of Jews by Vichy France, far beyond the metropole. The measures taken by the colonial administration in FWA, in keeping with Vichy laws regarding Jews, thus shed light on the obsessive nature of Vichy policy and its blind and often irrational implementation.

The Federation of French West Africa on the Eve of World War II

The federation of FWA was officially established in 1895. However, French presence and some form of governance, at least in certain regions, had existed since the seventeenth century. The federation was composed of seven territories: Senegal, Ivory Coast, Niger, Dahomey (now Benin), French Sudan (now Mali), French Guinea (now Guinea Conakry), Mauritania, and Togo, which fell under French mandate after it was wrested from German control during World War I. The overall territory of the federation was 4.7 million square kilometers, and on the eve of World War II its population stood at 15 million, including many diverse ethnic groups.[4] A governor-general ruled the federation from its capital, Dakar, and was also directly responsible for the governor of each territory. Under the governor a highly hierarchical system was created, beginning with the *commandant de cercle* and ending with the village chief, usually an African appointed by the French. Although the French colonial method of governing clearly favored direct rule down to the lowest level, in some areas, based on administrative and economic considerations, the precolonial ruler was kept in place, though he was divested of most of his power.

The first region in FWA that was exposed to French influence already in the seventeenth century was the coast of Senegal. The towns of Dakar, Rufisque, Gorée, and Saint Louis became in 1848 an experimental ground for the theory of assimilation, and their inhabitants, referred to as *originaires*, were granted the right to send a representative to the National Assembly in Paris. Until 1914 all the candidates for the National Assembly and those for local institutions were either French or métis.[5] In 1914, however, Blaise Diagne became the first African to be sent to the French parliament. At this time Africans also began to form their own political parties in Senegal.[6]

This political activity among the colonized was rare in the French empire and had no equivalent in other colonial systems either. However, it is important to bear in mind that the *originaires* were only a tiny portion of the Africans of FWA. The rest of this vast population was under harsh colonial rule and subjected to forced labor and to the *indigénat*, a legal system that enabled any French official to inflict limited punishment on Africans without trying them. Most Africans were considered subjects (*sujets*) and had no political rights whatsoever.

Before discussing the circumstances of World War II in FWA, it is important to consider the period that preceded the war and brought certain winds of change to French rule in the federation, namely, the period of the Popular Front.

The 1936 electoral victory of the Popular Front in France raised hopes for improvements in the empire, because two of the parties of which it was composed, the Communist and the Socialist, were anticolonial in their views.[7] However, it soon became apparent that the Popular Front had no coherent colonial program. Colonial affairs did not interest the French public and therefore remained marginalized.[8] In fact, the Popular Front government came to power when colonialism was universally accepted, with the exception of a small minority on the radical left. Therefore it could not have been anticolonial.

Nevertheless, the proclaimed aim of the Popular Front was to establish a maximum of social justice within the context of colonialism. This aim proved difficult to realize. In Algeria the reforms of the Popular Front led to a legislative attempt to extend French citizenship to 10,000 Muslims. However, because of settlers' pressure, even this limited reform failed.

In FWA the newly appointed governor–general, Marcel de Coppet, implemented some reforms.[9] These reforms affected only some of the colonies
in the federation, mainly Senegal, Ivory Coast, and Dahomey. The most
significant reform was the authorization of trade unions, but it too had its
limitations. To join a union, one had to be literate in French, and Africans
living outside the four communes had to present a school diploma. People
who had been imprisoned for more than a month could not join a union.
In addition to these limitations, union heads had to present a yearly report
on their activities to the colonial authorities.[10] In the context of prewar colonialism, these were not reforms to be easily dismissed. They undoubtedly
carried with them some hope for change among the African urban workers
and Western-educated elites. It is possible that these hopes raised by the
Popular Front, though not completely fulfilled, made the period of war,
especially the Vichy years, look even more thorny and repressive.[11]

Outbreak of the War and the Fall of France

By the time World War II broke out, all of the Popular Front's reforms
had been abolished, including the right to organize in trade unions. The
federation had entered an emergency situation, and the French began a
program of massive recruitment for the army. Between September 1939 and
June 1940, 100,000 Africans enlisted to fight the Germans.[12]

At the outset of the war France and Britain decided on tight cooperation all over the world. This cooperation was clearly seen in FWA.[13] For the
combatting parties in Europe, sub-Saharan French Africa was strategically
important for two reasons, apart from the human and material resources
it provided. First, the port of Dakar was the largest French harbor after
Marseille and Le Havre. Second, Niger and Chad (in French Equatorial
Africa [FEA]) had common boundaries with the Italian colony of Libya
(Tripolitania), and Chad also allowed access to Anglo-Egyptian Sudan and
British colonies in East Africa.[14]

With France's defeat by Germany in June 1940, the colonial administration in FWA, like that in other parts of the French empire, found
itself in a quandary. The colonial administrators had to decide whether
to answer Free French leader Charles de Gaulle's call, made in his June
18 speech from London, to continue the struggle against Germany from
the land of the empire or to accept the authority of Marshal Pétain, the
legitimate leader of France. It is important to bear in mind that Pétain's

credentials as the hero of Verdun were extremely strong. De Gaulle, on the other hand, was at the time a relatively unknown and marginal figure. During that June, when events in the metropole were not yet clear, the tendency of most administrators was to continue the war as a united African body, with FEA. But when Marshal Pétain declared his intention to sign an armistice with Germany, the situation dramatically shifted. On June 25, 1940, the day of the signing of the armistice, FEA governor-general Pierre Boisson declared his support for Pétain and was swiftly promoted to high commissioner of French (sub-Saharan) Africa (*haut-commissaire de l'Afrique française*) and transferred to Dakar.[15]

FWA's support for Vichy ruptured Anglo-French relations. Upon his arrival in Dakar, Boisson declared that he intended to protect the territory entrusted to him against the Germans and the Italians, as well as against the British and the Gaullists, but this declaration did little to improve the atmosphere. The British were concerned that FWA would easily fall to German troops. The relations between Vichy France and Britain further deteriorated following the British attack on Mers el-Kebir on July 3–4, 1940. This attack followed a British ultimatum to the French to surrender their fleet or destroy it so that the Germans would not be able to use it. When the French refused, the British sank the entire fleet, causing 1,200 French sailors to meet their death at sea.[16] This attack contributed a great deal to the growth of support for the Vichy regime in FWA.[17]

At the same time, Chad's governor, Félix Eboué, pledged his allegiance to de Gaulle and was promptly appointed governor-general of FEA, which turned officially to de Gaulle's side on August 26.[18] Encouraged by this support, the British and the Gaullists launched an unsuccessful attempt to win over FWA on September 23–25, 1940, which caused the final break in the Anglo-French bond. The British and the Gaullists dispatched a delegation to Boisson before the attack, asking him to join them voluntarily. His response was to imprison the members of the delegation and shoot its commander. The British retaliated by bombing Dakar for three days, injuring 200 people, most of them Africans, but they did not succeed in taking over the federation.[19]

In October–November 1940 fighting erupted between pro-Vichy forces in Gabon (FEA) and the Gaullists, but within a few weeks Gabon joined the rest of FEA in its support for the Free French.[20] The failure of the attack on Dakar and the Free French victory over Gabon ended the military phase in FWA, and the new governor-general of the federation could turn his focus to the difficult mission ahead of him: ruling the vast area in his hands while a major part of his own country was being ruled by others.

Vichy Propaganda and the National Revolution in French West Africa

The new regime that was established after France's defeat to Germany quickly endorsed an ideology that came to be known as the National Revolution. The old Republican values—liberty, equality, fraternity—were replaced by work, family, and fatherland. The first step of this so-called revolution was to return France to the "true French." That translated as action against Jews, Freemasons, and communists. In general, the National Revolution was based on a collection of right-wing ideas that had developed over the previous fifty years—an unoriginal blend of ideals spanning antidemocratic elitism; the reshaping of society, organization, and order; and a brand of nationalism that determined its enemies to be within its own ranks.[21]

The empire held an important part in this new ideology. Pétain had already referred to the French colonies in his maiden speech after signing the armistice. His words clearly show how important the empire was in his view: "I was no less concerned about our colonies than about metropolitan France. The Armistice protects the links that bind us to them. France has the right to count on their loyalty."[22]

Although the loss to Prussia in 1871 and the consequent loss of Alsace and Lorraine encouraged some French politicians to seek compensation overseas, the debacle of 1940, which left France with control over only one-third of its territory, turned the empire into a real lifesaver. It became the last opportunity to restore French honor. For the Vichy regime the empire was both a diplomatic and political playing card and a myth that was to compensate France for its defeat. The empire enabled France to prove to the world that it was still an independent state with resources, territory, and enormous manpower in its service.[23]

One of the many publications dealing with the empire, produced under Vichy, described to its readers how much worse their country's destiny would have been without the empire.

Thanks to this empire, France though defeated and reduced in Europe, is not a people without space, not a nation without men, not a state without resources. . . . The French should only consider how their country would have been wiped out if it was limited in 1940 to its metropolitan territory and its scant 39 million inhabitants! Deprived of all communication with the outside world, erased from the rank of the sovereign nations for an undetermined period, condemned to wait in the future for only the pity and generosity of others, France would have been, for years, just another Poland or a slightly larger Belgium.[24]

The empire, then, is presented as the supplier of the three necessities France had lost in the defeat to Germany—territory, manpower, and resources—and as a way in which the humiliated French nation might regain some of its lost honor. But the importance of the empire was not limited to the present. It also had a major role to play in the rehabilitation of France as a great nation in the world that would arise after the war. The Vichy regime perceived this world as an arena in which Germany, after defeating Britain or reaching some sort of agreement with it, would be the dominant power. However, a hope was expressed that France would be able to find for itself a respected status in this new world. Only the empire could secure such a status for France, and this would happen only if France invested efforts to nurture and protect it.[25]

The place the Vichy regime accorded in its ideology to the empire in general and to FWA specifically was manifested in its treatment of the colonies as an integral part of France. One important aspect of this view of the colonies as simple extensions of the metropole was the attempt to implement the ideology of the National Revolution in the colonies and propagate its messages to the local populations. As Eric Jennings shows, this was no easy move. Metropolitan ideologies had never been imported to the colonies before Vichy rule, and the two words *National* and *Revolution* carried connotations that no colonial power would have been happy to encourage locally.[26]

Indeed, in the West African case we cannot speak of the importation of the National Revolution but rather of its adjustment to suit the colonial reality. On the one hand, Vichy ideas and the new trinity of family, work, and fatherland were far more suitable for governing colonial subjects than were the republican values of liberty, equality, and fraternity; therefore their implementation in FWA went rather smoothly and was welcomed by the colonial administration. On the other hand, Boisson refused to copy in the colonies the National Revolution as it was. Occasionally he tried to protect the autonomy of the colonial administration from the Vichy center by blocking Vichy's more radical elements. He did this, for example, by preventing certain metropolitan organizations from opening branches in FWA. Not everything that was considered good for France was perceived as good for the colonized populations, and a certain process of selection informed the implementation of the National Revolution on African soil.

Propaganda directed at various segments of the colonial population in FWA was the principal tool that the colonial administration used to implement the National Revolution in the federation. In general, the main ideas of the National Revolution that were promoted in France were transmitted to Africans as well. The importance of work, family, and fatherland (the fatherland being France, of course) was emphasized again and again, as was its greater compatibility with African tradition over the old liberty, equality, and fraternity. Islam was used in FWA in the same way that Christianity was used in France. Muslim Africans were told that by embracing the values of Pétain's ideology, they were in fact following the commandments of their own religion.[27]

Vichy propaganda in France and in Africa had a few key differences. Some themes in this propaganda were relevant only in France, whereas French colonial achievements and advantages for the Africans were discussed mainly in Africa. One major subject in Vichy metropolitan propaganda that was totally absent in FWA was anti-Semitic messages. This can be mainly explained by the small number of Jews living in the federation. Nevertheless, as we will see in the next section, when it came to the implementation of Vichy anti-Jewish legislation, the situation was totally different.

Implementation of Vichy Anti-Jewish Legislation in French West Africa

In contrast to North Africa, in FWA there was no local Jewish community before the French arrival, and even later not many Jews were attracted to the federation, because the harsh climate in general did not encourage European settlement. As opposed to the large Jewish communities of France and North Africa,[28] only 110 Jews inhabited FWA during the war. This number included twelve children. Most Jews were French; some North African and other Jews came from other countries, such as Greece, Syria, the Netherlands, England, Hungary, and Poland. Professionally, most were merchants; four worked in medicine-related professions, two were bankers, one was a lawyer, and one worked as an accountant. Others engaged in trades related to agriculture, hotels, and industry.[29]

The Vichy government published the first Jewish status laws on October 3, 1940, with no German demand. The laws opened with a definition of who was considered a Jew in the eyes of the French state and then prohibited all of those included in this definition from holding senior positions in public service, the military, and trades that could influence public opinion, such as teaching, journalism, radio, cinema, and theater. In addition, the law established quotas of Jews who were allowed to hold free trades so as to limit the number of Jews.[30]

On June 2, 1941, the amended Jewish status laws were published, destined to replace the first ones. The new set of laws filled the gaps that existed in the former laws and added a few categories of public positions closed to Jews. In a series of decrees published after this legislation, quotas for Jews in the free trades were limited to 2%. Quotas of Jewish university students were limited to 3%. The new legislation also established a detailed census of all Jews living in the non-occupied territory and extended the Aryanization of Jewish businesses and property to this area as well.[31]

Until November 1942 the Vichy regime enjoyed an autonomy that could have permitted a different treatment of the Jews in France and more so in the colonies. This is especially true for FWA, which was distanced from the main arenas of the war. The Vichy government insisted on implementing the anti-Jewish laws in the colonies, but the distance from the metropole delayed their implementation and left a certain amount of maneuvering in the hands of the colonial administrations. It is thus interesting to examine the ways in which the colonial regime in FWA treated the few Jews who lived under its rule and the extent to which it implemented the decrees with regard to them.

FWA and French North Africa differed greatly in their response to the Vichy regime's implementation of anti-Jewish laws. First, as already mentioned, the Jewish population in FWA was insignificant compared to that of North Africa. This population also had no communal structure or leadership. Second, because of their small numbers and distribution in the vast territory of the West African federation, the issue of the Jews' relation to African society was insignificant in the eyes of the colonial authorities. Certain matters that concerned the authorities in North Africa did not concern those in FWA; the French fear of Muslim resentment of policy that favored Jews, for example, was irrelevant in FWA, as was administrators' concern that the local economy would be harmed through the implementation of the second anti-Jewish law.

What's more, because the territories of FWA were colonies rather than protectorates (except Togo), the French also did not have to take into consideration the sentiments of local political leadership, as was necessary in the case of the Moroccan sultan. In Morocco local French authorities, headed by General Charles Noguès, demanded that Jews be defined on a religious basis and not on a racial one so as not to upset the sultan. (The sultan could not have accepted the idea that a Jew who had converted to Islam was still considered a Jew.)[32] In FWA no such adjustments were required. All these differences have to be taken into consideration when evaluating the case of FWA.

The first Jewish status laws published in France on October 3, 1940, were published in West Africa only on November 8.[33] The second status law of June 1941 and the decree extending the list of prohibited professions for Jews were also published with a certain delay in the federation. From Boisson's correspondence with the Commissariat Général aux Questions Juives (CGQJ) in Vichy, it is quite clear that he was not especially enthusiastic about this legislation. Usually, when the instructions seemed vague to him, he chose to wait for further clarifications before implementing them.[34]

However, as soon as the clarifications arrived, Boisson instructed the governors to make sure the laws were fully implemented. When asked to perform a census of the Jews in FWA, he explained to his governors how to fill in the declaration forms and instructed them to check every form carefully so that he would not have to send them back. He also remarked that, because French Jews did not hurry to submit declarations, the governors would need to remind them of their duty and the severe sanctions that might be applied against them if they did not comply.[35]

A document discussing the spirit in which the anti-Jewish legislation in FWA should be implemented justified the full implementation of the metropolitan laws, despite the limited number of Jews in the region, in these words: "On first impression until now, it does not seem that the territories of French Africa are severely contaminated by Jewish interference. In fact . . . Jewish influence was, in our opinion, quite restrained. Even so, the future might hold unexpected surprises."[36]

The main issue occupying the colonial regime in the Vichy period with regard to Jews was their employment in prohibited positions according to Vichy metropolitan laws. The detailed correspondence about the dismissal of Jews from such posts clarifies the position of the administration with regard to the implementation of the anti-Jewish legislation.

The most well-known case is that of Léon Geismar, the secretary-general of FWA and thus the highest ranking Jew in the colonial hierarchy. Boisson dismissed Geismar from his post, offering as compensation to nominate him as the treasurer of the Ivory Coast. Geismar's post as secretary-general was offered to Armand Annet, who recounted this episode in his memoirs. Annet writes that Boisson explained to him that Geismar had to be dismissed within a month because "he belonged to the Jewish race" and asked Annet to take his place. Annet was the one who had to break the news to Geismar, and he did so by explaining to him that he, Annet, was not involved in his dismissal and that he disapproved of the decision. It did not prevent him, though, from accepting Geismar's job. Furthermore, Annet did not object to the principle of dismissing an official only because he was Jewish. He just thought that Geismar was a "positive Jew" and did not merit this destiny: "Although as an Alsatian he was incorporated into the German army in 1914, he left to join the French army. The racial law that touched him was even more unjust in his case."[37]

Sometime later, before he was sent to Madagascar as the new governor-general there, Annet went to Vichy to receive his formal nomination from the minister of the colonies, Admiral René-Charles Platon. He then took the opportunity to mention Geismar's case and to note the urgency of nominating him as the treasurer of the Ivory Coast. Platon promised to do his best, admitting that "this was one of the most painful cases."[38]

Although Geismar was dismissed from his senior position, for some French inhabitants of the colonies the compensation Boisson offered him was no less than offensive. A letter written by a French couple residing in Dakar and seized by the censors in March 1941 demonstrates the level of anti-Semitism that existed among the few French inhabitants of FWA. The letter describes what its writers refer to as an "instructive story." It severely criticizes the decision to nominate Geismar to the alternative position instead of definitively getting rid of him. The vicious and cynical tone of the letter is crucial to understanding the extent of hatred toward Jews, Free-masons, and all those who represented in the eyes of the writers the "evil spirit" of the Third Republic.

Once upon a time there were two Jews, both lived in Dakar for a period of time. One was the Secretary-General of FWA, the other was employed by the navigation company Paquet and was also the regional commissar of the French Scouts movement. A national revolution had swept a country called France. It presented itself as a movement destined to repair the stupidities of the past, especially those related to Jews.

There were plans to implement this movement in the colonies, but this was done with the little gentle spirit of the past, which was fairly Freemasonry. The first, not being able to continue to serve as Secretary-General, but still being a "big shot," was chased away with some noise so that the good idiotic and naïve public be content and then nominated treasurer-general. . . . The wolves, so they say, never eat each other![39]

Admittedly, even if Boisson wanted to object to the principle of removing Jews from administrative posts, he could not have avoided dismissing such a high-ranking official as Geismar, who was under the watchful eye of the Vichy government in France. Boisson's attempt to recompense Geismar, which attracted some criticism among the French inhabitants of the colonies, as we have seen, can be seen as a sort of resistance to the Vichy rules. An outright rejection of the principle of the laws was an unlikely possibility, if Boisson wanted to keep his own position. This attempt to avoid implementing a harsh Vichy policy was also evident in the way Boisson dealt with cases of lower-ranked Jews living in the federation.

Unlike in France, where posts of discharged Jews were easily filled by non-Jews, because of the scarcity of French inhabitants in FWA, it was often quite difficult to find replacements for the Jews who had lost their positions. This was the case with Sylvain Simon, a Jewish employee of the National Bank of Commerce and Industry of the Ivory Coast. When Boisson instructed the bank manager to dismiss Simon, the manager claimed that Simon was a subaltern employee and thus the anti-Jewish laws did not apply to him. Boisson forwarded the request to the CGQJ, which rejected it. The bank manager then explained to Boisson the enormous difficulties that Simon's dismissal would entail, because it would take a replacement three months to arrive from France. He also pleaded for Boisson's compassion, saying that Simon would have to leave the apartment the bank offered him and that it would be difficult for him to find alternative lodging. Again, Boisson transmitted the request to the CGQJ only to be rejected a second time.[40]

Abundant correspondence illustrates the ill treatment of Simon Hassid, an apprentice lawyer from Conakry, capital of French Guinea. In this case the correspondence reached extreme absurdity because Hassid was the only Jewish apprentice lawyer in the entire federation. This fact caused some embarrassment to Boisson when he had to implement the *numerus clausus* in the legal professions. In a report to the CGQJ with regard to Hassid's case, Boisson wrote, "The law assigns a percentage of 2% for Jewish lawyers and apprentices of law. In whole of FWA there are less than 100 lawyers and apprentices of law. Should we indeed deduce that no Jew can be a lawyer? Would not such an interpretation be exaggeratedly rigid?" The colonial administration thus suggested changing the law in this particular case by authorizing one Jewish lawyer when there were fewer than 100 lawyers in general.[41]

Despite the error in calculation intended or not (the minimum number of lawyers in FWA that would allow authorizing 1 Jewish lawyer according to the law was 50, not 100), we can see here a genuine attempt on Boisson's part to adapt the Vichy anti-Jewish laws to the reality of FWA. This attempt might be a result of Boisson's concern about the difficulty of finding replacements for Jews who would lose their jobs in the federation. It can also be explained by his rejection of an unjust law and the Vichy obsession with reaching even the few Jews who lived in remote colonies. Whatever the explanation, the attempt to change the laws failed. The Vichy government in France rejected Boisson's request, and Hassid was forced to leave his post. Hassid's case demonstrates well the Vichy obsession with anti-Jewish laws. The fact that there was only one Jewish legal apprentice in FWA did not prevent the absurd and irrational implementation of these laws.

In other cases, dismissed Jews claimed to be holding subaltern positions or to not being Jewish at all so as to keep their jobs. For example, Lucien Bloch, a police officer from Porto Novo, Dahomey, stated that he was born Catholic and was adopted by a Jew in 1929.[42] Most of these claims were met with complete distrust and were rejected. Nevertheless, some Jews managed to keep their jobs because their positions were proved to be subaltern or because they were engaged in trades that were not prohibited to Jews. One of these was, unsurprisingly perhaps, a butcher from French Guinea specializing in pork.[43]

Right after the Allied landing in North Africa on the night between November 7 and 8, 1942, Boisson declared his intention to protect the federation from the Anglo-American forces.[44] He also suspended all his relations with the American consulate in Dakar and put the consul under tight control.[45] However, after the landing, Admiral François Darlan signed an agreement with the Anglo-American forces that allowed the Vichy regime to continue its rule in North Africa under the patronage of the Allies. Darlan did not abolish the Vichy legislation, including the anti-Jewish laws.[46]

After Darlan's transfer to the American side, the situation in FWA changed. Boisson understood that there was no point in continued support for Pétain and changed his position accordingly. At the end of November he began negotiating with the Americans and eventually signed an agreement with Eisenhower. FWA was to move to the Allied side but keep its sovereignty and be free from foreign occupation or Gaullist intervention. The agreement did not force Boisson to renounce Vichy ideology, and he chose not to.[47]

On Christmas eve, 1942, Darlan was murdered and General Henri Giraud replaced him. In January 1943 Giraud wrote to Noguès and advised him that, although Jews should no longer be removed from the liberal professions, he should exercise caution and avoid returning them to their previous positions and restoring their seized property, because this might destabilize the situation. Indeed, until mid-March 1943 Giraud refused to consider any change in the Vichy legislation. The excuse he gave the Americans, and which they easily accepted, was that the immediate annulment of the Vichy laws, especially the restoration of the Crémieux Decree, which accorded Algerian Jews French citizenship in 1870 and which was annulled under Vichy rule, might cause riots among the Muslim population. Only consistent and persistent pressure of Jewish American and North African organizations on the American and French authorities gradually led to the annulment of these laws in French North Africa.[48]

In FWA it was difficult to claim that there was some sort of tension between the African population and the few dozens of Jews spread all over the federation, but this fact did not change Giraud's basic attitude toward this issue in the region. In a letter to Boisson from January 6, 1943, Giraud instructed Boisson, just as he had written to Noguès, to stop the suspension of Jews in the free trades but emphasized that a massive return of Jews to public service was out of the question. He also mentioned the congestion that might be created if all Jewish children returned immediately to school, an especially absurd claim in light of the fact that only twelve Jewish children were living in FWA at the time. Giraud also asked that Jews not be allowed to hold positions of authority. He closed his letter by stating that it would be best to postpone dealing with "political problems" until after the war ends and France regains its sovereignty.

It seems that Giraud simply sent Boisson an exact copy of the letter he had sent Noguès, ignoring completely the different situation of the Jews living in FWA. Only the final victory of de Gaulle in North Africa at the end of May 1943 brought the condemnation of the Vichy regime in FWA, the transfer of these colonies to the Free French Forces, and the formal end of the Vichy era in this region, including the anti-Jewish legislation.

Compared with the horrors that European Jews experienced during World War II, the dismissal of a few Jews seems almost insignificant. But it is precisely the small number of the potential victims of the Vichy laws and the distance of FWA from the main theaters of World War II that highlight the obsessive nature of the Vichy regime in its persecution of Jews. In a time of severe crisis, when two-thirds of the metropolitan territory was under Nazi occupation, the Vichy authorities were concerned with a Jewish banker in the Ivory Coast and a Jewish lawyer in French Guinea.

Conclusions

The federation of FWA was certainly not a central arena of World War II. It held some importance to the British and the French, because of its location, the port of Dakar, and the resources it offered, but it was not important enough for the Germans, who, in the framework of the armistice agreement they forced on Vichy France, had agreed to stay away from these French colonies. In fact, during the entire period that the federation was under Vichy rule, there was only one visit by a German official. Even then, the Germans accepted the French demand that the visitor, Eitel Fridrich Mülhausen, would pretend to be a French official by the name of René Martin.[49] Unlike French North Africa, which was a vital bridge to the Allied liberation of Western Europe after the Allied landing in November 1942, in the colonies of FWA military activities were limited and ended within a few months after the war had begun. Whereas the Germans invested efforts in distributing propaganda among Muslims living in French and British colonies, the federation of FWA with its minuscule Jewish population and limited strategic importance did not attract their attention.

But as I have shown, for Vichy France FWA was not a marginal territory. The dire circumstances of France after the defeat made the empire vital for its survival. The new regime was determined to fight against all those who it believed had brought the defeat and to regenerate the French nation under its hospice. The colonies, including those in sub-Saharan Africa, were a vital part of this plan. The Vichy regime therefore diffused the National Revolution in them, despite the dangerous aspects of this measure, and made sure that every anti-Jewish law would be implemented to its last detail, even when such an implementation became absurd in view of the insignificant number of Jews in the federation. This attitude of the Vichy regime toward a region that hardly interested the French in times of peace can teach us a great deal about this regime's characteristics and the ways it perceived reality during the war and in its aftermath.

Part II Experiences of Occupation, Internment, and Race Laws

4

"Other Places of Confinement"
Bedeau Internment Camp for Algerian Jewish Soldiers

Susan Slyomovics

THE ORIGINS OF THE CAMP in all its ominous gradations and nomenclatures—concentration camp, slave labor camp, internment camp, regroupment camp, prison camp, hospital camp, psychiatric hospital prison camp, transit camp, and more—are intimately linked to colonialism and colonial wars. Looking back to the 1896 Spanish camps in Cuba and the 1899 English camps in South Africa created to imprison the Boers, Giorgio Agamben concludes that "what matters here is that in both cases one is dealing with the extension to an entire civilian population of a state of exception linked to a colonial war."[1] Similarly, Isabel Hull's study of the German army underscores the ways in which Germany's African colonies provided the army with free rein to activate *Ausnahmezustände*, "declarations of emergency" or "states of exception," which suspended constraints on the military because all wars are "unlimited, existential emergencies."[2] Likewise, Hannah Arendt, in *Origins of Totalitarianism*, points to colonial violence in Africa as a precursor to the Nazi and Stalinist regimes. She singles out the two devices that frame this case study of Bedeau internment camp for the World War II Jewish soldiers of Algeria.

Two new devices for political organization and rule over foreign peoples were discovered during the first decades of imperialism. One was race as a principle of the body politic, and the other a bureaucracy as a principle of foreign domination.[3]

Both devices characterize France's imperial era in Algeria from its 1830 conquest to Algerian independence in 1962; they sustained a military culture that operated in racial and bureaucratic terms according to the brutal logic of always fighting a war. In actual wartime, such as World War II, the violence of French military culture in Algeria was intensified by Vichy-era fascism expanded to the overseas North African colonies against those racially classed by the colonial bureaucracy as *indigènes*, or "natives," a term perennially applied to the Muslim and temporarily, between 1940 and 1943, to the Jew.

Histories of Bedeau Camp

Beginning with France's 1830 conquest of Algeria, an archipelago of carceral sites was created and built throughout the colony. They were continually operational, and maintained and multiplied after World War II and into the Algerian War of Independence (1954–1962). A chronicle of France's Algerian Bedeau camp uncovers one among many sites of repression that represent the intersection of nineteenth- and twentieth-century histories, when colonialism met fascism.[4] Perhaps peripheral to the main theater of war where the Holocaust in Europe took place, this case study of a Vichy-era Algerian work and prison camp, designated uniquely for Algerian Jewish soldiers, foregrounds an important trend in Holocaust historiography: the understudied and underappreciated role of post–World War II reparations organizations in excavating, aggregating, and indemnifying individual victims and survivors of Nazi-era camps of every variety, even outside Europe. Knowledge about Bedeau, along with numerous sites of World War II imprisonment in North Africa, relies as much on the scattered incomplete archives by perpetrators, uncovered by researchers at various reparations organizations, as on the collections of oral and written testimonies by victims. As such, Bedeau's former inmates exemplify the intertwined processes of both deepening archival evidence and extending the geographic reach of the Holocaust to include North African camps. Finally, the story of Bedeau camp adds a somber footnote to the millennia of Jewish presence in Algeria and permits me to end this essay with speculative conclusions and structural interpretations as to what happened to Algerian Jewry after Algeria became independent from France.

Long before Bedeau camp there was the Algerian village of Ras-el-Ma, renamed Bedeau in 1883 to honor General Marie-Alphonse Bedeau (1804–1863). A French military figure of the conquest and pacification of Algeria, Bedeau was noted for logistical contributions that helped crush the Algerian resistance led by Emir 'Abd al-Qadir from the 1840s on. As an energetic proponent of European immigration and colonization, Bedeau undertook to create the requisite colonial infrastructure that produced settler villages through land expropriation, agricultural water projects to support plantation settlements, and the roads and bridges for transportation networks. At the same time, he placed these new colonial rural outposts under administrative structures that ensured settler domination in the countryside.[5] Thus the village of Bedeau was established as a *commune mixte*, an appellation to fit one of Arendt's devices through which the colonial bureaucracy reinvented France's metropolitan districting system of "communes." In France the commune resembled the American incorporated municipality, but for Algeria and other overseas colonies, an entire edifice of settler governance was fashioned. The *commune mixte*, in place from 1868 until the beginnings of the Algerian War of Independence in 1956, was mixed insofar as its structure and organization assured minority European settler population rule over the majority indigenous population in rural areas. The *commune mixte* of Bedeau was located approximately 62 miles south of Sidi-Bel-Abbès, a town first constructed as a fort by General Bedeau in 1843 that later headquartered the French Foreign Legion until Algerian independence. The eponymous founder, the history of the town of Bedeau as a *commune mixte*, the adjacent military camp, and the presence of the Foreign Legion worked in tandem to sustain colonial subjugation of the autochthonous population.

Photos of Bedeau camp from June 1936 portray a temporary encampment of military tents, known as *marabout*, set up to facilitate the French Foreign Legion's artillery maneuvers. *Marabout* is a colonial Algerian military term that began as a French deformation of the Arabic *murabit*, or Muslim religious leader, and was semantically extended to encompass native habitations such as tribal tents. By 1938 postcards of the Bedeau camp site were circulating, marketed to send back to the metropole by French soldiers serving in western Algeria. One such image captions Bedeau as a *camp d'instruction*, or "training camp," attesting to an early stage for bivouacking the army's artillery units in tents. A second photo depicts none of the ephemeral white tents but instead new sturdy circular stone structures for the French Foreign Legion camp.[6]

World War II in Vichy Algeria allocated an additional role for the military training facility at Bedeau camp: It became an internment camp for a minority of Algeria's Jewish population, namely, soldiers mobilized for war but instead dispatched to inhabit the *marabout* tents. Although camps and prisons had often been attached to military facilities since the French conquest, the story of Bedeau camp and why and how Algerian Jews went from soldier to camp prisoner within the French army is a chronicle of bureaucratic and racist reversals to the assured place of Jews in France's military hierarchy.

Algerian Jews, a far poorer community than their coreligionists in France, enlisted or signed contracts as civil servants or career military in the French army in higher numbers than in the metropole.[7] Historically, since World War I, 14,000 Algerian Jews mobilized to fight for France alongside 125,000 Algerian Muslims and 92,000 European settlers of Algeria. Again, the Jews of France and Algeria answered the call to arms to defend France during the so-called phony war that lasted from September 1939 to April 1940. In May 1940, after Germany defeated France, conquered France was divided between the Nazi-occupied zone (two-thirds of the country, including Paris) and the so-called unoccupied free zone to the south, headquartered in Vichy. With little delay, a cascading series of anti-Jewish laws were enacted that same year. Vichy's Statut des Juifs of October 3, 1940, defined a Jew as a person with three grandparents "of the Jewish race" or with two Jewish grandparents if the spouse was Jewish. Article 3 set into motion the exclusion of Jewish officers and cadets from the French army. The Statut des Juifs was followed on June 2, 1941, by another statute that comprehensively proscribed any Jewish presence in the military. The law of October 3, 1940, ordered foreign Jews to be placed in special camps or under house arrest.

Because Jews were singled out and foreign Jews were targeted for special abuse in France, juridical strategies unique to Algeria came to undermine the legal foundations of the Algerian Jewish community put in place by the French colonial regime. Within days of France's Statut des Juifs, a law passed on October 7, 1940 abrogated the Crémieux Decree, which had granted French citizenship to Algerian Jews since 1870. Once stripped collectively of their status as French citizens, the community of more than 110,000 Algerian Jews, a figure drawn from the 1931 census, was subjected to discrimination in every sphere. Before World War II most Algerian Jews had relegated their origins as an Arabic- and Berber-speaking native people to the past, but they had maintained forms of remembrance and allegiance to North African Jewish religious practices. This rare case of French citizenship conferred by the colonizing French empire on a community hitherto considered autochthonous radically realigned Algerian Jews' language, education, and cultural allegiances to France.[8]

Additional factors unique to the Algerian context under the Vichy regime were new laws that eliminated any possibility for Algerian Jews to request French citizenship in ways made contingently possible on behalf of Algerian Muslim natives since 1919, notably through service in the French armed forces. Vichy jurists swiftly revoked these possibilities specifically for Jews who served in the French military during World War I (according to a law enacted on October 11, 1940).[9] Many Vichy functionaries in Algeria, who were often members of the European settler population, were notorious for virulent anti-Semitism of more than one variety: They were both anti-Jewish and anti-Muslim Algerian.

In addition to the spoliation of property and expulsions from education and the professions beginning in 1940, further laws stripped Jews of French citizenship in Algeria and metropolitan strictures excluded Jews from the military and ordered foreign Jews into camps, culminating in a small number of Algerian Jews being confined in camps. They were a minority in the vast network of North African camps, which were predominantly populated by a variety of other groups labeled by the Vichy regime as "dangerous individuals" and "undesirable foreigners." Algeria's wartime imprisoned population included the overlapping categories of Spanish Republicans (both families and soldiers fleeing Franco's Spain), foreign and local communists, union leaders, Algerian militants (e.g., Messali Hadj and his political adherents in the Parti Populaire Algérien), fighters from the International Brigades who had left Spain in 1938–1939 and were deported later to North Africa, Freemasons, and a flood of European refugees, including German antifascists. By 1942 an estimated 2,000–3,000 Jews were placed in Algerian camps alongside political prisoners of various nationalities, forming an approximate amalgamated prisoner population of 15,000–20,000 people.[10]

One group, singled out by the "Picquendar *circulaire*" of March 27, 1941, which mandated "internment camps" (*camps d'internement*) for Algerian Jewish males of conscription age, was issued by General Odilon Picquendar: "Algerian Jewish soldiers, recently stripped of French nationality, will be combined into one unit of workers until the liberation of the class [i.e., the year conscripted] to which they are attached."[11] Picquendar's justification was to maintain Jewish males conscripted in 1938 and 1939 "under the French flag." Within the archipelago of Algerian camps of confinement, Bedeau was one of four sites designated primarily for Algerian Jewish soldiers; the others were Telergma for the Constantine region and two newly created camps in Cheragas and El Guerra.

By April 1941 the first group of Algerian Jews arrived at Bedeau camp under the rubric *groupes de travailleurs israélites* (GTIs), or "groups of Jewish workers." The GTI was a category specific to Algerian Jews; it was legally and administratively preceded by the French decree of November 29, 1940, which created *groupes de travailleurs étrangers* (groups of foreign workers, or GTEs) for foreigners in France. In France, GTEs entirely composed of Jews were called *groupes palestiniens* (Palestinian groups) or *groupes juifs homogènes* (all-Jewish groups), and by August 1942 the designations were way stations to deportation and death in eastern concentration camps.[12] In contrast in Algeria, as Aomar Boum argues in Chapter 7 of this volume, "North African camps exemplify a different model of internment, where captives had a margin of hope of survival despite the harsh topography of the desert and environmental conditions that restricted their movements in and out of the camp."[13] Correspondingly, Norbert Bel Ange summarizes the condition of Algerian Jewish soldiers, both volunteers and conscripts, after they arrived at Bedeau camp in 1941 as "denationalized, demilitarized, degraded but not demobilized."[14]

Bedeau Camp and Postwar German Compensation: First Phase, October 1940–November 1942

Memoirs, histories, and testimonies as well as archived French military reports have been deployed to attest to the abject conditions in Bedeau and other camps. However, amassing documentation and reviving legal and economic scrutiny for World War II sites of repression owe much to Germany's April 2004 official compensation program for Jews who were interned in an approved list of World War II labor camps located in North Africa. Funds came from the German state, based on the 2000 German Law for the Creation of the "Remembrance, Responsibility, and the Future" Foundation (Gesetz zur Errichtung einer Stiftung "Erinnerung, Verantwortung, Zukunft") and supplemented by a consortium of German private industries implicated in Nazi-era slave and forced labor. The goal was to compensate individual survivors of National Socialist injustice committed by the German Reich between 1933 and 1945.[15] The underlying purpose of the Foundation fund was to cover all further claims by forced laborers from the Nazi era, specifically those hitherto excluded from reparations, in order to assure "legal peace"[16] for those German industries that had profited from their servitude. North African Jewry was among the later additions to Germany's sustained redress program that had begun in 1952; the redress program is an ongoing landmark process that has paid out more than $60 billion, and it has set into motion a global legal transformation in how abuses by a state can be evaluated.[17] The "Remembrance, Responsibility, and the Future" Foundation determined that of some 3,000 Jews interned in North African camps, 300 were still alive and eligible in 2004 for compensation.

The various names assigned to those sent to sites of repression such as Bedeau attest to ongoing battles about acknowledgment, recognition, and compensation. Bedeau was categorized by the Foundation researchers as a work camp (*camp de travail* in French and *Arbeitslager* in German) but not classed as a compensable "concentration camp" according to the Federal Compensation Act, which enumerated lists of camps in Germany's *Federal Law Gazette* (*Bundesgesetzblatt*).[18]

In contrast to Germany's reparation protocols, German courts in the 1950s had decided in favor of compensating Jewish inmates of Algerian camps based on court decisions made in individual litigated cases that attested to forced labor and concentration camp–like conditions.[19] Successful litigants became eligible for a onetime German indemnification payment under the Federal Indemnification Law (Bundesentschädigungsgesetz; BEG) calibrated according to the period of incarceration. For example, one Djelfa inmate and survivor received a lump sum of 150 deutsche marks per month of incarceration, resulting in 3,600 deutsche marks for twenty-four months (in 1970 the equivalent of US$900).

At first, court decisions were valid for that single case, but these court decisions influenced the BEG authorities, who later elected to follow many of the German court decisions. According to Jens Hoppe, historian for the Claims Conference office in Germany, German courts could overrule decisions made by BEG authorities, but only after a survivor sued those very same BEG authorities. In many cases the survivors were counseled by the United Restitution Organization, which in turn was funded for many years by the Claims Conference, thereby achieving financial and legal circularity: Money that the Germans paid to the Claims Conference was used to help survivors obtain compensation denied by the BEG through German court decisions.[20]

At the dawn of the twenty-first century, a reorientation toward compensation occurred despite the sticking point long maintained by German researchers that, although some camp conditions for North African

Jewish prisoners resembled concentration camps in essential points, none-theless during World War II North African camps did not belong to the Nazi concentration camp system. Finally, in 2000, belated recognition was accorded to "other places of confinement or detention" (*anderer Haft-stätten*),[21] a catchall German category based on the features of inhuman conditions, inadequate nutrition, lack of medical care, and forced labor by inmates. Because the first German reparation protocols emerged in 1952, new and nuanced understandings of arbitrary detention and confinement had developed such that German legislation more broadly defined "forced labor" not only as compulsory work for which noncompliance entailed punishment but also as labor for the Nazi regime or other German ben-eficiaries that was not of an economic nature but rather work whose sole purpose was humiliation of the victim.[22] For French overseas colonies, Germany acknowledged that slave labor deported across national borders and forced labor within borders, the latter exemplified by Bedeau camp, resulted in equally abusive camp conditions. German compensation pro-tocols for North African Jews in camps allocated a small and symbolic "benefit entitlement," but only to Jews in North African camps whose camp confinement was entirely due to racial persecution based on religion (*Eine Leistungsberechtigung besteht nur aufgrund rassischer Verfolgung*).[23]

At stake was yet another German classification, namely, the official title of "political internee" (in French *interné politique*), which entitled holders to a monthly German pension of €291. Once this pension was ex-tended to the Jews of Tunisia, Morocco, and Algeria, based on their intern-ment in certain forced labor camps, qualified beneficiaries were defined as individuals who, being Jewish, were detained for at least six months in a camp in Tunisia, Morocco, and Algeria. Bedeau was among the thirty-six Algerian camps that the German government recognized as sites of deten-tion, and therefore inmates were entitled to compensation.

In contrast, despite decades of appeals and protests to the French government, the French National Assembly again in 2007 underscored its refusal to designate Algerian Jewish interned conscripts during Vichy rule as eligible to hold the political internee card (*carte d'interné politique*), as determined by the Office National des Anciens Combattants et Vic-times de Guerre (National Office of Veterans and Victims of War). As with Germany, France's determination rested on camp conditions, but its con-clusions were the opposite: Because Algerian Jewish conscripts were not placed in genuine prisons or internment camps, such as the *centres de séjour surveillé* at Djelfa, Bossuet, and Djenien-Bou-Rezg, but rather merely "regrouped" in labor units (*unités de travailleurs*) at the behest of the chief of the French armed forces, any and all indemnifications and recognition as political internees were refused.[24]

As with all compensation programs regulating human suffering linked to financial benefits, classification of camps and their duration became paramount. The "Remembrance, Responsibility, and the Future" Foundation assigned the beginning dates for Algerian Jewish soldiers' persecution in Algeria to October 1940, because it included not only the October 7, 1940, law abrogating French citizenship for Algerian Jews but also the dismissal of Jewish career soldiers in the French military and demobilization of all Jewish recruits called up for military service in 1939 to defend France. The end of the compensable imprisonment period was arbitrarily set as November 1942, the month of Operation Torch, the code name for the Allied forces landing in Morocco and Algeria. The legal principle underlying German indemnification (articulated in BEG, Section 43) was that the role of the German Reich as instigator for camp incarceration was over once the Allies entered Algeria. Presumably there was the assumption by all parties (Algerian Jews, Free France, postwar Germany) that the travails of Algerian Jews and their interned soldiers were over. This was not the case. In the following sections, inmate designations chronicle the prolongation of Vichy control even after Vichy fell.

March–December 1942:
Groupement de Travailleurs Algériens

German reparation protocols presumed that the 1942 Allied landing and liberation of North Africa, an operation in which the Algerian Jewish resistance fighters network played an outsized role on the ground,[25] included the reinstatement of French nationality for Algerian Jews and the closing of internment camps. This did not happen in the military, among the last French institutions in Algeria to abolish racial discrimination against Algerian Jews and reintegrate them as French citizens into combat units. Thus in March 1942, Bedeau camp detainees discovered that their liberation was not at hand. Rather, new bureaucratic devices reclassified and integrated them into the *groupement de travailleurs algériens* (GTA), a grouping of Algerian civilian workers already established in 1940 under the decree of November 23, 1940. The camp was placed under the direct authority of the Direction d'Économie Algérienne of the General Government of Algeria, seemingly removing camp inmates from military authority. This next phase made them subservient to a new civilian organization, one founded in 1942 and emanating directly from the Vichy government: the Service d'Ordre Légionnaire (SOL), a precursor to Vichy's dreaded collaborationist paramilitary *Milice*. Bedeau camp authorities were "Legionnaires," a term unrelated to the French Foreign Legion. The Legionnaires were anti-Jewish fascist units whose oversight of the camps signaled the next demeaning and confusing phase of prolonged internment.[26]

It is specifically during this phase of the GTA that disagreements emerge about whether Bedeau had taken on the form of a concentration camp, a designation that postwar Germany's reparation protocols and France's Ministry of Defense both rejected. In contrast, a contemporary undated report on Bedeau pointed to degraded material conditions and psychological abuse.

From the political and moral viewpoint: *impression of a concentration camp*, fights with civilians of Bedeau, insults by those in charge and by the Foreign Legion, with the themes: dirty Yids, dirty crows. *NOTE.*—This stage marked an indelible imprint on Camp Bedeau; despite all the notes and all the orders, the Camp remains today under a kind of spell of petty-mindedness and inferiority from which neither leaders nor men can rid themselves.[27]

The anonymous reporter describes a cordoned-off domain under a malevolent spell, an irrational sphere in which Algerian Jewish soldiers were relegated to civilian status, overseen by anti-Semitic authorities, both civilian and military, and hidden away in the remote reaches of southern Algeria, far from the central authority command's ability to break the spell of mistreatment that the Allied landing should have lifted. Postwar theorists of colonial psychology, although anachronistic to World War II, usefully describe the Prospero complex, which French psychoanalyst Octave Mannoni coined for the perverse enmeshment between colonizer and colonized, who were locked in a spellbinding unbreakable dyad: The colonizer, fleeing the father complex interpretable as the French metropole, scapegoats the colonized, and the colonized, forced into dependency by colonialism, is obliged to dissimulate deep resentments.[28]

The report's conclusions notwithstanding, according to Norbert Bel Ange's study of Bedeau, most Algerian Jewish soldiers continued to wear military regalia between 1941 and 1942 in Bedeau camp, and there were never watchtowers or barbed wire fences circumscribing the camp grounds, as there were in Telergma, the Constantine region camp for Algerian Jewish soldiers.[29] Photographs in Bel Ange's book depict internees still in the khaki military attire and *chéchia* caps of the French colonial army Zouave regiments. One caption states that the demeaning black outfits of internment were not imposed in Bedeau. After becoming civilian "Jewish workers" (*travailleurs israélites*), Bedeau camp inmates were subjected to new regulations that officially prohibited them from wearing military outfits, but these seem not to have been enforced; instead, housing, food, and the reported black outfits (hence the disparaging nickname *corbeaux*, or "crows") were supposedly furnished by the military but charged to workers through salary deductions. In symbolic protest Bedeau detainees deposited their derisory native pay (*solde indigène*) in the French national Secours National, a fund established during World War I to aid prisoners of war and civilians suffering in wartime.[30]

In addition, the Bedeau detainees were routinely loaned out as manual labor to European settlers for agricultural work during harvests or to the nearby Bossuet internment camp, or they were sent to do forestry work and trench digging. The photographs in Bel Ange's book remind viewers that a camera was available, and the images, staged outdoors, show posed groups, which makes it unclear who determined what to photograph. All images paradoxically are entirely positive in content, with groups of smiling young suntanned soldiers busily at their tasks, thereby occulting why they were there, who they were, and what they were doing.[31]

December 1942–May 1943: Jewish Pioneer Battalions to Camp Dissolution

In December 1942, as the French army began mobilizing for the invasions of France and Italy, those Jewish workers inducted into the GTIs, or *groupes de travailleurs israélites*, were switched back to quasi-military status from civilian control and reclassed as *bataillons de pionniers israélites* (BPIs, or Jewish pioneer battalions). Reattached to the French army but as mere auxiliary work units, the detainees were reattired officially in military uniforms. In addition, they were encouraged to volunteer for combat units, but only as *indigènes*, or "natives," in the infantry, because they still could not claim French nationality. Some did so to leave Bedeau and demonstrate their patriotism but fell into the trap of volunteering for worse conditions in the nearby Magenta camp. Most refused native status made available by joining Algerian Muslim units, whose food and housing conditions were known to be substandard and insalubrious. They also justifiably feared the loss of previous military ranking and time in the service, which was indeed confirmed in the postwar decades.

BPI status, or for that matter any worker unit status, did not entitle them to veterans benefits, nor could they attain the appellation of "political detainee," which France's Ministry of Defense in 2003 denied to BPI units because, as the ministry argued, when the units were created, Vichy France was no more.[32] The double humiliation of Vichy orders—to exclude Jews from the military and to force them into work units in detention camps—remained deliberately in place in post-Vichy liberated Algeria, historical facts denied by the French military command to this day. Nor should the role of American forces be discounted; the French Vichy-oriented administration in Algeria remained unchanged and the anti-Semitism of the authorities continued under the Allied forces.

From Bedeau, a collective response to the latest bureaucratic affronts that restricted the internees to the work camp emerged in the "Manifeste des juifs de Bedeau."[33] Among the manifesto's chief authors was Sidney Chouraqui, then a lawyer barred from practice under Vichy laws and incarcerated in Bedeau as of January 1943. Because Chouraqui arrived in Bedeau after the Allied liberation of North Africa, his sense of betrayal found its trenchant expression in calling Bedeau at this period "Vichy after Vichy."[34]

Chouraqui's co-author on the manifesto was Germain Ayache, a member of the contingent of conscripted Moroccan Jewish soldiers who swelled Bedeau's numbers and were similarly transformed into the corps of detainees called Jewish pioneers. Ayache became one of the most important historians of Morocco after the war as well as a noted political activist. Although his family had been granted French nationality under the Crémieux Decree through a Moroccan grandfather who worked in Algeria, Ayache was also interned in Bedeau camp after volunteering for combat.[35]

The manifesto sent to General Giraud included these sections:

We Jews mobilized to Bedeau, declare the following:

We hate Nazism, we hate it because it tortures a wounded France and because it specifically persecutes Jews.

Two months ago a great hope was born in us, to take on again fighting with modern armies and contribute to the final crushing of the enemy of humanity.

The realization of this wish was denied us.

Gathered pell-mell, infantry, artillery, cavalry, airmen, we have been turned into pioneers. . . .

That we were withdrawn from our respective units and all transformed into workers, disregarding the use of our skills, this fact has only one consequence for the public: to present us as suspect or unable to fight with weapons in hand.

We declare that no one has the right to doubt our fighting capacity: it would be an insult to the memory of our elders who rest by the thousands in the ground in France.

We express profound regret at seeing ourselves deliberately excluded from the current fighting for which we remain ardent champions. . . .

In 1940, we fought as French. Since then we were excluded from the national community.

Let us all automatically be assigned to the units to which we were normally intended, that we be allowed to fight each according to our skills, but with dignity like other soldiers.

Let this be permitted, and all united we will answer: "Present."[36]

Slowly conditions improved in Bedeau throughout 1943. By March 1943 the Jewish BPI units were officially dissolved. Between April and July 1943 the camp was emptied of internees, who joined 5,000 other Jewish males drawn from all other internment camps assigned to various fighting units. Finally, on October 20, 1943, almost a year after the Allied landing in Algeria, Vichy's abrogation of the Crémieux Decree was itself revoked and Algerian Jews regained French nationality. In her 1943 campaign for the restoration of French citizenship to Algerian Jews, Hannah Arendt clearly laid the blame for its unnecessary prolongation after the Allied liberation on the venal foot-dragging of the French military commanders of North Africa.

General Giraud, instead of abolishing the Crémieux Decree, had extended French citizenship to all natives prepared to accept French civil law—General Giraud pretends to have nullified the Crémieux Decree because it caused inequality among the natives and gave a privileged position to the Jews. Actually, he has acted as an agent of those French colonials who always wanted to bring under their "dictatorship" the only part of the Algerian population that so far escaped their arbitrary and selfish rule. The French colonials, in other words, took advantage of France's defeat and of their freedom from control of the mother country to introduce into Algeria a measure which they would have never been able to obtain through legal means.[37]

Inspired by Nazi Germany's racial classifications of the Jew, Giraud's policies were the logical extension of Vichy Algeria's legal concept of race, which was based on a long-standing application to indigenous Muslim colonial subjects and subsequently to Algerian Jews. Relegating the Jew to the Muslim category of native served to stabilize and strengthen those who inhabited that very category of indigene by claiming to render both equal—rather, equally without the rights of citizenship while holding out the possibility of a controlled naturalization process to become French. There could be no starker ideological evidence for colonial manipulation than Giraud paternalistically proffering the ability to assimilate as citizens into the wholly masculine universe of the French military, but withholding this from Muslims and Jews.

Camp Testimonies

Research on Jewish inmates of Vichy-era camps in the Maghreb is influenced by many considerations, especially the implacable experiential hesitations and silences of those interned. Some remain unwilling to speak about a past that was both personally shameful and nationally disgraceful to France and about their allegiances and subsequent patriotic service in the French army. Each phase of the Algerian Jewish soldier in the Bedeau camp, from draftee or seasoned veteran before France's 1940 defeat, to military internee, to civilian worker, to volunteer native infantryman, has influenced testimonies about conditions in Bedeau. Vichy's disciplinary regime in Algeria of penal servitude, forced labor, and administrative detention waxed and waned between 1940 and 1942 and throughout the extra year after Vichy fell. Accounts about Bedeau also vary because camp populations changed; Jewish soldiers often endured multiple transfers among several internment locations.[38]

Testimonies by Sidney Chouraqui, Maurice Benkemoun, Léon Benhamou, and Léon Askénasi, published some fifty years after World War II, are inevitably affected by such ruptures as Algerian independence and the mass departure of Algerian Jews, primarily to France. For example, former Bedeau prisoner Léon Benhamou vividly recalls camp conditions and personnel in his 1994 article, which describes the first camp phase under French Foreign Legion oversight.

There we lived for two long years under *marabout* tents, attired in an old uniform and a black cap, under the orders of a detachment of Legionnaires from the 1st Foreign Legion Regiment, commanded by a French officer, Captain Orsini, who never missed communicating to his subordinates his hateful hostility against Jews.

We were subjected to the most strenuous forced labor: hygiene was absent, and, by way of latrines, pits were dug in nature, allowing a stench to escape that poisoned us.

The food was to match. A terrible heat overwhelmed us in the day, and we froze from the cold at night. As lighting and heating, we used oil from sardine cans preciously preserved.

We were deprived of radio, newspapers, any means of communication with the outside.[39]

Other accounts emphasize later phases, when Algerian Jews, who would have conventionally been called up for military service from 1940 to 1942, were instead dispatched to Bedeau and given no training other than the make-work of manual labor. Unlike many previous internees, who had known army service training between 1939 and 1940, Maurice Benkemoun volunteered after the Allied landings overthrew the Vichy government.

It was entirely in good faith that we naïvely responded to the call-up for general mobilization addressed to the French, affixed to the walls of all our communes, that we perceived, to our great surprise that our grouping place, Bedeau camp, was specific to Jews. Everything had then been prepared in secret by French officers as well as the top administration to set up this camp in which, finally, cynicism about its management and our humiliation helping, the worst could have happened. Hypocrisy, fanatical racism, duplicity, and betrayal, we learned later that this was essential to the Nazi method. In Bedeau, the very rare complaints were brutally punished without comment. It was the intelligence and discipline of Jewish youth who saw to it that no serious rebellion took place: it would have been fatal for us because we were not armed to confront a situation and procedure so barbarous.[40]

In the last year of the camp's existence, the atmosphere among the detainees turned toward religious practices and deepening Jewish affiliations, attributable to the charismatic presence of the Oran-born son of Algeria's last chief rabbi: Léon Askénasi, a rabbi, educator, and towering scholarly figure of postwar French Judaism. He was assigned as a military chaplain to the French Foreign Legion, which was the absurd alternative unit available to Algerian Jews unwilling or unable to join the native Algerian Muslim regiments. His choice of the Foreign Legion transformed him into a foreign Jew in his own country, as opposed to a native Jew; either status entailed the loss of his prewar identity as "French of Algeria of the Jewish religion" (*français d'Algérie de religion juive*). His sojourn in Bedeau camp in 1943–1944 produced the following nuanced reflections (written in 2001) on the untenable future for his Algerian Jewish compatriots after the war.

We were mobilized as foreigners and in particular in the Foreign Legion. The vast majority of Jews mustered in the Legion camp thought that this was the vicissitude of history and that the time would come when French citizenship would be returned to us. I was in Bedeau Camp between 1943 and 1944, then I was a soldier in the war in the Colonial Army, a regular corps in the French infantry. What I lived during this period certainly affected me in a subterranean way, and the moment I encountered the Israeli reality, that was the way it was settled naturally. Fundamentally, if I had to live in the diaspora, I would have been seen more as an Algerian Jew of French culture than as a French Jew of Algerian culture. Algeria became later an Arab country and I could not consider myself an Arab.

Even today, I cannot comprehend the way in which North African Jews consider themselves French. Independent of the anti-Jewish and anti-Israel character of Arab countries, it does not occur to them to consider themselves Arabs but as French. This attitude is a kind of racism. It can be explained by the fact that Jews consider the mark of French culture superior to the mark of Arab culture. Objectively this is nonsense because cultures cannot be measured by the same criteria. But there is evidence for a Jew who has lived in an Islamic country: the difference between Jew and Arab is not only according to religion, it is also national. This double difference does not exist in relation to the European. This explains the continuity of the diaspora in a European milieu.

After the fact, it was a very enriching experience for me to know the milieu of the Foreign Legion, but we were not organized as Jews in order for us to develop a national conscience. We considered ourselves as a kind of minority of the diaspora type. Religious life in the camp was very intense, and it was there perhaps that I began to understand the condition of exile, which I have completely rid myself of on becoming Israeli. I felt that I was not at home and consequently, that I had no rights to claim. I could only attempt, through a strategy of submission, to obtain favors.[41]

Askénazi, deprived of control over his life in Bedeau and profoundly alienated from his prewar Oran life, reflects an acute self-awareness and radical clarity about Algerian Jewry. He remarks on the inherent racism of his own community that rejected Arab culture but embraced all things French at the expense of its own past. At the same time, there could be neither a return to the status quo antebellum for these three communities nor a future for Jews under Islam. Religion, Askénasi notes, was racialized and equated with nationality in the new post-1962 Algerian republic, an independent nation-state that in turn effaced its Jewish and Berber minority elements. Thus Vichy's innovation, which was to include Jews in the colonial racialization of religious communities, continued to reverberate postwar and globally.

One way for Rabbi Askénazi to resolve the intractable contradictions of Arabs, Jews, and French of Algeria was to move to France. In contrast to the more than 90% of Algerian Jews who settled permanently in France after Algerian independence in 1962, Askénazi ultimately left for Israel in 1968, when mass North African immigration became part of a different Zionist story of both dispossessing the native Palestinians Arabs and the creation of Mizrahim, or "Oriental Jews," which included North African Jewry. Once again but on the eastern shores of the Mediterranean Sea, Algerian Jewry was inserted into another settler colonial matrix, albeit this time and place through the establishment of the State of Israel, where they precariously resided between the superior caste of European Jews and the subordinated native Palestinians.[42]

Bedeau: Caste, Coercion, Race

Whereas Arendt, Agamben, and Hull locate the rise of mass internment to colonial wars, more specific to French colonial Algeria is Frantz Fanon's 1961 *The Wretched of the Earth*, which was preceded by Pierre Bourdieu's work. Bourdieu's first book, *Sociologie de l'Algérie*, appeared in 1958 as he was completing his French military service in Algeria. Although both Bourdieu and Fanon lived in Algeria after World War II and through much of the Algerian War (1954–1962) and both supported Algerian independence, Bourdieu's ethnography is structured according to the ways in which race always upstages social class in the colonial order: "Caste spirit stifles class consciousness. . . . Political life and political consciousness have become Manichean in form."[43] Bourdieu concludes that membership in the superior caste, determined by race and hegemonic political power, enables the radical deprivation of the colonized as the basis for colonizer domination.

In hindsight, Bourdieu's system is more relevant to the racialized anti-Jewish microcosm of Bedeau: "The function of racism is none other than to provide a rationalization of the existing state of affairs so as to make it appear to be a lawfully instituted order."[44] From 1940 to 1943 the Algerian Jewish interned soldiers were subjected to states of deprivation that were more extreme than those usually reserved even for native Muslims, because there was a war, Vichy France was on the losing side, and anti-Jewish laws were legal. Thus the brutal and humiliating nexus of race and Bourdieusian definitions of caste imposed on Algerian Jews was exacerbated and exposed by war.

The war plainly revealed the true basis for the colonial order: the relation backed by force, which allows the dominant caste to keep the dominated caste in a position of

inferiority. . . . Without the exercise of force, there would be nothing to counterbalance the force directed at the very roots of the system—the rebellion against an inferior
social position.[45]

Bedeau camp exemplified the intertwined devices of social exclusion, geographic isolation, and spatial concentration combined with racial special-
ization of the camp population in which Algerian Jews lost their caste
privilege conferred by French nationality. They experienced the precariousness of their situation through the system of French colonial hierarchies of
racial domination underpinned by naked coercion in which "the exercise
of the power of choice, which theoretically belongs to those societies that
confront one another, has not been granted to the dominated society."[46]

Bourdieu's vision of colonial Algeria is ethnographically bleak. Both
Fanon and Bourdieu believed that this settler colony was not reformable.
At least Mannoni's psychological studies of French colonialism, based on
his Prospero complex, hold out the faint hope of a happy ending. In this
scenario, as with Shakespeare's protagonist in *The Tempest*, Prospero the
colonizer lifts the spell of enslavement from the rightful hereditary native
ruler Caliban and sails back home across the sea. The case of the incarcerated Algerian Jewish soldier, seemingly a brief historical footnote, is a
crucial reminder that colonialism not only creates the category of native or
indigene in the first place but also, having created the category, incessantly
destabilizes, indeed plays havoc with nativeness. Consequently, Algerian
Jewry, returned to its former realignment after World War II within the
settler colonial superior caste, departed en masse in 1962 as part of the great
population exodus across the Mediterranean Sea from Algeria to France.
Prospero's aspirational metaphor became a reality for the majority of Jews
when they set out for France alongside the European *colons* of Algeria.
There in France they were folded, if only for bureaucratic and legal purposes, into their latest apotheosis, namely, the so-called *pied noirs* and the
"repatriated" (*rapatriés*) of Algeria. Both the communities of Algerian Jews
and former European settlers hold French citizenship and have benefited
from several post-1962 programs of reparation and financial indemnification, yet neither group in the metropole believes that they are accorded the
requisite characteristics of genuine French rootedness, or *français de souche*.

5

Blessing of the *Bled*
Rural Moroccan Jewry During World War II

Aomar Boum and Mohammed Hatimi

IN THIS CHAPTER we highlight some aspects of Jewish-Muslim relations during World War II in the pre-Saharan region of rural Morocco, also known as the *bled*, focusing on settlements of the Anti-Atlas (Foum Zguid, Akka, Tata, Tissint), Sus (Tiznit, Tahala, Tafraout, Iligh, Ifrane, Agadir), and Tafilalt (Erfoud, Ksar Souk [Errachidia], Rissani, Boudnib, Rich). Before the *bled* assumed a strategic military significance for the French colonial administration, the region had long been a liminal space of interaction and communal encounters between Jewish and Muslim communities, between Arabs and Amazigh, and between sedentary populations and Bedouins.[1] It is in light of this history of relatively peaceful coexistence[2] that the impact of World War II on the *bled* is of particular interest. The *bled*, despite the harshness of the desert, has always been blessed by geographic remoteness, which allowed it to be the last place to be affected by humans, even though it was always the first place to be affected by natural drought and plagues.[3]

In 2004 Aomar Boum interviewed Mbark, a native of the southeastern oasis of Foum Zguid, about his memories of World War II.[4] In the 1930s, Mbark, a former day laborer and descendent of a family of slaves, was occasionally ordered by the local tribal leader to travel on foot to neighboring villages and towns as far north as Marrakesh. He was tasked with delivering letters to colonial administrators updating them on local social and political affairs in this pre-Saharan Moroccan region, which French authorities had fully colonized by the early 1930s. During the interviews, Mbark provided vivid accounts of the French colonial impact in the region and the nature of Muslim-Jewish relations during the war. "I heard about

Hitler for the first time when I delivered a telegram to Thami el Glaoui, the Pasha of Marrakesh, in 1942," he revealed. A political ally of the colonial administration in Morocco, el Glaoui benefited from French support, because he served their military interests in southern Morocco.[5] Mbark recalled:

When I arrived at the Kasbah Telouet, his hometown in the High Atlas mountains, I was informed of el Glaoui's hasty departure to Marrakesh in a car provided by the bus company CTM. I was ordered to head to Marrakesh where he was meeting with French administrators. After I delivered my message, I learned that Americans troops had just landed in Safi.

Despite the state of emergency invoked by the war, Mbark reported that the native populations of rural communities in the region of the Anti-Atlas, Draa, and Tafilalt were scarcely aware of or politically affected by Vichy authorities.

Based on oral histories and a limited set of military and civilian archives and documentation held by the Service Historique de la Défense à Vincennes, the Centre des Archives Diplomatiques de Nantes, the Alliance Israélite Universelle in Paris, and the Archives du Maroc in Rabat, we argue that World War II had minimal negative effects on Muslim perceptions of Jews in the southern rural hinterlands, or the *bled*, a term explained in more detail in the next section, "Jewish Society in the Bled." Despite the impact of the war on the region, we claim that it did not mark a turning point in Jewish-Muslim relations in the *bled* or worsen Muslim attitudes toward or treatment of local Jews.

The Jewish population of the Saharan margins numbered between 10,000 and 20,000 individuals, settled in various oasis hamlets throughout the Anti-Atlas and southeastern Morocco (see Table 1 and Map 4).[6] Like Muslims, the Jews of the Saharan hinterlands saw the war in Europe largely as a confrontation between "Christian" nations, of little local import.[7] Jewish peddlers continued to move around the villages, towns, and communities affected by severe drought. They attended weekly markets, providing credit and trading in commodities such as sugar and tea throughout the southern and southeastern regions. In these remote areas of Morocco, international politics did not penetrate down to the level of people's daily social concerns. Even when the war negatively affected livelihoods in the region, as a result of the decreased supply of basic commodities, rural Jews and Muslims initially took little notice because they were accustomed to economic hardship and to making do with few resources. However, by the

TABLE 1: Jewish population of select mellahs (Jewish settlements) in the bled (pre-Saharan rural Morocco)

Mellah	1936	1947	1951
Oufrane	122	40	141
Guelmim	12	115	113
Tagadirt (Akka)	102	—	118
Tata	20	—	—
Foum el Hisn	4	2	—
Agadir Tissint	—	5	—
Foum Zguid	13	—	—
Anzi	—	—	150
Agadir	503	1,340	1,650
Inzgane	68		300
Taroundant	926	953	953
Tiznit	357	457	244

These numbers are compiled from Flamand, Diaspora en terre d'Islam; Flamand, "Quelques renseignements statistiques"; de Foucauld, Reconnaissance au Maroc; La Porte des Vaux, Tribus du Haut Sous; and Secrétariat Général du Protectorat, Dénombrement général de la population.

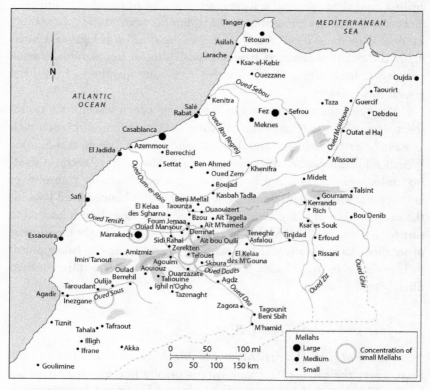

MAP 4: Principal *mellahs* (Jewish settlements) of the *bled* (pre-Saharan rural Morocco) during the colonial period.

time of the American landing in 1942 and the end of the war, the economic impact of the war together with the coinciding drought would end up affecting these communities, leading to waves of migration to urban centers such as Agadir, Marrakesh, Taroudant, Guelmim, and later Casablanca.

Therefore, although some French colonial authorities tried to take advantage of the emerging anti-Jewish laws to stir up communal conflict between some local Jews and Muslims over landownership, Jewish-Muslim relations remained calm and local French military officers refrained from imposing anti-Jewish laws in these remote settlements for fear of indirectly encouraging urban migration. They were reluctant to subject the Jews of these remote hinterlands to the same political and economic confinement and restrictions as those imposed on the urban Jewish population because they were aware that such measures would disrupt economic life in and the supply of goods to communities already in dire need.

Despite this cautionary attitude, in response to Muslim protests against food shortages in the region, a major case of Jewish-Muslim conflict around property ownership in the region did occur during the war. As we discuss in the section "Anti-Semites in the *Bled*," this legal case highlights the complex relations between local Muslim populations, French military administrators, the monarchy, and some members of the local Jewish community.

Yet this official French policy toward rural Jews was not always respected, especially in villages and communities close to military bases, such as Ksar Souk (Errachidia) and Tafilalt, where a number of anti-Semitic French soldiers were based. In the months following the American landing, as local populations continued to struggle economically, a number of anti-Semitic French civilian and military authorities blamed local Jews for the deterioration of living conditions. In response, local Jewish leadership turned to the sultan, Sidi Mohammed ben Youssef, and sought the support of sharifian representatives (Muslims from a noble religious background) in the region; in many cases, Jews complained about their mistreatment directly to the sultan.

Jewish Society in the *Bled*

The *bled* is the Darija (Moroccan Arabic) term that refers to rural areas where the sultan's legal authority is usually not applied. First used by Ibn Khaldoun,[8] the term was later adopted by official Muslim jurists to denote the lands that could fall under Makhzan (central government) power but where the government's jurisdiction could also be limited. In this case the political and legal vacuum is usually filled by tribal lords who apply customary law or by independent judges, many of whom emigrated to the *bled* when they disagreed with the central government.[9] By the nineteenth century, the term was adopted by the French to identify wide regions in the interior of Morocco. In her classic book *In Morocco*, Pulitzer Prize-winning American novelist and short story writer Edith Wharton describes the distinctive landscape of the region.

Between these nomad colonies lies the *bled*, the immense waste of fallow land and palmetto desert: an earth as void of life as the sky above it of clouds. The scenery is always the same; but if one has the love of great emptinesses, and of the play of light on long stretches of parched earth and rock, the sameness is part of the enchantment. In such a scene every landmark takes on an extreme value. For miles one watches the little white dome of a saint's grave rising and disappearing with the undulations of the trail. . . . The two-draped riders passing single file up the red slope to that ring of tents on the ridge have a mysterious and inexplicable importance. . . . More exciting still is the encounter of the first veiled women heading a little cavalcade from the south. All of the mystery that awaits us looks out through the eye-slits in the grave-clothes muffling her. Where have they come from, where are they going, all the slow wayfarers out of the unknown? Probably only from one thatched *douar* (village of tents) to another; but interminable distances unroll behind them, they breathe of Timbuctoo and the farthest desert.[10]

This short passage reflects the French and Western view of the *bled*: exotic, empty, barren, unwelcoming, and sometimes threatening. The colonial classical view divided Morocco into the "*bled al-Makhzan* which obeyed the Sultan and the *bled al-Siba*, which did not."[11] The *bled al-Siba* became a symbol of dissidence and insolence, a region that escaped government control and French pacification.

The term *bled* was used for the first time by the French army during the period of the military "pacification" of the Berber tribal revolt (1912–1934), but its meaning was later extended by civilian administrators and colonial officers to refer to rural areas regardless of their geographic location in colonial Morocco. This vast region was deemed "useless" Morocco, as opposed to the "useful" urban regions, which extended from the Sus region to the farthest east, following the railway line from Marrakesh to Fez. Powerful local tribal leaders (*caid*s), such as Thami el Glaoui, and their regional representatives throughout the *bled* ruled these areas on behalf of the central government and the colonial authorities in return for personal benefits and political control of the region. The *bled* consisted of self-sufficient communities of subsistence farmers and artisans living in complex Berber and Arab social systems where different socially stratified groups coexisted and supported each other in a precarious economic and social balance.[12] Within this system each community contributed in one way or another to its own survival and to that of the whole by performing predefined roles and tasks.

Given that the World War II period was a difficult time for urban and rural Moroccan and other Maghrebi Jews, the near absence of references to North African Jewish experiences in autobiographies written by members of Jewish communities who lived during the 1940s is striking.[13] Notwithstanding the negative effect of Vichy laws on Jewish life in North Africa, we can argue without reservation that, although European Jews were undergoing a collective trauma under Nazi rule, most rural Moroccan Jews were exposed to the genocidal atrocities and horrors of the Holocaust only after the end of the war, mostly after most of them left Morocco for Israel between 1950 and 1962. It is thus outside rural and urban Moroccan society that the Jews of the *bled* discovered the horrors of World War II and realized the blessing of being from marginal hamlets in southern Morocco, despite the economic challenges they faced during the war.

Even though firsthand accounts of the impact of the war on the lives of ordinary Jewish and non-Jewish communities are scarce, we know that economic hardships and military abuses were visited on the local population, including Jews, by the colonial administrators. Recent autobiographies of urban North African Jews shed a considerable light on part of this history, but rural communities have remained outside this historical narrative, resulting in a historical erasure of rural Jewish lives. Yet, despite the silence around Jewish lives in the *bled* during the war, by aggregating various references in colonial and national private and state archives together with the oral testimony of Muslim informants from the region, we can assemble a picture of the experiences of the Jewish communities of the southern tribal hinterlands.

By the end of the nineteenth century, Morocco had begun to witness major social and political transformations, which coincided with serious financial instability. The advance of European modernization led to a slow economic upheaval that negatively affected the indigenous economic structure, which had long operated according to a guild system based on craftsmanship.[14] The precapitalist Moroccan economic system, located largely in Fez, Marrakesh, and Rabat-Salé, began to face competition from Europe in the domestic market. The dumping of competitive and affordable European products onto local markets undermined local artisans and merchants. At the end of the 1920s, French settlers managed to disrupt many aspects of the local economy. The development of the mining and agribusiness industries tied many families to daily wages. The French disruption of the local economy led to the migration of indigenous labor workers to many urban settlements and the emergence of labor unions. Moreover, colonial legal frameworks challenged and undermined the traditional social and religious hierarchies that structured Jewish-Muslim as well as Arab-Amazigh relations.

Despite these dramatic social transformations, local rural Jewry remained largely untouched by modernization. French authorities were careful not to expand capitalism into the *bled*, especially because they wanted to control population movements in order to discourage people from pouring into cities and aggravating the labor problem. Equally important, the Alliance Israélite Universelle did not extend its networks of schools to these communities of the southeastern *bled* until the late 1930s and early 1940s.[15] In the absence of modern schools, local rabbis continued to exercise their social and religious authority in these communities, meaning that schooling was largely limited to boys or was nonexistent in many parts of the countryside. Hence the Jews of the *bled* were illiterate and therefore unable to access modern professions, such as law, banking, and the media.[16]

Finally, the absence of infrastructure and roads restricted both the Jewish and the Muslim communities' contact with the outside world. News and information were limited to what the authorities decided to share with the local community. In 1941, while the war was raging in Europe and elsewhere, a French officer responsible for ensuring the political stability of the population of a hamlet south of the region of Foum Zguid wrote to his commander in Rabat that the population does "not seem to realize the seriousness of the situation. For them, what is going on in Europe is a simple confrontation, yet another one among Christian nations (infidels)."[17]

Tafilalt and Draa are vast arid regions where precipitation is low and droughts are the norm. In the 1940s a famine resulting from a drought was exacerbated by a shortage of food supplied by the French colonial authorities to the region.[18] The local population resided in tribal settlements known as *ksours* along dry riverbanks, forming small oasis communities whose economy was primarily based on subsistence farming. Historically, these villages also served as resting places on the trans-Saharan caravan routes that connected sub-Saharan Africa to North African urban centers. In these southern communities Jews lived in quarters neighboring Arab and Amazigh Muslims. During their long presence in the region, Jews had maintained strong social ties with their tribal neighbors, despite isolated instances of animosity. Several factors contributed to these relatively peaceful social relations, including remoteness from the central authority, frequent tribal attacks, famine, recurring epidemics, adverse topography, and chronic droughts. These environmental, political, and geographic challenges have historically forced Jewish and Muslim communities to transcend their religious differences and tolerate each other for their mutual welfare.

Unlike the general focus on the Jewish society in the *bled* as closed, Jews expanded their social ties and personal political networks within and outside Muslim communities where they lived. In the *bled* Jews managed many aspects of economic activity, at the levels of production, distribution, transportation, and trading.[19] They were also key craftsmen and artisans without whose services farming activities would have been crippled. Their neutral *dhimmi* status meant that they enjoyed legal protection, which freed them to move around and trade among rival Muslim communities.[20] The tribal economy made it easy for Jews to be part of tribal social closures. Villagers throughout southern Morocco allowed Jews to live inside their *ksours* to sustain their economic and farming needs. Over time this economic bond became personal, developing into lifelong partnerships, sometimes for generations.

Farming is a context where we can see the development of social relations between Jews and Muslims, contrary to the silences and misinterpretations of European travelers who wrote about the region. Throughout the *bled* many Jews were indirectly participating in agricultural activities.[21] Landownership and water rights are two of the most valuable resources in southern Moroccan oases. Despite their regulation by tribal customary and Sharia laws, Jews were able to acquire land and water rights from Muslims.[22]

It is important to emphasize that, despite religious differences, southern rural Muslim and Jewish communities also shared linguistic, customary, and cultural belief systems.[23] During an interview, Izza, a great grandmother in her late 90s, described the daily interactions between Jewish and Muslim women in Zaouit Sidi Abdenbi.

There were a few Jewish families in the region. They were protected by the community. When Jewish men leave their women and children behind, sometimes for a month, their wives mingle with Muslim women. We sometimes weave and sing together outside the walls of the *ksar* [village]. Just like us, they prepared barley couscous and spoke *tashelhit* [an Amazigh dialect].

Because they spoke the local dialects such as Darija (Moroccan Arabic) and Tamazight, Jewish merchants and peddlers could maintain and expand their trade networks and enhance their social and economic relations with Muslims. Because movement in the *bled* could be treacherous, Jewish merchants required safe passage and protection, and, despite some cases in which Jews were attacked and their caravans pillaged, Mbark noted that even during the famine of the 1940s, he rarely heard of Jewish peddlers being affected or targeted. Masoud, a descendent of local nobility, noted in an interview in July 2004 that tribal conflict sometimes erupted because of the targeting of a Jewish peddler.

In the late 1930s, a peddler by the name of Moshe was attacked by a group of men of a neighboring village as he returned from a trading expedition that took him to Taznakht and villages as far as Ouarzazate. War almost broke out between both communities. Despite their religious status, Jews who resided among us were seen as one of us [*oulad la bled*].

This anecdote demonstrates that Jews were seen as belonging to and identified with the larger Muslim community in which they dwelled to the extent that an assault against one Jew from one village, or *ksour*, by Muslims from another village could be grounds for conflict between the two villages.

After the first year of French colonialism in Morocco, colonial military and civilian administrators began to limit the legal and religious regulations (also known as the *dhimmi* laws) that governed Muslim-Jewish relations, in effect reducing the protections traditionally accorded to Jews under Islamic law.[24] Remote from urban centers such Fez and Rabat, where religious scholars (*'ulama*) held and exercised religious authority, collective survival in the southern hamlets forced many religious scholars to prioritize custom over Islamic jurisprudence. During the precolonial period, Jewish merchants and litigants crossed religious boundaries, bringing legal cases before Muslim judges or courts when they could have stayed within the Jewish legal system.

The crossing of legal systems by many Jews of the *bled* highlights how the relationship between the sultan, tribal lords, and Jews was based on the bond of protection, which allowed Jews to petition the sultan or his representatives when they felt that they were the victims of legal or religious abuse.[25] The protection of Jews was a matter of survival for tribal leaders and religious scholars, as well as brotherhoods (*zawiyyas*) and communities, because it ensured the protection of trade. Given the already limited supply of food in the region, local French military authorities wanted to avoid disruption of the food supply and distribution system by any and all means, which meant a largely hands-off stance toward local Jews. However, despite the circumspection of French authorities, the colonial period marked the beginning of a shift not only in Jewish-Muslim relations in the *bled* but also in the nature of the limited encounters between the two communities in their respective religious courts. The impact of the European legal framework, colonial rule, and consular foreign protection ushered in the first stages of Jewish-Muslim separation as a result of colonial legal policies toward Jews that weakened their status as *dhimmi*.

After the French "military pacification of the south," a competition between French and Spanish colonial authorities grew over the control and management of trade across the border between the French-administered southeastern *bled* and the Spanish Sahara. To control trade in the southeast, France opened the port of Agadir, undermining local trade connections with the Spanish-controlled city of Sidi Ifni and limiting the Spanish trading hegemony in the region. During the 1930s, the French colonial authorities relied on some local Jewish merchants, such as Shalom ben Haroun Ohana from Ait Jarar, to play a role in the distribution of French commercial products along the traditional trading routes of the southeastern *bled*.[26] As the economy of the Spanish Sahara became negatively affected by the penetration of French products, its colonial authorities tried to convince Jewish families and merchants to settle in Sidi Ifni, threatening to otherwise limit their access to its controlled region.[27]

Jewish-Muslim Relations Under Vichy

The establishment of the French protectorate did not initially alter the region's equilibrium, thanks to the colonial authorities' adoption of a simple and clear policy: avoid anything that could disturb the local balance. Certainly, living conditions deteriorated as a result of the pacification operations led by the French military authorities and the reallocation of certain roles to the benefit of new local actors. Inevitably, local populations resented those who benefited, whether rich Jews or rich Muslims. Yet this was balanced by the prevailing belief that it was God's will that some people were fortunate and wealthy, whereas others were poor and underprivileged. Such religious beliefs contributed to political docility and strengthened mutual understanding and social coexistence. Against this backdrop, World War II had little impact on intercommunal relations in rural areas and did little to affect Jewish-Muslim religious and social relations.

As difficult as Vichy laws were to implement in the cities, they were even more difficult to implement in the *bled*.[28] The French protectorate faced a real dilemma when it was obliged by the Vichy regime to institute anti-Jewish legislation in Morocco. Aware of the danger that could result from hasty measures, General Charles Noguès at first sought to buy time.[29] When it became evident that the resident-general and his close associates had not complied with the directives coming from Xavier Vallat, the commissioner-general for Jewish questions,[30] Vichy authorities opted to send a special emissary to remind everyone of the rules. In August 1941 Vallat himself toured North Africa.[31]

Nevertheless, it proved impossible to subject Jews in the *bled* to *numeri clausi*, to evict them from European areas, or to force them from their jobs. For example, in the newly controlled city of Agadir, Jews and Muslims already lived side by side in the modern quarter of the city, where they were later joined by European settlers. Most professions prohibited to Moroccan Jews by Article 4 of the *dahir* (decree) of August 5, 1941, were nonexistent in southern Morocco. Meanwhile, it was impossible to restrict Jews from wholesale trade (although by the end of the war European settlers had begun to expand their control over such trade between Marrakesh, Essaouira, Agadir, and the *bled*). To Vichy representatives in the south, prohibiting Jews from many professions would have meant economic suicide.

Most of the ordinary inhabitants of the Anti-Atlas whom Boum interviewed,[32] like Mbark, knew nothing about Nazi and Vichy anti-Semitism and its effect on Jews until the end of the war and the beginning of Jewish emigration. In fact, many of the interviewees, now in their early 90s, reported that anti-Jewish propaganda had no impact on Jewish-Muslim relations in this region. Overall, the import and character of

European anti-Semitism was alien and incomprehensible to the Muslim population. Despite long-standing attitudes, both Islamic and traditional, that stigmatized Jews as inferior, the local population could not envision their survival in the *bled* without a Jewish presence, as Lahcen, a farmer in his late 80s noted.

Moreover, it was the same *dhimmi* status that marked Jews as inferior that also granted them special protection—and limited the potential effect of French and European anti-Semitism on them. As long as Jews paid the *jizya* tax levied on *dhimmi*, they were accorded rights under Islamic law.[33] Thus, though defining Jews as inferior, the Islamic principle of "dhimmitude" legally protected them from Nazi policies. Furthermore, it is important to understand that Jews were never collectively held responsible for Morocco's political misfortunes. Indeed, it was difficult for most Muslims to picture their "poor and humble" Jewish neighbors as fitting the anti-Semitic stereotypes perpetrated by European powers during the period.

For French authorities the social peace of the *bled* during the war was a major priority. Like el Glaoui, Muslim agents of the colonial administration throughout the southern rural regions facilitated this political stability. The vast majority of the population could not imagine modern warfare with its mobilization, bombardment, mass destruction, deportation raids, boycotts, deportations, and resistance. In the *bled* there was no appreciable military presence or concentration of war matériel, no safe havens, searches, deportations, or even arrests. In short, the war was far away, even though many European prisoners and Jewish refugees were held captive in labor camps in settlements throughout the *bled*.[34] The local population did not know the reason for these camps. Only two things brought home the harsh reality of the war to the local people: food rationing (especially tea and sugar) and the recruitment of a small number of young men from the region into the French army.

For the local population the adversity of war meant that several products became scarce and their prices increased. Merchants struggled to maintain supplies, because these products were not available in large cities either. There was no opportunity for speculation, especially on "strategic" products such as tea and sugar, because the French government ensured that merchants would not get rich at the expense of a population already tested by natural disasters.[35] It should be recalled that the decade preceding the war had been a period of tough economic times. In addition to the negative effects of the global crisis of 1929, Morocco had experienced successive years of drought, locust infestations, and famine.

By the middle of April 1930, trains were being delayed by drifting mounds of locusts, and a severe drought had begun a month earlier. The locust invasion by itself devastated some 860,000 hectares of cropland. . . . Famine was developing. Imports of sugar and tea—staples of the native Moroccan diet—fell sharply. Livestock perished on a massive scale. In all, the native Moroccan loss from locusts and drought was estimated at a half-billion francs.[36]

In the rural areas destitution and poverty became the norm even after World War II, despite the agricultural relief program introduced by the protectorate administration in the south after Noguès's visit to the region of Agadir.[37] Hence the French protectorate in Morocco was careful to control the price of commodities, including tea and sugar.[38]

The conscription of young villagers into the French army was blessed by the sultan himself and facilitated by local agents of the Makhzan. A number of families (both Muslim and Jewish) saw military service as a means to achieve social and economic mobility instead of as a hardship. Serving in the French military provided advantages and opportunities to these households, including access to monetary payment, clothes, shoes, and food. Hajj Driss, one of the few individuals from the *bled* who served in the French army in Europe, noted that serving in the military allowed him to move up the highly stratified social ranks in the village after the war by providing him with a monthly pension after independence. At the same time, local Jews were exempt from being drafted. According to local customs, Jews were historically exempt from carrying weapons and participating in tribal feuds. Before the Vichy era, many young urban North African Jews had wished to fight on behalf of the French army and had experienced their denial as a rejection and humiliation; however, the Jews of the *bled* were mostly not affected by these colonial policies, given the local custom to deny Jews the right to bear arms.

In addition to these factors, censorship and the limited access to information throughout the *bled* contributed to limited awareness of the political and military global events on the part of both Jews and Muslims. In addition to the high rate of illiteracy among both Jewish and Muslim populations, the few available means of communication were controlled by the colonial administration. Newspapers rarely reached remote areas, and those who did receive them, mostly a few French settlers, did so only sporadically.[39] It is notable, though, that unlike Spanish northern Morocco, the French press in Morocco did not simply parrot Nazism and its anti-Semitism. As for radio, the colonial authorities had long considered it to be "the most lethal weapon of propaganda,"[40] so the administration took great care not to grant authorizations to purchase and use the airwaves except in a few trusted cases, and it revoked such permission upon the merest suspicion. Radio Berlin and Radio Bari were not transmitted in the region, limiting the circulation of any propaganda among the native population.[41]

Anti-Semites in the *Bled*: A Jewish-Muslim Legal Crisis

Despite the relative peace that Jews experienced in the rural south, several colonial documents suggest that a few French officials harassed the local population, especially after the American landing. The affair, known as The Plundered Lands case, exemplifies how French anti-Semitism in many parts of the southern *bled* created animosity between Jews and Muslims. This incident demonstrates the degree and nature of the external manipulations and pressures that were brought to bear on the Jewish-Muslim relationship during the war years and how that relationship withstood French colonial attempts to stir animosity between members of the two communities.

During the 1920s many Jews legally acquired farming lands in the *bled* through what is known as a *rahn*. Thomas Park discusses this phenomenon in his work on the region of Essaouira between the 1930s and 1950s.

The transactions dealing with rural property that are most significant are sales/purchases and mortgage (*rahn*). All those interviewed in Essaouira maintained that a mortgage would only be entered into in an emergency. In Morocco, a *rahn* usually involved a contract which specified that the owner of a piece of land agreed, in return for a sum of money or quantity of grain to (a) grant the lender the usufruct [legal right to use and enjoy profits of something belonging to someone else] of that piece of land for a given number of years and (b) return the same quantity of money or grain to the lender at the expiration of that period. On successful conclusion of this contract, the owner would recuperate but if he was unable to fulfill his obligation to repay the amount borrowed, he could sell the land or, as was usual, take out a second or further mortgage (at more disadvantageous terms). In the latter case, the lender got further usufruct of the land for a similar or longer period in return for lending an additional smaller sum. A series of mortgages almost inevitably led to the loss of the land.[42]

Accordingly, in the interwar period many Jewish families became major landowners largely through the mortgage of lands. However, in 1940 a new *dahir* called for canceling all existing *rahn*s and suggested that farmers should repossess their lands by means of installments from the colonial state that would help them pay off their loans.[43]

Although the introduction of the decree coincided with the anti-Jewish laws, it arose from a different motivation. During the 1930s, the French colonial administration had been interested in maintaining agricultural production in the southern oases to limit emigration to the cities, especially in the context of intermittent droughts and famine. Given that Jews were rarely directly involved in farming, colonial administrators argued that if these lands were kept as Jewish property, Muslim families would lose their only source of subsistence, forcing them to leave the *bled* for the crowded cities. Many Muslim families throughout the *bled* began petitioning for the repossession of the lands they had lost during previous droughts and famine, but one of the best-known cases, one that captured the attention of the colonial authorities and the public, is that of the Jews of Tafilalt, who went to court to regain the lands that were taken from them in 1940 as a result of the decree.[44]

This case reveals that many pro-Vichy supporters in military administrative circles served in rural areas. Unable to divert and distract attention of the local population and leaders (including tribal lords and administrative *caid*s) from the rising costs of food, these officials occasionally directly administered local affairs based on their own racist and anti-Semitic beliefs by scapegoating local Jews. It was no accident that in the wake of the defeat of France, for which French colonial authorities held the Jews partly to blame, many legal "affairs" involving conflicts between Jews and Muslims emerged, especially after 1943. They included various complaints of Muslims against abuses linked to Jewish "usury," the harmful results of alleged exploitation of common lands and water resources by Jews, wholesale monopolies allegedly granted to Jews, and alleged price gouging by Jews. It is within this framework that the plundered lands affair took place and caught the attention of a large part of the local public during the years of war.[45]

The anti-Jewish feelings at the root of the plundered lands affair of 1943 were triggered by the economic crisis that had earlier affected communities throughout the Tafilalt region in the 1920s. The French military missions to control the south and break up pockets of resistance to colonial rule affected economic and social networks. Colonial authorities disrupted

movement between the urban centers and weekly markets, which exacerbated the effects of the drought and successive dry seasons. A number of
Muslim families found themselves forced to sell or mortgage their farming plots, palm or olive trees, water shares, and sometimes their houses to
meet their family needs.[46] Some wealthy Jews and Muslims took advantage of these circumstances to acquire land and houses at low prices. The
transactions were registered with local Muslim judges and notaries (*aduls*)
according to the rules of use and thus acquired legal force and authentic
documentation. During the interwar period, no one had contested these
sales. Both Jews and Muslims accepted their Islamic and customary legal
standing.

During the first year of World War II, poverty and the collective
malaise that followed put the colonial authorities in a sensitive position.
Taking advantage of the expansion of anti-Semitic ideas, military officers
successfully manipulated Muslim economic anger and redirected it toward
local Jews.[47] Colonial reports referred to economic disparity, the illegal origin of wealth acquired by Jews, and its disastrous effects on social equilibrium.[48] It should be noted that the term *Jew* in the administrative military
reports acquired, over time, a generic connotation referring to any category
of landowners except Muslims. Therefore, and despite the fact that anti-
Jewish Vichy laws did not affect Jews in the *bled*, anti-Semitic propaganda
began to influence the local military officers, who in turn influenced those
under their authority.

The warning signs of the crisis appeared as early as 1941. Several families who had willingly sold their property to local Jews suddenly considered
themselves victims and registered complaints in their local Sharia court.
French military officers encouraged Muslim parties to register their complaints and approved them.[49] In the *ksours*, such as Tezimi, Ouled Ezzahra,
and Ouled Hnabou, tensions ran high; some plaintiffs threatened to resort
to collective retribution.[50] Whereas some thought that the transactions
in question had strong legal foundation, because they were conducted in
accordance with Islamic jurisprudence and customary standards, others
thought that the sales were originally illegitimate and unfair, because they
took place when Muslims families were facing famine.

Members of the Jewish community claimed that French colonial
administrators were encouraging Muslim plaintiffs to press these complaints to distract attention from the government's failure to solve the food
shortage. Colonial authorities also started implementing a census of Jew-

ish property in the region.[51] Nevertheless, many Jewish owners, confident in their legal rights and bearing certified documents, stood their ground. They maintained that the sales had been conducted according to the rules; the local Jewish population produced notarized Islamic legal documents stating that there had been neither coercion nor duress; amounts paid corresponded perfectly to the market prices of the time and had been negotiated and accepted by the seller. The Jews relied on the support of the *caid*s and Muslim wealthy landowners. The latter were aware of the colonial administration's complicity yet were unable or unwilling to defend the Jewish owners.

During a visit of Sultan Sidi Mohammed ben Youssef to the region in 1941, the Muslim plaintiffs presented their grievances. The sultan instructed his associates to form a commission of inquiry. Shortly thereafter, the commission pronounced its unequivocal decision (Decision 2278/15, September 1941): The Jews were obliged to return any properties acquired through a *rahn* and, contrary to the procedures of Sharia, were to do so within a period not to exceed six months. The Jewish landowners denounced the decision and rejected its conclusions. They appealed their case. The court criticized the complicity of the French military and civil authorities in the region. Jewish representatives managed to approach the royal palace with their grievance and succeeded in persuading the sultan of the merits of their complaints. As a result, a new commission was set up to reconsider the case.[52]

The reliance on the sultan's arbitration attests to the close relationship between the Jewish "subjects" and the sultan, "the Commander of the Faithful" (*amir al-mu'minin*). The sultan had always been the last recourse for Jews to seek protection from the abuses of the local French administration. For his part, the sultan could not refuse the appeals that the Jews submitted to him. His function as a symbolic protector of *dhimmi*s required him to meet the obligation of ensuring justice for them and, if need be, to decide in their favor. Moreover, the sultan was in a politically weak position in relation to his Jewish subjects after the adoption of Vichy laws, which had been approved by his cabinet. Fully aware of the harm that the Jews were subjected to, the sultan did his best to reassure them and to meet their requests for support and protection. Meanwhile, military authorities in the Tafilalt strongly resented "the refusal of Jews to obey," "the arrogance of the Jews," and "the Jewish resistance," calling it outrageous, derogatory, and harmful to the "interests of the French presence."[53]

The second commission came to the same conclusions as the first one: The Jewish landowners were obliged to return the acquired properties, and a specific deadline was given (January 31, 1943). Given his weak political position, the sultan had to give his seal of approval to the court's decision. The Jewish owners responded by requesting the intervention of the United States authorities, claiming that the committee's decision against them was made in compliance with anti-Semitic Vichy laws. The French authorities ended up revoking these laws after the American landing in November 1942.

It would be difficult to talk about this issue without discussing the anti-Semitic sentiments among some French officers. There is nothing in the documentation of the day that suggests any kind of complicity between French officers and anti-Semitic French settlers in the southern region. The settlers, who were few in number in the region, depended on the Jews to ensure essential functions for maintaining local balance. It is hard to see how they could espouse anti-Jewish feelings that were harmful to their own interests. From the standpoint of French administrators, adopting an apologetic stance in relation to Nazi ideology was tantamount to supporting German propaganda and thus harmful to the authority of France and its political capital in the *bled*, which the French had not been able to pacify until 1934. Any restriction on the mobility of Jewish merchants could have undermined stability in the *bled*, especially when drought had begun to affect the local economy. It was necessary to maintain, at all costs, good relations between Jews and Muslims and to limit the harmful effects of anti-Semitic laws in the region.

In any event, the plundered lands affair ultimately had only limited impact on the relationship between the Muslim majority and the Jewish minority. The crisis was reduced to a simple quarrel between the two parties concerned. However, the French administration's policy of cleansing itself of Vichyists immediately after the American landing did not contribute substantially to the restoration of social peace. As we have seen, the Jews of the southeastern *bled* had long played a major role in the tribal histories of the communities of southern Morocco. As peddlers, merchants, and artisans, they represented key social categories in the hierarchical society. For the most part, the French colonial authorities understood the strategic importance of Jews' economic and social roles in the *bled* and tried to maintain the native customary order. The plundered lands case demonstrates how, against this background, the unremitting onslaught of droughts, famine, and disease negatively affected these relations, especially in the early 1940s. Whereas Muslim families struggled to survive the economic crisis and the lingering effects of the droughts, Jewish families were adversely affected by the shortage of trade and restrictions by French colonial authorities on their economic activities. Overall, despite such setbacks, relations between Jews and Muslims remained positive.

The real economic impact of the war on Jewish-Muslim relations was felt most dramatically in the postwar years, when Jewish families began to leave the rural *bled* for the cities, especially Marrakesh, Agadir, and Casablanca. By 1947 many Jewish settlements (*mellah*s) ceased to exist, because their Jewish residents either relocated to prosperous Jewish communities in the *bled* or moved to the cities, where they could at least have access to daily rations of soup, even in the crowded Jewish neighborhoods of Marrakesh and Casablanca before their final emigration out of Morocco after the war.

6

The Commissariat Général aux Questions Juives in Tunisia and the Implementation of Vichy's Anti-Jewish Legislation

Daniel Lee

IN LATE SEPTEMBER 1941, Victor Assal, a 40-year old office clerk living on the outskirts of Tunis, sat down and began to fill out a detailed administrative form.[1] As required by anti-Semitic legislation, Assal declared that he and his family were Jewish. He also listed their most valuable possessions and what they were worth. Victor Assal's declaration is interesting for many reasons, not least the date Assal completed the form: September 25, 1941. A law passed by the Vichy government at the beginning of June 1941 ordered Jews to declare themselves as such by mid-July of that year. All of Vichy's laws were automatically applicable in France's colonies, as set out by the armistice with Germany that had awarded the French government control of the empire. This meant that Tunisia's 80,000 Jews had a month to complete the paperwork. Anyone who did not return their form before then could be penalized.

Given the publicity surrounding the census and the consequences for noncompletion, why did Victor Assal wait so long to send in his family's declaration? By delving deeper into the archives, we can see that Assal was not alone in filling out his form late. Almost all the Jews in Tunisia fulfilled their census obligations toward the end of September, months after their coreligionists in France had completed the process.

The discrepancy over the return of the census in metropolitan France and Tunisia cannot be attributed to a paper shortage on the other side of the Mediterranean; nor were the country's Jews given a different deadline by which they had to register. Rather, as will become clear in the pages that follow, this unremarkable two-month interval over the summer of 1941 is of crucial importance to our understanding of *how* the new Vichy state attempted to fit in with the more long-standing political order of French colonialism.

. . .

After having been virtually ignored for decades, since the turn of the twenty-first century the experiences of Tunisian Jews during World War II have become a center of frenzied interest. As can be seen from the other chapters in this book, Tunisia experienced the war differently from Algeria or Morocco. Unlike the other countries in the Maghreb, Tunisia, a French protectorate since 1881, fell to the Nazis in November 1942. The period that followed provides a fascinating opportunity to uncover the interplay between Nazi Germany and the French empire in the realm of Jewish affairs. Moreover, it allows scholars to examine modern French history through the combination of two prisms: colonialism and the Holocaust.

Recent attention on Tunisia has extended far beyond academic circles, thanks in part to a renewed thirst for knowledge by the large number of Jews of Tunisian origin who live in France. Explorations of wartime themes, which include persecution and Jewish-Muslim relations, have been captured in the highly successful films *Le chant des mariées* (2008) and *Villa Jasmin* (2008), each set predominantly during World War II. Frédéric Gasquet's acclaimed memoir *La lettre de mon père* (2006) appeared at the same time as a flurry of studies on the Jews of Tunisia during the war, only a few of which were ever intended for academic audiences.[2]

Perhaps more than anyone else in France, Claude Nataf has raised the awareness of the plight of Tunisian Jewry during the dark years.[3] As President of the Société d'Histoire des Juifs de Tunisie (SHJT), Nataf has organized events open to *le grand public* and even secured funding from the Fondation pour la Mémoire de la Shoah—an organization that had hitherto only rarely supported studies that fell outside the purview of the European continent—to publish three key texts from the period of the war.[4] Arguably, Nataf's most defining achievement came in 2006, when he introduced to the Mémorial de la Shoah in Paris, France's official Holocaust museum, an annual ceremony bringing in dignitaries and community representatives to commemorate the mass roundup that took place in Tunis on December 9, 1942.

By enshrining this commemoration on the Mémorial's official calendar of events, Nataf secured Tunisian Jewry's entry into the mainstream

Holocaust narrative. Even though studies of Tunisian Jewry during the war are unlikely ever to eclipse those of Jews in continental Europe, a recent surge in interest by writers and artists to retrace the roundups and deportations that accompanied the war years has ensured that the persecution of Tunisian Jewry is, for now, anything but marginal.[5]

Closer examination, however, reveals a major omission from most academic studies and literary and cinematic representations of the Jews of Tunisia during World War II. The Vichy regime, which controlled Tunisia from the summer of 1940 until November 1942, is almost entirely absent from these studies and accounts, which take as their focus the German occupation of the country (November 1942–May 1943). Despite the existence of a number of excellent investigations dedicated to the Vichy era and the Jews in North Africa by Michel Abitbol, Michael M. Laskier, and Colette Zytnicki, Tunisia is the sole principal focus of inquiry in a 1992 article by Claude Nataf.[6] The recent interest in Vichy's Commissariat Général aux Questions Juives (CGQJ; Commissariat-General for Jewish Affairs) in North Africa has concentrated only on Algeria and Morocco.[7]

The virtual absence of the Vichy regime in the historiography is not a recent phenomenon. The title of Jacques Sabille's groundbreaking 1954 work, *Les juifs de Tunisie sous Vichy et l'occupation*, is misleading, for only 6 of the book's 158 pages actually concern the Vichy years.[8] Similarly, autobiographical accounts by Jews living in Tunisia during World War II, such as those written by Paul Ghez and Robert Borgel, generally begin at the end of 1942. Most literary and cinematic representations also follow this trend; the opening scenes of *Le chant des mariées* take place in November 1942. In the *Pillar of Salt* Albert Memmi describes his experiences under Vichy rule in a single page, compared to almost forty pages on the German occupation.[9]

Vichy's absence is curious. France's armistice with Germany ensured that the Vichy administration exercised sovereignty over the nation's vast overseas empire. Just as in Marseille, Lyon, and Toulouse, from the summer of 1940 French government officials in Tunis, Sousse, and Sfax fell under the auspices of the *État français*. The individual responsible for enforcing the implementation of French laws was Vichy's chief representative in the regency, the country's resident-general. Marcel Peyrouton assumed this role in June 1940, before he was swiftly recalled to Vichy a week after parliament awarded full powers to Pétain on July 10, 1940. His replacement as resident-general was Admiral Jean-Pierre Esteva, who remained in the regency until May 1943. In the period before the German invasion,

Esteva enacted Vichy's acts and decrees into Tunisian law, by means of the *Journal Officiel Tunisien*. The regime's racial laws were not exempt. Vichy's first Statut des Juifs of October 1940 made clear in Article 9 that the law was to be applied in "Algeria, the colonies, the countries under protectorates, the countries under mandates."[10]

To ignore the Jews' experience under Vichy rule and to concentrate almost entirely on the German occupation offers only a partial insight into the totality of the Jewish experience of World War II. What explains Vichy's absence from the historical and personal accounts of Tunisian Jewry during the war? One reason is, of course, the drastic changes that affected everyday life during the German occupation. It is understandable that the events of 1943—the roundups, deportations, pillaging, forced labor, and bombings—have come to overshadow the earlier Vichy years. Writing many years after the events, Jewish victims of German atrocities can be excused for wanting to gloss over the Vichy years, a period that in hindsight must have seemed uneventful compared with the devastation that followed.[11] Such ways of remembering are, of course, not unique to Tunisia; scores of written and oral testimonies of Jews living in the non-occupied zone also gloss over the 1940–1942 period and concentrate on the roundups and deportations that began in 1942.[12]

Elevating the memory of the German occupation offers, however, only one explanation for why Vichy authority in Tunisia has been forgotten. Another possibility revolves around the idea that Vichy's eighty-nine anti-Semitic laws and decrees that appeared in the *Journal Officiel Tunisien* between August 1940 and November 1942 had little impact in the regency. It was a claim often made in the aftermath of the liberation by colonial officials seeking to defend their wartime actions. As Pierre de Font-Réaulx, counselor on judicial and legislative matters to the Tunisian government, noted, the racial laws were applied with "the very greatest moderation. . . . It was possible to get around them."[13] Historians generally agree that the implementation of the racial laws in Tunisia occurred at a much slower pace and never reached the same intense level of persecution as that experienced by Jews in the metropole.[14] Some historians have pointed to the ineptitude of Vichy's CGQJ, which for these scholars might explain why persecution in Tunisia was enforced differently from what was occurring at the same time in the non-occupied zone.[15]

Because of Vichy's perceived moderation in applying the racial laws in Tunisia, most scholars have tended to gloss over the actual consequences of the anti-Semitic legislation that appeared in published legal texts, widely made available in the Tunisian press. As has already been suggested for the French non-occupied zone, this concentration by historians on the period *after* the Nazis arrived in Tunisia in late 1942 does not follow the same pattern as research into Jews living in European countries before there was a visible German presence. Studies of Italian, Hungarian, and Romanian Jews, for example, analyze in depth the local anti-Semitic measures that were enacted locally *before* the Nazis arrived and implemented their own ways of dealing with the Jewish question.

In this chapter I reinsert Vichy back into the story of the experience of Tunisian Jewry during World War II. To do so, I analyze the position in the protectorate of the CGQJ, which was created in March 1941 and led by the notorious anti-Semite Xavier Vallat. North Africa has been entirely absent from early studies of the CGQJ, which focused solely on the role of the institution in metropolitan France.[16] Later studies of the Vichy era that consider the CGQJ in North Africa, such as those by Michael Marrus and Robert Paxton and Laurent Joly, have concentrated only on Algeria, where the lawyer Roger Franceschi, Vallat's representative, was directly responsible for the regime's Aryanization measures.[17] In Algeria significant progress was made before Operation Torch, with 2,900 *administrateurs provisoires* in place, approved by the CGQJ, to administer the government's spoliation laws.[18]

As we will see, by late 1942 the results of the CGQJ's efforts in Tunisia to implement Vichy's racial laws were not as successful as Vallat had initially hoped. Unlike in the non-occupied zone, by the time the Germans arrived, the CGQJ had only a small presence in the regency. The CGQJ's mediocre results have profound implications for our understanding of some of the larger issues that were at stake with the racial laws and their implementation in Tunisia. Paradoxically, a closer examination of the intricacies of the failed CGQJ project on the ground reveals the ambiguities of the French colonial order as it coexisted and was bolstered by the new, untried, and untested Vichy regime. It allows for an understanding of why anti-Semitic legislation was implemented and experienced so intensely in Tunisia at some moments between 1940 and 1942, whereas at other times it was able to pass almost unnoticed.

The study of the CGQJ in Tunisia and its interaction with Jews, the Résidence Générale, and the Tunisian government can shed important new light on the stop-start attitude toward Jewish affairs in the regency. The dominant school of thought, advanced by Michel Abitbol and supported by other important scholars such as Claude Nataf, considers Admiral Esteva, the resident-general, a reluctant persecutor who, as he explained at his trial, held off the discriminatory measures for as long as he could.[19] Nataf argues that Esteva attempted to soften the impact of the anti-Semitic legislation, which was often based on staunch Catholic arguments.[20] Terrence Peterson has recently challenged this idea and has argued convincingly that Vichy's racial laws were not applied in Tunisia because their enactment might have disrupted the Tunisian economy and damaged it so much that the protectorate might have fallen under Italian control.[21]

Analyzing the CGQJ's place alongside existing actors in the colonial administration requires teasing out the nuances in existing approaches. Although Esteva's position on Jewish affairs and the danger posed by Italy in the French imaginary were undoubtedly crucial factors, these accounts hinge on the principle that at no point did the implementation of Vichy anti-Semitism in the regency become a matter worthy of serious attention for administrators in Tunisia. As we will see, the presence of the CGQJ in Tunisia ensured that enacting the racial laws became a matter of principal concern in the protectorate. Long-standing colonial administrators were suddenly terrified at the prospect of potentially losing sovereignty of a local issue to a newly created Vichy institution that was seeking to assert itself in a foreign environment. After the summer of 1941, they dusted off their copies of the Statut des Juifs and looked at the legislation with fresh eyes.

Summer, 1941: The Crucial Moment

Just as in Vichy's non-occupied zone, Tunisian Jewry experienced Vichy's racial laws unevenly and at varying paces. Despite a climate of fear and uncertainty about the future, most Jews in the protectorate did not experience tangible effects of the racial decrees during the first eighteen months of the new order. This was different from the experience in the non-occupied zone. In the summer of 1941 many Jews in the south of France felt the impact of the racial laws for the first time. In June 1941 the second Statut des Juifs enlarged the number of professions barred to Jews and introduced a *numerus clausus* to limit the number of Jews studying in universities. It also called for a compulsory census of Jews in the non-occupied zone and in France's overseas territories. The next month, Aryanization laws were passed that forbade Jews from owning properties and businesses. All these laws were supposed to be implemented in Tunisia.

Even though the CGQJ had problems when it came to executing many of these measures in the non-occupied zone, such setbacks paled in comparison to the CGQJ's efficiency in Tunisia, where, in the summer and autumn of 1941, the organization proved entirely impotent.

Some local figures, eager to marginalize the Jewish population, commented on the lack of enforcement of the Statut des Juifs. In one letter, from the autumn of 1941, business leaders in Tunis were astonished at the discrepancy between the enforcement of the laws in France and Tunisia. They sought the swift implementation of the racial laws in the protectorate.[22] The signatories of this letter would not have long to wait to see substantial changes. In the months between the spring of 1942 and Operation Torch in November 1942, large swaths of Tunisian Jewry were subject to the same discriminatory measures that had gradually engulfed Jews in France in 1941. During the spring and summer of 1942, laws that had been passed earlier, and virtually ignored, were quickly put into practice. Jewish lawyers and newspaper and cinema owners were removed from their jobs. So too were Jews in commercial positions such as banking, property, and insurance. Elsewhere, Jewish youth movements were forbidden and a *numerus clausus* was put in place in secondary schools, something the Vichy regime never attempted in metropolitan France. By the summer of 1942, spoliation measures had advanced and 160 potential *administrateurs provisoires* were in place to take over Jewish property.[23]

The spring of 1942 thus represents a critical change in the day-to-day lives of ordinary Tunisian Jews, who came to experience—albeit almost a year later—the same racial laws as their coreligionists in the non-occupied zone who were engaged in the same jobs and who had similar financial investments. But the change in tempo did not occur overnight. Unbeknownst to the business leaders who had complained and to ordinary Tunisian Jews, such as Victor Assal, who felt discrimination daily from the spring of 1942, events took place behind the scenes during the summer of 1941. These events, shaped by a triangular set of officials from the French colonial administration, the Tunisian government, and representatives of the Vichy regime, paved the way for the Jews' later discrimination. Seemingly innocuous, the events of that summer were, in fact, decisive in the history of the persecution of Tunisian Jewry. It was precisely at this time that we notice a drastic change in tempo over how local officials administered Vichy's discriminatory measures. Laws that had hitherto been marginal or even ignored suddenly became a priority for bureaucrats.

What might account for the sudden change? In August 1941, four months after the creation of the CGQJ, Vallat undertook a two-week tour of North Africa to inspect how the racial laws were being administered. As he was later to make clear in his memoirs, the situation of Jews in North Africa was never an afterthought for him; he was the man responsible for settling Vichy's Jewish question.[24] He was all too aware of North Africa's large Jewish population, who, when it came to reducing Jewish influence in the French state and economy, were to be treated in precisely the same way as Jews in metropolitan France. Vallat's visit included trips to Tunisia and Morocco.

His visit to North Africa proved significant. Vallat made little secret of his annoyance that Aryanization and spoliation measures were not being implemented in the colonies as quickly as he wanted. More than anyone else, he knew that the racial laws could be enforced only once the personnel and bureaucracy, whose sole responsibility would be to oversee Jewish affairs, were in place. He had firsthand experience of this in mainland France. Even though the first Statut des Juifs had been passed on October 3, 1940, officials at the local level regularly had other tasks that they deemed more important than enacting the new racial laws. The fact that so few Jews had been evicted from professions in metropolitan France by the spring of 1941 led the Vichy government to create Vallat's ministry to deal with Jewish affairs.

Before his summer 1941 visit, the Jewish question was one of many hundreds of matters of legislation left to local colonial officials. Vallat was made aware of just how far down the agenda the Jewish question was for local officials when he saw firsthand the meager results of the first and second Statuts des Juifs in the protectorate. For Vallat, protectorate officials, who were used to a particular way of working, were not up to the task of effectively implementing the racial laws. Vallat believed that only the introduction of a Vichy body to administer the racial laws would remedy the situation. During his meeting in August 1941 with Resident-General Esteva, Vallat made clear his intention to send a CGQJ representative from Vichy to Tunis; that representative would be charged with putting into action the racial laws in the regency.[25] This decision had significant consequences that even Vallat could never have foreseen.

The injection of the CGQJ into Tunisia drastically altered the policy-making chain of command overseeing the Jewish question in Tunisia. Alongside the colonial administration and the Tunisian government, a third actor, Vichy officials, was suddenly on the scene, equipped with the authority to take measures against Jews. Subsequent events in the autumn of 1941 reveal the extent to which the arrival of the CGQJ in Tunisia unsettled local officials and forced their hand over Jewish affairs. Esteva, the Résidence Générale, and the Tunisian government, all of which were responsible for administering the Jewish question since the autumn of 1940, had to reckon with a newly created Vichy agency that was not under its jurisdiction and was ignorant of and seemed to exist outside the traditional parameters of colonial governance.

The CGQJ as an Impetus

The presence of the CGQJ in Tunisia from the autumn of 1941 spurred the enforcement of previously neglected persecutory measures. Officials at the Résidence Générale and the Tunisian government did not want the running of Jewish affairs to be left entirely in the hands of the CGQJ. Although some, such as Raphaël Alibert's former right-hand man Pierre de Font Réaux, sought to implement the Statut des Juifs in order to fulfill their own anti-Semitic convictions, most of Esteva's officials pushed through the racial laws to assert their authority and protect their fiefdom against the CGQJ, this alien and Vichy-imposed creation that it thought was going to meddle in the local administration. Of course, local officials' irritation with the CGQJ was not unique to a colonial setting. A similar situation had already arisen in France, where local officials in the provinces saw the CGQJ as nothing more than a nuisance whose local influence needed to be reduced. Some prefects even went so far as refusing to open mail sent by the CGQJ.[26] Unlike in the non-occupied zone, where officials tried to ignore the CGQJ, an opposite situation took place in the colonies: Local officials watched every move of the CGQJ closely and sought a strategy to counteract its apparent power.

The creation of the CGQJ served as an impetus for colonial officials to usurp control of the racial laws and to enact them with vigor. We see the greatest proof of this in the obligatory census of the summer of 1941. A law putting into place a compulsory Jewish census for all Jews in France was passed on June 2, 1941. Article 3 rendered it applicable to the empire. Because he was responsible for drawing up the law in May 1941, Vallat, the lawyer, made sure that special provisions would be in place to best carry out the census effectively in the colonies. He knew that difficulties might arise because of the "very particular conditions in which certain North African Jews live" and proposed that the various governors and resident-generals would find the best way of conducting the census *after* first discussing the situation with Vallat.[27] All Jews were ordered to declare themselves as such by July 31. Whereas in the metropole the process of compiling the census did not go as smoothly as Vallat would have liked—with delays resulting from various *départements* not receiving the forms on time—the compilation of the census in Tunisia did not even get off the ground. By the end of July a notice was published in the protectorate postponing until further notice the date on which the declarations for the census were to be submitted by Jewish residents.[28]

In the days that followed Vallat's visit to Tunisia in late August, however, the situation drastically changed, and local officials at the residency scrambled to revive the census. In a dispatch to Washington on September 3, 1941, Hooker Doolittle, the U.S. consul in Tunis, wrote that Vallat's visit "seems to have jarred the Tunisian authorities out of their lethargy into applying the order regarding the census of the Jews."[29] Census forms were quickly printed and sent out to Victor Assal and the rest of Tunisia's Jewish population to fill in and return.

Vallat's Representative in Tunisia: Hayaux du Tilly

The compulsory census was the first instance in which protectorate officials bent over backward to enact the racial laws. Over the course of the next year there was constant tension between the CGQJ and Esteva's officials at the Residency. This escalated following Vallat's appointment in mid-September 1941 of Colonel François Hayaux du Tilly as the CGQJ's representative in Tunisia. Until now, scholars have paid little consideration to Hayaux's position in the protectorate. Despite being the local official responsible for Vichy's anti-Semitic policies, he was not mentioned in Jacques Sabille's classic account *Les juifs de Tunisie sous Vichy et l'occupation*. Paying closer attention to Hayaux reveals why persecution in Tunisia took the form that it did.

Hayaux arrived in Tunisia with his wife and teenage daughter in early December 1941. Like so many officials in Vichy's newly created agencies, Hayaux had military nepotism to thank for his appointment. The reduction in size of the French army led former military men to seek new positions in the administration.[30] Career officers such as Hayaux could rely on their military connections to help them gain entry to an array of Vichy's ministries and institutions. In Hayaux's case, he had the support of François Valentin, head of Vichy's veterans organization, the Légion Française des Combattants, who wrote to his trusted friend Vallat to intervene on Hayaux's behalf.[31]

As a representative of a Vichy-created institution, Hayaux was able to operate freely and did not fall under the responsibility of the Tunisian government or the Residency. It is curious that Hayaux, like his counterpart in Morocco, Jacques de Bernonville, reported directly to Vallat in Vichy and not to Roger Franceschi in Algiers. The CGQJ in North Africa did not adopt the same regional hierarchy that it and all other Vichy creations had in the metropole. CGQJ officials in, for example, the *départements* of the Tarn or the Tarn-et-Garonne, would report their findings to Joseph Lécussan, the regional director of the CGQJ in Toulouse, and not directly to Vallat in Vichy. It is also surprising that, despite being sent to perform several months' training in various CGQJ offices across non-occupied France, Hayaux was not sent to Algeria. His lack of preparation for the role in French North Africa would have angered local officials in Tunisia, who would have found him ill-equipped to deal with Jewish affairs in an entirely colonial setting.

Esteva was immediately livid at Hayaux's appointment, a reaction that matched Maxime Weygand's sentiment following Franceschi's arrival in Algeria.[32] Within days of the announcement, Esteva complained to Admiral François Darlan, head of the Vichy government, that there was no need for an agent of the CGQJ in the protectorate, because local officials had the situation of Jews under control.[33] His protests were unsuccessful. Between December 1941 and June 1942, Hayaux repaid Vallat's faith in him by zealously overseeing the development of the racial laws in Tunisia.

Hayaux's letters from this time display an angry man and a rabid anti-Semite, intent above all on persecuting Jews.[34] It is ironic that he ended the war as the assistant director general of the French Red Cross.[35] The list of letters that were sent from the CGQJ in the metropole to Hayaux in Tunis point to the expansion in activity of this Vichy institution in North Africa.[36] Throughout his spell, Hayaux sought to oversee the implementation of the Aryanization and spoliation decrees. In 1942 he was active in locating Jewish businesses and bank accounts to liquidate and in finding provisional administrators to take over Jewish homes and businesses.[37] In his monthly reports to Vichy, Hayaux revealed the extent to which he planned to eliminate Jews from the regency's economic and political land-scape. In May 1942 he claimed to have vetted forty Frenchmen who were ready to become provisional administrators of Jewish properties.[38]

Inadvertently, Hayaux's presence in the regency led to the active par-ticipation of local officials in enforcing the racial laws. In the spring of 1942 the Residency appointed a few personnel and a consultative commit-tee on Jewish questions that was entirely separate from the CGQJ. Such newfound zeal by colonial officials ensured that coexistence between the Residency and the CGQJ could only exist for so long. Esteva and his sup-porters at the Résidence Générale sought to wrestle control of the Jewish question away from the CGQJ. Their efforts were successful. In June 1942 Esteva took the astonishing step of asking Pierre Laval to remove Hayaux. Not only did Laval acquiesce, but he also denied Louis Darquier de Pellepoix, Vallat's successor as head of the CGQJ, a replacement.[39] Hayaux left Tunisia in the summer of 1942, hoping to put to good use the skills he had learned in Tunisia to banish once and for all "the Jewish enemy" that threatened to destroy France. Without work and with a family to feed, he had nothing other than Darquier's word that he would find employment in the metropole.[40]

Esteva had triumphed over Vallat, but at what cost? His desire to maintain sovereignty in all areas of policy making led him to take action against Jews in the protectorate, a population he had tried to shelter until 1941. Thus by the summer of 1942, Esteva and officials at the Residency and the Tunisian government had proven that they could handle the implemen-tation of the Jewish affairs briefing within the confines of the pre-Vichy colonial infrastructure. Hayaux's dismissal did not lead to a relaxation of the laws. On the contrary, a dangerous precedent had been set and the marginalization of the Jews had become a permanent feature on the mosaic of the colonial authorities. On the eve of the Nazi occupation, discrimina-tory measures against Jews were increasing and continuing to be actively enforced.

Attention to Tunisia illuminates important differences concerning the role of the CGQJ in France and Tunisia before and during the period of German occupation. The Jews of North Africa were an afterthought in the imaginary of Darquier, Vallat's successor as head of the CGQJ from the spring of 1942. Unlike in France, where he meddled constantly in the busi-ness of other Vichy ministries, hoping to exert greater control in the realm of Jewish affairs, in North Africa Darquier did not seek to extend his purview. He did not even visit the territory, claiming in the spring of 1942 to have more pressing matters in the occupied and non-occupied zones that required his attention.[41] Although he welcomed the possibility of taking action against Jews in the Maghreb when presented with the opportunity, Darquier's chief concern was always the marginalization of Jews in metropolitan France.[42] He did not contest Laval's decision to remove Hayaux from Tunis.

The German invasion of the non-occupied zone did not lead to a decline in the functioning of the CGQJ. On the contrary, right up to the eve of the liberation, CGQJ officials across the metropole continued to propose and oversee anti-Semitic legislation. Darquier was not afforded the opportunity to cooperate with the Germans in Tunisia, an interaction that he relished in metropolitan France. Instead, the Nazis did not require his services. The German occupation of Tunisia did not lead to the CGQJ's reemergence in the protectorate. In the realm of anti-Jewish legislation, the Germans were content with the work of the resident-general and the Tunisian government, whose willingness to implement legislation had become, by November 1942, the status quo. Naturally, as vanquishers, the Germans could take their own action when required against Jews who operated beyond the protectorate's habitual actions. For example, on December 22, 1942, General Hans-Jürgen von Arnim, commander of the German army, signed an order requiring Jews to pay 20 million francs for the Anglo-American bombings of non-Jewish property, for which the Jews were said to be responsible. This was André Gide's only diary entry for that day, commenting that notices for the fine were "abundantly posted on the walls of the city" in French, Arabic, and Italian.[43]

Conclusion

A renewed focus on Jewish affairs in Tunisia in the spring of 1942 was not the result of Laval's return to power at that time; nor was it a direct consequence of Darquier's appointment as head of the CGQJ. As we have seen, it was Vallat's visit to North Africa in the summer of 1941 that spurred a renewed interest in the racial laws and that later led to important changes affecting the local Jewish population. Even though, as most previous studies have rightly pointed out, Jewish lawyers and cinema owners felt the laws most severely, other elements of the Jewish population were not intended to be spared. The Aryanization and spoliation measures had not been forgotten in Tunisia. Their enforcement simply lagged behind the metropole. The enforcement of the compulsory Jewish census in September 1941 shows that Vallat's visit in the summer of 1941 and news of Hayaux's appointment led local colonial officials to look again at the racial laws. In taking control of Jewish affairs, colonial officials intended to marginalize the CGQJ, which some felt threatened to upset the traditional hierarchy of power in the protectorate.

This new energy to apply anti-Semitic decrees locally even led protectorate officials to *propose* new directives to Vichy. In the spring of 1942 civil servants in Tunis sought to deny Jewish women from being able to marry non-Jewish men. Probing this exchange between colonial and Vichy authorities overturns the long-held view by Vichy historians that Vichy was not interested in questions of mixed marriages between Jews and non-Jews. But the discussions on mixed marriage are important for another reason. They reveal that Vichy was actually importing specific colonial methods of dealing with the local Jewish population in French North Africa back to metropolitan France. Using a lens that looks for interactions between France and the colonies in the realm of Jewish affairs fits with the recent turn in French imperial history that has challenged nationalist histories, by tracing how imperial concepts and ideas were multidirectional, a conversation from which Vichy and the Jews have been entirely absent.

The Nazi occupation of Tunisia was never inevitable. To elevate the focus onto the six-month occupation at the expense of two years of Vichy rule conceals a series of exchanges, discussions, and events that, taken together, shed important new light on the implementation of the racial laws in the colonies. To bring Vichy back in from the cold exposes the strategies used by an otherwise invisible cast of actors intent on maneuvering for control of Jewish affairs.

Part III   Narrative and Political Reverberations

7

Eyewitness Djelfa
Daily Life in a Saharan Vichy Labor Camp

Aomar Boum

IN *HOMO SACER* Giorgio Agamben discusses the meanings and logics of the camp as space and place where jurisdictional rules and political regulations turn ordinary law-abiding individuals into suspects for the security of the state.[1] Inside the camp walls individuals live "bare life," with no civil or legal rights.[2] Their guards could kill, mistreat, and subject them to all forms of slavery and forced labor without any legal consequences.

Forced labor camps and detention centers have been historical and geographic realities of many societies. Yet, as Richard Overy argues, historians have focused on concentration camps as defining institutions of Hitler's Third Reich.[3] Since the end of World War II, historical and autobiographical works on Nazi camps throughout Europe have dominated Holocaust and genocide literature.[4] Compared with Nazi history of detention and concentration camps, the relative historical amnesia and historiographic silence toward other camp experiences is largely reflected in the absence of broad historical studies that detail the complexities of camps established by other governments during World War II, such as the United States, Japan, Italy, Spain, and France, on their mainlands as well as in their colonies.[5] Despite the growing historical interest in concentration and labor camps across the world today, the memory of World War II is finally becoming a regular topic of academic interest in a few North African and Middle Eastern academic circles. These intellectual conversations promise to break through the walls of taboo in societies where Jews and non-Jews were affected by colonial regulations.[6]

In this chapter, using the memoir and literary works of Max Aub,[7] a

Mexican-Spanish Jew and a survivor of the camp of Djelfa,[8] I shed a needed light on Vichy camps in North Africa through the example of Djelfa.[9] I address the functions and bureaucratic management of camps and prisoners' relations and daily lives within them. I also analyze the movement of internees between French labor and internment camps in French North African colonies and their connections to camps in the French mainland. I contend that the collective experience of the camp by Jews and non-Jews is essential to our understanding and reevaluation of the war period in the daily lives of the internees. I argue that North African camps exemplify a different model of internment, where captives had a margin of hope of survival despite the harsh topography of the desert and environmental conditions that restricted their movements in and out of the camp.

Vichy Camps: Between Official Silencing and Literary Remembering

During and after World War II, prisoners and refugees who were interned in many detention centers throughout the world published memoirs about their daily lives behind barbed wire. In North Africa, during the German occupation of France, refugees and prisoners who fled to French North African colonies were not allowed by Vichy guards to record the daily events of Saharan camps. For example, in his work on Max Aub, Eric Dickey notes that the

entire *Diario de Djelfa* was written on the front and back of an 8.5 cm by 13.4 cm note card. What stands out is the complete illegibility of the document to the naked eye, as the handwriting is so minute that it is impossible to discern any words. Aub was prohibited from writing in the concentration camp of Djelfa, which forced him to turn to these measures in order to conceal his writing. This reinforces the trauma of the camp as it sought to eliminate one's voice.[10]

Many tried to keep a record of their internment, but their notes were confiscated and destroyed by camp guards. In his memoir on the detention and disciplinary camp of Djenien-Bou-Rezg in south Oran between 1940 and 1943, Mohamed Arezki Berkani,[11] who wrote the only surviving Muslim memoir about a Vichy camp in Algeria and Morocco, states, "During our imprisonment we were not authorized to take notes about our lived experiences and the activities of the police force in the camps. . . . Some militants took notes in Arabic or French, but they were forced to burn them later."[12] This explains the meager number of oral testimonies on Vichy North Africa by Spanish Republican, Jewish, and Muslim survivors of labor camps throughout Morocco and Algeria.[13]

This shortage of autobiographies written during the war can also be attributed to what Claudine Kahan terms the "shame of eyewitness."[14] Psychological studies argue that survivors of traumatic events struggle to report the sadistic treatments of their guards and torturers. Motivated by avoiding the shame and the reliving of trauma, survivors of Vichy North African camps blocked memories of the war, suppressing experiences of maltreatment and dehumanization.[15] In addition, some former detainees coped with trauma by minimizing the importance of their testimonies after they left the camps and by avoiding writing about their experiences or even acknowledging the value of their voice in the burgeoning literature of camps in the aftermath of World War II.[16]

In marginal regions outside Europe, testimonies of refugees and survivors who fled Nazi Europe and were interned in North Africa were always seen as secondary to those of Third Reich victims, given the historical focus on European death camps.[17] Until recently, the Vichy North African camp remained a topic outside the history of World War II in North Africa, Spain, and France.[18]

The local population that surrounded the camps also saw forced labor as part of the general colonial bureaucracy that France established throughout its colonies. For many members of the local Jewish and Muslim population, there was nothing unusual about the newly set-up camps throughout the Algerian and Moroccan Saharan territories, established to extend the railroad networks to the Mediterranean ports.[19] In his book *Two Arabs, a Berber, and a Jew: Entangled Lives in Morocco*, Lawrence Rosen notes:

Although little remarked upon by Westerners, the camps were not altogether unknown to people in Morocco. One was even located in Missour, not far from El Mers, where Shimon was living during the war years. . . . Shimon was never aware of the camp's existence. Even after the American troops landed in 1942, Roosevelt did not move to have the camps closed immediately, as he and Eisenhower were intent on keeping the local French forces . . . from doing anything that might interfere with the allies' push toward Italy.[20]

Few studies have been published on the relationship between the different nationalities of camp prisoners, camp guards, and the local population of Saharan communities during Vichy rule of French North Africa.[21]

Until recently, the dilapidated barracks of detention camps and disciplinary centers along miles of railroads received little attention from historians, archaeologists, and other social scientists, largely because of the general perception that there is little evidence of this historical chapter in North African Jewish-Muslim relations. In addition, the French colonial authorities left little paperwork that described life at these sites. On some occasions, colonial military administrators had a lot of time to destroy evidence of internees' abuse, even after the American landing in Morocco and Algeria. Despite the major lacunae of documentation, a few sources have emerged recently that shed light on the social, political, religious, and cultural life in camps managed by Vichy military administrators in Morocco and Algeria. These include the American Friends Service Committee Archive,[22] the private collection of Hélène Cazès Benatar,[23] and the personal testimonies of Muslim and Jewish survivors of the camps.[24]

In *How to Accept German Reparations* Susan Slyomovics sets out questions pertinent to how archives serve as living memories and narratives that could help us understand and analyze social and historical events, which anthropologists have historically conceived as the job of historians.[25] In this chapter I expand the repertoire of archives to include testimonial literary works written by prisoners during their forced stay and after their release from internment camps. In this context I rely largely on the work of Max Aub, especially *Diario de Djelfa* (Journal of Djelfa) and *El Cementerio de Djelfa* (The Cemetery of Djelfa). *Diario de Djelfa* includes forty-seven poems chosen from the many poems Aub wrote inside the camp between November 28, 1941, and May 18, 1942.

Although Aub's writings have largely been read outside North African studies and Holocaust studies, I argue that any analysis of Vichy interment camps would be limited without his literary works on camps as sites of memory.[26] As a literary critic, playwright, and novelist, Aub wrote in Spanish. The relative absence of translation of his works in French, English, and Arabic has also preserved the silence over his memories of Vichy camps. Aub acknowledged this limitation, arguing that "writing in Spanish has never been good business."[27] In addition, Aub's past political experience as a Spanish Republican barred him from entering France as well as Spain, especially after he wrote a book critical of Franco. Aub was not able to return to Spain until a few years before his death in 1972. Moreover, his writings never gained popularity in Spain; mainstream publishing companies showed little interest in either publishing or translating his work.

Because his work received little official and public attention, Aub founded his own journal, *Sala de espera*, in 1948 to disseminate his work in Spain and Mexico. The publication closed in 1951. Before his death Aub noted:

Neither Losada, nor [Espasa] Calpe, nor Porrúa, nor anyone has ever wanted to publish a single book of mine. . . . And now the Fondo [de Cultura Económica] even refuses to distribute them. That is, for he who does not know, even though I am paying they refuse to distribute them in bookstores. The truth is that the lack of confidence that I have in my work is based on the fact that my books are not sold.[28]

The politically motivated rejection of Aub's work by Franco's government limited its access to readers in Spain, France, and the United States. In addition, and despite his long stay in Mexico, few academic works and little historical attention have been given to Aub's literary publications.

For Aub, *Diario de Djelfa* and *El Cementerio de Djelfa* are about the remembrance of life in the camp of Djelfa. Despite their literary orientation, the works are full of references to real-life stories and events that took place inside Djelfa. In his writing Aub tries to capture the relationship between guards and prisoners and the interactions between prisoners and the neighboring villages and their Jewish and Muslim communities. Aub is conscious of the interpretation of his testimonial literature as fiction instead of fact.

This awareness of the possible limitation of these works as factual testimonies is also reflected in Mohamed Arezki Berkani's memoir on the detention and disciplinary camp of Djenien-Bou-Rezg. In the introduction to this memoir, Arezki Berkani cautions the reader not to let the weaknesses of his memory during the period of his detention undermine the historical value of his experience.

This work is borne out of my memories, which I try to write with objectivity, without hate towards the French. I will say what comes to my mind at this moment. There remain many events that I have forgotten. I specify here that I started writing this memoir starting December 1946. I could not do so earlier because of certain circumstances.[29]

Vichy Camps, the Saharan Railway, and an Economy of Forced Labor

In the last decades of the nineteenth century, French colonial authorities began discussing and planning a trans-Saharan railroad between the port of Dakar and Algerian and Moroccan coastal cities.[30] After many

years of military and geographic expeditions. which led to the French taking political control of sub-Saharan, North, and West African territories,
a heated debate erupted between supporters of the railways proposal and
advocates of a system of motor roads that would cross the Sahara. Neither
plan materialized until the German Reich defeated France in 1940. The
limited railroad lines connecting North African ports with West African
and sub-Saharan mines and regions and the need to maintain French colonial power in the region were two key reasons that pushed Marshal Henri
Philippe Pétain to authorize the construction of the Mediterranean-Niger
railway system in March 1941.

The labor for building the railroad came from the refugees, who were
organized into forced labor groups known as *groupes de travailleurs étrangers*
(GTEs). GTEs 1, 4, 9, and 12 were stationed at camp Bou Arfa;[31] GTEs 3,
5, 6, and 10 were housed in camp Colomb-Béchar, south of Oran;[32] GTE 2
was based in the disciplinary camp of Kenadza, and GTE 7 around Constantine. The camps of Djelfa and Berrouaghia[33] were largely reserved for
political undesirables.

FIGURE 5: Rosenthal, a German Jewish prisoner, pushes a cart in the stone quarry
of the Im Fout labor camp in Morocco, 1941–1942. Source: United States Holocaust
Memorial Museum Archives, Washington, D.C., Photograph 50721, courtesy of Sami
Dorra. Reprinted with permission.

The Vichy railroad project was widely supported by Hitler's officers, who later saw its strategic advantage as a potentially viable route to
transport Senegalese troops through Saharan interiors instead of the risky
maritime routes. Vichy authorities envisioned the future connection of
North and West Africa through the Mediterranean-Niger (Mer-Niger)
Railroad. A number of military internment camps were set up in southwestern Mali, eastern and western Guinea, and Senegal. Vichy authorities
set up three internment camps, known as Conakry, Kindia (Kinda), and
Kankan, in French Guinea (known today as Guinea).[34] These camps were
established to hold Allied prisoners of war. In southwestern Mali, camp
Koulikoro was built to intern the crews of British, Dutch, Danish, and
Greek ships.[35] Finally, the camp of Sebikotane (also known as Dakar) was
established east of Dakar and housed mostly Belgian and British mer-
chant sailors.[36]

When the French authorities began the discussion of these large
railroad systems connecting French West Africa and North Africa, they
were faced with the challenge of recruiting a labor force willing to work
under extreme Saharan weather conditions. The answer was to use the
political prisoners in metropolitan France and especially the large number of refugees in France's North African colonies who were regarded
as undesirable. Although escaping near certain death that would have
awaited them in German concentration and extermination camps in
Europe, refugees were faced with an extremely harsh new reality as the
Vichy government began their enlistment in forced labor camps. Herded
in chains to the harbors of Vichy, political prisoners and refugees were
deported on freighters to Oran, Algeria, and driven to Algiers and then
to Djelfa in the south.

At this point, most of the humanitarian organizations in charge
of Jewish and non-Jewish relief relocated from Paris to neutral Lisbon.
The Hebrew Immigrant Aid Society (HICEM) and the American Joint
Distribution Committee (JDC) moved their offices to Lisbon, as they
cooperated to provide Jewish refugees with tickets and visa information
and to secure their transportation.[37] In Casablanca the JDC and the
HICEM relied on the services of Hélène Cazès Benatar (1898–1979), a
Moroccan Jewish lawyer born and raised in Tangier before she moved
to Casablanca, where she married and became active in many associations.[38] In 1939 Benatar opened an office to support internees in French
camps and refugees who waited in Casablanca for a visa. Before she

began collaborating with the JDC, she worked as a volunteer for the Red Cross in Casablanca.

With the introduction of the Vichy anti-Jewish laws in Algeria and the formal revoking of French citizenship for Algerian Jews, Morocco became a destination for many.[39] Many survivors mentioned the poorer food rations for Jews and anti-Semitic acts in Algeria. Moroccan Jews were not persecuted in the same way as Jews in Algeria were; however, almost all Jewish families were affected in one way or another. Nevertheless, Moroccan Jews were not widely affected by the new anti-Jewish laws, despite the fact that Mohammed V was forced to sign the *dahir*s of October 31, 1940, and August 8, 1941. Unlike in Algeria, where French right-wing and anti-Semitic European settlers had a large presence in urban centers, in Morocco the *dahir*s had a limited impact, though a few Moroccan Jews were affected. The extent depended on the regional and local administration of the anti-Jewish measures, which were "designed to deprive Jews from working in a wide array of professions, including real estate, moneylending, banking, non-Jewish journalism, and radio broadcasting. Jews were allowed to engage in the crafts and wholesale trading."[40]

In Morocco, although pogroms took place at different times and in different places, for example, Fez in 1912, relations between Jews and Muslims were relatively calm compared with Algeria.[41] Given the widespread poverty among Muslim and Jewish communities, the American Friends Service Committee office opted to deal with the question of thousands of men interned in labor camps.

In July 1942, four months before the Allied landing, the Quakers opened an office in Casablanca under the leadership of Leslie Heath, Ken Kimberland, and David Hartley. The Quakers approached the issue of Vichy camp internees through a program that identified three major points of relief. According to Howard Wriggins,

> They provided used clothing from Quakers stocks for the worst-off internees. With the help of French social workers, they identified destitute families of internees and provided small cash supplements or emergency food. They assisted disabled veterans among Spanish refugees who were not in camps. On occasion they were able to act as intermediaries between the internees and the authorities.[42]

To provide these forms of relief to internees throughout Morocco and Algeria, the Quakers had to rely on bureaucratic networks of management without clashing or interfering with government activities. Before and during the first stages of the war, they began reporting to consulates and State Department agencies on the struggles and the sufferings of European refugees in Saharan camps.

An OSS report dated August 26, 1942, states that close to 1,000 internees were held in tents in the Djelfa camp in Algeria. All the internees fought in the Spanish Civil War as members of the International Brigade, which was composed of volunteers from more than fifty countries, including Cuba, Canada, Mexico, the United States, Germany, and Argentina. Mostly recruited and organized by the Communist International, these fighters came to Spain to support Republican forces against the Nationalists led by Franco and supported by Germany and Italy. At the end of the Spanish Civil War an influx of refugees, including women and children, crossed French borders and were interned in concentration camps, such as Gurs and Le Vernet, both constructed as a result of decisions made by the democratic government of France; those suspected of being communists or anarchists were interned in separate prison camps and subjected to hard labor. In mid-1939 Spanish Republican prisoners were given the choice of freedom if they enlisted in the French Army and the Foreign Legion. However, after the fall of France in June 1940, Spanish Republicans, including members of the International Brigade who had played a key role in the French Foreign Legion, were transferred to labor camps to serve in different labor units.

In the summer of 1941, thousands of former volunteers from the International Brigade and other refugees were herded into camps in crowded tents and barracks, sometimes with no protection from the heat or cold. Although the Vichy government directly managed the railroad project, Nazi German experts provided technical assistance. The inmates lived in small brick houses or in Arab tents, organized by GTE or by *groupe de travailleurs démobilisés* (GTD).

Agamben argues that the concentration camp is the embodiment of the state of exception, where the *Muselmann*, the hopeless prisoner, awaits death. In this sense, the camp is outside normal and conventional law. Unlike Agamben's definition of the Nazi camps, I argue that Djelfa, as a Vichy North African camp, exemplified a different model of the camp, where internees had a margin of hope of survival despite all the restrictions put on their movements in and out of the camp. Prisoners communicated with the outside world through Quakers, Moroccan Jews, and Jewish organization volunteers in Casablanca, Algiers, Madrid, and Lisbon (in particular, until 1941, in many German *Konzentrationslager*, prisoners could communicate with the outside world).

The internees had some access to books, medical services, food, letters, and even cigarettes. They were also allowed to communicate with each other, to write personal biographies, and to go outside the camp for a weekend trip to neighboring Arab and Berber villages. But this relative movement and access to some basic human services was misleading, especially after the Allied landing, as José Campos Peral, the former editor of *Lucha* who was interned at the camp of Cherchell in Algeria, argues.

The French had even invented the fiction that internees remaining in the camps were now free men working under legitimate contract, after the manner of contract workers in metropolitan France. Technical freedom in Bou Arfa was meaningless. The camp is surrounded by razorbacks which could be scaled only with difficulty and even if one got out of the bowl it would be hundreds of miles through the desert to civilization.[43]

Like the majority of European Nazi death and internment camps, French North African labor camps in Algeria and Morocco had the same "forced labor" purpose. Labeled as labor camps, these internment centers were designed to intern Allied prisoners of war and to serve as disciplinary and isolation camps, a forced labor camp for foreign workers, and a refugee center for members of the Foreign Legion or displaced persons. Most of the camps were intended to be a source of inexpensive forced labor for French-operated railroads and mines.

Like German camps, however, intolerable conditions reigned in the North African camps, where weak, undernourished, undesirable political prisoners and refugees were "being annihilated through work," even if the mortality rate was much lower in comparison.[44] The Vichy North African camps were deliberately constructed in dry, barren, and isolated Saharan regions as part of a system of brutality and terror, with the intention of creating a sense of helplessness. To survive, internees in the camps attempted to use the bureaucratic means at their disposal within the inhumane structures of the camp. Although subjected to forced labor, internees were to a degree aware of the fate of inmates in Nazi death camps and strategically understood that their compliance with the authorities could postpone or prevent a transfer to Nazi death camps or to a disciplinary internment prison, where the mortality rate was quite high.

Djelfa and the Topography of Isolation

In 1852, after the French military occupation of the Sahara, a French military post was set up on the outskirts of the village of Djelfa.[45] In 1867 Reverend J. Lowitz described a missionary journey throughout Laghouat Province for the *Jewish Herald* under the superintendence of the British Society for the Propagation of the Gospel Among the Jews. Lowitz was part of a British project to convert Jews in remote areas to Christianity. He talked about his interaction with local Jewish rabbis and described schools that were open to the education of Jewish and Protestant children. He recounted visiting Jews in their homes and shops. Although he gave specific statistics about the population of different villages surrounding the city of Laghouat, he noted that, during his passage through Djelfa, he met "with a few Jews."[46] Historically, Djelfa had a considerable number of Jews who lived alongside Muslim communities and played a central role in the local economy, largely as peddlers.

Djelfa is located at the crossroads between Laghouat, Bou-Saada, and Aflou, 306 kilometers (190 miles) south of Algiers. In 1921 Djelfa became the southern terminus of the railroad to Blida. As a central colonial post, Djelfa attracted a Jewish community of about 400 people, mostly from Ghardaia[47] and Bou-Saada.[48] In 1930 the population of Djelfa numbered 3,000 inhabitants. Under the Vichy regime the Djelfa camp served as a center for residential assignment (*assignation à résidence*) and as a forced labor camp. On March 25, 1941, the camp became a *centre de séjour surveillé* under the authority of Jules César Caboche, who served between April 7, 1941, and June 23, 1943. In the unpublished "Campo de Djelfa, Argelia" (Camp of Djelfa, Algeria), Max Aub describes the journey from France to Djelfa.

We left Port-Vendres at dusk; out of the port, they removed our handcuffs. . . . We were two Spaniards in the expedition, we would have liked to see the Spanish soil. . . . Three days after we arrived in Algiers, . . . they locked us in an old fortress. . . . Until that time our luggage was transported (I could not travel without books, I was carrying a lot of clothes and my manuscripts). . . . At six o'clock we were ordered to line up to go to the station.[49]

After sixteen hours of travel by train, Aub and other prisoners arrived in Djelfa and were forced to walk 4 kilometers before their arrival at the camp site, where they were met by adjutant Jean Gravelle, the commander of the camp. Aub recounted how prisoners had to abandon their bags and luggage.

Max Aub, who was born French with a Jewish French mother and a German father and who was adopted by Spain and later Mexico, returned to France after the fall of Barcelona. As the Vichy administration took over, he was denounced as a "red" and was first imprisoned as a militant communist at the Vichy penal camp in Le Vernet d'Ariège before his deportation to Djelfa. In 1942 he escaped and hid in a Jewish maternity hospital in Casablanca with the help of the HICEM. On September 10, 1942, after he was granted Mexican protection and a visa, he fled to Mexico City aboard the Portuguese ship *Serpa Pinto*. Aub was one of the few prisoners in Djelfa who recorded memories of life in the camp in his works and poetry.

Djelfa camp held a number of prominent French and Spanish personalities. The most notable prisoner was Bernard Lecache, the president of the International League Against Antisemitism (Ligue Internationale contre l'antisémitisme).[50] Another well-known prisoner was the French communist Roger Garaudy, who was interned during the first weeks of the camp in 1941. Both Lecache and Garaudy were later transferred to the Bossuet camp.[51] In *Parole d'homme* Garaudy notes that, when he was interned in Djelfa, he was saved from near death when the Ibadi Muslim (a sect in Islam) guards defied orders to shoot him and other prisoners.[52]

In the prologue to *Diario de Djelfa* (Journal of Djelfa), Aub talks about secret casual readings of his poems about life in the camp to other prisoners: "We used to read them hungry and livid at the light of an oil lamp carefully kept underneath the camping tent keeping them from the imbecile cruelty of our blind guardians."[53]

Despite the shortage of personal narratives on daily life in Djelfa and other camps, ample historical data highlight how prisoners lived in these remote pre-Saharan internment camps. Yet any historical assessment of life in Vichy North African camps requires a careful consideration of Max Aub's literary works. In this context I explain the general characteristics of Djelfa as a disciplinary camp of forced labor through the literary works of Aub and through the reports by American Friends Service Committee representatives and the official report of André Jean-Faure, the Vichy inspector general of North African camps. Despite its inconsistencies, Jean-Faure's report about Djelfa as an example of a detention labor camp is an important document that contextualizes Aub's testimonial literary perspective.

The official document includes maps of the camp that describe its geographic placement. In the description of the camp, Jean-Faure fails to give the impression that Djelfa camp is a detention center. In his work on the camp, Bernard Sicot demonstrates how Jean-Faure describes the camp as a center protected from outside forces instead of highlighting the isolation and loneliness of the prisoners. There was no reference to the special section in the camp where prisoners faced harsh treatment and death.

In 1941 Djelfa opened its doors to receive 1,200 French "undesirables" (*indésirables*), who were later transferred to different camps. The camp was also used to detain Spanish Republicans, former members of the French Foreign Legion, the International Brigade, Jews, and other nationalities.[54] In his visit to the camp, Dr. Edouard Wyss-Dunant, the International Committee of the Red Cross representative who visited the camp on August 16, 1942, counted 899 prisoners (189 of whom were Jewish). Internees included Spaniards (444), Poles (52, including 44 Jews), stateless people (118), Germans (50, including 16 Jews), Austrians (15, including 11 Jews), Hungarians (15, including 11 Jews), Romanians (11, all Jewish), Russians (39, including 17 Jews), Soviets (85, including 37 Jews), Czechs (8), Armenians (6), British (2), Belgians (3), Italians (2), Serbians (1), and Argentinians (3). The remaining 43 prisoners were of various other nationalities.[55]

Built on the right bank of Oued Djelfa, about 1 kilometer north of the military post, the Djelfa camp consisted mostly of tents known as Arab *marabout*. Twelve to twenty men occupied each tent. In "Campo de Djelfa, Argelia" Aub writes, "Parked behind barbs, the prisoners lived in tents. They started to construct barracks, which were used not to house the first workers or protect them from cold and heat but to work in different productive trades for the administration."[56]

In March 1941, François Darlan, serving in the pro-German government, asked French administrators in the Algerian colony to treat refugees in Vichy camps without subjecting them to repressive measures. He notified the general government of Algeria that the refugees held in the *centres de séjour surveillé* in Algeria and Morocco were not condemned individuals and should be treated as administrative internees and not be subjected to forced labor. At the same time, using the law of November 19, 1938, Darlan underscored that camp administrators could use internees for specific tasks, noting that military commanders of the southern Algerian territories could use the internees in workshops in the camp with the purpose of making objects that could be sold for their benefit.[57] The camp authorities in Algeria were allowed by the Ministry of Interior to establish workshops in the camps, using the detainees' hobbies and skills to make

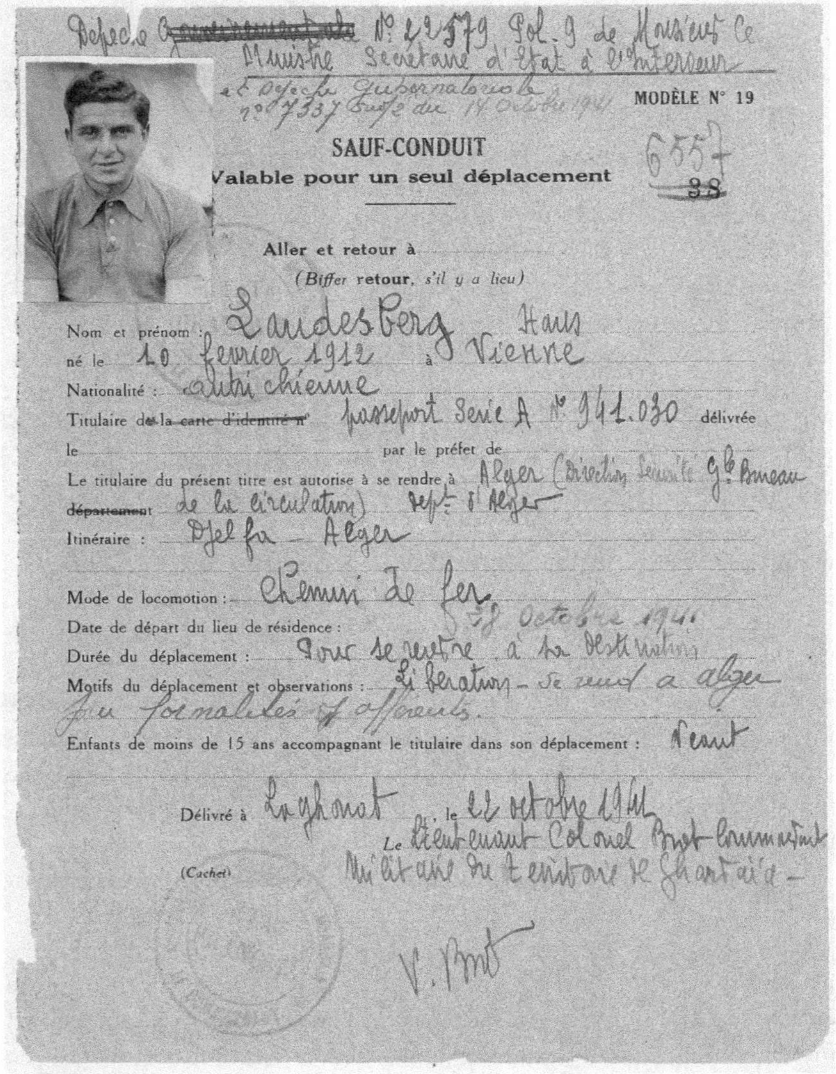

Dépêche ~~Gouvernementale~~ N° 22579 Pol. 9 de Monsieur le Ministre Secrétaire d'Etat à l'Intérieur
et Dépêche Gubernatoriale n° 7337 du 14 Octobre 1941

MODÈLE N° 19

6557
~~38~~

SAUF-CONDUIT

Valable pour un seul déplacement

Aller et retour à ....

(*Biffer* **retour**, *s'il y a lieu*)

Nom et prénom : Landesberg Hans

né le 10 fevrier 1912 à Vienne

Nationalité : autrichienne

Titulaire de ~~la carte d'identité n°~~ passeport Serie A N° 941.030 délivrée

le .... par le préfet de ....

Le titulaire du présent titre est autorisé à se rendre à Alger (Direction Sécurité Gle Bureau

~~département~~ de la circulation) Dept d'Alger

Itinéraire : Djelfa - Alger

Mode de locomotion : Chemin de fer

Date de départ du lieu de résidence : 28 octobre 1941

Durée du déplacement : Pour se rendre à la destination

Motifs du déplacement et observations : Libération - se rend à Alger pour formalités afferents.

Enfants de moins de 15 ans accompagnant le titulaire dans son déplacement : Néant

Délivré à Laghouat, le 22 octobre 1941

Le Lieutenant Colonel ... Commandant Militaire du territoire de Ghardaïa

(*Cachet*)

FIGURE 6: Safe conduct pass issued to Hans Landesberg in the Djelfa internment camp releasing him to leave for Algiers. Source: United States Holocaust Memorial Museum, Washington, D.C., Photograph 65539, courtesy of Hans Landesberg. Reprinted with permission.

objects that could be sold in Algerian markets. The camp authorities used halfah grass, which was widespread in the region of Djelfa, to launch a set of activities making sacks, baskets, sandals, and ropes. Many of these objects targeted the harvesting and packing of dates.

According to Wyss-Dunant, the camp commandant used the prisoners in such a way as to make the camp virtually autonomous. The commandant accomplished this feat by "dividing the men according to their specialties and in initiating workshops where these skills could be utilized."[58] The prisoners erected the barracks and manufactured everything for the camp.

The blacksmiths built a complete forge, some carpenters their workshop, and they made all the necessary things. There were some tanners in the group and the commandant in anticipation of the coming winter put them to work making clothing (and shoes) from sheepskin. Moreover as halfah grass (*Stipa tenacissima*, a widespread perennial plant which dominates the landscape of the valleys and mountains around Djelfa) is very plentiful in the country . . . he set up a workshop for the manufacture of hammocks, sandals, mats and mattresses.[59]

Later, the prisoners built a canteen and community hall and operated a soap factory. The prisoners worked from 6 a.m. to 11 a.m. and from 3 p.m. to 6 p.m. The detainees who worked in the town of Djelfa were paid 20 Francs a day, 10 of which was put into the camp's general account and 5 in an account reserved for their eventual release. The prisoners who worked inside the camp were paid 16 francs a day.

Although official Vichy reports claim that workers were fairly paid for their work, Aub argues that the prisoners were exploited for the personal enrichment of Caboche and other camp guards and commanders. For instance, during the period of April–May 1942, Aub notes that the gains of Caboche, the camp commander, were close to 200,000 francs from halfah grass. Prisoners harvested the plant to be used for making sandals, mats, and baskets. Aub witnessed how prisoners were "hired" as carriers, charcoal makers, painters, and masons. They were given 20 francs per day, usually paid as 100 grams of bread. Other prisoners served at the village administrative hall. It was estimated that the daily gains of the camp from prisoners' labor were between 15,000 and 18,000 francs.

In one of the few critical assessments of the forced labor practices in the camp, Jean-Faure recommended that prisoners be paid extra money for the work they did outside the camp. The report states, "Workers should be paid a normal salary when they work outside the camp [and they should be] given a reasonable minimum pay of 2 to 3 francs per hour when they work outside the camp." Workers were not forced to work, but the consequences of not doing so were undesirable; prisoners who refused to participate in the camp activities were afforded fewer privileges. Aub notes how "at Djelfa work is not obligatory, but those who do not work do not eat. . . . Forced labor was usually rewarded through one hundred grams of bread." Therefore and even though work did not improve the prisoners' conditions or earn them money, it did allow them to have the opportunity to be outside the camp, visit the village, and have access to more food.

Jewish prisoners were subjected to anti-Semitic treatment and abuse. In *El Cementerio de Djelfa* Aub talks about a Jew who was forced to work on Saturday, despite the religious laws against it. Jacob Oliel provides the example of Gaston Gundelfinger, a German Jew, who faced a set of disciplinary procedures from the camp guards when he refused to work.[60] Unlike other groups, Jews did not enjoy benefits similar to those of other prisoners. Yet they were occasionally allowed to visit neighboring synagogues and to meet with the local Jewish community of Djelfa during certain religious festivities.

Life in the camp was unbearable because of the cold winds of the High Plains of Algeria. Aub notes how Djelfa is "the land of cold wind."[61] During the winter, prisoners were not allowed to make a fire inside their tents for heating. The prisoners slept on wooden beds, sometimes on bed irons. But most slept on the ground on hay. There was a shortage of mats and blankets. They ate 50 grams (1.7 ounces) of bread per day and meat three times a week. They raised cattle in the camp and maintained small fruit and vegetable gardens. According to many prisoners, there was little food, and some resorted to eating rats and dogs to survive.[62] The prisoners did not have shoes, underwear, or towels. Prisoners suffered from malnutrition, typhoid, dysentery, and dehydration. Many suffered from the extreme cold during the winter and from the heat in the summer. The lack of shoes also put the prisoners at risk of scorpion and snake bites. In January 1943 Aub reported that 57 prisoners died, largely because of typhoid fever (i.e., about 6% of the 900 camp inmates).

The simple act of building a fire was punishable by spending the night in a special area of the camp and sleeping in the *cachot*, a stone bed without blankets and full of lice, where the temperature dropped to

15 degrees Celsius. Internees complained of the shortage of blankets and clothes. In this context many prisoners died in the camp, especially during the winter. Aub described how he saw people die of cold. The camp authorities made sure that dying prisoners were transported to the neighboring civilian hospitals. By making sure that dying internees were moved to the village of Djelfa, Caboche avoided filing paperwork for their deaths and therefore left no historical trace of them in the camp.

In the camp the relationship between the prisoners and their guards varied depending on the individuals. Caboche relied on spahis (members of the cavalry regiments of the French army recruited primarily from the indigenous population), Moroccan *goumiers* (soldiers who served in the auxiliary unit), Senegalese *tirailleurs* (infantry), and local *douaïr* (mobilized Muslims engaged in the police auxiliary service) to control and discipline the internees in Djelfa. Although many local Muslim camp guards refused to participate in the torture of internees, a few Arab soldiers did not opt out of Caboche's harsh policies toward some prisoners. Muslim guards were transferred to other places monthly to disrupt any sympathy with the prisoners. This disobedience was noted in many camps in Morocco as well as in Italy.[63]

In the *Diario de Djelfa* Aub wrote a poem with the title "Dice el Moroen Cuclillas" (The Moor Says as He Is Squatting) in which he references many historical tropes that reflect the connection between Christian Spaniards and Muslims in the context of the history of Spain. Aub highlights that both groups are victims of the French-Spanish past and present traumatic histories.

> The moor says as he is squatting
> Oh my al-Hambra
> And the fatigued Christian said
> Oh my *alambre* [Spanish, barbed-wire]
> The moor greenish black
> From the cold in his jellaba
> Looks at his minaret
> And maybe remembers Spain
> With his ancestors,
> Their jewels and their turbans
> Waterwheel in the *sakia* [Arabic, irrigation canal)
> The farms and their waterways
> And the colorfully dressed people

> The moor says as he is squatting
> Oh my al-Hambra
> And the fatigued Christian said
> Oh my *alambre*
>
> . . .
>
> They say that we speak loudly
> With great shouts
> And they say that we are
> Imprisoned with a Muslim guard
> It looks as though both of us
> Are guarded in the same way
> And one day the day will come
> When we have the same fate
> The Moor says as he is squatting
> Oh my al-Hambra
> And the fatigued Christian said
> Oh my *alambre*

Caboche announced to the prisoners that he was their enemy and that his task was to send as many as possible to the cemetery. In the poem "You Already Stink, Julian Castillo,"[64] Aub describes death and burial in the camp:

> At the door of the Church
> Twenty Moors have gathered
> Because the word got out
> That another refugee has died

In 1959 a German court decided that the living conditions inside Djelfa camp had been degrading. Therefore a survivor who had been incarcerated first in Le Vernet and then sent to Djelfa received a onetime indemnification payment from Germany for the months of incarceration in Djelfa.

On January 22, 1945, as a commitment to testimonial realism, Aub noted, "I think I have no right to be silent in what I saw in favor of writing what I imagine."[65] Despite the marginalization of Vichy labor camps in the history of World War II and North African studies, Max Aub's voice and writings have managed to lift the veil of silence from the memory of Vichy labor camps in North Africa. Unlike the Nazi death camps, North African Vichy camps were internment centers that did not benefit from the exposure to the military cameras of the American Allied forces when they landed on the Atlantic and Mediterranean coasts of Morocco and Algeria. Instead, the American army left the management of camps to French authorities, despite the illegal internment of Jewish and non-Jewish refugees.

Max Aub managed to challenge this official silencing, giving voice to life and death inside Vichy labor camps. His literary description of Djelfa is one of the most important historical accounts we have today about the lives of refugees and internees of the war on the southern margins of the Mediterranean. In the context of the larger Mediterranean context of World War II, Aub's work offers a connected story of life inside the camps of Spain, France, and Vichy North Africa. His writings should allow historians to follow the journey of refugees of war as they managed the French bureaucracy during the Vichy period. In addition, most of Aub's literary work is memories and descriptions of events and encounters involving Jews, Muslims, Senegalese soldiers, and French administrators. These accounts highlight a set of human affects, which have an ethnographic value insofar as they are a repository of human feelings of fear, anxiety, anger, defeat, and hope. From an anthropological perspective, we could benefit from a rereading of these archives of emotion as we rewrite the Vichy camp and its topography of Saharan internment through ethnographic texts that rely on testimonial fiction.

8

The Ethics and Aesthetics of Restraint
Judeo-Tunisian Narratives of Occupation

Lia Brozgal

FOR SIX MONTHS during World War II, from November 1942 to May 1943, the Jewish communities of Tunisia bore the vicissitudes of Nazi occupation while the specter of the Final Solution hovered on the not-so-distant horizon. At the time, the Jews of Tunisia, like their coreligionists in Morocco and Algeria, had already seen their civil, political, and economic rights curtailed by the anti-Jewish laws conceived under the Vichy regime and promulgated throughout France's North African territories.[1] But if institutional anti-Semitism was the common lot of North African Jewry during this period, the experience of German occupation was unique to Tunisia, where the arrival of Colonel Walter Rauff and his forces made the Hitlerian *Weltanschauung* a quotidian reality for the country's 85,000 Jews. In Tunis but also in Sfax, Sousse, Bizerte, and other urban areas, Jews were targets of harassment, physical violence, unexplained arrests, internments, and generalized spoliation. Men between the ages of 16 and 60 were transported to camps, where they were compelled to perform arduous labor. Onerous fines were levied on the community. Members of the elite were arrested in their homes in the middle of the night, and some individuals were assassinated or deported to concentration camps in Europe.[2] Midnight raids on the Jewish quarter of Tunis were a pretext for ransacking and rape.

Deeply significant for Tunisian Jewry and unique in the context of World War II in North Africa, this historical episode has been recounted in a handful of chronicles, nearly all of which were written in French and published in Tunisia between 1943 and 1946. The chronicles give voice to the subjective experiences of micro-aggression and abject anti-Semitic violence but also to the logistics and politics of occupation.

The first text to appear in print was Paul Ghez's *Six mois sous la botte: les juifs de Tunis aux prises avec les SS* (Six Months Under the Boot: The Jews of Tunis Grapple with the SS), published in Tunis immediately after the Allied liberation of the capital in 1943.[3] *Six mois* appears to be Ghez's personal diary; complete with dated entries, it records the author's interactions with the Nazi command and his own internal turmoil.[4]

In 1944 Robert Borgel—son of Moïse Borgel, the aging leader of the Jewish community in Tunis—published a longer and more detailed account of the occupation, titled *Étoile jaune et croix gammée* (Yellow Star and Swastika).[5] Several years later, Gaston Guez, a mohel from Tunis, edited *Nos martyrs sous la botte allemande: où les ex-travailleurs juifs de Tunisie racontent leurs souffrances* (Our Martyrs Under the German Boot: The Jewish Workers of Tunis Recount Their Suffering). Unlike the highly narrativized accounts by Ghez and Borgel, Guez's self-published document is a compendium of transcribed testimonials, photos, and letters collected from the families of fallen Jewish workers.[6]

Although the chronicles by Ghez, Borgel, and Guez are the product of insiders—members of the Jewish community animated by their personal connection to the events—the corpus also contains two texts written by outsiders: *Tunis sous la croix gammée* (Tunis Under the Swastika), published by Eugène Boretz in 1944 and *La croix gammée s'aventure en Tunisie* (The Swastika Ventures into Tunisia), written by Maximilien Trenner in the fall of 1943.[7]

In this chapter I am concerned with recuperating this little-known corpus of primary materials, for like the events they describe, the chronicles register only faintly in specialized scholarship on World War II and the Holocaust and hardly at all in the realm of general knowledge. Works of historiography refer to them in footnotes and occasionally call on them to bolster factual assertions, but the chronicles have never been rigorously mined for the rich microhistories they contain. Nor, moreover, have they been read through a literary lens, despite the established place of literature in the study of the Holocaust and the undeniable literary qualities of the chronicles themselves.[8]

Facts certainly matter when it comes to writing about episodes of historical trauma, and the chronicles are valuable insofar as they fill in the gaps in knowledge about little-known events generally considered mar-

FIGURE 7: A Jewish forced laborer in Tunisia wearing the obligatory Star of David, with a German officer in the background. Source: Bundesarchiv, Bild 101I-556-0937-30; photo: Dr. Stocker, 1942/1943. Reprinted with permission.

ginal to the Holocaust. But the very act of writing this story, of "poetizing" or "narrativizing" lived experience, is central to the expression of that experience and to the reader's understanding of it.[9] In this regard, the significance of the chronicles also resides in their strategies of representation, which have influenced the broader construction of this historical episode. Through historicized close reading of the accounts by Ghez and Borgel, I explore how the works' *poetics*—their tropes, narrative techniques, and discursive strategies—shape their production of historical evidence and our interpretation of the events they represent.

. . .

In his work on the Tunisian chronicles, historian Claude Nataf articulates a causal link between their limited impact and the Tunisian Jews' general sense of *pudeur* (restraint) when evoking the German occupation.

L'écho de ces récits et témoignages est demeuré faible. Il faut reconnaître que, comparées aux souffrances subies par les Communautés juives d'Europe, celles de la Communauté juive de Tunisie sont apparues insignifiantes, et les juifs originaires de Tunisie eux-mêmes ont jugé que *la pudeur* leur commandait de ravaler leurs douleurs au rang de mauvais souvenirs qu'on n'évoque pas.[10] (my emphasis)

But the echo of these chronicles and testimonials has remained weak. It must be recognized that, compared to the suffering of the European Jewish communities, the suffering of the Jewish community of Tunisia appeared insignificant, and the Jews from Tunisia decided of their own accord that decency required them to swallow their pain, like bad memories that one doesn't bring up.

Nataf hints at an ethical conundrum that haunts the chronicles written by Jewish community insiders and manifests in their poetics, particularly in the accounts produced by Paul Ghez and Robert Borgel.[11] A close reading of the discursive and rhetorical strategies deployed in their narratives illuminates a paradox at the core of the chronicles: The sense of duty to recount—to become "historians of themselves"—vies with an ethics of *pudeur*, or restraint.[12] In both texts the tension created by the coexistence of these seemingly irreconcilable missions plays out at the level of craft: in lexical choices, narrative decisions, and rhetorical and discursive strategies.

The titles of the two works offer the first clues to decoding their ethical and aesthetic restraint. In Ghez's *Six mois sous la botte: les juifs de Tunis aux prises avec les SS*, the titular "six months" is a transparent reference to the duration of the occupation but also a sign of temporal limitation. By emphasizing the relative brevity of the episode, the title reassures readers that the trials depicted will be brought to an end within the space of the text. Recourse to irony, which emerges as a key rhetorical strategy in *Six mois*, is also foregrounded in the title: the notion that "the Jews of Tunis grapple with the SS" suggests a struggle between equals or a bout between well-matched opponents. Its intended meaning, of course, is the opposite; the Jews constituted a vulnerable population with few resources to counter an all-powerful occupier.

The capacity of irony to minimize the appearance of sentimentality or maudlin self-pity is also mobilized in Borgel's title, *Étoile jaune et croix gammée*. Here, the literary technique of parataxis draws a grammatical and structural equivalency between the Jews and the Nazis (metonymically represented by the yellow star and the swastika, respectively). With its parallel syntax, *Étoile jaune et croix gammée* gestures to a conflict of equals, evincing a subtle irony whereby the explicit grammar of coordination masks an implicit reality of subordination. If the notion of a level playing field (rhetorically and actually) between the "yellow star" and the "swastika" smacks of bravura, it also functions to diminish Judeo-Tunisian

FIGURE 8: Portrait of an unidentified Jewish forced laborer in Tunisia wearing the obligatory Star of David. Source: Bundesarchiv, Bild 101I-556-0937-10; photo: Dr. Stocker, 1942/1943. Reprinted with permission.

victimhood and assert the Jews' status as capable opponents. In both titles ostensibly clear language contains rhetorical and literary devices that ultimately downplay the episode's severity.

In *Six mois* Ghez's aesthetic restraint is nearly always mobilized to subtly obfuscate his knowledge of specific events in Europe and the Final Solution. His status as a prominent lawyer, a distinguished member of the Jewish community, and a decorated veteran of both world wars makes it likely that he knew the extent of the Nazis' plans for the Jews.[13] In the entry dated November 20, 1942, shortly after the arrival of the Gestapo in Tunis, Ghez reveals a sense of deep foreboding.

Les Boches se multiplient et étendent leur emprise. On commence à parler des réquisitions de villas dans le secteur du Belvédère. Bien entendu, les Juifs font les frais de ces opérations et les expulsions se font avec une brutalité inhumaine. Pouvait-on attendre autre chose des soldats à croix gammée? L'inquiétude est grande, surtout chez les Juifs. Les récits des atrocités d'Europe Centrale sont présents à l'esprit. J'ai beaucoup voyagé en France depuis l'Armistice et j'ai causé avec des transfuges de la zone occupée. Leurs récits donnent le frisson aux plus endurcis. Tristes pressentiments![14]

The Krauts are growing in number and casting a wider net. There is talk of requisitioning villas in the Belvedere area. Of course, the Jews bear the brunt of these operations, and the expulsions are carried out with inhumane brutality. But what else could one expect from the swastika troops? Anxieties run high, especially among the Jews. The stories of the atrocities of Eastern Europe are on everyone's mind. I have traveled extensively in France since the Armistice, and I have spoken with refugees from the occupied zone. Their tales make even the toughest man shudder. Sad premonitions!

Ghez is sufficiently informed about the practices of the Third Reich to label them atrocities. Even though any number of the stories emerging from the occupied zone between 1940 and 1942 would have been atrocious enough to make even the "toughest man shudder," it seems reasonable to read Ghez's "sad premonitions" as proof of his detailed knowledge about the Final Solution. Indeed, this passage is notable within the context of *Six mois* because it constitutes Ghez's most transparent admission of what he knows, and it is the only time he refers to his direct contact with Jews in Europe.

As the situation intensifies, however, Ghez's language becomes increasingly steeped in euphemism. On December 8, he explains his decision to submit to the Germans' demand that the community take charge of recruiting Jewish men for the labor camps; Ghez fears that even the small act of refusing to organize the recruitment effort will result in retaliation on the part of the SS.

Le colonel [Rauff] est catégorique. Si la population n'exécute pas, il fera fusiller des otages, et les SS procèderont eux-mêmes au recrutement. C'est un pogrome en perspective. . . . Après avoir emprisonnée et peut-être fusillé des otages, les SS . . . procèderont eux-mêmes à une rafle imposante et barbare. Ils l'ont fait à Varsovie, ils l'ont fait à Paris.[15]

Rauff is categorical. If the population does not execute his orders, he will have the hostages shot, and the SS will take over the recruitment themselves. It is a pogrom in the making. . . . After having imprisoned and perhaps shot the hostages, the SS . . . would undertake a wide-scale and barbarian roundup. They did it in Warsaw; they did it in Paris.

Ghez reveals knowledge of the events in Europe while at the same refusing to name them explicitly or comment further on their implications for the situation in Tunisia. The "pogrom in the making" may or may not refer to the pogroms carried out in Europe (the term was also used to describe Arab raids on the Jewish ghettos of North Africa), but the references to Warsaw and Paris are unequivocal. Based on the time of Ghez's writing and the context of "wide-scale and barbarian" roundups, "Warsaw" refers to the establishment of the Warsaw ghetto in 1940 and "Paris" to the Vél d'Hiv roundup in the French capital on July 16, 1942. The text, however, uses a rhetorical shorthand, allowing toponyms—Warsaw, Paris—to stand in for the actual events that took place at those sites, signaling knowledge metonymically rather than directly.

The author's unexpected use of apostrophe to refer to himself as Don Quixote also participates in the text's aesthetic of restraint by leveraging the symbolic valences of Cervantes' "ingenious *hidalgo*"—that idealistic but delusional knight who mistook windmills for giants. When senior members of the Jewish community are arrested and held hostage for seven days, Ghez considers his options, certain that his turn will come. After rejecting the possibility of running away or hiding, he lights on the notion of going to Algeria to join the Allied forces.

Rejoindre la frontière algérienne à la rencontre des libérateurs? C'est bien tentant et je me sens déjà les fourmis dans les jambes. Silence Don Quichotte! Tu oublies cette malheureuse qui vit ses derniers jours.[16]

Join the liberators at the Algerian border? It is very tempting and I'm already itching to go. Be quiet, Don Quixote! You are forgetting this miserable woman who is living her final days.

The "miserable woman" in question is Ghez's ailing wife, who would die of cancer several weeks later, in January 1943, and whose story is yet another tragedy the author prefers to envelop in the language of discretion.

Were it the lone example in the chronicle, the intertextuality of this bizarre and sudden self-apostrophe could perhaps be written off as incidental, a turn of phrase unremarkable for an educated man of the time. Over the course of this brief text, however, the half-dozen instances where Ghez refers to himself as Don Quixote underscore the author's resistance to naming the German atrocities while, at the same time, revealing a deeper ambivalence about his own role in the unfolding drama. For example, on December 6, the day Ghez announces to the community that he will take charge of the recruitment efforts, despite his earlier decision to withdraw from public life, he writes:

Je m'étais pourtant promis de ne plus tenter d'aventure, de rester au chevet de ma femme, de veiller sur mes petits. La phrase est lancée, il faut y aller. Ajuste ta lance, Don Quichotte, et pars devant.[17]

And yet I had promised not to go off on adventures, to stay by my wife's bedside, to take care of my children. Now the word is out, I have to go. Sword up, Don Quixote, and off you go.

Ghez's self-fashioning as an incarnation of Cervantes' hero is almost painfully ironic: the enemies of Don Quixote, after all, would turn out to be figments of his imagination.

Furthermore, Ghez attributes quixotic ideals to his children. Recounting his family's expulsion from their home under the brutal encouragement of the SS, Ghez describes his children's reactions.

Le petit Roland, qui vient d'avoir 8 ans, maudit nos persécuteurs et pense à les exterminer. Sa petite soeur Edith fait chorus. Seront-ils aussi des Don Quichotte?[18]

Young Roland, who just turned 8, curses our persecutors and imagines exterminating them. His little sister Edith chimes in. Are they also a couple of Don Quixotes?

Here, in one of the few scenes in which Ghez reveals the intimacy of his domestic life, he worries that his children, in their railings against their persecutors, resemble him: obsessed with doing battle against enemies who cannot be beaten.

So far, the atrocities committed in Europe have only been suggested, never named explicitly, appearing in the text cloaked in the language of euphemism and metaphor. At this point, however, "le petit Roland, mau-

dit nos persécuteurs et pense à les *exterminer*" (emphasis mine). Significantly, Ghez's son does not think of beating up his persecutors, nor of
fighting or even simply killing them, but rather of *exterminating* them. By
the time of Ghez's writing, the connotations of "exterminate" were widely
understood. Here, the highly charged word produces a double effect. The
mere use of the expression might be read as a tacit admission that Ghez
knows about and can adequately describe the nature of the atrocities.[19]
At the same time, by attributing its use to a child and imagining it, in a
vengeful twist, applied to the persecutors rather than the victims, Ghez
decontextualizes "exterminate" and avoids associating it with the plight of
the Tunisian Jews.

Whereas *Six mois* deploys a variety of rhetorical strategies to avoid
explicitly naming the unnamable reality that hovered like a specter over
the Jewish community of Tunisia, *Étoile jaune et croix gammée* is both more
transparent about its knowledge of the Final Solution and the fate of European Jewry and more forthcoming in its narrative of suffering. Borgel
begins by historicizing the experience of Tunisian Jewry within a broader
context of anti-Semitism.

Quelles misères, quels procédés de terreur renouvelés d'un Moyen Âge d'Inquisition
allaient connaître nos Juifs, coupables du seul fait de leur naissance; quels moyens
d'y échapper, d'y soustraire femmes, enfants, vieillards, telle était l'angoissante question qui allait se poser à la Communauté israélite, privée de la protection d'un gouvernement qui n'était plus libre, et dont la compassion aurait pu difficilement se
manifester.[20]

What miseries, what methods of Inquisition-style medieval terror would become all
too familiar to our Jews, guilty simply because they were born Jewish? How to escape,
to save the women, children, and the elderly: this was the agonizing question the
Israelite community would have to ask itself, abandoned as it was by a government
that was no longer free, and whose compassion would have been difficult to express.

Compared to *Six mois*, Borgel's chronicle is more robustly historical, more
prone to luxuriate in pathos, and more apt to state its knowledge clearly.[21]
Beyond placing the community's situation on a historical continuum, Borgel reveals himself to be a self-conscious documentarian, a writer of history responsible for translating the experience for a broader audience.[22]
Although Ghez is the more sensitive and self-reflective writer, his *Six mois*
proffers no such authorial mission statement and refrains from commenting on the task of writing itself. Borgel, however, uses his introduction to

situate his intervention and his goals and to shore up his bona fides as an eyewitness and thus as an ostensibly reliable narrator.

Ma seule ambition est d'apporter ici un témoignage objectif sur ce passage difficile qui comptera dans la mémoire de nos juifs. . . . Ayant été amené, au secrétariat particulier de la présidence, à suivre et vivre, heure par heure, toutes les étapes de cette dangereuse aventure, j'ai l'unique dessein d'en retracer le récit dénué d'artifice.[23]

My only goal here is to provide an objective account of this difficult moment that will be important in our Jews' memory. . . . Having had the opportunity, as the personal secretary of the president of the Community, to participate hour by hour in all stages of this dangerous adventure, I have a single mission: to tell this story without embellishment.

Notwithstanding its claims to objectivity and authenticity, Borgel's text does produce moments of restraint, or *pudeur*, albeit in a fashion quite different from that observed in *Six mois*. In *Étoile jaune* Borgel tends to mix rhetorically elusive gestures with strong statements of fact. The first line of his introduction, for example, refers to Tunisia as suffering "les affres sombres de l'occupation allemande" ("the somber pangs of German occupation"),[24] thus allowing a polysemic noun to introduce a wrinkle of ambiguity: *les affres* could be translated as "agonies" or "horrors" but also more gently as "pangs." The vocabulary of the sentence that follows, however, is a trenchant litany of exactions endured by all Tunisians: "l'odieux déroulement de tyrannie policière, de travail forcé, de contraintes et d'impostures" ("the odious unfolding of police tyranny, forced labor, intimidation, duplicities").

The text briskly segues to the specificity of the Jews, who find themselves

aux prises avec le Nazi, l'ennemi cruel qui avait déjà inscrit dans les ghettos de Lodz et de Varsovie, dans les ruines fumantes des synagogues d'Allemagne et de Pologne, en Ukraine, à Kiev, à Krasnoe, à Chamovo, et jusqu'en France enfin, sa volonté hystérique d'extermination.[25]

grappling with the Nazis, those cruel enemies who had already stamped their hysterical will to exterminate on the Lodz and Warsaw ghettos; on the smoking ruins of the synagogues of Germany and Poland; on Ukraine, Kiev, Krasny, and Chamovo, and finally, on France.

Like Ghez, Borgel has recourse to evocative toponyms (Lodz, Warsaw) but refuses to take for granted their signification. Rather, he instructs readers in their individual specificity as sites of ghettos, ravaged synagogues, and massive deportations of Jews, as well as in their collective importance as sites where Hitler's "hysterical will to exterminate" is forever inscribed.

Whereas *Six mois* remains sufficiently ambiguous about the Holocaust as to hint that perhaps the Jews of Tunisia were unaware of the fate of European Jewry, *Étoile jaune* is abundantly detailed, with Borgel leaving no doubt that his coreligionists were amply informed of the Third Reich's activities. On occasion, however, Borgel's restraint manifests through rhetorical tactics that leave the reader to surmise his meaning. Narrating the anxiety of several members of the Jewish community as they are summoned before the German field officers, Borgel notes that the men are haunted by the memory of a cousin "arrêté par la Gestapo, alors qu'il cherchait à fuir la zone occupée, emmené jusqu'au camp de Drancy, puis de là en Pologne où, depuis . . . " ("arrested by the Gestapo as he attempted to flee the occupied zone, taken to Drancy, and from there to Poland, where, since then . . . ").[26] In a rare poetic flair, *Étoile jaune* uses an ellipsis, the rhetorical figure that signals aposiopesis, or "becoming silent," to stand in for the fate of the cousin deported to Poland.

Comparatively, *Étoile jaune* appears to be more transparent than *Six mois*. Its instances of restraint are fleeting, stylistic rather than substantive, and any potential extrapolation from form to meaning is arguably subverted by ample doses of historical detail. Yet the publishing history of *Étoile jaune* is important to the interpretation of Borgel's chronicle. Although *Six mois* was the first chronicle published, *Étoile jaune* was the first to be reprinted by the Fondation pour la Mémoire de la Shoah in its series Témoignages de la Shoah, directed by Serge Klarsfeld. Borgel's text, then, was the first Tunisian Holocaust narrative to be pulled from the proverbial footnotes of history and given full status as a text, complete with a developed critical apparatus in the form of multiple prefaces by historians Klarsfeld and Nataf, extensive footnotes, and more than fifty pages of primary historical documents, including photos and facsimiles of official correspondence. Before its 2007 reprint, *Étoile jaune* had been out of print for years, available only in a few university libraries; today it can be purchased directly on the Internet, in paperback and as an e-book.

If Borgel's restraint initially appears worth mentioning only insofar as it might provide a comparative foil to Ghez's text, the experience of reading *Étoile jaune* in tandem with its historical supplements suggests that any given text's *pudeur* may be as much a function of its reader as of its writer. Whereas I have underscored the relative paucity of aesthetic, or stylistic, restraint in Borgel's chronicle itself, Nataf's notes reveal instances of what one might call factual, or historical, restraint, all of which use similar wording to describe the author's strategy. Nataf qualifies his commentary with expressions such as "Borgel passe *pudiquement* sur la scène" ("Borgel describes the scene with great *discretion*"); "Borgel passe *pudiquement* sur les raisons" ("Borgel discretely *sidesteps* the reasons"); "Robert Borgel décrit ici avec *pudeur* la mise à sac par les soldats de la Hara . . . dépouillement accompagné de viols" ("Robert Borgel uses *discretion* in describing the soldiers' ransacking of the ghetto . . . robbery accompanied by rape"); and "Borgel abord ici avec beaucoup de *délicatesse* les différences d'attitude" ("Borgel *delicately* treats the differences in attitude") (my emphasis throughout).[27]

The restraint identified by Nataf in the four notes differs from the restraint in *Six mois*. In *Étolie jaune* Borgel seems determined to gloss over some of the internal rifts within the elite of the Jewish community or to protect the innocent. For example, in the short, ironically titled chapter "La soldatesque se distrait" ("The Troops Have Some Fun"), he reports for the record the German soldiers' propensity for ransacking the Jewish ghetto and raping Jewish women. Yet the tone of the section is clearly one of restraint; Borgel uses the word *violenté* (treated brutally) rather than *viol* (rape).[28] Without deep historical knowledge of the events in question and without reading comparatively across the chronicles, a reader might not notice that Borgel's restraint resides in his selection and presentation of details. Nataf's notes add missing historical context, but they have the effect of shedding light on the very details that Borgel has preferred to deal with euphemistically.

Despite its relatively unequivocal narrative, *Étoile jaune* concludes with a gesture that, perhaps surprisingly, diminishes its entire enterprise: After having spent its time narrativizing the suffering of the Tunisian Jews, the chronicle ends by underscoring the community's relative good fortune, having avoided

profondes douleurs, d'atroces épreuves . . . les wagons de l'asphyxie . . . et à nos femmes—qui sait—le transport aux maisons publiques et la souillure "FMM" (*Freies Militär-Mädchen*).[29]

deep wounds, horrible ordeals . . . the mobile gas vans . . . and seeing our women—who knows?—transported to "public houses" and stained with the shame of the "FMM."

Borgel then switches to an explicitly comparative mode.

Dans le moment même où la Tunisie vivait sous l'oppression, quelque part là-bas, en Pologne ukrainienne, les gardes noirs et les SS entassaient des Juifs, vieillards, femmes, enfants innocents dans des wagons où ils avaient jeté de la chaux vive. *Nach himmel,* répondaient par dérision les Nazis à qui on demandait la destination de ces convois d'épouvante. Plus près de nous, en France captive, a-t-on perdu le souvenir de cette nuit du 15 au 16 juillet 1942 où on arracha aux mères les enfants de 4 ans, où on parqua plus de 60,000 malheureux pour les faire mourir ensuite plus loin, vers l'est, dans un camp de misère?[30]

At the very same moment when Tunisia was living the oppression, somewhere else, in Ukrainian Poland, the black guards and the SS were piling the Jews—the elderly, women, and innocent children—into wagons with quicklime. *Nach himmel* [to heaven], responded the Nazis derisively when asked the destination of these convoys of terror. Still closer to us, in occupied France, has the memory of the night of July 15 been forgotten? The night when young children were torn from their mothers, when more than 60,000 miserable souls were arrested only to be murdered later, somewhere in the east, in a wretched camp?

By giving the proverbial and quite nearly the literal last word to the Jews of Europe, Borgel ensures that readers are not left with the impression that Tunisian Jewry—in its experiences or in the representation of those experiences—might seek to place itself in the same discursive space as European Jewry. In a few lines he relegates the story of his own people to the background of history.

Notwithstanding their respective differences in style, both *Six mois sous la botte* and *Étoile jaune et croix gammée* constitute textual testaments to an important moment in history, offering readers a glimpse of a particular Jewish community's response to Nazi persecution. Yet both chronicles confirm Nataf's suggestion that the Jews of Tunisia diminished the representation of their own suffering and tamped down painful memories, even as they sought to document their experiences at the hands of the Germans. The chronicles indeed produce an ambivalent subtext when it comes to assigning meaning and importance to the events they represent. At the same time, the texts' restraint—regardless of its origins and manifestations—does not, in and of itself, explain their "limited impact."

. . .

Like the chronicles, the historical scholarship on the period of Nazi occupation and its impact on the Tunisian Jews also produces an ambivalent discourse. Although the experiences of Maghrebi Jews during World War II have not been robustly incorporated Holocaust scholarship, a small handful of scholars have taken up the question within the specific framework of Sephardi or North African Jewry or in the narrower context of a particular Jewish community.[31] Their work evinces a canny awareness of their topic's liminal position with respect to larger conversations. M. Mitchell Serels, for example, openly deplores the Sephardi Jews' elision from Holocaust history, noting, "We have forgotten this sad chapter. It has been overshadowed by the tragedy in Europe. But the tragedy in Africa, particularly in Tunisia and Libya, is part of the history of the Jews and part of the history of the Holocaust."[32] Similarly, French historian André Kaspi openly laments, "This silence, so rarely broken, on the Jews of North Africa, as if they hadn't also suffered the effects of racial persecution, as if they had been preserved from the hardships of war, in a word, *as if they had been sheltered from the Shoah*" (my emphasis).[33]

Yet those same historians who tell the tale of the Tunisian Jews often remind readers that their fate paled in comparison to that of European Jewry.[34] Michel Abitbol, one of the first scholars to highlight the specific experiences of North African Jews during the war, is nevertheless cool in his assessment of their situation, effectively minimizing the Nazi's treatment of the Tunisian Jews, which bore "very little similarity to the deadly treatment that European Jews suffered at the time of the Final Solution."[35] Even Kaspi, whose quoted comment implies that the Jews of Tunisia did experience the Shoah, inexplicably reverses his position by the end of his analysis: "Let us not dramatize excessively. Nothing here compares to what happened in France. It was a period of just a few months."[36] This scholarly discourse on the occupation of Tunisia produces an ambivalent metanarrative in which an explicit desire to fill in gaps in knowledge and reveal a blind spot in the historical record competes with an implicit, ethical imperative to contextualize the story by acknowledging a hierarchy of suffering. Although such historiographers have done important work to excavate the story of the Tunisian Jews, they have also minimized the story's global importance, forestalling comparisons between the fate of European Jewry and what might be described as a minor episode of persecution.[37]

Although both the chronicles and the scholarship evince a similar ambivalence when it comes to assigning importance to the events they represent, it is not at all clear that the motivations and origins of the two forms of ambivalence are the same. Given Ghez and Borgel's positionality and proximity to both the events and the people in question and given the contemporaneous nature of their writings, the roots of their ambivalence can be located in an instinctive restraint. Born of empathy and identification with their European brethren, this same restraint is exemplified in Albert Memmi's novel *The Pillar of Salt*, in which the protagonist, a Tunisian Jew who survived the Nazi occupation and labor camps, laments:

Parce que je n'ai pas perdu un bras ou une jambe au camp de travail, parce que je n'ai pas été embarqué pour l'enfer, ou parce qu'on ne m'a pas arraché les ongles, je me sens débiteur envers mon siècle. Victime ou bourreau, l'époque l'exige. Je ne me sens pas assez victime, voilà pourquoi ma conscience reste torturée.[38]

Because I didn't lose an arm or a leg in the labor camp, because I wasn't carted off to hell, and because my fingernails weren't torn out, I feel a tremendous debt to history. You're either a victim or the hangman: these are times that force you to choose. I am not enough of a victim; that is why my conscience is tortured.[39]

Comparatively, however, the ambivalence of the historians appears at once more problematic and more politically charged. Of course, the tenor of the chronicles themselves may have informed the historians' works, but because scholars are in no way obligated to take up the ethical positions of their subjects, it seems worth considering their hesitation as, at least in part, a by-product of the cultural-political context in which it was conceived. From the works cited here, we might extrapolate a certain anxiety about placing the suffering of the Tunisian and European Jews in the same discursive space: Tunisian Jews, after all, were not deported and exterminated en masse. Historians who have written about the Jews of Tunisia have shied away from the vocabulary of catastrophe, as though calling these faraway victims "survivors" of the Holocaust or the Shoah would somehow mitigate the tragedy in Europe.

A literal construal of terms and events may be at stake here. How closely one hews to the original meanings of "Shoah" ("annihilation," in Hebrew) and "Holocaust" ("a sacrifice entirely consumed by fire," from the Greek) and to the various geographic limits or categories of the victims they have historically implied is an issue laden with both pathos and politics.[40] Moreover, in the context of the "politicization of the Holocaust," comparative acts are particularly fraught;[41] for some, the mere gesture of comparison risks diluting the potency of the narrative of the Shoah or allowing it to function as a metaphor for catastrophe rather than as catastrophe itself, hence, perhaps, the need to define the Tunisian experience as "not at all comparable" (Laski) or dissimilar (Abitbol) to what happened in Europe. After all, decentering the Holocaust from its geographic and epistemological moorings in a climate when negationism or even attacks on the "uniqueness" of the Holocaust appear to threaten its factual and discursive status might allow cracks to appear in the bedrock of "never forget."[42]

To complicate matters further, the difficulty in placing North African Jewish suffering in the same discursive field as European Jewish suffering may be more than a side effect of the politicization of the Holocaust or the result of literal interpretation; it may be related to historically encoded attitudes toward Jewish memory. For David Roskies, the concepts of Jewish history and memory are relatively new, born out of the nineteenth-century culture wars between the traditional Hasidim and the Enlightenment-minded *maskilim*.[43] Before their "hearts and minds" battle for Jews' imagination, " 'memory' per se was not even an operative category in Judaism. Rather, Jews in each period had their master metaphors. . . . In times of crisis, the function of Jewish memory was to transcend the ruptures of history."[44] Before the schism between tradition and modernity created the possibility for what Roskies calls "a free market of pasthoods"[45]—thus fostering an environment where rabbis and scholars competed for Jewish history and memory—the sacred texts had served, and sufficed, to offer Jews a set of narratives and archetypes that could be pressed into service to explain anything.[46]

To extend Roskies' capitalist metaphor, opening the field to competition meant offering "consumers" more memory options but not necessarily the opportunity to acquire multiple options at once. In other words, the new availability of multiple "usable pasts" created the need for a choice where one had not existed before, and "choosing one set of memories entailed actively opposing another set."[47] If Roskies' explanation of the change over time in the concept of Jewish memory articulates a shift from a unique "usable past" to the existence of multiple narrative possibilities for memory and history, it nonetheless underscores a need to select a single grand narrative. This would point, then, to a historically encoded resistance to allowing for multiple, competing, and contradictory narratives.

As scholars continue to look for new vocabularies that invert the traditional relationship between the putative center and its periphery, new frameworks for the representation of memory and history may offer ways to think through the Tunisian chronicles as participating in the literature of the Holocaust without setting off a contest for victimhood. Models such as Michael Rothberg's "multidirectional memory" or Max Silverman's "palimpsestic memory" argue for the fruitful coexistence of multiple and even contradictory acts of remembrance.[48] *Six mois sous la botte* and *Étoile jaune et croix gammée* exemplify, *avant la lettre*, such a praxis. Ghez and Borgel faced an irresolvable dilemma: Write a history that competes with a more catastrophic one, or be written out of history. Rather than resolve this paradox, they turned it into a project at once ethical and aesthetic.

9

Fissures and Fusions
Moroccan Jewish Communists and World War II

Alma Rachel Heckman

Devoured by his own words, he couldn't know what fate was ripening
in the enclosed space of his imagination. "I will be a professional
revolutionary," he wrote in his journal.[1]

THE WORLD WAR II YEARS were pivotal for Moroccan Jews and for
global communism. The war years were a watershed moment in several
preexisting political trends for Moroccan Jews: communism, Zionism, and
Gallicism.[2] Even though these political ideologies were fluid during the
interwar period, the fissures between these predominant three trajectories
hardened during the Vichy period (1940–1942 in Morocco). Moroccan
Jewish communists ultimately became marginalized in narratives of World
War II, Morocco's national liberation movement, and global communism.

Through the life and works of Moroccan Jewish novelist and former
Moroccan Communist Party (PCM) leader Edmond Amran El Maleh
(1917–2010), in this chapter I address Jewish engagement in the PCM
through the crucible of the Vichy years. North Africa and the Middle East
have long been treated as peripheral to the main stage of World War II,
the Holocaust, and global communist politics, but El Maleh's work, con-
textualized within the broader political landscape of Jewish and Moroccan politics, contributes to a richer regional understanding of the period,
rehabilitating the margins of the margins into a new "standard" narrative.

It is impossible to generalize the experiences of Moroccan Jews during
the war years—whether urban or rural, in the Spanish or French protectorates, wealthy or poor. The diversity of Moroccan Jews was compounded
by an influx of European Jewish refugees, themselves experiencing widely
varied fates as political prisoners in labor camps, or even living in relative
comfort. These diverse Jewish populations lived and worked in a divided
Morocco that was under colonial occupation by France and Spain (as of

1912), with European workers arriving from Italy, France, and Spain. This European population increased with the arrival of refugees from the Spanish Civil War and Europe's fascist regimes in the 1930s. Nascent Zionist politics in the region added to the alphabet soup of political discourses available to Jews, intersecting with communism and the Gallicism espoused by educational and philanthropic institutions such as the Alliance Israélite Universelle.[3]

Communism arrived in Morocco during the interwar period as a branch of the French Communist Party (PCF), with a vexed relationship to its twin metropoles of Moscow and Paris. After the rupture of the infamous 1939 Hitler-Stalin Pact, the USSR became the self-appointed vanguard of the global struggle against fascism, combined with a preexisting overt opposition to imperialism. This had deep ramifications for the immediate postwar period and pressed the issue of global communist support for national liberation movements from imperialist powers such as France. It also led to a complicated dance of support and denial of independence on the part of the PCF relative to its sibling parties in North Africa.[4] This dance coincided with an accelerating struggle for national liberation across the region, the establishment of the State of Israel in 1948, the ascendance of the United States in the region, and France's postwar imperial weakness. El Maleh's own biography, refracted through the alienated personae of his semi-autobiographical fiction (particularly *Parcours immobile* [1980] and *Mille ans, un jour* ([1986]), provides a compelling narrative thread to traverse these upheavals at the intersection of many margins on the periphery of a global war.

Edmond Amran El Maleh was of the first generation of children born under the French and Spanish protectorates over Morocco (established in 1912). He died in 2010 after a long career in political activism, journalism, education, and, finally, novel writing. Born in the Moroccan Atlantic coastal city of Safi in 1917, El Maleh came of age during the 1920s, a period of intellectual and political ferment compounded by immigration from France, Spain, and Italy and large-scale rural migration to Moroccan cities. El Maleh's family historically hailed from the coastal city of Essaouira (formerly known as Mogador), south of Safi and the traditional entrepôt of the *tujjar al-sultan* (the Jewish merchant-diplomats of the sultan in the early modern era).[5] El Maleh received a typical French-language education and a Jewish education. He was active in the communist party in 1930s Casablanca as a member of the Jeunesses Communistes (Youth

Communists) and was crucial to the party's agitation during the war years and the movement for national independence, achieved in 1956. After King Hassan II's bloody crushing of the Casablancan student protests in 1965, El Maleh left Morocco to live in self-imposed exile in France. He had left the PCM a few years before this exile under somewhat mysterious circumstances, possibly because, rumor has it, he was passed up for leadership based on his Jewish background.[6] In addition, El Maleh came to oppose what he saw as the party's strict Stalinist orthodoxy.

El Maleh published his first novel in 1980 at the age of 63 while living in Paris. This novel, *Parcours immobile*, is part fiction, part autobiography, and part pastiche of Jewish Moroccan character "types." It follows the political trajectory of a triptych of type personalities rolled into one protagonist, Josua/Edgar/Aïssa, as he navigates his interwar colonial surroundings, the war years, and recruitment into the PCM, which focused on national liberation. The abiding, repeating motif of this novel is the phrase "It's understood that Moroccan Jews don't do politics,"[7] highlighting the transgressive nature of both El Maleh's and his protagonist's political engagement and marginality, both of which are crucial to a more complete understanding of Moroccan Jewish deracination and political engagement.

El Maleh pursues these themes in his second published novel, *Mille ans, un jour* (1986), which follows a similarly isolated, pastiche-type characterization of Moroccan Jewish identities and affiliations. The novel begins with the protagonist, a Moroccan Jew named Nessim, reading a newspaper article depicting the death of a Palestinian child during the Sabra and Shatila massacre of 1982. The image of the Palestinian boy launches Nessim into a narrative historical time warp, wending the reader through centuries of Maghrebi Jewish history, starting with Nessim's *tujjar al-sultan* progenitors.

Whereas *Parcours immobile* focuses particularly on the protagonist's engagement in the PCM and disillusion, the primary concern of *Mille ans, un jour* is the uprooting of a deep Moroccan Jewish past. Each book situates its narrative in the interwar period, the war years, and the immediate postwar independence struggle and documents the crushing oppression meted out on the PCM (and other opposition groups) during the 1960s and 1970s. This semi-autobiographical work mirrors events in El Maleh's own life during this crucial period of midcentury Jewish political activism.

How was the PCM first established? Why were Jews attracted to it? What did the larger Jewish political universe of Jews look like on the eve of World War II? How did the varied experiences of Jews during the Vichy period change such affiliations? First, the interwar period included an array of Jewish political options. In this era, French cultural affinity, communist politics, and Zionist activism were fluid and not at all mutually exclusive, as they would become in the postwar period. Second, in the crucible of the Vichy years the borders between such ideologies would harden, a trajectory that ultimately would render Moroccan Jews engaged in the PCM marginal even to the margins. The shape of postwar Moroccan politics, including Jewish politics, was largely defined by the Vichy years, the de facto American administration of Morocco after the success of Operation Torch (1942), and the demonstrable weakness of France compared with the USSR, the United States, and the United Kingdom. For those Jews committed to the national liberation project (however few in number), the PCM often proved the most viable political option. Ultimately, however, Jewish communists would be marginalized from the predominant Moroccan Jewish community and communists would be marginalized from mainstream national liberation politics. From each marginal story a clearer picture of the whole emerges, whether of the diversity of Jewish experiences during World War II, global communism, or the accelerating demands for national liberation across the colonized world following the conclusion of war.

Interwar Fusions: The Beginning of Leftist Radical Politics in Morocco

As the epigraph to this chapter indicates, the young adult Josua/Edgar/Aïssa in El Maleh's *Parcours immobile* dreams of becoming a "professional revolutionary" in the midst of the ideological fervor of the 1930s.[8] Josua/Edgar/Aïssa is born to an old Essaouira family on the eve of Passover, either in 1912 or 1915,[9] a time replete with significance for the story of Exodus, perhaps foreshadowing the Moroccan Jewish exodus of the 1950s–1970s. El Maleh describes a calm childhood home in which the Jewish men and women of the family split generationally as to dressing in the "European" style or the more "traditional" style, speaking French, Arabic, or Berber. El Maleh hints at "silent" forces creeping into the "the happy, luminous, preserved kingdom of this well-to-do Jewish family, with a respected lineage of great merchants and rabbis. New things were silently creeping in on tiptoe like silent messengers."[10] The ominous "new things" are none other than the seeds of political and social trajectories for Moroccan Jews in the interwar period, growing and splitting off after World War II.

The three primary political trajectories available to Moroccan Jews on the eve of World War II were Republicanism through Gallic cultural identity informed by the Alliance Israélite Universelle, communism, and Zionism. Each of these ideologies was predicated on a *mission civilisatrice* in its own right. The Alliance Israélite Universelle was founded in 1860 by a group of first- and second-generation emancipated French Jews led by Adolphe Crémieux (French Jewish emancipation occurred in two waves, 1790 and 1791). This philanthropic and educational organization had as its founding motto *kol yisrael arevim ze lazeh*—"all Jews are responsible for one another."

As a former student of the Alliance Israélite Universelle, Josua had been taught to identify with France. In the process he became divorced from his surrounding Moroccan Arabo- and Berberophone context, as with so many Moroccan Jews, in the name of "donning the bright uniform of progress and hygiene."[11] It is in this context that Josua and so many other Moroccan Jews gained political consciousness, triangulated between aspirations for Moroccan independence, French citizenship aspirations, and Zionism. Josua chooses communism, because he is personally galvanized by exposure to refugees of the Spanish Civil War fleeing to Morocco and the infusion of radicalism they brought to the preexisting Moroccan branch of the PCF. Josua reflects, "It was the period when his sympathies, his friends were Spanish, he discovered Spain, the first militants he knew were Spanish militants."[12]

The Spanish Civil War and indeed the roots of the PCF's engagement in Morocco lie in the Rif war of 1921–1926 (explored at greater length later in this chapter). It is impossible to understand Jewish engagement in leftist politics in Morocco, and hence national liberation politics, without such background. Further still, the communist party and affiliated leftist networks in the 1920s and 1930s owed their appeal in large part to the arrival of refugee and working populations mixing with indigenous Jews and Muslims on the docks, ports, and railroads.

The conclusion of World War I brought a significant number of European settlers to Morocco. The European workers who arrived in Morocco following World War I brought their ideological affinities with them. Moroccan branches of the French General Labor Confederation were established, and Moroccan workers were increasingly drawn to them. Morocco's first labor union, the Association Générale, was founded in

1919, just two years after the Russian Revolution in 1917. Protectorate officials legally barred Moroccan workers from joining, but it would only be a matter of time before Moroccans, working alongside Europeans, became inspired and even radicalized, a profound fear of protectorate authorities.[13]

At the same time, far away from Casablanca in the Rif mountains under the Spanish protectorate, a new war broke out. Muhammed ibn Abd el-Krim al-Khattabi (often just referred to as Abd el-Krim), a Berber *qadi* (Muslim judge) and journalist, inflicted damage to Spain's protectorate authority when he and his Riffian Berber troops crushed Spanish forces on July 20, 1921, in the northeastern Moroccan town of Annual.[14] Abd el-Krim's forces were so successful against the Spanish that they were able to declare an independent Rif Republic (independent from both Spain and the sultan in French Morocco) by September 1921. As Spanish-controlled towns fell to the Riffian fighters, French Morocco and the sultan looked with alarm at the northern upstart. In April 1925 Abd el-Krim and his troops struck within the French zone, provoking France and Spain to form a military alliance.[15] By September 8, 1925, this alliance dealt a crushing blow to Abd el-Krim's forces. The war was brutal; chemical weapons, beheadings, and grotesque violence were commonplace.

The brutality of the war coincided with ongoing events in France and Syria. These events ultimately enabled the establishment of a branch of the PCF. The eighteenth national congress of the French Section of the Workers' International in 1920 resolved a long-running debate within the French left, namely, between the communists and the socialists, and formally established the PCF as a member of the Third International. To join the Third International, the PCF had to adopt twenty-one conditions furnished by Moscow, two of which directly addressed colonialism.[16] One condition required the dissemination of propaganda within the military, including among indigenous soldiers in the French army as well as among French soldiers wherever they may be posted. Another condition mandated clear and unwavering militant support for national liberation in colonized lands. The first resident-general of the Moroccan protectorate, General Hubert Lyautey (term in Morocco, 1912–1925), who had cut his administrative teeth in Indochina, Madagascar, and Algeria, was adamantly opposed to any leftist activity in Morocco. His successor, Théodore Steeg (who governed from 1925 to 1929), proved more amenable.[17] The PCF was not legally able to establish a Moroccan branch until Théodore Steeg became resident-general. However, pursuant to the demands of Moscow and feeling the pressure to prove itself on the international stage, the PCF began acting on the twenty-one conditions almost immediately.[18]

News of the intense violence in the Moroccan Rif outraged French leftists, provoking large demonstrations in Paris (thousands protested) and political action.[19] The PCF's main newspaper, *l'Humanité*, was available in North Africa during the interwar years. It was banned in May 1925, because it called for fraternization between French and Riffian fighters and the spread of communist propaganda, but it remained illegally obtainable.[20] Moscow excoriated PCF members Jacques Doriot and André Chasseigne at the Fifth Congress of the Communist International (June–July 1924) for not doing enough regarding France's colonies. Chasseigne returned to France and reported that "the most immediate task of the PCF is work in Morocco."[21] In the summer of 1925, the Jeunesses Communistes of the PCF visited Morocco in the hopes of establishing contact with local nationalist activists and Abd el-Krim himself.[22]

PCF leaders aimed to increase indigenous exposure to labor unions, communist propaganda, and leftist political groups. These efforts were directed from the metropole but rested firmly in the hands of local communist representatives. The representatives were largely French, but with the Spanish Civil War these numbers were augmented, as new ideological elements poured in from across the Strait of Gibraltar. Once the Republican forces at last gave way to Franco, political refugees streamed across the Pyrenees into France and across the Strait of Gibraltar into French Morocco.

In Morocco the Spanish refugees flocked to large urban centers such as Casablanca, Rabat, Meknes, Fez, and Marrakesh. Spanish and European Jewish leftists in cities such as Meknes and Casablanca sparked the invigoration of leftist organizations in those locales as well as in others. Meknes in the 1930s hosted numerous Spanish communist fundraisers, dances, film projections, and more. Police surveillance indicates that Jews attended these events in high numbers. Even those Jews who opposed this political trend could not help but be influenced by the many posters pasted on the walls of the *mellah* (the Jewish quarter) and medina (the "old city," or Muslim quarter) and in the predominant political cafés that abounded in the city.[23]

This leftist culture was bolstered by other universalist, antifascist and human-rights-based organizations that Jews often led or joined, prominently the International League Against Anti-Semitism (Ligue internationale contre l'antisémitisme), the League for Human Rights, and the Young Autonomous Socialists, which was an entirely local and nearly entirely Jewish leftist organization. Each of these groups hosted events to benefit the Spanish Civil War refugees, combat anti-Semitism, and agitate for human rights and national liberation pursuant to the promises of Moscow. Jews, both indigenous and European, joined by Muslims and European leftists hailing primarily from France and Spain, mixed in cafés and at formal meetings and overlapped in a heady atmosphere of possibility increasingly channeled toward a common goal of opposition to fascism.

Fissures: The War Against Fascism and the Vichy Years

The Vichy period was crucial for the political galvanization of Moroccan Jewry and, in the long term, for its marginalization. This galvanization manifested in many different directions, most notably Zionism and communism. Some Moroccan Jews joined the prevailing mainstream Istiqlal ("independence," in Arabic) party. There were many more Jews (likely a majority) who could claim no hard and fast political ideology but who observed alternately alarming and promising events leading to their political and geographic choices. The porous nature of Jewish political possibilities in the interwar period eventually narrowed into distinct political organizations and a choice following World War II: to remain in Morocco or to leave, either for France or, more commonly, for Israel following the state's establishment in 1948. During the Vichy period, preexisting fissures and fusions among Moroccan Jews regarding their place in their homeland intensified, as did their fears and hopes.

France fell to Germany after a brief campaign in the spring of 1940 that included many soldiers from North Africa, Jews as well as Muslims. Marshal Henri Phillipe Pétain, a World War I hero, came to head the Vichy government, so named for the new capital of southern unoccupied France, whereas northern France and Paris came under direct Nazi authority. Until recently, the extent of Vichy policy in France's colonial holdings had been a neglected field, marginal to the European main stage.[24] Currently, an efflorescence of critical scholarship is filling in these lacunae and redefining scholarly and popular understandings of World War II, Jewish studies, and Middle Eastern and North African studies at the critical mid-twentieth-century juncture.[25] This new scholarship demonstrates the extent of Vichy policy, including anti-Semitic policy, in the part of the French empire with the largest Jewish concentration: North Africa.

Before the installation of the Vichy regime, a wave of European Jewish refugees arrived in Morocco and were deposited in refugee camps and homes directed by the Joint Distribution Committee (JDC), with the indefatigable Hélène Cazès Benatar at the helm.[26] Those refugees deemed politically dangerous (Jews and non-Jews), largely those suspected of communist sympathies, were pushed into forced labor camps to work on the illusory trans-Saharan railroad (an old French imperial dream to connect by rail the northern Mediterranean port of Oran to Timbuktu). Most of the residents of these camps were Spanish radicals who informed many political trajectories of the interwar period.

Moroccan Jews became intensely politically active upon Hitler's ascent to power in 1933, organizing meetings and boycotts. In March 1933 alone, 5,000 people attended a rally held at the Regent cinema in Casablanca, including organizers from local human rights organizations, members of the International League Against Anti-Semitism, and communists. Leaflets encouraging boycotts were distributed in synagogues and were written in both French and Judeo-Arabic. On the eve of World War II many Moroccan Jews wanted to enlist and fight for France; they were largely denied out of a concern for "French prestige."[27] Thousands of Jews fled Central Europe between 1933 and 1940. Many ended up in Morocco and informed a mounting climate of anxiety.[28]

When the Vichy laws were applied, it was not without care for the precarious political stability of the 1930s. Resident-General Noguès enforced Vichy legislation stamped with the sultan's seal but also sought to prevent Jewish "subversion" in opposition to France.[29] The laws published in the *Journal Officiel* in November 1940 and August 1941

limited to only 2% the number of Jews who could serve as medical doctors and lawyers and to 10% the number of Jews allowed to teach in the secondary schools. Similar restrictions were imposed on other professions such as cinema operators, real estate agents, pharmacists, and lawyers. Discriminatory laws required Jews who had recently bought or rented houses or flats in modern European neighborhoods to return to the old Jewish quarters.[30]

In addition to such legal restrictions, pro-Vichy Europeans spread graffiti and pamphlets and fliers replete with anti-Semitic slogans, such as "This is a Jewish business, a business of profiteers"; "Buying from Jews

FIGURE 9: Sause (Sami) Dorra (left) and Dunn (right), prisoners in the Im Fout Labor Camp in Morocco, 1941–1942. Born in Beirut, Dorra lived in Vienna, Paris, and Algiers before the war. During the conflict, Dorra, an Iranian national, was arrested for lacking proper legal paperwork. Dunn, an Irishman, was in North Africa studying with the White Fathers before his arrest. Source: United States Holocaust Memorial Museum Archives, Washington, D.C., Photograph 50722, courtesy of Sami Dorra. Reprinted with permission.

destroys French commerce"; "Worker, your enemy is the Jew; he exploits you and derives his ill-gotten gains from your misery."[31] In addition to such fliers, pro-Vichy Europeans, most notably those in the Moroccan branches of the Croix de Feu encouraged Moroccan Muslims to identify Jews as a common, exploitive enemy.[32]

Nazi representatives in northern Morocco blamed the Spanish Civil War and the current economic suffering on Jews. Nazi Germany maintained an office at the Hotel National in Melilla, founded the International Anti-Jewish League in Tangier, made appeals to Moroccan nationalists, and enabled broadcasts from Radio Berlin.[33] Propaganda in Arabic claimed that "Jews would enslave Muslims if the Communists should win the war."[34] Faced with the legal restrictions, many Moroccan Jews sought foreign intervention from American Jewish organizations.[35] Barring that, they sought exemptions, which were possible, although difficult, to procure.

Meanwhile, pro-Vichy European settlers in Morocco placed increasing pressure on Resident-General Noguès. Historian Mohammed Kenbib argues that, in response:

Some of the 7,700, mostly Jewish, refugees documented by the residency between June 1940 and February 1941 awaiting departure for America or Palestine were moved to detention centers located far from the cities. Jewish refugees denounced by Vichy activists as "dangerous" and others who did not hold transit visas or held visas that were no longer valid, were sent to forced labor camps such as Agdz and Bou Denib located in remote and desolate parts of the country.[36]

For Moroccan Jews, the period wrought grave legal, economic, and political instability, in addition to raising the increasingly urgent question of belonging and the naked truth of a fickle French Republicanism.[37]

El Maleh's 1986 novel *Mille ans, un jour* begins with a Jewish man—the protagonist, Nessim—looking at a photograph of a dead child in Lebanon. This photograph serves as a Proustian madeleine—and the reader is jolted into several different intervals of the Moroccan Jewish past. One of these moments is 1933, when Hitler rose to power and the news media shockwaves spread to North Africa. One day in 1933 Nessim goes to a local restaurant where he regularly meets his friends, a group almost entirely composed of Europeans.[38] Nessim does not keep kosher and looks with disdain on the "pious and traditional Jewish community," a community in which his family has a long history of producing notable rabbis. Nessim is an *évolué*, a Moroccan Jew thoroughly educated and acculturated to France.[39] The table conversation turns to Hitler, "something that hap-pened over there, in another universe."[40] El Maleh paints a vignette that encapsulates much of the *évolué* identity.

"Hitler! How funny," said De Bergerac with a humor that this time irritated his companions.

"Don't believe it old boy," said Mr. Angrand with all seriousness. . . .

Nessim listened without saying anything. It all struck him as being very far away. At the Alliance Israélite [Universelle] school, the only education had been that of French history. . . .

"Don't you see," Mr. Angrand said to Nessim—to whom he continued to speak in the formal *vous* form despite a long, old friendship—"Don't you see that what's happen-ing in Germany is very bad for you Jews!"

"Drink, drink," shouted Morgane and Petitburon, who were not inclined to cast a pall over this merry meal, among friends, a concentrated form of this small colonial soci-ety into which Nessim had been admitted, but without fully participating. He had been well assimilated, but he held onto a deep difference that he himself still didn't fully grasp.[41]

Nessim, a product of the Alliance who surrounded himself with European, distinctly non-Jewish friends, cannot escape an abiding sense of alienation. The obvious understatement—"What's happening in Germany is very bad for you Jews!"—highlights Nessim's alterity: "you Jews." El Maleh writes Nessim to be dimly but perhaps increasingly conscious of the fact that his Gallicizing Alliance education, his perfect French, and his disdain for and even abandonment of his "traditional" Jewish background have left him somewhat stranded. "Jewishness" comes to the fore and challenges Nes-sim's French identity further with the arrival of European, Yiddish-speaking Jewish refugees in Morocco and the increase of anti-Semitic propaganda distributed by European settlers in Morocco well before the installation of the Vichy government.[42] El Maleh's depiction of anti-Semitic propa-ganda clashes tragically with images of French assimilated Jewish women, "corseted, their hair in *chignons*, the mirror image of French women," forced, by an abrupt shift in the politically acceptable air, to "change partners!"[43]

Nessim is not politicized by these experiences; rather, he is confused, unsure of his place in society. He describes one friend, another Moroccan Jew, Messaoud, as being remarkably politically active.

No Jew ventured into politics, no one joined an activity about which we knew noth-ing and which could bring trouble; better to remain Jewish without history, separated from everything, like the authorities, the friendly paternalism of the French entourage pushing you imperatively to do so. A blue shirt and red tie, a certain Messaoud, a petty worker from a poor family, regarded with a certain distance by the [Jewish] community aristocracy, Messaoud thus dressed went to Casablanca one day. They say he went to attend a meeting, that he sold a newspaper in the city streets, even that he got in a fight with some Frenchmen, something extraordinary! . . . Nessim didn't wear any particular color or any external sign, he disliked any ostentation, but he harbored many ardent [political] beliefs, which were not settled on any one program and didn't amount to any particular activity.[44]

Nessim's confusion is met with decisiveness in the broader Jewish communal setting. Although Jews "don't do politics" in this world, El Maleh depicts cracks in the perceived apolitical Jewish atmosphere, first through characters like Messaoud, who embrace leftist political activism, and then through the synagogues: "Hitler was there in that faraway geographic space, the first German Jews fleeing their country were arriving, the announcement had been made in the synagogue one Saturday to urge the community's solidarity."[45] El Maleh depicts the Jews of Safi as perplexed on how to channel their feelings of Jewish solidarity with the European refugees: "No one knew a single word of Yiddish in the Safi community and it wasn't even certain that our two extra-terrestrials knew how to speak it, but they could more or less speak German-sounding words. Only Ruben knew a little bit."[46] The only reason that Ruben knows any Yiddish is because he reads an imported Zionist magazine and has come to identify Yiddish with Zionism rather than Hebrew.

The enigmatic character of the Ashkenazi writer for the Zionist paper remains a vaguely threatening outside force, "about whom we knew nothing,"[47] figuring perhaps as a stand-in for Moroccan Jews' lack of understanding of Yishuv Palestine itself. Nessim likes to tease Ruben about the Zionist paper and relates that he "didn't understand why Ruben devoted himself to that paper," for he had read about Herzl, the miracles performed by the settlers in Palestine, and all about kibbutzim and was still not persuaded.[48] Yet many were persuaded by their experiences under Vichy to embrace Zionism, even as many others preferred to view the Vichy regime as a blip in the trajectory of humanist French Republicanism. Ultimately, the Vichy years encouraged Moroccan Jews to identify more firmly with global Jewish national identity or to entrench themselves further in Moroccan national identity.

The second alter-ago of *Mille ans, un jour* is a Berber Jew in the Atlas mountains by the name of Yeshuaa (a nod to Josua of *Parcours immobile*).

Unlike Josua/Edgar/Aïssa or Nessim, Yeshuaa's news of the war filters in from Casablanca and is marinated in the anxiety of distant rumor. Yeshuaa reflects:

Hitler, Haman, the bloody shadow or evil bubbled up from the night. . . . The black days of Hitler, cruel days of Haman, even worse because no one could have stopped the massacres. The news was bad, the threat so close by. The news arrived from Casablanca. They were kicking Jews out of their schools, their jobs, their businesses; the houses where they lived were marked with a cross, indicating them for massacre; at the entrance to the old medina French people had beaten some Jews to death for wearing a beret instead of a skullcap. Yeshuaa himself had seen in Gueliz, in Marrakesh, French people like this marching in a blue shirt and a beret, "Shab ["youth" in Arabic] Pétain," someone told him. . . . There was typhus and people were dying like flies. Jews from the community were asking what sin they could have committed to unleash such wrath from God.[49]

Documents across archives corroborate the narration of El Maleh's Yeshuaa. Rumors raced across the country that Hitler had expressed support for Moroccan nationalists and would soon free those who had been imprisoned or exiled in 1937 and that Germany would establish an airbase in Port-Lyautey. German radio, broadcast in Arabic, repeated its propaganda "endlessly"; swastikas appeared on the medina walls "in several cities."[50] An Italian commission arrived in Rabat in July 1940. Their arrival, alongside the landing of a Lufthansa flight in Casablanca en route between Seville and Dakar, caused heightened tension.[51] Casablanca witnessed stones thrown through the windows of Jewish-owned stores, alongside fliers bearing anti-Semitic slogans.[52]

In general, Moroccan Jews continued to publicly affirm loyalty to France, hoping it would grant them some leeway, and "bowed their heads before the storm," circulating less in public and expressing utmost deference.[53] Jews were prohibited from any political organizing or meeting, except for strictly religious purposes, to take place in synagogues. Under no circumstances were Jews to take advantage of the space of the synagogues to make political statements. A protectorate report says, "These indications were received graciously [by the Jews] who took advantage of the occasion to affirm their sentiments of perfect loyalty [to France]. They demonstrated, in fact, that current events have left the Jews profoundly demoralized. They feel threatened from all sides and seek, above all, to go unnoticed."[54] With the Anglo-American Allied landings in Morocco in November 1942, some

Jewish hopes were increasingly pinned on political avenues other than the French emancipatory dream, whereas others awaited the return of what they saw as the true, enlightened Republican France.

Fused Fissures: Immediate Postwar Conditions and Ramifications

The Allied victory in World War II proved a boon for the spread and popularity of communism. The PCM rode this tide of antifascist, pro-Soviet, and even pro-American victory. In this period, the PCM began to shift from a largely European-dominated organization to one involving more Moroccans. Despite the PCF's outspoken resistance to the immediate colonial liberation of North Africa during the war years (out of a purported fear of fascist inroads), certain members of the PCM had their own ideas.[55] At first, the PCM leadership embraced the PCF line that the goal for communist parties in North Africa was to "convince the vast majority of autochthonous [inhabitants] that their best interests lie with the people of France, which is different from the official France that they have known thus far."[56] However, as with interwar-era labor unions, increased indigenous membership and intervention challenged the PCF's colonial policy.

Building on a prewar legacy of universalist activism against racism and anti-Semitism through the International League Against Anti-Semitism and many other groups, the PCM appealed to a wide swath of the Moroccan Jewish political landscape. The PCM welcomed "the entire Moroccan population regardless of race, language or religion."[57] This held great appeal for many Moroccan Jews, particularly the urban, educated elite, who were often educated at Alliance schools by left-leaning teachers. Zionism also grew in appeal following the Vichy betrayal. Even though some Moroccan Jews embraced Moroccan nationalism through the lens of communist universalism, many more embraced Zionism.[58]

For those Jews who would become engaged in Morocco's national liberation movement (who were, it is important to emphasize, in the distinct minority), the PCM was the inclusive avenue of participation. In addition to the PCM's less than entirely effective literacy programs, participating in the PCM's activities was itself a kind of school, according to Simon Lévy, another prominent Jewish PCM leader.[59] This school was largely taught by the Spanish workers and political refugees, solidarity with whom sparked so many Moroccan Jewish communist trajectories before and after World War II, particularly because so many had populated the forced labor camps.

The PCM worked in a clandestine manner during the Vichy years through dedicated resistance groups that included indigenous and European Jews, European non-Jews, and indigenous Muslims. This activity focused on gaining new adherents, distributing propaganda around cities (primarily Casablanca), and posting fliers.[60] The PCM's first secretary-general after post-Vichy reconstitution was Léon René Sultan.[61] Léon Sultan was an Algerian-born Jew and thus had French citizenship pursuant to the dictates of the Crémieux Decree of 1870. He was a lawyer in Casablanca and a staunch member of the Communist Party of Morocco (the prewar, intermittently legal predecessor of the Moroccan Communist Party). He was disbarred as a result of enforced Vichy legislation and subsequently petitioned the protectorate authorities for an exemption. Although he was unsuccessful in this endeavor, Sultan also petitioned on behalf of other Jews who had lost their jobs or placement in schools and on behalf of political prisoners in the Vichy labor camps. After the Allied liberation, Sultan worked with Hélène Cazès Benatar to help liberate the political prisoners and find them jobs and exit visas. After resurrecting the PCM in 1943, Sultan joined the Free French Forces after the success of Operation Torch and ultimately perished in 1945 from injuries sustained while fighting for France.

One year after Sultan's death, the PCM convened its first national congress in Casablanca (April 1946). Two years earlier, in January 1944, the mainstream Istiqlal party had made its stand for national liberation of Morocco from France and Spain. The primary purpose of the 1946 congress was to confirm the PCM's Moroccanization. With this Moroccanization a new Moroccan Muslim secretary-general (Ali Yata) was appointed and the PCM débuted as a national liberation party.

The published brochure commemorating this first congress featured a photograph of Léon Sultan on the cover and a dedication to him below the main title: "Léon-René Sultan (1905–1945), Secretary-General of the Moroccan Communist Party, died for France and Morocco."[62] Emerging out of the settling dust of war, the pamphlet lionized the USSR and the PCF and PCM's own antifascist activities. Characteristic of postwar communist parties in the Middle East and North Africa and Europe, the emphasis of the pamphlet was not on the particularities of compromised Republicanism in Morocco or even the anxieties of Vichy anti-Semitic legislation.[63] Rather, the emphasis was on the exploitation of the *fellahin* (peasants) for wartime grain stores to fuel the Vichy forces and "the Vichyists and Pétain- ists who took positions of authority in administration as well as the army, and the owners of land and mines that delivered all Moroccan production to their Nazi masters."[64]

Another focus of the pamphlet was the human cost of Moroccans serving in the French forces alongside others from the broader colonial world. All of this, insist the pamphlet's authors, was directly parallel to the "serfs of France before the great revolution of 1789."[65] Such language placed the party firmly in the camp of national revolution for the cause of independence from France and Spain.

The timeline the PCM draws for itself at this momentous first na- tional congress converges neatly with that of El Maleh's Josua/Edgar/Aïssa character. The party's retrospective pamphlet on the occasion of the first national congress cites the beginning of Arabic-language political tracts in 1935 and 1936, in which the party decried fascism and informed Moroccans that Hitler and the Nazi Party considered Arabs among the "degenerate" races.[66] It goes on to declare the PCM as one of the staunchest supporters of the Spanish Republicans, sending its own members to fight in Spain under party leaders André Marty and Henri Ramos, for "the communists of Franc knew that the Spanish Republicans were not only defending their own country, but also that of the world and the Moroccan people."[67]

The narrative continues to discuss the Vichy labor camps that in- terned "political undesirables," largely communists, in Morocco, survivors of which were hailed as heroes at the first national congress.[68] After situ- ating the destruction of Nazi Germany as critical for Morocco's political future, the congress notes a common call for unity: "We emphasize the im- portance of the unity of all populations in our country in order to secure the future Morocco and we denounce the division between Europeans, Jews and Muslims, which only benefits the very worst enemies of the Mo- roccan people."[69] Following a long discourse on access to reasonable em- ployment and health care for all, the speaker, as recorded by the pamphlet, again returns to the theme of unity: "The worst enemies of the Moroccan people have only one thing to do: pit Muslims against Jews, Moroccans against the French. They have always known how to use the nationalist inclinations of the Muslim and they have striven to maintain and even develop the colonial spirit of the European and the Zionist movement among Jews."[70] The pamphlet (and, one imagines, the congress) concludes with a call for more propaganda distribution in Arabic and the growth of educational programs; finally, they were "happy to announce today that the number of Moroccans is greater than that of the Europeans" in the party, marking a firm transition to the Moroccanization of the party under the leadership of Ali Yata.[71]

El Maleh's writing on the subject is somewhat more disenchanted. At the 1946 national congress, Josua, in his militant underground persona of Aïssa, is given more weighty responsibilities in the propagandizing for the party in the Jeunesses Communistes.[72] He describes the moment of declaring the party's direction in favor of independence as "a happy period! None had yet tasted the poisoned fruit of lucid critique."[73] Two years later, in the fateful year of 1948, El Maleh paints a picture of frivolous ignorance and self-righteous revolutionary spirit at the regular meeting spot of the PCM: "Against the backdrop of a dancehall, the Moulin de la Gaieté, in Casablanca, in that naïve year of '48, the frivolous, the serious, in staged performances, overlap. A party [parti, "political party"] is taking shape, a youth in the age of innocence, learning to venture out of his dreams to perhaps reach the shores of the Revolution."[74]

El Maleh's Josua/Aïssa is blended grammatically with the PCM itself, each imbued with naïveté as each launches into a revolutionary struggle for Moroccan independence. At that congress the internationalism of the Communist International is blended with the national liberation fervor of the era, as the crowd intones the International, in the midst of the merriment, willfully ignorant of the establishment of the State of Israel and all that would mean for the country's Jewish population. "That day!" writes a sardonic El Maleh, "Historians will reconstruct the momentous events of that congress, material to reconstruct the destroyed theater [the Moulin de la Gaieté]."[75] Astonished at his own tremendous political revolutionary trajectory, Josua/Aïssa reflects:

He, Josua, a Moroccan Jew, perfectly assimilated . . . he, Josua, me, Josua, it doesn't matter through which character but the story had already begun, undermined by suspicion, the invisible mechanism behind the *mise en scène*, simply he, Josua Aïssa, dull and without pomp, without the pressure of a bubble that bursts at the forefront, found himself every day with the dockers on the port of Casablanca.[76]

El Maleh positions both himself and Josua/Aïssa as representative and yet thoroughly marginal in that representation. It is important to point out that the vast majority of Moroccan Jews were not members of the PCM, or Zionist activists. Most, as El Maleh reminds the reader repeatedly through the text, "don't do politics."

In the immediate postwar years, however, the political trajectories of both Zionism and communism gained momentum. Josua/Aïssa plunges ever deeper into the PCM's politics of national liberation, and this tension comes to the fore when his family is investigated by a French police officer while the man himself is underground.

A brutal violation of a familial Jewish life, calm and dignified, enclosed in its traditional framework, dreaming neither of politics nor of revolution. "Your son, madame, is working against the French. This will cost him dearly." And the mother doesn't understand at all, except for the anguish that seizes her heart at "he does politics" and the distance, the gap that was growing between Josua Aïssa and his parents, his childhood friends.[77]

This was the common fate of Moroccan Jewish communists. Having become conscious pariahs in the Arendtian understanding and alienated in the Marxian vein, the historical personages of Edmond Amran El Maleh, Simon Lévy, and Abraham Serfaty, just to name the most prominent among them, each found themselves caught in the crosshairs of national liberation politics informed by the experience of the Vichy years, formed by a bourgeois French educational system that rendered them elites and at the margins of Morocco, Jewish life, and the mainstream Islam-informed national liberation movement.[78] The gap between generations, between political affiliations, would only continue to grow through the 1950s, 1960s, and 1970s (a period that extends far beyond the purview of this chapter). Josua/Aïssa ultimately abandons his family, his wife and child, for his role in the national movement; it all seems worthwhile "for a beautiful story to come."[79]

Conclusion: "A Game of Complex Margins"

The Vichy years in Morocco accelerated preexisting political and social fissures among Moroccan Jews. The ideological fluidity and fusions that were possible during the interwar period hardened into starkly differing trajectories, marginalizing Moroccan communist Jews from the broader Moroccan Jewish population as well as marginalizing the communists from mainstream national liberation politics. The Vichy period proved to be a period of betrayal of French Republican values for Gallicized Moroccan Jews, pushing them to reimagine their political futures inside and outside Morocco. The pastiche Jewish characters of Edmond Amran El Maleh elucidate the fissures and fusions of Jewish politics surrounding Morocco's Vichy period. The characters of Josua/Edgar/Aïssa in *Parcours immobile* and Nessim/Yeshuaa in *Mille ans, un jour* grapple with the Vichy period and their own political awakenings, nuancing the story of the Holocaust in its marginal theaters. These characters and the story of El Maleh's own political engagement are themselves pastiche examples of the deeply radical yet marginal experiences of many Moroccan Jews. As such, they elucidate the "game of complex margins."[80] Those margins must be integrated into the narrative whole, not only of Jewish lived experience and ramifications of World War II, but also of global communist politics.

Part IV Commentary

10

Recentering the Holocaust (Again)

Omer Bartov

THE POSTWAR HISTORY OF THE HOLOCAUST has seen many twists and turns. Initially, although Nazi crimes were condemned by all and sundry, the precise nature of these crimes was anything but clear. To be sure, it was known that Jews had been persecuted and murdered, but so were many others. Europe lay prostrate: its cities reduced to piles of rubble, its millions of people displaced and on the way, on trains and horse-drawn carts and on foot, from one end of the continent to the other. The Jews in the displaced persons (DP) camps appeared especially irritating to some of the liberators (or the new occupiers, as others perceived them): They were distraught, filthy, traumatized, and insistent on their victimhood. But what about all the others, people asked, what about the millions of Germans expelled from the East, the millions of Soviet prisoners of war and citizens who died at the hands of the Germans, the brave resistance fighters across the continent, not least the Poles, the French, the Italians? What's so special about the Jews?[1]

Not long after the war, the particular condition of the Jews in the DP camps was recognized; they had been victims of genocide, a newly coined term that was just beginning to make the rounds, and they mostly could not return to where they had come from. Jewish survivors were thus given special treatment—not the kind that the SS had meted out to them in the gas chambers but actual preferential treatment in recognition of the singularity of their victimhood among so many other cases of horror and suffering.[2] But this administrative decision, especially by the American occupiers in Germany, did not have immediate legal or political ramifications. The Nuremberg International Tribunal famously did not request testimonies from Jews and ended up paying little attention to the Final Solution.[3] The British authorities made immigration to Palestine an offense for which Holocaust survivors could be, and were, incarcerated in detention camps in Cyprus or returned to Europe; the Americans, who had resisted Jewish immigration before the Holocaust, were biding their time in letting in those who survived the slaughter.[4]

This too changed. The State of Israel was established and absorbed hundreds of thousands of survivors; the United States, as well as other countries, took in many more; and the Eichmann trial of 1961–1962 finally focused on the Holocaust as a major component of Nazi policy rather than just one element, and possibly not the most important, of the regime's criminality.[5] Yet even then, not least among historians, the genocide of the Jews was not recognized as part and parcel of World War II and as a central event in the history of the twentieth century. Whereas the Federal Republic of Germany recognized in the mid-1950s that its predecessor had committed crimes "in the name of the German people," France, whose collaborationist regime participated actively in the deportation and murder of 75,000 Jews living in the country at the time, took another four decades to recognize its own responsibility as the successor state of the Vichy regime.[6] Indeed, it was only in the 1980s, and increasingly in the 1990s, that the Holocaust was recognized not only as an important historical event but also as one whose acknowledgment by European states (and increasingly also non-European states and, of course, the United States) symbolized their coming to terms with the past and their presumed commitment to defend human rights and international law.[7] Eastern European states wishing to join the European Union after the fall of communism were expected to face up to their past and to commemorate the Holocaust. Initial resentment and resistance to such conditions were also transformed into international competition over slick new exhibits celebrating Jewish life before the Holocaust and mourning its extinction, such as the Jewish Museum in Berlin, the Polin Museum in Warsaw, and other museums in Vilnius, Budapest, and Moscow, not to mention the new Yad Vashem Museum in Jerusalem and the United States Holocaust Memorial Museum in Washington, D.C., which in many ways set the standard for all the others.

To be sure, the competition of victimhood never ceased. In fact, just as the Holocaust came to be recognized as the major European crime of the modern era, the newly liberated states of Eastern Europe began to increasingly insist on their own long-suppressed victimhood: first under the Nazis and then, for a much longer period, under the Soviets.[8] Museums commemorating the Holocaust came under competition from museums commemorating local fallen heroes, nationalists who coincidentally had often also participated in the murder of the Jews. Today, even though everyone wants to demonstrate their recognition of the genocide of the Jews, such recognition comes at the price of others' will to acknowledge "their own" genocide: President Viktor Yushchenko of Ukraine, for instance, wanted Israel to recognize the Holodomor, the mass famine in Ukraine in the early 1930s, as Ukraine's genocide as part of his own recognition of the Jewish genocide (but not of the massive role of Ukrainian policemen and nationalists in the Holocaust).[9]

Of course, the competition of victimhood is not just a matter of national or nationalist rhetoric. Other ethnic and religious groups came to realize in the 1980s and 1990s that claims of past victimization could provide political capital in the present. Numerous new types of genocide, victimhood, and survival were discovered, because the world we inhabit today and inhabited in the past has generated endless cases of violence, oppression, and inhumanity, a rich and murky source from which one could mold new identities or remake old ones. In this process the Holocaust came to play an ambiguous role. On the one hand, it was the model that everyone wanted to emulate; not the event itself, of course, but the manner in which it became a focus of Jewish identity and provided Jews around the world with a certain moral superiority as survivors—real, imagined, and virtual—of the worst case of modern inhumanity. In other words, everyone wanted to have their own Holocaust too. Yet, on the other hand, the Holocaust came to be seen as an obstacle and an irritation, because no one could quite match its ferocity and totality, and, once invoked, it always seemed to diminish the horrors suffered by others, as had indeed been the argument in the immediate aftermath of the war.[10]

Nor can the competition of victimhood be found only in Eastern Europe or among scholars of comparative genocide, imperialism, and colonialism; it has also played a major role in debates over the State of Israel and among its own citizens. The survivors arriving in Israel after the war were not uniformly greeted with love and empathy. For native-born Israelis, or even immigrants who went there before the war, the survivors often represented everything that they detested: They were weak, defeated, demoralized, and always whining. The project was to transform them as quickly as possible into healthy, optimistic, forward-looking Israelis; nothing could be worse than to linger on that ignominious past, in which native Israelis always suspected the survivors of having been somehow complicit, because otherwise why had they survived while so many others perished? In other words, the Holocaust in Israel was hardly a source of pride but rather a shameful episode, whose legacy of national humiliation was epitomized by the survivors. At the same time, the Holocaust was also the main raison d'être of the Jewish state, which defined itself as the refuge of all persecuted Jews and enacted the Law of Return as the symbol of its mission. Had there been a Jewish state before the Holocaust, it was implied, indeed asserted, the genocide would not have happened. This was the fault of the Jewish masses who had not come just as much as the guilt of the rest of the world for not facilitating the creation of the state, not least the British, who had limited immigration, and the Palestinians, who had opposed it.[11]

But there was another vast wave of immigration to Israel in the 1950s and 1960s, not from Europe but from North Africa and the Middle East, altogether over half a million people, about the same number as that of postwar European Jewish immigrants. These were not the masses that such Zionist leaders as David Ben-Gurion had hoped to entice. As he saw it, Jews would become the majority in Palestine when their brethren in Eastern Europe immigrated there. But those "human reserves" had become severely depleted thanks to Nazi extermination policies.[12] To be sure, the Jews did become a majority in Palestine in the aftermath of the War of 1948, but that was only in part because of the arrival of Holocaust survivors. The second, indeed primary reason was the expulsion of three-quarters of a million Palestinians, who were overwhelmingly never allowed to return after the war.[13] This made newly established Israel into a Jewish majority state, most of whose population was made up of European Jews, many of them Holocaust survivors in one sense or another (because large numbers of them had actually fled the Nazis to the USSR, where they experienced a different kind of hell under Stalin's rule).[14] But within two decades of the state's creation, the Jewish European majority was greatly diminished, as Sephardi Jews flooded into the country, forced out of lands where they had lived for centuries, in some cases millennia, not least in response to the creation of Israel and the expulsion of the Palestinians.[15]

The growing presence of Jews from North Africa and the Middle East in Israel occurred just as the Holocaust was changing its status in the perception of the Israeli Jewish public. In the early years of the state, survivors often avoided mentioning the Shoah as a personal experience—not least because others preferred not to hear about it; usually the event was invoked either as an abstract yet decisive reason for the righteousness of Zionism or as an instance of Jewish heroism, especially in the Warsaw Ghetto Uprising, thereby implicitly justifying the expulsion of the Palestinians, which was rarely openly admitted, and linking the fighters of the ghetto with the newly minted Zionist warriors. But following the Eichmann trial, and especially in the wake of the wars of 1967 and 1973, the Holocaust became a focus of Israeli identity akin in some ways to the manner in which it constituted the easiest way for American Jews to invoke their own Jewish identity (as the offspring of survivors and as eternally potential victims).[16] The sense of superiority over the Mizrahim—those easterners "from the Atlas Mountains," the primitive, quasi-Arab Jews of North Africa and the Middle East—combined with an assertion of moral superiority of victimhood; and victimhood on this scale made it entirely impossible to concede the price of prejudices against and marginalization of the Sephardim. To be sure, they too had been forced out of their homes and lands, but, it was claimed, there was no comparison between their victimization and what had occurred in the Holocaust. Seen as culturally inferior, settled in the periphery, and forced into the margins of society, economy, and politics, the Mizrahim could not even make a claim of victimhood in the face of superior Ashkenazi victimization.[17]

This in turn triggered an increasing insistence on recognizing the Holocaust in North Africa, both the reality of persecution and suffering and the potential of overall genocide. Ironically, this competition over victimhood between Ashkenazim and Sephardim mirrored the one between Jewish Israelis and Palestinians, with the latter claiming that they had become the victims of Jews who insisted on the superiority of the Holocaust compared to the Nakba—the Palestinian catastrophe of mass expulsion in 1948—and thus on their absolute right to a state of their own. It also mirrors the competition between those who strive to revive the repressed memory of the Holocaust and enhance its commemoration in Europe, and those who insist on balancing the persecution of the Jews by local fascists, nationalists, and collaborators with the repression of such self-described liberation fighters by the Soviets, who are in turn often perceived as synonymous with Jews. In short, victimhood provides both political capital and license in a vicious circle that is exceedingly difficult to break.[18]

As this book demonstrates, the story of North African Jews can be placed in a variety of contexts, none of which invalidates the other. North

African Jewry had a rich, diverse, and deeply rooted culture; Jews were an integral part of their societies but at the same time maintained their own traditions and communities; relations between Jews and Arabs and those between Jews and Berbers and increasingly also European settlers were deeply affected by colonization, which in many ways exacerbated Jewish-Muslim tensions.[19] World War II, the imposition of anti-Jewish policies, and news about the mass murder in Europe were often experienced by North African Jews as traumatic, both because of their real effects and as a threat of worse things to come. Most important, perhaps, whereas the creation of the State of Israel was seen as a panacea by the inhabitants of DP camps in Europe seeking to build a new life, it heralded catastrophe for Jews throughout North Africa and the Middle East and played a major role in the destruction of these ancient Jewish civilizations. Possibly just as traumatizing as the forced departure from their homes was the fact that for the majority Ashkenazim, absorbing the new Sephardi arrivals not only denied their culture and way of life but also denied their own share of responsibility for the catastrophe of this Jewry, indeed, presented it as a final triumph of Zionism. Although North African and Middle Eastern Jews were seen as a poor replacement for the murdered masses of European Jewry, the Ashkenazi Jews in Israel perceived themselves as taking on the burden of a new civilizing mission on behalf of their less fortunate Eastern brethren, an altruistic, albeit patronizing undertaking of elevating them to certain European standards and expectation, even as Israeli statehood as such was justified by the perceived need to escape Europe and create an independent Jewish state.

Still, taking the long view, one must acknowledge two positive developments in a story made up of cycles of victimization and its abuse. First, as the contributors to this book demonstrate, there is a growing body of scholarship, as well as literature and film, on this other, largely forgotten world of North African Jewry, akin to the attempts made (also often belatedly) to resurrect in representation and research the lost world of Eastern European Jewry. This process is only in its early stages but it will no doubt serve to undermine the simplistic and misleading stereotypes and obfuscations that have long marred Jewish scholarship and Israeli perceptions of North African Jewish society and culture. This will also bring a more complex understanding of the extra-European dimension of the Holocaust and its deep and long-term effects on North African Jewry.

Second, it must be said that, for better or for worse, the Holocaust has become a national asset in Israel. A couple of decades ago the film

Don't Touch My Holocaust (1994, dir. Asher Tlalim) was one of the first attempts to interrogate the manner in which the genocide of the Jews had affected, and in many ways infected, second-generation Jewish Israelis, including very much those of North African and Middle Eastern origin and, in numerous complex ways, Israeli Arabs, none of whom could evade the incessant discourse on the catastrophe that had preceded their own birth.[20] Since then, the Holocaust has come to dominate Israeli life more than ever. I cannot say that this is a positive development in terms of Israeli politics and self-perception; the integrating dynamic of the genocide of European Jewry has made too many Israelis, no matter their ancestry, see themselves as potential victims of a genocide that happened on another continent, under different circumstances, more than seven decades ago. This perception has a deeply distorting effect on politics, education, and national identity.

On the positive side, a different kind of integration has been taking place. Despite the ongoing rhetoric of tribal warfare between the Mizrahim and Ashkenazim, which is exploited on the one hand by right-wing politicians courting Mizrahi resentments and, on the other, by self-appointed intellectual defenders of Western civilization, Israeli culture has been transformed in radical ways. Claims of being a Euro-American enclave in the Middle East notwithstanding, Israel's contemporary culture, music, cuisine, its very ethnicity, resemble the region in which it exists—and from which its Sephardi communities came—more than at any other time since its establishment. In that, not only have Ashkenazim and Mizrahim drawn closer, but also Israeli Jews as a whole and Israeli Arabs—the politics of division, violence, and oppression notwithstanding—are increasingly difficult to distinguish from each other. In this sense we can perhaps say that what may eventually bring history and people together is not a shared catastrophe but the unstoppable dynamic of coexistence.[21]

11

Paradigms and Differences

Susan Rubin Suleiman

TO SCHOLARS OF THE HOLOCAUST, the essays in this book offer both a revelation and a challenge. They are a revelation because, as many of the contributors and the editors emphasize, the persecution of Jews in North Africa during World War II is a subject that has come late to Holocaust studies, if at all. Many Holocaust scholars, including me, have had only a hazy idea of what went on in North Africa, and they have never truly considered what it would mean to the field if we included North Africa in the history and cultural productions (literature, film) by or about Jews who experienced exclusion, internment, and other modes of persecution that are associated with the Holocaust but occurred outside the boundaries of continental Europe. As several of the contributors here emphasize, the question has not only intellectual and disciplinary implications but also juridical and financial ones: The demand for recognition of the traumas experienced by Jews in North Africa as a result of Germany's actions during the war has gone hand in hand with demands for reparations. Although reparation payments from the German government were granted to Jews persecuted in Europe as early as the 1950s, comparable reparations for Jews who suffered persecution in North Africa were not negotiated until decades later, some as late as 2011.

It is in the intellectual and disciplinary realm, however, that the work displayed in the essays in this volume acquires its full importance and poses its most interesting challenges. How does the inclusion of North Africa affect the paradigms that Holocaust scholars have constructed in thinking about the fate of Jews in Nazi-occupied Europe? How can we think about the significant differences that existed between the two geographic areas, both during the war and afterward, without falling into the trap of "competing victimhoods"? On the other side of the geographic-disciplinary divide, how can scholars who work chiefly on North Africa benefit from adopting, or at least considering, certain conceptual models that have been developed over recent decades by scholars of the Holocaust?

Inclusion with Diversity

The experiences of Jews in North Africa during the war differed significantly from those of Jews in Europe. If North Africa is to be included in Holocaust studies, it must be in a way that acknowledges both its resemblances to and its diversions from the familiar paradigms of Holocaust historiography. Consider the narrative paradigm of exclusion, ghettoization, deportation (camps), and death that is most familiar to Holocaust scholars who study the fate of Jews in countries occupied by the Nazis. (The other major paradigm is "the Holocaust by bullets," which designates the mass murders of Jews by Einsatzgruppen on the Eastern front after the Nazis invaded the Soviet Union in June 1941; it is not relevant to North Africa.) Clearly, the Jews of North Africa did not live out the full paradigm, not even during the Nazi occupation of Tunisia (November 1942–May 1943). They did endure exclusion and internment, however. In the French colonial regimes of Algeria, Morocco, and Tunisia before the Nazi occupation, Vichy exclusionary laws that deprived Jews of civil rights in France were applied with varying degrees of efficiency and zeal, but sufficiently so that Jews felt persecuted. In Libya, which was under Italian rule, anti-Jewish laws were similarly imported from the mainland. Punitive forced labor camps were set up in all these countries, again with variations but in a pattern that corresponded to many camps in Europe. As the ongoing project of the *Encyclopedia of Camps and Ghettos* published by the United States Holocaust Memorial Museum makes clear, continental Europe itself had a large variety of punitive detention sites, ranging from small ghettos or detention centers to industrial extermination camps.[1]

One major effect of the inclusion of North Africa in Holocaust studies, then, is to confirm the diversity of Jewish fates during the war, all of which can find their place under the rubric of "the Holocaust." The trend in Holocaust studies in general since the turn of the twenty-first century has in fact been to emphasize specificities. Whereas earlier scholars sought to define categories such as "the survivor" as though all those who survived persecution were overwhelmingly similar, today the emphasis is on the diversity of traumatic experiences in the Holocaust and of victims' responses to them. There is no such thing as "the survivor," only *survivors* who underwent different kinds of suffering and whose responses at the time, as well as their postwar lives, were not uniform, even if many of their wartime experiences were similar. Historians today are asking more and more detailed questions: Microhistories of Jews in a single town or region or of conditions in a specific camp are at the forefront of this trend. Historians are also including diaries and testimonies by victims and survivors in their broader accounts, thus emphasizing that the Holocaust victimized not nameless masses but individuals, each with his or her unique history within the collective.[2]

The concept of inclusion with diversity that I am proposing here differs significantly from Michael Rothberg's influential concept of multidirectional memory, although it shares with it the goal of overcoming competitive models of victimhood. Rothberg, in defining multidirectional memory as the productive and dynamic "interaction of different historical memories" in a "heterogeneous and changing post–World War II present,"[3] has in mind the interactions between *different* historical events and different groups' memories of them: the Holocaust, colonialism, the slave trade. The concept of inclusion with diversity refers to the *same* historical event but seen from different perspectives; it can apply to the Holocaust as well as to colonialism, the slave trade, or the genocides that have plagued the post–World War II world (Rwanda, Srebrenica). The two concepts are complementary: Multidirectional memory puts into play differences *between* events, groups, and memories, whereas inclusion with diversity grapples with differences *within* them.

One major difference that distinguishes North Africa within the larger domain of Holocaust studies is the particular situation of Jews in the colonial context. In Europe Jews were for centuries despised and persecuted as the Other of the Christian population; in the French colonial context Jews were often pitted against an even more despised population, the Arabs and Berbers (almost of whom were Muslims), who constituted the large majority of North Africa's inhabitants but who under colonialism were its most oppressed subjects. This unique triangular situation, where Jews found themselves between the European colonizers and the Muslim colonized, created a shifting ground. Thus in Algeria, where Jews had been granted

French citizenship by the Crémieux Decree of 1870, they still remained the object of anti-Semitic prejudice on the part of many European settlers, just as though they had been in France! At the same time, their privileged status in relation to Muslims (most of whom never acquired French citizenship) put them at odds with the Muslim majority and made alliances between the two groups difficult if not impossible. During the war, the Vichy decrees of 1940 and 1941 stripped Jews of citizenship (it was later restored), without, however, creating any solidarity with the Muslim colonized. A similarly ambiguous situation for Jews existed, with variations, in Tunisia, Morocco, and Libya. In many places the colonial government consciously sought to foment hostility between the two groups, encouraging Muslims to attack Jews or else turning a blind eye when they did.

In discussing the fate of Jews in North Africa during the war, therefore, one has to keep in mind the specificity of the colonial situation, which does not apply to discussions of the Holocaust in Europe. The fact that after the creation of the State of Israel, which was a direct outcome of the persecution of Jews during the war, the large majority of Jews in North Africa (as in the Middle East generally) ended up emigrating from countries where they had lived for centuries is of course another major phenomenon that distinguishes North Africa from Europe. Many Jews who survived the Holocaust on the continent also emigrated after the war, but most of them were from Eastern Europe. In France, where, despite the existence of popular anti-Semitism, Jews had enjoyed safety and full civil rights for more than a century before the war, survivors generally stayed and even thrived in the postwar decades; and as we know, France became a favored destination for Jews fleeing North Africa in the 1960s, after the former colonies gained their independence. Holocaust scholars who study not only the events of the Holocaust proper but also their consequences after the war have a wide open field to explore in North Africa.

On a more theoretical level, the inclusion of North Africa in Holocaust studies raises provocative and productive questions. Just as Holocaust scholars still ponder the question of exactly when the Holocaust began (was it 1933, when Hitler came to power and the book burnings started? Or later, and if so, when? 1935 with the Nuremberg Laws? 1938 with Kristallnacht? 1941 with the mass shootings in the East?), so the inclusion of North Africa allows them to think about another parameter: not time, but space. Did the Holocaust occur only in countries invaded by Germany, as was the case in continental Europe? Or was it sufficient that the persecution of

Jews be undertaken by a regime (like Vichy France or Mussolini's Italy) that collaborated with the Nazis, even without the actual presence of Nazis? In North Africa only Tunisia was actually occupied by German troops, and for a relatively short time. Yet the persecution of Jews by the Vichy regime and Mussolini in Morocco, Algeria, Libya, and Tunisia (before the German occupation) is also discussed by contributors to this volume—and the fact that reparation payments have been made to Jews in those countries confirms that Germany's responsibility in the Holocaust went beyond areas actually occupied by it.

Generations of Memory

Turning the question around, how can conceptual models developed by scholars of the Holocaust be useful to specialists who study North Africa? One major field in Holocaust studies over the past several decades has been that of memory. The question it asks is not, What happened during the Holocaust? but, How is it remembered? This trend has overlapped with the larger trend of memory studies, which became a dominant model in historiography after the publication, in the 1980s, of the multivolume collective project spearheaded by Pierre Nora, *Les lieux de mémoire*. As concerns specifically French memory of the war years, Henry Rousso's *Le syndrome de Vichy*, first published in 1987, set the tone for a whole generation of scholars, not only in history but also in literary and cultural studies.

But memory is closely linked to generations. What is remembered depends on who is doing the remembering, and a large part of that is determined by the proximity of the rememberer to the events in question. Technically, only someone who was "there" can remember an event as part of personal memory; but it makes a huge difference whether one was a young child, an adolescent, or a mature adult at the time. I have formulated the concept of the 1.5 generation to take account of the way child survivors have negotiated issues of trauma and memory.[4] As we know from theorists of collective memory, however, memories can also be transmitted from generation to generation, independently of personal memory in the strict sense. Marianne Hirsch's influential concept of postmemory goes far in theorizing how people (individuals and groups) relate to traumatic events that they themselves did not live through but that they have in a sense adopted by way of family membership (memories transmitted directly from those who were there to their descendants) or else by a chosen affiliation, in which case a person or group that has no direct involvement in the past event feels sufficiently concerned to join in collective remembrance of it.[5]

Scholars who work on North Africa have a rich field if they adopt the generational model (or even merely try it on, the way one tries on a garment to see if it fits). Because my own area of scholarship is in literary and cultural studies, I would be especially interested in learning more about the way that child survivors of the war years, both Jews and non-Jews, have remembered those years and represented them in written memoirs or other forms of testimony and also whether their ways of remembering differ from those of people who were adults during the war. Autobiographical texts by Jacques Derrida and Hélène Cixous, two of the best-known Algerian-Jewish transplants to France, have provided moving accounts of what it felt like, as a young child, to be suddenly stripped of rights (such as the right to attend a French school) circa 1941; they have also explored their uneasy position, both linguistic and social, between French settlers and Muslim subjects in Algeria, during the war and afterward.[6] The Franco-Algerian novelist Leila Sebbar (born in 1941), who left Algeria as a teenager in 1958, has not only written fictional and autobiographical texts about her childhood during and after the war but also in recent years published testimonies by many others, Jews and non-Jews, who grew up in North Africa before emigrating to France.[7]

If we extend the inquiry to the realm of postmemory, we can ask how the generations that were born after the war, and after emigration, "remember" those years. Obviously, these questions also apply to Muslims and their descendants, especially those who for their own reasons left North Africa after the war or after independence. Boualem Sansal's well-known novel *Le village de l'Allemand* makes an explicit multidirectional link between Jewish and Muslim memory and postmemory of World War II. But even on just its own terms, the study of Muslim memories of that time, and of the battles for independence that followed, can usefully adopt concepts elaborated in the study of the Holocaust.

12

Sephardim and Holocaust Historiography

Susan Gilson Miller

IT HAS TAKEN ALMOST SEVENTY YEARS since the end of World War II for scholars to acknowledge that the Holocaust affected Sephardi Jews in a manner that was quite different from the way it impacted Ashkenazi Jews. Yet the scope of that difference has been difficult to establish, because research and writing on the Sephardi experience is so lacking. Henry Abramson has said that the persecution of Sephardi Jewry in the Nazi era is under "a double occlusion": The Holocaust is "widely understood to be principally a European phenomenon" and Sephardim, including North African Jews, have been largely ignored when it comes to retelling the story of those terrible times.[1] Moreover, the number of scholars working on the topic of Sephardim during the Holocaust is minuscule, compared with those working on Europe and especially Eastern Europe. Abramson concludes, "Hidden from both public view and academic attention, the plight of Sephardic Jews during the war has remained understudied and undervalued."[2]

There are some exceptions to this rule. When we turn to southeastern Europe and the Balkans, where communities of Ladino-speaking Sephardim thrived for hundreds of years under Ottoman dominion, accounts of their genocide are slowly coming to light. But these histories are often woven into larger narratives of evolving political aims, military developments, and mass killings that were unfolding farther north. That the fate of these southern Jews followed the same familiar pattern of stigmatization, ghettoization, and extermination as the Jews of Central and Eastern Europe may explain their inclusion in more global histories, lending credence to the (now contested) theory of a Nazi master plan. Yet even these well-documented local histories from southeastern Europe, undoubtedly compelling in their own right, are treated as marginalia and usually consigned to footnotes, a result of the optic of most scholars who write on the Holocaust.[3]

It is my contention that historicizing the role of Sephardim from all parts of the non-European world into Holocaust history is a project of critical need, not only to fill the glaring omissions but also to correct a serious imbalance that has distorted Sephardi self-regard for more than three generations. Furthermore, I argue that the mechanisms that have deprived Sephardim of their rightful place in this central drama of modern Jewish history has not only put them at a disadvantage in relation to other Jews but also perpetuated the myth that Jews of the non-European world were mere bystanders to the catastrophic events that enveloped the Jewish world at midcentury. The aim of this chapter is to explore how this egregious absence came about and what we might do to correct it.

Occlusion or Exclusion?

Let us start with a question: Why this forgetfulness? Is it really "occlusion," as Abramson maintains, a kind of impersonal "closing off"? Or is it more correctly a purposeful occultation, which captures the idea of concealment, obstruction, and exclusivity, that is, a conscious effort to remove the Sephardim as a group from the grand narrative of World War II? In considering this notion, I make a few general observations.

First, most scholars of Jewish studies worldwide have been trained in a Eurocentric tradition and know little about the histories and peoples of the non-Western world. They do not read or speak languages other than European languages, though they may know modern Hebrew. With few exceptions, they have no acquaintance with Arabic, Turkish, or Persian literature and languages and are unable to use them as historical sources. In other words, they do not have the basic tools needed for scholarly research on the countries of the Middle East and North Africa, where most of the Sephardim who were victims of the Holocaust once lived.

Second, even in Israel, or especially in Israel, the gatekeepers to Holocaust learning come from a European background. Institutions such as Yad Vashem were founded to preserve and validate a specifically European experience—the destruction of European Jewry—to gather testimonies, to put up a bulwark against Holocaust deniers, to honor the "righteous" Gentiles, ninety-nine point nine percent of whom are Europeans, and to establish institutions that would preserve the memory of those events for future generations. Yad Vashem at its creation was intended more as an institutional home for survivor memories and as a repository for their stories and less as a center for impartial scholarly research. It was only some years after its founding that a "scientific" research arm was added. It is not unreasonable to assert, and I am not alone in this, that Yad Vashem exists in part to validate Israel's role as guarantor of Jewish survival and to make perfectly manifest the pledge "Never again" that is so central to Zionist thinking. Processes of memorializing the Shoah are at the heart of Yad Vashem's mission; those same processes direct and shape the ideology and political dynamics of the Jewish state. It follows, then, that the memorialization achieved thus far in the context of Yad Vashem has been built on a solidly European Jewish foundation. This reality at the core of Yad Vashem's raison d'être has created the conditions for treating non-European experiences as ancillary to the "main story" of what happened in Europe.

Third, and finally, it is an incontrovertible fact that the 6 million were almost all Ashkenazi Jews, whose terrible fate was not shared by non-European Jews. Indeed, for many people, professional historians and laypeople alike, this fact is the source of the insurmountable difference between Ashkenazim and Sephardim in terms of the Holocaust. The structural exclusion of Sephardim from the near-sacred category of "survivor" has placed them at a permanent disadvantage relative to their European coreligionists, creating in effect two separate narratives, one of a "European" Shoah and the other of a Shoah of all the rest. The potential risks in this distinction have caused alarm even among European-oriented scholars, leading them to take a second look at Sephardi histories to redress an imbalance that is dysfunctional in terms of building a universally shared Jewish historical memory.

Is North Africa Part of the Shoah?

Dan Michman, a professor at Bar-Ilan University, former head of the research unit at Yad Vashem, and a prolific author of books and articles on the Holocaust, recently turned to the question of the Sephardim and their place in Holocaust historiography in an effort to explain these disparities. In his unpublished article "The Fate of North African Jews During World

War II: Does It Belong to the Shoah?" Michman offers insight into the state of research in establishment circles.[4] He begins by asking, "To what extent can North African Jews be considered as part of the Shoah?" Initially, he observes, no recognized scholars entertained the idea that North Africa had a role to play in Holocaust historiography, but as the years have passed, the idea has become more generally accepted. For Michman, the crucial question regarding the historical representation of these events is one of genocide and the extent to which North African Jews were included in the Final Solution. His argument unfolds as follows.

First, the numbers. According to a protocol presented at the infamous Wannsee Conference of January 1942 for coordinating actions leading up to the program of mass genocide, a census was made of all the Jews left in Europe. This census claimed that 700,000 Jews were living in France. Scholars have observed that this number is quite high and in need of explanation. German Holocaust historian Peter Longerich responds that the reason for the inflated number is that the Nazis included the Jews of French North Africa in their calculations.[5] Other scholars, such as Raul Hilberg, argue that the Final Solution applied only to the European continent; without explaining the high number, Hilberg says that it does not include the Jews of North Africa.[6] The disagreement about numbers among scholars is critical, because it provides the background to an even more important debate about inclusiveness. For Michman, the Wannsee census is pivotal: Did it include Jews of North Africa or not? He concludes that the Nazi numbers are wrong and that the Jews of North Africa were not part of the Nazi program of genocide. Oddly enough, Michman refers to the testimony of Eichmann at his trial in Jerusalem—Eichmann, who was perhaps the world's greatest liar—as evidence to support his position.[7]

Historians whose life work has been the collection of quantitative data on the Holocaust to prove its veracity rarely ask "what if" questions. Yet Michman does exactly that: "What if the German occupation had been completed, would the Jews of North Africa [then] have been included in the Final Solution?" Prefacing his answer by warning that historians like himself prefer to avoid the conditional, he concedes that it is quite possible that the Nazi regime would have applied the techniques developed in Europe outside Europe's borders, "had that been possible."[8] But clearly, it was not possible, at least in Morocco and Algeria, to realize such a plan because of the turn of events, making the subject moot. (Tunisia is a different story, and Michman's argument has some footing there, thus requiring special treatment.) Michman's conclusion is that North African Jews were not part of the Nazi genocide and hence, according to criteria established by Yad Vashem, not entitled to the status of "victims." This decision has significant consequences, not only in regard to the matter of victim compensation but also in terms of the far more important work of memory, memorialization, and knowledge production.

If the question of Maghrebi Jewish participation in the Shoah were left to Yad Vashem scholars, we would probably have to stop here. My own experience while doing research at the Yad Vashem archives in the summer of 2015 may be relevant. When I requested the only dossier in the finding aid relating to the Holocaust in North Africa, it arrived completely empty. I was told by the archivist that the contents had been transferred to the Ben-Zvi Institute, Israel's official home for the study of Jews of the non-Western world.[9] Absence was also the theme in my visit to Yad Vashem's museum. Only one half of one small wall in this vast exhibition space was dedicated to Tunisia, where Jews were deported and Jewish civilians were subjected to forced labor. What do we conclude from this? The principal Israeli institution for memorializing the Holocaust has passed over the question of Sephardi involvement, handing it over to "specialists" at the chronically underfunded Ben-Zvi Institute, where it remains in the custodianship of a scholar and two assistants who have created a website offering selective access to a small portion of the documents in the collection.

Looking for Other Signs

With such an important topic, however, matters do not end there. By setting aside the notion that actors must be "survivors" in the usual sense of the term and by paying attention to more recent trends in Holocaust historiography, we can begin to visualize new thematic opportunities for constructing a Sephardi history of the Holocaust on its own terms. Using the vast array of source material currently available—documents, voice and video recordings, visual images, newspaper accounts, letters, and memoirs—historians can begin the process of filling the void.[10]

Of particular relevance are new ways of thinking about Holocaust historiography that depend not so much on positivist facts and figures but on adopting a more innovative approach. Foremost among them is the new cultural history, first constituted as a disciplinary field in the early part of the twentieth century. With its emphasis on nonelite groups and their relation to concepts of power, class, race, gender, religious difference, aesthetics, and communication (to name only a few), cultural historians seize on the experiences of ordinary people that have eluded more conventional historical interpretations. Whereas previous Holocaust historiography focused to an overwhelming degree on the actions and intentions of states toward their Jewish victims, the new cultural history puts the emphasis on broader societal participation that includes both Jews and the non-Jews who were also victims of mass violence.[11]

British historian Dan Stone, a proponent of the cultural turn, observes that most "traditional" historiography of the Holocaust, for all its enormity, is dominated by "a more or less positivist—that is to say, nontheorized, empiricist historical method."[12] Stone's idea is that historical data cannot be considered separate from memory and that memory is a concrete cultural practice of pivotal importance to Holocaust narratology that embraces wider circles than the victimhood of certain protected groups. For Stone, memory is essential, with all memories being equally valid in making sense of the past. Memory embraces facts and figures, to be sure, but it also embraces the sentient aspects of historical construction: the feelings, emotions, self-understandings, and relationships behind events and numbers that are distributed across societies. Taking Stone's argument one step further, we can imagine how, if we move to this level of engagement with the sources, we might find new ways of talking about the Holocaust in North Africa that would have meaning for scholars and laypeople alike, without having to argue the case for victimhood, witnessing, or even survival.

My own project on the war years in North Africa concerns European refugees in Morocco and the activities of Hélène Cazès Benatar, a Moroccan lawyer who was the primary agent for their relief. I focus on the context, personalities, narratives, and modalities of her efforts to help refugees who escaped Europe to answer questions that up to now have not been asked: What were the immediate and long-term effects of the encounter between masses of European refugees, mostly Jewish, and local populations? In what ways did refugees who arrived in Morocco—somewhere between 10,000 and 20,000 by the end of the war—react to French colonial rule, to the Moroccan nationalist movement, and to the aspirations of Moroccan Jewry for long-term political equality, keeping in mind that Moroccan Jews were at the time the largest community of Sephardi Jews in the non-Western world?[13] How do we understand the effects of war on Muslim-Jewish relations, Sephardi-Ashkenazi relations, Vichy-colonial and Moroccan-colonized relations, East-West relations (Westerners in this case being the occupying Allied troops and Easterners being the indigenous people, both Jewish and Muslim)?

In the process of developing a specific North African narrative, I find many points of comparison and crossover with the European experience of the Holocaust. Racial discrimination, radicalization, prison camps, forced labor, the texture of refugee lives, questions of anti-Semitism and racialization—all aspects of Hitler's Europe—were indeed also part of the Sephardi experience in North Africa.[14] Unpacking those experiences through ethnographic means and using the thick description techniques of cultural anthropologist Clifford Geertz, for example, or the symbolic sensibility of Victor Turner open the way to radically altering our understanding of North African Jews in wartime that should have bearing on the larger picture of Holocaust historiography. Some specific examples of historical revisionism based on methods of cultural analysis should make this point clearer.

The theme of *exclusion*, for example, is familiar to us from the European context, and it has its own North African iteration. Vichy officials used various methods to exclude Jews from the rest of society. How successful were they in imposing Nazi-inspired race laws in North Africa? We find a replication of many of the steps taken in France—the firing of Jews from public jobs, the banishment of children from schools, orders to return to the ghetto—but in North Africa it appears that efforts at exclusion had only qualified success. What cultural factors shaped a specifically North African response to race laws and modified their impact? My own inquiries suggest that Vichy restrictions made only limited inroads because native Jews quietly fought back, exercising their traditional means of access, mobilizing long-standing networks, and finding countless ways to counteract the most crippling effects of the race laws. The Jewish counterattack is evident between the lines of the official documentation, showing up not only in facts and figures but also in the quality of relations between native Jews on the one hand and Vichy authorities on the other, reminding us that these interactions took place in a cultural context that was fundamentally different from Jewish-Gentile relations in the European setting.

Another question best answered by reading cultural signs is to what extent Jews were protected by Muslims, an issue that has been the source of much journalistic bravado.[15] The answer not only is in the data but also depends on paying closer attention to the social and political context.

Reading the local press, we find that the main tormenters of Moroccan Jews were not Muslim Moroccans but rather colonial settlers, who saw in the race laws an opportunity to profit from looting Jewish businesses and limiting perceived Jewish advantages. Resentment was based on a particularly European form of anti-Semitism that was not normative in Muslim society. We also see a marked inertia in the French colonial administration to apply restrictions to Jews, because of a culture of co-option that goes back to the earliest years of the protectorate. Seasoned colonial officials held deep-seated ideas about the importance of Jews to native society and the local economy, and, though by no means free of prejudice, they resisted as long as they could the orders of doctrinaire Vichyites, such as Pierre Laval, who were outsiders to the colonial enterprise. We can observe a sharp demarcation between what happened in the metropole and what happened in the colonies based on an array of inherited cultural values.

Another thematic thread concerns *community organization* and community activism. Here, too, cultural analysis is key. How were Jewish communities traditionally organized, and how did their patterns of organization come into play in the midst of crisis? Practically speaking, how were refugees housed, fed, and clothed, and by whom? In Morocco, authorities for the most part left this matter up to local Jews. How communities organized to help Jews from abroad, most of whom knew little or no French, regarded Morocco as an uncivilized place, and considered its inhabitants, including its Jews, to be one step above "primitive" nomads on the scale of human development, is a story unto itself. Networking, housing, food, financial help, compassion, religious comfort, and other forms of generosity and solidarity were qualities that emerged from local Jewish communities in this time of crisis. The role of the American Joint Distribution Committee and other foreign agencies was actually quite limited in the early years of the war and did not come into play until after 1942. Before that time, the burden of handling the refugee crisis fell largely on local Jews.

The *Ashkenazi-Sephardi encounter* in wartime is another topic ripe for cultural analysis. In many ways it foreshadows the disastrous encounter between Ashkenazim and Sephardim/Mizrahim in postindependence Israel. Facts such as sexual relations and marriage between Jewish refugees and local Jews are described in culturally laden language that paints a layered image of how European Jews intermingled with local Jewish society, which, it should be noted, was as complex and diversified in education, class, religious sensibility, and worldliness as its Ashkenazi guests.

Questions of *quality of life*. Scholars like Dan Michman have concluded that Sephardi Jews in North Africa were exempt from the threat of genocide and therefore were not victims in the European sense; if one insists on their victimhood, then it is a victimhood of a different ontological order. Whereas genocide, as we define it in the European context, clearly did not occur, Maghrebi Jews reacted as though the Nazis were on their doorstep. It would be untrue to say that they felt safe or that the wartime situation was not one of trauma and deprivation. Indeed, they could easily have been Nazi victims, as American historian Norman Goda points out, if the Allied forces had not landed on the shores of North Africa in November 1942, upsetting German plans. Goda argues that it was Hitler's plan to invade North Africa, once (and this is a very big "once") Russia and Great Britain had been defeated.[16] It is safe to conclude that life for North African Jews, living in the shadow of the Nazi threat and enduring the daily insults, stresses, and anxieties of Vichy oppression, was a psychological nightmare and thus a subject worthy of further exploration.

In conclusion, there are numerous points where narratives of the Holocaust in North Africa become intertwined with those of the European Holocaust, where bringing the two discourses together in one cohesive account could be revelatory. Not only writing Sephardi experiences into Holocaust studies but also applying them to the theorizing of Holocaust histories is another worthwhile enterprise. Introducing the signs, symbols, rituals, dreams, memories, and cultural templates that are emerging from the non-Western matrix into the analysis of what has up to now been a strictly European endeavor is a tantalizing possibility that might lend meaning to the Holocaust for legions of people, both Jewish and non-Jewish, who presently regard it as an abstraction lacking relevance to their own life experiences. It is not unreasonable to imagine that the recovery of Sephardi histories and their integration into the whole could produce a revitalized historiography in the widest possible sense.

13

Stages in Jewish Historiography and Collective Memory

Haim Saadoun

WORDS HAVE MEANING; language can determine one's conceptions and even perceptions. Thus the title of this book, *The Holocaust and North Africa*, will initiate (or continue) a debate regarding the correct way to define events in North Africa in relation to the Holocaust. Should it be "The Holocaust in North Africa" or "The Holocaust and North Africa" or perhaps just "World War II in North Africa"?

Is the subject of North African Jewry during the Holocaust a marginal topic? And if so, what can we learn from this so-called marginal topic about the Holocaust itself? Indeed, how does one define "a marginal issue" in the context of the Holocaust? Is the suffering of one individual or of one community more or less important than that of any other? Does the fact that mass murder did not take place in North Africa mean that the Jewish communities there should not be considered Holocaust survivors? Should "Holocaust survivors" be defined by historians, lawyers, or perhaps by the "survivors" themselves? Would a Jew in one of the countries of North Africa consider him- or herself a Holocaust survivor? Perhaps it is safer to examine the subject in each country separately than to generalize. Moreover, do we even know enough about the events in each country to be able to discuss the subject? These are only some of the important questions that arise in the current book.

Because this book reflects the tendencies of the current stage of development of historiography in this area, it is useful to consider what has come before, that is, the main stages in the development of the historiography of World War II in North Africa and its impact on the collective memory of Jews from North Africa, mainly in Israel but also in France. This consideration is at the heart of this think piece.

1944–1954: Shaping Collective Memory and the Beginning of Research

A disparity lies between the relative silence of ordinary Jews who suffered during the war and Jewish community leaders, who were determined to write and publish their versions of events immediately after the end of the war in North Africa. Today, two diaries in particular are of great historical interest: *Six mois sous la botte*, the diary of Paul Ghez, who was head of the labor force recruitment committee for the Germans in Tunisia; and *Étoile jaune et croix gammée*, the diary of Moïse Borgel, who was the president of the Tunisian Jewish community. Both were composed during the Nazi occupation of Tunisia, between November 1942 and May 1943. Because these diaries represent the first time Tunisian Jewish leaders provided accounts of their own actions at this time, they are particularly crucial to our understanding of the community's most severe crisis of the modern period. These two diaries are mentioned in almost all studies of Tunisia during this period and in particular form the basis of Lia Brozgal's close examination of what she calls "The Ethics and Aesthetics of Restraint" in the current volume (Chapter 8).

Ghez and Borgel were not alone. Maurice Eisenbeth, the chief rabbi of Algeria, published his diaries from the war in 1945.[1] A year later, a Tunisian Jewish mohel (circumciser) published a book in which he presented biographies and photographs of all the Jews killed during the Nazi rule of Tunisia.[2] Other Tunisian Jews wrote lamentations, and Jews from Morocco wrote *qassidas* (long poems) about the war in general. As I show here, the last and current stage in Jewish historiography is characterized by, among other things, the discovery of more unpublished diaries from World War II in North Africa.

Notwithstanding the literature described so far, periodicals, newspapers, and other sources dating from after the war omit any account of the suffering of Jews during this period. It would seem that most Jews who suffered during the war, from a death in the family or otherwise, tried to hide their feelings, as though this were not an occasion for communal mourning. It seems that the Jewish leadership "asked" the Jews to return to a "normal" routine. The truth is that Jews did write diaries during and just after the war, but they did not publish them; the publication of this material would only begin at the end of the twentieth century.[3] Typically, as Jews went about trying to rehabilitate their lives after the war's end, they maintained a silence regarding their wartime experiences, so we do not have real sources to support our assumptions about the community's reaction to the war. The only public expression was the commemorative monument to the victims of World War II at Le Borgel Cemetery, which was inaugurated on April 16, 1948, and the yearly commemoration ceremony.

The first explanation for this relative silence is the simple fact that Jews, especially those in Libya and Tunisia, were preoccupied with the physical rehabilitation of their communities following the wreckage caused by fighting, and this work constituted a part of the general rehabilitation taking place in these countries. Real financial assistance from the colonial powers was nonexistent at this time, because Italy and France were still at war and were therefore faced with financial problems of their own. As a result, the economic situation in French North Africa deteriorated. Jews in French North Africa tried to return to the prewar positions from which they had been fired under the Vichy regime's decrees.

The second explanation for the absence of publications about the war in its immediate aftermath is that the prevailing public and political agenda was North Africa's independence; this cause was taken up by nationalists, who were encouraged by the international atmosphere during and after the war and by the weakness of France and Italy. Great Britain declared that, as in the case of India and Palestine, their rule over Libya would soon come to an end. France, for a variety of reasons, did not make a similar declaration, thus fueling the nationalist struggle.

For the Jewish communities any future independence was a highly relevant issue, and it is not surprising that the war became a turning point in the history of the Jewish communities, from which point onward they went into decline. One of the first expressions of this process was the exodus to Palestine of small groups of young people, mainly Zionists, from North Africa before the establishment of the State of Israel. The first illegal ship left the Algerian coast on May 12, 1947, with more than 400 illegal Jewish immigrants, mainly from Morocco. The end of Jewish existence in the countries and among the peoples with whom they had lived for hundreds years had begun.

The third explanation for the immediate postwar silence is that, paradoxically, the decade between the end of the war and the independence of the North African countries was relatively good for Jewish communities, mainly because of the increase in communal and cultural organizations and energized political (including Zionist) activities.

Two important and quite different books conclude this first stage of historiography: one a work of fiction and the other a work of academic research. The first is the autobiographical novel *La statue de sel* (The Pillar of Salt), written by Albert Memmi and published in 1953. Memmi was a 33-year-old Tunisian Jew, assimilated into French culture, who was deeply frustrated by French anti-Semitism and worried about his future as part of the French culture that he admired so much. At the time, the Tunisian Jewish community rejected and was angered by this autobiographical novel because of its naturalistic descriptions of their own community, not because of his description of the war. Memmi focuses on five key points in Tunisian Jewish collective memory: the influence of the Jewish leadership, the role of the French authorities, Jews' existence in the camps, Jewish daily life during the occupation, and the significance of the period of World War II.[4]

The second important publication marking the end of this period of immediate postwar historiography is the first piece of academic research regarding the war: Jacque Sabille's *Les juifs de Tunisie sous Vichy et l'occupation*. This work was published as part of the activities of the Center for Contemporary Jewish Documentation, established in 1944 by Isaac Schneersohn. Schneersohn sent Sabille and another scholar, Michael Ansky, to North Africa to document what had happened there during the war.[5] Whereas Ansky is a well-known figure, we have little information about Sabille and his mission to Tunisia at the beginning of the 1950s to collect documents and testimonies of wartime. Nonetheless, it is Sabille's work that constitutes the basis of all future research. Sabille posits that the Vichy regime and the German occupation should be seen as one period and that the anti-Semitism of the early 1930s was simply a prelude to the ultimate destruction of the Jews. This perception should be reexamined in connection to our current knowledge about the war in North Africa.

The first historiographic period (1944–1954) is thus characterized by the first documentation and testimonies of those who lived through this period. Recently, we have become aware that other diaries were indeed written during this period but not published until later, for unknown reasons.

1954–1984: Silence and Ignorance

The second historiographic period, dating from 1954 to 1984, is bookended by two events. The period has its preface in 1953, when Memmi published his *La statue de sel*, and that work is significant to the understanding of the modernization process of the Jewish community in Tunisia and perhaps also other Jewish communities in the Muslim world. But 1954 marks the beginning of negotiations regarding the independence of North African countries and its impact on the faith of the Jewish communities. This stage ends in 1984, when Michel Abitbol published his research on the Vichy period in North Africa in *Les juifs d'Afrique du Nord sous Vichy*.[6]

Silence and ignorance of the subject prevailed during the long period in between the publication of Memmi's and Abitbol's works, as an examination of Robert Attal's *Les juifs d'Afrique du Nord: Bibliographie* (1993) bears out: It shows that there were almost no publications of any kind during this period.[7] Moreover, even during Eichmann's trial in 1961, the suffering of North African Jewry was not mentioned.[8] Nor did the first Israeli museums include the story of North Africa in their exhibits.

So what are the reasons for this prevailing silence and ignorance? At the beginning of the period, North African Jewry in Israel was preoccupied with the problems attending integration, because of the immigrant communities' economic and social problems. Issues such as history, heritage, and collective memory were placed on the back burner in the interest of focusing on immediate pragmatic challenges. As North African Jews grappled with the significant difficulties of assimilation into Israeli society, the writing of memoirs and the publishing of scholarly research understandably took a back seat.

Another factor contributing to the historiographic lacuna is the fact that at that time the French archives were almost completely closed to research. The regulations regarding re-opening the archives from this period would loosen only at the end of the twentieth century.

A final contributor to the silence of this period is the singular preoccupation with the unprecedented challenge to historical memory posed by the Holocaust. Ceremonies of Holocaust remembrance took priority in shaping the collective memory of this period. Because the most characteristic element of Holocaust, the annihilation of Jewish communities and mass murder, did not take place in North Africa, North African Jews were excluded from this "story," from the collective memory of the period, and in a sense from one of the fundaments of the Israeli ethos.

1984–1997: Research Establishment and Expansion

The third historiographic period opens with Michel Abitbol's *The Jews of North Africa During the Second World War*, originally published in French in 1983.[9] Abitbol had begun his research several years earlier and had published a few articles on the subject. The importance of his research lies in the comparative analysis of all North African countries and his thematic overview. Another milestone, published the same year, was a three-volume series in the journal *Pe'amim* that surveyed all Oriental Jewish communities during World War II.[10] This work served as the database for high school curricula in Israel.

The recognition by the Israeli academy of North African Jewry as a scholarly subject was a crucial factor in the development of the historiography. One reason for this recognition is that by the end of the 1980s Holocaust research had reached a point of maturity; there was a consensus about most of the mechanisms and ideology responsible for the extermination of Jews. The time was thus ripe for other avenues of research to open up—or in the words of the editors of *Pe'amim*, there was reason for "pushing the boundaries of the Holocaust." Understanding what happened during the war outside Europe therefore became important, especially to scholars born in North Africa.

At around this same time, Israeli public opinion began to open up to the challenges of including Sephardim and Mizrahim in the main narratives of what can be called the Israeli story. Accordingly, North African Jews in Israel began to explore their past as part of the coalescing Israeli master narrative. Most of the important research on Jews in Muslim countries in general and on our subject in particular was carried out during this period.

The first results of this resurgent scholarship began to be published in the middle of the twentieth century. For the first time, scholars could rely on a comparative picture of events across different countries. In addition, we had high-quality scholarship on specific subjects, such as the Jewish underground in Algeria, the Italian attitude toward Jews (mainly in Tunisia), and the conduct of the Jewish leadership. The Center for the Heritage of Oriental Jews in the Ministry of Education, created in 1976, became an important source of support that fed the flourishing of research in this area.

During this period, North African Jews in Israel were trying to find their place in Israeli society. Thus the main topics of the collective memory were their contributions to Zionism, to illegal immigration, to self-defense, and to tragedy as an anchor of this memory. The Holocaust as a subject in collective memory was pushed aside.

From an academic point of view, this period ends with the publication of Yad Vashem's *Pinkas Hakehilot: Encyclopedia of the Jewish Communities from Their Foundation Until After the Holocaust.*[11] This was the first attempt to describe the history of Jewish communities in Libya and Tunisia; the Holocaust was not the main focus but was treated as just a part of the chronological history. The decision not to include Vichy-controlled Algeria and Morocco in *Pinkas Hakehilot* was based on the academic perception that the events in those countries were different from those in Libya and Tunisia, where Germany and Italy ruled directly. The inclusion of North Africa in *Pinkas Hakehilot*, the first publication of the most important memorial institute of the Holocaust in Israel, meant that the Jews of these communities were understood to have been part of the Holocaust. Yad Vashem in effect determined the borders of the Holocaust. From that time on, Yad Vashem became deeply involved in various aspects of research, exhibitions, conferences, and the like concerning these North African communities.

1997–2009: Increase in Public Interest and Contraction of Research

The fourth historiographic period is characterized by an overall contraction of the field, as the teaching of the humanities in Israeli universities, as elsewhere, lost ground to science and technology. Courses concerning Sephardi and Maghrebi communities diminished, as did the number of doctoral students who chose to study these subjects. Many thought that the main historical sources had been explored. But countertrends were emerging at the same time.

One such countertrend was fueled by a growing public interest in efforts by Jewish organizations—along with the involvement of President Bill Clinton and the U.S. Congress—to compensate Jews for property confiscated during the Holocaust. The Israeli laws regarding compensation for Holocaust survivors for the first time included Jews from Libya and Tunisia. Another counterpressure came about as a function of the fact that, at the turn of twenty-first century, Jews who had emigrated to Israel in the 1950s were reaching an age at which they felt it was their last opportunity to tell their stories.

A side effect of the American role in helping Jews recover their property was the pressure the United States applied to European governments to allow greater access to their archives. The French accordingly changed the relevant laws to allow more access to files from World War II. The results were a boon to scholars researching such topics as Jewish daily life, daily life in the camps, gender issues, and relations with non-Jewish society.

I posit 2009 as the terminus of this period because it was the year in which the important conference "North Africa and Its Jews in the Second World War" (July 13–24, 2009), organized by the United States Holocaust Memorial Museum, was held. This conference marked the end of one period and the beginning of another.[12] It was the first conference focused solely on North African Jewry (and not on Sephardim) and the first to devote an entire two weeks to the subject; in addition, although it was not the first time that scholars from North Africa were part of an academic meeting, the conference represented the first time such scholars played an essential and dominant role in a larger conversation.

2009–2017: New Tendencies

The past decade is characterized by new research trends among scholars from North Africa. One important development was the establishment in 2006 of the Documentation Center of North African Jewry During World War II at the Ben-Zvi Institute; the center was created to raise public, educational, and academic awareness of the lesser known story of North African Jews during the Holocaust. Seventy years after the end of World War II, collected materials are being uploaded for availability to the general public. North African scholars took part in a conference organized by the Société d'Histoire des Juifs de Tunisie in Paris. The fact that only Moroccan and Tunisian scholars participated in this meeting underscores the local governments' positive but sensitive attitude toward their Jewish history and heritage, unlike other North African countries.

The current period is characterized by a new tendency among institutions and organizations to deal forthrightly with the subject of the Holocaust. I mention in particular the United States Holocaust Memorial Museum (in Washington, D.C.), Yad Vashem (in Jerusalem), and Le Mémorial de la Shoah (in Paris). These distinguished institutions are collecting documents, organizing workshops and conferences, and encouraging scholars to research the topic. Universities have taken the initiative to organize conferences or to publish research. The academy's support of this tendency is of great importance, as is the support of the Claims Conference, the Israeli Parliament, and other organizations.

The recent decade has also seen an outpouring of documentary films and movies on the subject, just a few of which are the documentaries *A Matter of Time* (dir. Marco Carmel, 2005; Hebrew and English), *Tunisian Heroes of the Holocaust* (dir. Robert Satloff, 2011), and *Les juifs d'Afrique du Nord pendant la Seconde Guerre mondiale* (dir. Claude Santiago, 2015); and the movies *Le chant des mariées* (dir. Karin Albou, 2008), *Villa Jasmin* (dir. Férid Boughedir, 2008), *Les hommes libres* (dir. Ismael Ferroukhi, 2011), *Victor "Young" Perez* (dir. Jacques Ouaniche, 2013), and *Credulous Night* (dir. Rami Kimchi, 2015; Hebrew and French).

As a result of the increasing interest in the Holocaust, including its shaping in North Africa, we are facing a new wave of the publication of wartime diaries. Apart from the diaries published just after war, we have three others: Paul Sebag's *Communistes de Tunisie, 1939–1943: souvenirs et documents*, Jacob André Guez's *Au camp de Bizerte*, and Clément Houri's *L'occupation de la Tunisie*.[13] These three publications represent three different individuals' perspectives, feelings, and thoughts during this period. Political activist Sebag deals with the communist party in Tunis during World War II but also gives attention to French, Jewish, and Tunisian political activists. Guez's diary, on the other hand, is a close and sensitive description of daily life in the camp of Bizerte. Houri's perspective is different. He explores daily life during the occupation—problems such as meeting basic daily needs, how to get to work, dealing with electricity outages, and surviving the bombing of Tunis.

One contemporary historiographic tendency is to reopen and revisit topics that had been presumed closed. For example, the question of camps in North Africa demands further research, mainly because of the dearth of documentation. The chapters by Aomar Boum and Susan Slyomovics in the present book (Chapters 7 and 4, respectively) exemplify this new research direction, using sources such as personal diaries, websites, and recent information regarding compensation. The differences among the camps in various countries of North Africa—with respect to location, conditions, purposes, population, and duration—are significant, as are the differences between them and the camps in Europe. But the most important distinction is that, except for the camps in Tunisia, the North African camps were not established exclusively for Jews, whereas in Europe all the camps were primarily for Jews. Even in Tunisia, there were only forced labor camps, and most of them cannot really be called camps. We know neither the number nor the demographic character of the Jews who were interned at the camps. Boum's research has uncovered the remarkable diary of a Muslim, Mohamed Arezki Berkani, who was interned at the camp of Djenien-Bou-Rezg in Algeria. As far as I know, this is the only diary of a North African non-Jew ever found or published. The Bedeau camp was also unique because it was reserved for young Algerian Jews who served in the French army, not for all Algerian Jews. The two chapters by Boum and Slyomovics illustrate the problematic nature and challenges surrounding the topic of North African camps and the need for careful research.

Another example of the expansion of research subjects is the chapter by Boum and Mohammed Hatimi in this collection (Chapter 5), regarding Jewish-Muslim relations during the war in rural southern Morocco—that is, the periphery of a peripheral area of a peripheral issue in the history of the Jews in Morocco. As the first attempt to deal with this subject, the chapter demonstrates the willingness of North African scholars to push research in new directions.

Conclusions

We are now in the last moment when the possibility of obtaining eye-witness testimony from Jews, Muslims, and French who lived during the World War II period can still give their accounts. Although these testimonies are likely biased, their collection should be carried out, and urgently. We have the advantage of excellent archives of this unique period and an increasing public interest in the subject, driven in large part by second- and third-generation descendants of those who lived during this era. Among universities, academic centers, institutions, and organizations with an interest in the Holocaust in general, there is now an increasing awareness of the subject of North African Jewry during World War II. However, the small number of scholars dealing with this subject throughout the entire world is still notable. Hence it is important to encourage institutions to pay more attention to the cultivation and support of young researchers and to coordinate the exchange of knowledge among scholars.

14

A Memory That Is Not One

Michael Rothberg

IN *MONOLINGUALISM OF THE OTHER*, the philosopher Jacques Derrida uses the lens of language to explore what it means to have lived through the contradictions of French-Jewish-Algerian existence in the twentieth century. One of the refrains of Derrida's reflections is the phrase, "I only have one language; it is not mine."[1] The stakes of this initially mysterious paradox become clear as Derrida situates his account in the trajectory of Algerian Jewish experience from the Crémieux Decree, which granted indigenous Jews French citizenship in 1870, through the Vichy anti-Jewish statutes, which revoked that citizenship seventy years later.[2] Many Algerian Jews embraced the late-nineteenth-century invitation to become French, and by the time of Derrida's youth had—at least according to the philosopher—"lost" previously native languages such as Arabic and Berber and fallen into a half-chosen, half-imposed French monolingualism.[3] This affiliation with French language and culture was then violently severed by the Vichy statutes, which not only rendered Jews stateless but also expelled young members of the community like Derrida from the French educational system.

The application of Vichy's anti-Jewish statutes to Algerian Jews—and in different ways to Jews in other zones of the French empire, including Tunisia, Morocco, and even French West Africa—should not be surprising. Most of Algeria, after all, was a department of France at the time, and the colonial territories were central to France's self-understanding as an imperial power. Yet, as the present book documents, the North African (not to mention sub-Saharan African) contexts of World War II and the

Holocaust have rarely figured in accounts of the persecution and genocide of Jews.

The Holocaust and North Africa sets out to readjust our sense of the geography of the genocide and to bring attention to the histories and experiences that have never been a central part of the scholarship on, and collective memory of, the Holocaust. Paraphrasing Derrida, we might say, from the perspective of North African Jews, "I only have one memory; it is not mine." The "one memory" of the Holocaust that has existed is the memory of the persecution of *European* (and primarily *Ashkenazi*) Jews: a memory that is not in any way singular across the length and breadth of Europe but that over the decades has nevertheless consolidated into a coherent story with a global reach. That memory can only have been an awkward affair for Jews, like Derrida, with North African origins and direct experiences of fascism.

From the vantage point of late writings such as *Monolingualism of the Other* and "Circumfession," we can speculate that Derrida's multiply marginal location—as a member of an ambiguously situated minority in a colonized country—became a conceptual resource for his critical examination of the relation between centers and margins of political, intellectual, and cultural power. Deconstruction, Derrida's most well known philosophical innovation, offers a mode of reading that both recognizes the power of the center—along with the histories and memories that help shore it up and that it helps to shore up in return—and unsettles that power by revealing its reliance on what is only apparently marginal. The margins, in Derrida's thought, become a site for the radical reexamination of what is taken for granted. Such a critical examination from the margins is precisely what is called for and undertaken by the editors and contributors of *The Holocaust and North Africa*.

This volume offers, first and foremost, a rich collection of essays that challenge us to think in new ways about the Nazi genocide and its relation to colonialism, fascism, collaboration, resistance, and military occupation, among other topics. Before returning to the question of how the contributions here might help us unsettle the center and margins of our understanding of the Holocaust, it is important to point out that most of the essays are written in a historicist mode and offer fine-grained analyses of German, French, and Italian policies along with the ways that Jewish and Muslim North Africans experienced and responded to those policies across a remarkably diverse range of national and colonial contexts. In addition, a smaller number of essays, those by Aomar Boum, Lia Brozgal, and Alma Heckman, along with the editors' introduction, reflect on the cultural representation and memory of the events at stake. Brozgal (Chapter 8) especially draws our attention to the particular resources that literature and film can bring to bear on our understanding of the rich historical and anthropological insights of the other essays. As a literary critic with a special interest in memory, I find myself inspired by the new conceptualizations of history that become possible when we view events and their implications through the lens of cultural texts, including those of a figure such as Derrida.[4]

Because this volume takes up a topic long considered marginal to the understanding of the Nazi genocide, it is not surprising that the thematics of center and margin that are so important for Derrida also appear frequently in these essays. For our contributors, center and margin are spatial categories that they sometimes mobilize in a "literal" fashion. Location can matter enormously in the ways that histories play out: For example, Boum and Mohammed Hatimi point to the specificity of the historical experiences of the southern regions of Morocco in relation to the urban centers (Chapter 5), and the Algerian and Moroccan borderlands are mentioned as sites of porous Jewish identities in Daniel Schroeter's essay (Chapter 1).

Frequently this geography of centers and margins is overlaid with metaphorical meanings that indicate relations of geopolitical power in contexts of colonialism. These are often but not always Manichean relations between colonizers and the colonized. In the context of colonialism and occupation, the center-margin relation is a social and political fact, the outcome of hierarchical power relations. Yet one of the strengths of this volume is the way the contributors repeatedly draw attention to differences within the two sides of that only apparently fixed binary. On the side of the colonizers, for instance, Daniel Lee addresses the struggle that takes place between metropolitan officials in the center and the colonial administrators of the margins over how to define and enact policy towards Jews (Chapter 6). The category of the colonized is similarly shifting and tension-laden in North Africa, as Derrida's own work shows, because indigenous Jews sometimes experienced privileges that were not afforded to their Muslim compatriots, as with the Crémieux Decree; but in the context of fascism indigenous Jews were also exceptionally vulnerable to the loss of rights (and worse).

Some of the essays suggest the need not only to complicate but also to dismantle oppositions such as center and margin. For instance, Alma

Heckman cites Edmond Amran El Maleh's notion of the "game of complex margins" that has always existed in the interstices of the binary dynamics of power (Chapter 9). Although such a contribution is not offered in the philosophical vocabulary of Derrida's texts, it similarly highlights the privilege of the marginal perspective. In Heckman's words, "From each marginal story a clearer picture of the whole emerges."

The relation of (small) part to whole identified by Heckman also suggests the related importance of *scale* in this volume. One of the (many) challenges of writing about the Holocaust—along with other traumatic histories—is the problem of scale: How do we conceptualize or represent racial persecution and the perpetration of mass death as they unfold across vast geographies and over months and years? As a theater of the Holocaust, North Africa is both geographically marginal to the centers of policy making and extermination and also relatively small in terms of the number of Jews affected (though the geographic area is of course imposing). Some of the essays here take this problem of scale as an opportunity to rethink the status of historical evidence. For instance, Ruth Ginio foregrounds the epistemic possibilities of thinking the whole through small numbers in her account of how Vichy officials in the federation of French West Africa sought to expel Jews from certain professions (Chapter 3).

Compared with the horrors that European Jews experienced during World War II, the dismissal of a few Jews seems almost insignificant. But it is precisely the small number of the potential victims of the Vichy laws and the distance of [French West Africa] from the main theaters of World War II that highlight the obsessive nature of the Vichy regime in its persecution of Jews. In a time of severe crisis, when two-thirds of the metropolitan territory was under Nazi occupation, the Vichy authorities were concerned with a Jewish banker in the Ivory Coast and a Jewish lawyer in French Guinea. (p. 90)

Such a shift of scale from the small, minor, distant, and marginal to the preoccupations of the center bears a certain resemblance to Derrida's own strategies in *Monolingualism of the Other*. Derrida starts from a historical peculiarity—the experience of being a "Franco-Maghrebian" Jew—and derives from it certain structural features of language, such as the further paradox, "We only ever speak one language. . . . We never speak only one language."[5] The thrust of Derrida's paradoxical thinking is to move beyond a notion of language as property, as something a speaking subject could "own" or "possess." Can these propositions also shed light on the problems of memory and history at stake in this volume? Can we think about the Holocaust and North Africa beyond the logic of property and possession?

The dynamics of centers and margins, parts and wholes, small and large scales are indeed central to the question of the Holocaust and North Africa, but the answers they provoke are not necessarily simple or straightforward. That is, the essays here stand on their own as contributions to the understanding of the Nazi period, Vichy, and late colonialism in North Africa, but it remains to determine what "whole" they sketch when taken together. In Derridean deconstruction, two logical moves are necessary: first, a reversal that privileges the marginal concept over the central one; and second, a dispersal that rewrites the entire terrain beyond the terms of the opposition. In approaching a topic as understudied (relatively) as the Holocaust and North Africa, it is natural for the first tendency to predominate: Assert the centrality of what had been marginal, and claim the experience of North African Jews and societies as "proper" to the Holocaust.

The essays in this volume sometimes make such a move, but my sense is that they are ultimately at their best when they shift to another, less singular terrain, that is, when they do not simply try to write their way into the Holocaust narrative but also ask us to reconsider what *other*, less hegemonic frames might be available for thinking about North Africa during World War II. The experience of anti-Semitic policies, the loss of social positions, the harsh realities of forced labor and detention camps, and (in a small number of cases) deportation to Nazi camps are all elements of North African Jewish life and death during the war that should be included in the larger history of the Holocaust. But the most striking aspects of these histories lie, I believe, elsewhere: They reveal a layering of histories that are not "one," that are not singular, but rather, in my terms, multidirectional.[6]

What emerges most powerfully in this volume is not just the addition of new spaces to the history of the Holocaust, though this is also a significant contribution. Instead, what I take away is a more concrete understanding of the interaction of fascism and colonialism and the place of Jewish and Muslim communities within that dynamic.[7] Susan Slyomovics (Chapter 4) captures this interaction powerfully when—drawing on Arendt's genealogy of totalitarianism in colonial bureaucracy and racism—she describes how, in the context of war, "the violence of French military culture in Algeria was intensified by Vichy-era fascism expanded to the overseas North African colonies against those racially classed by the colonial bureaucracy as *indigènes* or 'natives,' a term perennially applied to the Muslim and temporarily, between 1940 and 1943, to the Jew" (p. 96). Schroeter (Chapter 1) makes a similarly crucial point when he concludes that, "as implemented in North Africa, Vichy's Jewish policy is legible only in the colonial context. Seen on a longer continuum, Vichy's anti-Semitic legislation was integral to French colonialism, embedded in the racial policy toward both Muslims and Jews across North Africa that both predated and followed the war" (p. 48). The unfolding of the war in North Africa, in other words, becomes a point of inflection between different historical trajectories of race and violence that cannot be entirely subsumed in the category "Holocaust."

In drawing our attention to this process of inflection, Slyomovics and Schroeter, along with others in this volume, direct us toward a project that is at once historically rich and intensely *current*. Most crucially, they bring Jews and Muslims into the same frame, describe comparative racial dynamics that are both historically embedded and dramatically malleable, and offer a model of how fascist and imperial politics interact and intensify each other. In a world that continues to be marked by colonial and imperial logics and that is also seeing the rise of movements that can be described as postfascist, the histories recovered here take on great urgency.[8] I do not believe we should attempt to collapse those recovered histories into a singular account of the Holocaust; nor should we read the present straightforwardly out of the experience of Nazi genocide. Rather, reading from the margins reveals an entangled, multidirectional history of fascism and colonialism that is not "one" and cannot be "owned" by any discipline or field but whose legacies nonetheless reach, unevenly and sometimes uncannily, into the present.

15

Intersectional Methodologies in Holocaust Studies

Todd Presner

NEARLY THREE DECADES AGO, Saul Friedländer organized a major conference at UCLA in which he asked a number of historians, philosophers, and literary scholars to reflect on the limits of representing the Holocaust.[1] Prompted by the controversy over Hayden White's theories of history, which Friedländer and others perceived to erase the boundary between fact and fiction, thereby leading to Holocaust revisionism and negationism, the conference attendees set out to examine how postmodernism challenged "the realities and truths of the Holocaust," or for that matter, any "stable truth as far as this past [the Final Solution] is concerned."[2] For Friedländer and other historians, such as Pierre Vidal-Naquet and Carlo Ginzburg, the truth and reality of the Holocaust must be upheld so that historians can establish and maintain its factuality. Postmodernism—considered by Friedländer to be the "rejection of the possibility of identifying some stable reality or truth beyond the constant polysemy and self-referentiality of linguistic constructs"[3]—seemed to deny this possibility and therefore opened the door to Holocaust deniers.

For White, however, historical narratives, like literary narratives, are foremost problems of emplotment, and all authors choose various kinds of narrative strategies, tropes, and modes of figuration to construct their objects of study. These narratives, White suggests, gain relative traction, cogency, and sometimes even canonicity in particular times for particular people and in particular situations. Departing from the claim that there is "an inexpungeable relativity in every representation of historical phenomena," White argues that injunctions of "realism" in the representation of events such as the Holocaust may be "inadequate" precisely because of the "modernist" nature of the Holocaust, by which he means its scale, scope, and resistance to conventional, realistic, storylike structures of emplotment.[4] For White, the Holocaust did not set any a priori "limits" on acceptable or unacceptable modes of its representation; rather, it gave rise to new, modernist representational strategies, some of which, like the writings of W. G. Sebald or Georges Perec, blurred the boundaries between the fictive and the factual. Although these anxieties may seem somewhat dated, particularly in light of the impact that literature, memoir, and film have had on creating a public Holocaust consciousness and on creating vital forms of transgenerational memory,[5] the debates over representation unleashed in the formative years of "Holocaust studies" played a critical role in both establishing and defending the contours of the discipline's object of study: the Holocaust.

As the tenor of these particular debates softened over the years, the positions of the two protagonists (Friedländer and White) appeared to move closer and closer together.[6] In fact, Friedländer would describe his own modes of historical emplotment in his magnum opus, *The Years of Extermination* (2007), as inspired by modernist literary and filmic techniques (such as montage, cutting and splicing, spatiotemporal dilations, and a multiplicity of voices and perspectives); however, he still insisted on the centrality of the archive and was steadfast in his refusal to blur the distinction between literature and history.[7] His goal was to evoke a sense of disbelief in his readers, "a kind of cognitive dissonance . . . [that refuses] to domesticate the unbelievable," something he detects in more conventional (linear and causal) historical narratives.[8] At the same time, White's own position—far from negationism or denial—evolved to stress the significance of the "practical past," that is, the ethical and moral dimensions of historical writing after "all of the factual information contained in the historical record" has been collected.[9]

In 2012, UCLA hosted a follow-up conference, "History Unlimited: Probing the Ethics of Holocaust Culture," to take stock of the salient controversies and debates that had shaped the prior two decades of Holocaust studies.[10] In the years following the first conference, the field not only had matured and diversified but also had expanded to include a second generation of scholars who no longer felt confined by the historical impulse to establish "the limits of representation" or to exorcise the specter of relativism. Instead, they were interested in comparative approaches to Holocaust studies that expanded the range of geographic, historical, and media dimensions of its study in ways that raised new methodological approaches, reimagined the archive, and proliferated narrative frameworks. The organizers of the second conference were particularly interested in capturing and scrutinizing some of the key debates surrounding the "exceptionality" of the Holocaust as a unique historical event using the methodological and disciplinary tools of comparative genocide studies and postcolonial studies.[11]

Friedländer's original volume *Probing the Limits of Representation* sought to assess narrative limits with regard to the representation of the Holocaust. In contrast, the follow-up volume (*Probing the Ethics of Holocaust Culture*, edited by Fogu, Kansteiner, and Presner) sought, among other things, to interrogate assumptions about the spatial and temporal limits of the Holocaust and thereby open up new historiographic strategies that linked the events of the Holocaust more broadly to the operative methodologies of postcolonial studies. Of course, it was Hannah Arendt who argued almost seven decades ago that Nazism was linked both spatially and temporally with imperialism and colonialism: spatially, because its conquest and occupation policy of the East was colonial; and temporally, because it drew on—experientially, epistemologically, and imaginatively—the broad European experiences that wed racism, bureaucracy, and mass murder in the colonization of the African continent in the late nineteenth century.[12] Significantly, it took nearly half a century for Arendt's theses to be taken up seriously by scholars in the fields of Holocaust and colonial studies, perhaps, as Jürgen Zimmerer speculates, because of highly charged political and emotional reasons that maintain "the singularity of the Holocaust."[13] As of this writing today, the field has burgeoned in numerous ways, with multiple variations of the "colonial paradigm" articulating continuities between European colonialism, European imperialism, and the Holocaust.[14]

The critical methodological interventions used in postcolonial studies and comparative genocide studies interrogate and problematize longstanding assumptions about the temporal and spatial boundaries of the Holocaust. Their scholars use narrative strategies that emphasize a broad range of continuities and discontinuities, multiple sites of contact, overlapping atrocities, and entangled histories and memories that move in more than one direction at once.[15] With regard to continuities, it is now generally accepted, as Alon Confino argues, that "the Holocaust cannot be understood without consideration of European colonialism," precisely because it became "thinkable" after the annihilation of millions of people by the colonial-imperial regimes set up by the British, French, Dutch, Belgians, and Germans around the world, and, particularly, the German extermination of the Herero and Namaqua in southwest Africa between 1904 and 1907.[16] Although this explanation is not complete by itself (e.g., it leaves out the long and variegated history of anti-Semitism in Europe), the connections with the history of European imperialism and colonialism in Africa now figure prominently in Holocaust studies, although not always comfortably.[17]

Concomitant with the reassessment of the temporal boundaries of the Holocaust is a reassessment of the spatial boundaries in ways that have shifted scholarly attention to the east and the south. With regard to the eastward shift, Timothy Snyder's *Bloodlands* stands out for its geographic focus on the region most affected by Hitlerism and Stalinism: the bloodlands, which, in today's terms, encompasses the western rim of the Russian Federation, most of Poland, the Baltic States, Belarus, and Ukraine.[18] Through deliberate mass murder, 14 million people were killed by starvation, bullets, or gassings by Nazi Germany and the Soviet Union between 1933 and 1945 in this specific geographic region, a fact that informs Snyder's comparative methodology of leaders, systems, utopian aspirations, ideologies, and violence. More recently, Snyder has expanded the geographic contours to a planetary scale to examine Hitler's idea of German *Lebensraum* in a global context, from the concrete Nazi aspiration to establish a German breadbasket in Ukraine to contemporary manifestations of "ecological panic" in which a state may decide to eliminate an internal or external enemy to preserve its own food supply or agricultural productivity.[19] In so doing, these new spatial and temporal continuities of the Holocaust give rise to an event and method that not only loses its absolute uniqueness but also provides a "practical" warning (to bring in White's ethical approach) for the future.

In line with scholarship on the spatial turn in Holocaust studies, renewed attention is being given to the geographic, spatially differentiated dimensions of the Holocaust, ranging from the expansive geographic concepts deployed by the Nazis (from *Lebensraum* to *Generalplan Ost*) to the experiential spaces occupied by the victims and the contemporary topographies of memory that mark sites of atrocity.[20] Deploying the computational methods of Geographic Information Systems (GIS), scholars and institutions have created extensive databases, maps, and spatial analyses that have begun to reveal relationships, patterns, networks, and pathways at various scales (from the individual body and homes to streets, cities, countries, and regions).[21] Much of this research has been spurred by such fields as geography and digital humanities, both of which bring methods from the margins, so to speak, to account for and interrogate the spatial dimensions of the Holocaust.

In 2015 UCLA hosted a third international Holocaust conference co-organized by two of the editors of this volume, Sarah Abrevaya Stein and Aomar Boum: "On the Margins of the Holocaust: Jews, Muslims, and Colonialism in North Africa During the Second World War."[22] The aim of the conference was to probe the margins (geographic, historiographic, political, and memorial) of the Holocaust by focusing attention on the overlapping experiences of Jews and Muslims in North Africa during World War II and in light of the longer history and aftermath of colonialism. Although many of the basic facts have been established in the scholarly literature,[23] constellated frameworks for comparative analysis are still in their early stages: What methods and approaches can help us think through the significance of the double overlay of fascism and colonialism in North Africa? What was the impact of both World War II and the longer history of colonialism on North African Jews and Muslims? What kinds of historical, cultural, and political narratives have to be developed to understand the differentiated experiences and fate of the nearly half a million Jews in Morocco, Algeria, Tunisia, and Libya, whose lives were affected by the French and Italian racial laws, who had property expropriated, who were professionally and economically disenfranchised, and who variously faced internment and forced labor as the Vichy authorities established labor and concentration camps across the Maghreb and the Sahara? And, finally, with respect to the intellectual and political affiliations of the discipline and institutional formations of Holocaust studies, in the Introduction to this volume the editors ask, How have "European-centered Holocaust studies . . . played a role in marginalizing the North African story?" (p. 8).

Within what we might call conventional (European-centered) Holocaust historiography, North Africa is usually mentioned (if at all) in a few pages. For example, in his seminal study of the Holocaust, Raul Hilberg mentions the effect of the abrogation of the Crémieux Decree on the Jews of Algeria, the effect of racial laws and Aryanization on Jews in Morocco and Tunisia, and the establishment of Vichy labor camps;[24] similarly, Leni

Yahil mentions the effect of the Statut de Juifs on Algerian Jews and the French protectorates in the context of the first systematic assaults against Europe's Jews between 1939 and 1940.[25] David Cesarani discusses the Vichy anti-Jewish laws and the establishment of Vichy forced labor camps, and both he and Peter Longerich state that the Jews of North Africa were, in fact, targets of the Nazis according to the Wannsee Conference protocols,[26] which list 700,000 Jews in the "unoccupied territory" (colonial territories) of France in its calculations.[27] The fate of Jews in North Africa barely figures in other major historical works, such as Christopher Browning's *Origins of the Final Solution* or Saul Friedländer's *Years of Extermination*.

The purpose of the present volume is not simply to reinsert North Africa into standard historical accounts of the Holocaust focused on Europe but rather to ask what can be known when we expand both the geographies affected and the temporal contours of the period to include the times leading up to, during, and after World War II. How might we more fully appreciate, for instance, the expansive reach of Vichy anti-Semitic laws and their imbrication with the long history of colonialism, racism, and bureaucratic administration far beyond continental Europe? To be sure, North African Jews did not suffer systematic mass murder, and the distinctions between their experiences and those of Jews in continental Europe are significant. But by broadening, shifting, and multiplying our historiographic frameworks, as the contributors to this volume show, other experiences—such as the relationships between Jews and Muslims in these doubly occupied zones—come into view and thus give rise to overlapping and entangled histories.[28]

By turning our attention to the intellectual debates, reception, and legacies of these three conferences, something that becomes quite evident is the way in which the seemingly obvious and seemingly fixed concept of the Holocaust has come under tremendous—and tremendously productive—scrutiny. This scrutiny is driven by attempts to explain it, to document its many complex contours, to represent it in various media forms, to comprehend its changing meaning and significance, and to study it using new disciplinary and methodological approaches. As such, it should be no surprise that the current volume builds even further on this tradition of critical scrutiny and research innovation in the field of Holocaust studies. Perhaps we will only understand the full significance of this conference and the resulting volume in the years to come, as the field continues to grow and diversify with significant linkages to North African studies and postcolonial studies. As the debates and interventions contained in this volume variously build on as well as depart from the legacies of the two earlier conferences, we can appreciate not only the dynamism and development of the field of Holocaust studies *writ large* but also the new research questions unlocked by truly intersectional methodologies.

Acknowledgments

This volume arose out of the 2015 conference "On the Margins of the Holocaust: Jews, Muslims, and Colonialism in North Africa During the Second World War," convened at the University of California, Los Angeles, and organized by the United States Holocaust Memorial Museum (USHMM), the UCLA Alan D. Leve Center for Jewish Studies, the UCLA Center for Near Eastern Studies, and the 1939 Society Program in Holocaust Studies at UCLA. Our first debt is to the many people who helped us realize that fruitful event, especially Todd Presner, the Sady and Ludwig Kahn Director of the UCLA Center for Jewish Studies (2010–2018); and Leah Wolfson, senior program officer at the USHMM. We are also grateful to the staff of the Center for Jewish Studies, who enabled the conference to unfold with such efficiency: Vivian Holenbeck, Mary Pinkerson, Saba Soomekh, Chelsea White, and David Wu. Additional thanks are due to Robert M. Ehrenreich, director of University Programs at the USHMM, for his support; the many scholars who participated in the 2015 conference; Paul Shapiro, the former director of the Jack, Joseph, and Morton Mandel Center of Advanced Holocaust Studies at the USHMM; and those who have contributed their work to the current volume.

Our colleagues have been copiously generous with offering additional expertise and insight—reading drafts of our Introduction and consulting with us about the volume and its various maps, images, and details. Our warmest thanks go to Daniel Schroeter, Susan Slyomovics, Omer Bartov, Aron Rodrigue, and Harvey Goldberg in this regard. They were always available when called on, and their contributions are immensely appreciated. At UCLA, we are blessed with wonderful colleagues from whom we have learned so much, including, in addition to those already mentioned, David N. Myers, Chris Silver (now of McGill University), and Alma Heckman (now of the University of California, Santa Cruz).

Various institutions and archives allowed us to reproduce the rare historical images in this book, and we thank them for their courtesy. Bill Nelson produced the maps and is, as ever, a wonderful collaborator. We also thank Geoffrey Megargee at the USHMM for sharing copies of maps from the *United States Holocaust Memorial Museum Encyclopedia of Camps and Ghettos, 1933–1945*, on which some of our maps have been based.

Funding for elements of this volume came from the Maurice Amado Chair in Sephardic Studies at UCLA, the UCLA Academic Senate, and the 1939 Society Program in Holocaust Studies at UCLA, with the generous assistance of the Alan D. Leve Center for Jewish Studies. Our thanks are due to all these parties.

We feel tremendously grateful to be based in California, home to a thriving community of scholars working on Jews and North Africa. A debt is owed to Emily Gottreich and Jessica Marglin for organizing the California Working Group on Jews in the Maghrib and the Middle East (Cal JEMM). The conversations and company fostered by that group are a wonderful asset to us all.

Both of the editors have worked with Kate Wahl, publishing director and editor-in-chief at Stanford University Press, on other projects. With this book, she displayed her trademark professionalism, vision, and care. One could take this for granted, were it not so very rare. Additional appreciation is due to the others at the Press who have lent their expertise and time.

Norma Mendoza Denton and Fred Zimmerman are brilliant partners in crime. Maggie, Ira, and Julius keep us smart and on our toes: thanks, most of all, to that dynamic trio for the best questions, jokes, and company.

Aomar Boum and Sarah Abrevaya Stein

Contributors

OMER BARTOV is the John P. Birkelund Distinguished Professor of European History at Brown University. His many books include *Hitler's Army* (1991), *Mirrors of Destruction* (2000), *Germany's War and the Holocaust* (2003), *The "Jew" in Cinema* (2005), *Erased: Vanishing Traces of Jewish Galicia in Present-Day Ukraine* (2007), and *Anatomy of a Genocide: The Life and Death of a Town Called Buczacz* (2018). He is currently engaged in researching a new book tentatively titled *Israel, Palestine: A Personal Political History.*

AOMAR BOUM is Associate Professor in the Department of Anthropology at the University of California, Los Angeles. He is interested in the place of religious minorities, such as Jews, Baha'is, Shias, and Christians, in post-independence Middle Eastern and North African nation-states. He is the author of *Memories of Absence: How Muslims Remember Jews in Morocco* (2013). Boum is currently finishing a book on the Baha'i question in Morocco and, with Daniel J. Schroeter, a book on Sultan Sidi Mohammed Ben Youssef, Jews, and Holocaust politics in Morocco.

LIA BROZGAL is Associate Professor of French and Francophone Studies at the University of California, Los Angeles, where she is also affiliated with the Leve Center for Jewish Studies and the graduate program in African studies. She is the author of *Against Autobiography: Albert Memmi and the Production of Theory* (2013); co-editor of *Being Contemporary: French Literature, Culture, and Politics Today* (2016): and co-editor of the first English-language translation of *Ninette of Sin Street*, a Tunisian novella by Vitalis Danon (2017). Her work has been recognized by the University of California President's Faculty Fellowship (2012–2013), the Camargo Foundation Scholar-in-Residence Program (2014), and the American Council of Learned Societies Fellowship (2015–2016).

RUTH GINIO is Associate Professor in the Department of History at Ben-Gurion University of the Negev and Director of the Inter-University Program for African Studies. Her current research project is murder investigations in French West Africa. She is the author of two books: *The French Army and Its African Soldiers: The Years of Decolonization* (2017) and *French Colonialism Unmasked: The Vichy Years in French West Africa* (2006). She has co-edited with Efrat Ben–Ze'ev and Jay Winter a volume titled *Shadows of War: A Social History of Silence in the 20th Century* (2007). Between 2010 and 2012 she served as the president of the French Colonial Historical Society.

MOHAMMED HATIMI is Professor of Modern History in the Faculty of Letters, Université Sidi Mohamed Ben Abdellah, Fès-Sais. His work explores the Jewish community of Morocco and the nationalist movement. His unpublished doctoral dissertation is titled "Moroccan Jewish Communities and the Difficult Choice Between Zionism and Moroccan Independence, 1947–1961" (in Arabic).

ALMA HECKMAN is Neufeld-Levin Chair of Holocaust Studies and Assistant Professor of History and Jewish Studies at the University of California, Santa Cruz. She specializes in modern Jewish history of North Africa and the Middle East with an interest in citizenship, the politics of belonging, transnationalism, and empire. She is currently at work on a book tentatively titled *Radical Nationalists: Moroccan Jewish Communists, 1925–1975*.

JENS HOPPE received his doctorate from the University of Muenster in 2001. Since 2001, he has worked as a historian for the New York City–based Conference on Jewish Material Claims Against Germany at their Office for Germany in Frankfurt am Main. He has conducted research on, among other topics, the persecution of Jews in Bulgaria, North Africa, and Yugoslavia during World War II, Judaica held by museums, Jewish museums, looted art, and provenance research.

DANIEL LEE is a Vice-Chancellor's Fellow in the Department of History at the University of Sheffield. Before joining Sheffield in 2015, Lee was a British Academy postdoctoral fellow at Brasenose College, Oxford. He is the author of *Pétain's Jewish Children: French Jewish Youth and the Vichy Regime, 1940–1942* (2014). He has held fellowships at the Institute of Historical Research, the European University Institute, Yad Vashem, and the United States Holocaust Memorial Museum. As a BBC Radio 3 New Generation Thinker, Lee is a regular broadcaster on radio.

SUSAN GILSON MILLER is Professor in the Department of History at the University of California, Davis. She specializes in North African history. Her publications include *The History of Modern Morocco* (2013), *Berbers and Others: Beyond Tribe and Nation in the Maghrib* (2010), *The Architecture and Memory of the Minority Quarter of the Muslim Mediterranean City* (2010), and *Disorienting Encounters: Travels of a Moroccan Scholar in France in 1845–1846* (1992). Her current project is a study of the refugee crisis in Morocco during World War II.

TODD PRESNER is Ross Professor of Germanic Languages and Comparative Literature at the University of California, Los Angeles. His recent publications are *HyperCities: Thick Mapping in the Digital Humanities* (2014), with David Shepard and Yoh Kawano, and *Probing the Ethics of Holocaust Culture* (2016), co-edited with Claudio Fogu and Wulf Kansteiner.

MICHAEL ROTHBERG is the 1939 Society Samuel Goetz Chair in Holocaust Studies and Professor of English and Comparative Literature at the University of California, Los Angeles. His latest book is *Multidirectional Memory: Remembering the Holocaust in the Age of Decolonization* (2009). He is also the author of *Traumatic Realism: The Demands of Holo-*

caust Representation (2000) and has co-edited *The Holocaust: Theoretical Readings* (2003). He is currently completing *The Implicated Subject: Beyond Victims and Perpetrators* and *Inheritance Trouble: Migrant Archives of Holocaust Remembrance* (with Yasemin Yildiz).

HAIM SAADOUN is Dean of Academic Studies at the Open University, Director of the Center for Documentation on North African Jewry During World War II at the Ben-Zvi Institute for the Study of Jewish Communities in the East in Jerusalem, and founding editor of the book series Jewish Communities in the East in the Nineteenth and Twentieth Centuries at the Ben-Zvi Institute in Jerusalem. He received the Gaon Prize for research on North African Jewish heritage and the President's Prize in honor of President Yitzhak Ben-Zvi for research on the Jewish communities of the Middle East. His recent publications include essays in *Pe'amim* and *The Journal of Clement Houri* (2011), a first-person account of the Nazi occupation of Tunis during World War II.

DANIEL J. SCHROETER is the Amos S. Deinard Memorial Chair in Jewish History at the University of Minnesota. He is author of *The Sultan's Jew: Morocco and the Sephardi World* (2002) and *Merchants of Essaouira: Urban Society and Imperialism in Southwestern Morocco, 1844–1886* (1988) and co-editor of *Jewish Culture and Society in North Africa* (2011). He was the 2014–2015 Ina Levine Scholar-in-Residence at the Jack, Joseph, and Morton Mandel Center for Advanced Holocaust Studies of the United States Holocaust Memorial Museum, and the Shoshana Shier Distinguished Visiting Professor, Center for Jewish Studies, at the University of Toronto in fall 2016.

SUSAN SLYOMOVICS is Distinguished Professor of Anthropology and Near Eastern Languages and Cultures at the University of California, Los Angeles. Her current research project is on the fates of French colonial monuments in Algeria. She is editor of several volumes and the author of *How to Accept German Reparations* (2014), *The Performance of Human Rights in Morocco* (2005), and *The Object of Memory: Arab and Jew Narrate the Palestinian Village* (1998).

SARAH ABREVAYA STEIN is Professor of History and Maurice Amado Chair in Sephardic Studies at the University of California, Los Angeles. A Guggenheim Fellow, her award-winning books include *Extraterritorial Dreams: European Citizenship, Sephardi Jews, and the Ottoman Twentieth Century* (2016), *Saharan Jews and the Fate of French Algeria* (2014), *Sephardi Lives: A Documentary History, 1700–1950* (edited with Julia Phillips Cohen, 2014), and *Plumes: Ostrich Feathers, Jews, and a Lost World of Global Commerce* (2008), available in a 2018 Arabic translation by the University of Mohammed V Press, with translation by Khalid Bensrhir.

SUSAN RUBIN SULEIMAN is the C. Douglas Dillon Research Professor of the Civilization of France and Research Professor of Comparative Literature at Harvard University. Her many books and edited volumes include *The Némirovsky Question: The Life, Death, and Legacy of a Jewish Writer in 20th-Century France* (2016), *French Global: A New Approach to Literary History* (2010), and *Crises of Memory and the Second World War* (2006). In addition to her scholarly work, Suleiman is the author of *Budapest Diary: In Search of the Motherbook* (1996), a memoir about Hungary.

Notes

Notes to Introduction

1. Mohamed Berkani, "Anouar Benmalek: "La Shoah a un peu commencé en Afrique avec les Hereros," *Géopolis* (August 28, 2015), http://geopolis.francetvinfo.fr/anouar-benmalek-la -shoah-a-un-peu-commence-en-afrique-avec-les-hereros-76463 (accessed November 2, 2016); English translation by authors. It is possible that the work of Boualem Sansal initiated the trend with his widely acclaimed *Le village de l'Allemand*.

2. See also "Littérature—Anouar Benmalek: 'En Afrique, il y a un déficit de mémoire," *Jeune Afrique* (August 24, 2015), www.jeuneafrique.com/mag/255284/culture/litterature-anouar -benmalek-en-afrique-il-y-a-un-deficit-de-memoire/ (accessed March 20, 2018); and "From the Shoah to the Herero Genocide: A Singular Journey for an Arab Writer Anouar Benmalek, May 2016," blog post (June 2, 2016), anouarbenmalek.blogspot.com/2016/06/from-shoah-to -herero-genocide-singular_2.html (accessed November 2, 2016).

3. For an exploration of this intellectual genealogy, see, for example, Cheyette, *Diasporas of the Mind*; Rothberg, *Multidirectional Memory*; and Slyomovics, *German Reparations*, esp. ch. 7. Exploration of the historical links between colonial violence and the Holocaust have been plentiful; see, for example, Baranowski, *Nazi Empire*; Hull, *Absolute Destruction*; Kossler, *Namibia and Germany*; Moses, "Holocaust and Colonialism," 68–80; Moses and Stone, *Colonialism and Genocide*; Olusoga and Erichsen, *Kaiser's Holocaust*; Traverso, *Origins of Nazi Violence*; Zimmerer, "Colonialism and the Holocaust"; and Zimmerer and Zeller, *Genocide*.

4. Schreier, *Arabs of the Jewish Faith*; Katz, *Burdens of Brotherhood*. For an exception to the trend, see Stein, *Saharan Jews*.

5. Marglin, *Across Legal Lines*; Lewis, *Divided Rule*.

6. Crespil, *Mogador*.

7. Laskier, *North African Jewry*; Ansky, *Juifs d'Algérie*.

8. Oliel, *Camps de Vichy*.

9. Klarsfeld, *Memorial to the Jews*.

10. This is an intentionally and inevitably partial list, as would be any single attempt to account for the diversity of Holocaust histories and scholarship. Work referenced herein includes Garbarini, *Numbered Days*; Dreyfus, *Impossible réparation*; Vincent, *Hitler's Silent Partners*; Lower, *Nazi Empire Building*; Fleming, *Greece*; Confino, *World Without Jews*; and Lipschitz, *Franco*.

11. Rothberg, *Multidirectional Memory*.

12. We contrast here two dialogic edited volumes, the first canonical and the second a newly published "bookend" to the first: Friedländer, *Probing the Limits of Representation*; and Fogu et al., *Probing the Ethics of Holocaust Culture*.

13. See, especially, Knowles and Jaskot, "Mapping the SS Concentration Camps."

14. Despite the increasing number of publications on the Holocaust and the Arab world, the impact of World War II on Middle Eastern societies requires more scholarly attention. For studies on the Holocaust and the Arab world, see Herf, *Nazi Propaganda*; Nicosia, *Nazi Germany*; Wien, "Coming to Terms"; Nordbruch, "Cultural Fusion"; Gershoni and Jankowski, *Confronting Fascism*; and Gershoni, *Arab Responses*. On recent public debates on the Holocaust in the Arab world, see Litvak and Webman, *From Empathy to Denial*; and Achkar, *Arabs and the Holocaust*.

15. This volume finds dialogue with a number of events focused on the history of the Holocaust in southeastern Europe and North Africa, regions little covered by the Holocaust canon thus far. These include the 1999 "Sephardic and Oriental Holocaust Workshop" sponsored by the United States Holocaust Memorial Museum (USHMM); lectures by Aron Rodrigue on Sephardim and the Holocaust delivered at the 2004 Ina Levine Annual Lecture at the USHMM and at the 2005 Samuel and Althea Stroum lectures for the University of Washington; the April 2003 conference "Sephardic Jewry and the Holocaust: the Future of the Field," held at the University of Washington and co-sponsored by the USHMM; the June 2009 conference "North Africa and Its Jews in the Second World War," convened by the USHMM; the June 2015 workshop "Historical Comprehension and Moral Judgment of World War II and the Holocaust: The View from North Africa—Morocco, Algeria, Tunisia, and Libya," sponsored by the Hebrew University, Jerusalem; and the UCLA event from which the current volume is derived, "On the Margins of the Holocaust: Jews, Muslims, and Colonialism in North Africa During the Second World War," organized by the USHMM, the UCLA Alan D. Leve Center for Jewish Studies, the UCLA Center for Near Eastern Studies, and the 1939 Society at UCLA.

16. Lower, *Hitler's Furies*, 78.

17. Ofer, "History."

18. Lidar Gravé-Lazi, "New Holocaust Education Program in Israel to Start in Kindergarten," *Jerusalem Post* (April 24, 2014).

19. The phrase is the title of a photograph by Meir Gal, in which the artist holds, in a hand outstretched before him, 9 pages of a 400-page textbook to illustrate just how little coverage is devoted to Mizrahi history in mainstream Israeli pedagogy. See meirgal .com/exhibitions/nine-out-of-four-hundred-the-west-and-the-rest-1997/5060044 (accessed March 20, 2018).

20. French literature includes Abitbol, *Juifs d'Afrique du Nord*; Levisse-Touzé, *Afrique*

du Nord; Laskier, *Yehudei ha-Maghreb*; and Laloum and Allouche, *Juifs d'Algérie*. For a finer-grained historiographic review of the literature pertaining to World War II in Morocco, see Miller, "Filling a Historical Parenthesis." Miller's article introduces a special issue of *The Journal of North African Studies* that includes relevant articles: Baida, "American Landing"; Boum, "Partners Against Anti-Semitism"; Kenbib, "Moroccan Jews"; and Maghraoui, "Goumiers." In addition, recent English-language literature includes Heckman, "Radical Nationalists"; Katz, *Burdens of Brotherhood*, esp. ch. 3; Katz, "Paris Mosque"; Slyomovics, *German Reparations*, esp. ch. 6; and Stein, *Saharan Jews*, esp. ch. 5.

21. Yad Vashem has included coverage of North Africa in their *Pinkas Hakehillot: Encyclopedia of Jewish Communities*, a multivolume work that focuses on specific communities: to wit, Abramski-Beligh's *Libya, Tunisia*. Representing the genre of memory book is Yaacov Haggiag-Liluf's *Toldot Yehude Luv: me-reshit hityashvut ha-Yehudim be-Luv ye-'ad 'aliyatam u-ķeliṭatam ba-arets* (Tel-Or, Israel: ha-Irgun ha-'olami shel Yehudim yots'e Luv, ha-Makhon le-limudim ule-meḥḳar Yahadut Luv, 2000).

22. The special issue is "Les juifs d'Orient face au nazisme et à la Shoah (1930–1945)," *Revue d'Histoire de la Shoah* 205 (October 2016). Select American and French scholars are represented in the volume as well.

23. Bensoussan, "Juifs d'Orient." Bensoussan's work stands in opposition to Robert Satloff's popular work, imagined as a quest for an "Arab" Righteous of the Nation. Satloff, *Among the Righteous*.

24. Oppenheimer, "Holocaust."

25. Yablonka, *Harhek meha-mesila*. Also see Schwartz, "Tragedy Shrouded in Silence"; and Kozlovsky-Golan, "Site of Amnesia."

26. On the history of Mizrahi activism more generally, see Roby, *Mizrahi Era*.

27. Yarden Skop, "Mizrahi Jewish Heritage to Be Taught as Required Matriculation Subject in Israeli Schools," *Ha'aretz* (August 9, 2016).

28. Rein, "Historiographie israélienne."

29. Sucary, *Benghazi to Bergen-Belsen*.

30. Yossi Sucary, "We Can No Longer Deny the Holocaust of Libya's Jews," *972 Magazine* (April 16, 2016), 972mag.com/we-can-no-longer-deny-the-holocaust-of-libyas-jews/105596/ (accessed November 5, 2016).

31. Sucary, "We Can No Longer Deny."

32. Faraz Rivli, "Fils du Sheol: Anouar Benmalek on Memory, Violence, and Fiction," *The Highlander* (October 18, 2016), www.highlandernews.org/25662/25662/ (accessed November 2, 2016).

33. For example, Slyomovics, "French Restitution"; and Slyomovics, *German Reparations*, esp. ch. 6.

Notes to Chapter 1

Research for this article was made possible thanks to my tenure as Ina Levine Invitational Scholar at the Jack, Joseph, and Morton Mandel Center for Advanced Holocaust Studies, United States Holocaust Memorial Museum.

1. For the first well-documented study of the Jews in Algeria and the question of res-

titution of their rights after the Allied landing, see Ansky, *Juifs d'Algérie*, 222–321. For a broader view of the process, see Abitbol, *Jews of North Africa*, 141–65.

2. The U.S. State Department's support for the French administration in Algiers, which was still composed predominantly of Vichy and pro-fascist supporters, is harshly criticized in a U.S. intelligence report: "The Situation in North Africa, 1940–1943," National Archives and Records Administration, RG 266, OSS, Algiers, AI 97, Box 31.

3. Ansky, *Juifs d'Algérie*, 285.

4. Arendt, "Crémieux Decree," (1943), 123. Arendt's article is discussed in Roberts, "Jews, Citizenship, and Anti-Semitism," 362–63.

5. The abrogation of the Crémieux Decree followed the promulgation of the Statut des Juifs, but the Crémieux Decree was promulgated in Algeria before the Statut des Juifs. Ansky refers to the first anti-Semitic measure implemented as the Law on the Press of August 27, 1940, which abrogated a previous law that had banned inciting racial or religious hatred and that was to prepare opinion for the envisaged anti-Jewish legislation. See Ansky, *Juifs d'Algérie*, 86–89. Numerous other works have studied the abrogation of the decree and its implications. See, for example, Cantier, *Algérie*, 72–76; Abitbol, *Jews of North Africa*, 59–62; Roberts, "Jews, Citizenship, and Anti-Semitism," 309–10; and Renucci, "Débat sur le statut politique."

6. Scholarship on the connection between colonialism, genocide in Africa, and the Holocaust has revived attention to Hannah Arendt's theories in *The Origins of Totalitarianism*, and thus her intervention in 1943 sheds light on the formulation of her thinking. A. Dirk Moses convincingly argues that scholars have misunderstood Arendt in invoking her theory on totalitarianism to link imperialism to the Holocaust. Moses argues that Arendt saw a kind of "*discontinuity* between what she called 'the Western tradition' and totalitarian crimes. . . . 'Continental imperialism,' as she called Pan-Germanism and Pan-Slavism, fed into totalitarianism and its unique crimes, while any abuses of 'Western imperialism' were rationally limited" (Moses, "Hannah Arendt," 73).

7. Satloff, *Among the Righteous*.

8. Abitbol's *Jews of North Africa*, first published in French in 1983, laid the groundwork for future studies. See also Laskier, *Yehudei ha-Magreb*; and Laskier, "Between Vichy Antisemitism."

9. The question of Mizrahim and the Holocaust in Israeli discourse and public institutions is exhaustively studied by Yablonka, *Harhek meha-mesila*. A second generation of Mizrahi activists are still fighting the cause of inscribing their history into the national narrative. See, for example, Yossi Sucary, "We Can No Longer Deny the Holocaust of Libya's Jews," +972 *Magazine* (April 16, 2015), 972mag.com/we-can-no-longer-deny-the-holocaust-of-libyas-jews/105596/ (accessed April 3, 2018). Sucary is the author of a Hebrew novel, *Benghazi–Bergen-Belsen* (Tel Aviv: 'Am 'Oved, 2013; English translation in 2016), which recounts the experience of Libyan Jews in concentration camps, based on memories of his grandmother and mother. The story, however, focuses on the ill-treatment by European Jewish prisoners in the camp to emphasize the attitude of Ashkenazi Jews toward the Libyan Jews, as analyzed by Batya Shimony, "Being a Mizrahi Jew, an Israeli, and Touching the Holocaust," +972 *Magazine* (May 10, 2014), 972mag.com/being-a-mizrahi-jew

-an-israeli-and-touching-the-holocaust/90722/ (accessed April 3, 2018). For a collection of histories and narratives compiled for educators with a plea for inclusion of the Sephardi experience in the Holocaust narrative, see Azses, *Shoah*.

10. See the discussion on reparations to North African and especially Algerian Jews in Slyomovics, *German Reparations*, 207–34.

11. "Claims Conference Obtains Approximately $26 Million for 7,000 Holocaust Victims Who Lived Under Persecutory Restrictions" (April 29, 2011), www.claimscon.org /2011/04/morocco/ (accessed January 5, 2017); Gil Stern Stern Shefler, "Berlin to Pay Moroccan Jews Who Suffered Under Vichy," *Jerusalem Post* (April 27, 2011), www.jpost.com /Jewish-World/Jewish-News/Berlin-to-pay-Moroccan-Jews-who-suffered-under-Vichy (accessed January 5, 2017). The question of whether Moroccan and Algerian Jews should receive regular stipends in Israel, through the German reparations, is still unresolved.

12. Lawyers are also representing Jews from Iraq, justified by the 1941 Farhud, the rioting and plunder that came in the wake of a pro-Nazi coup that left 179 Jews dead; it has been claimed that the Farhud was the direct result of Nazi incitement.

13. This information is based on my personal conversations and correspondence with lawyers and historians in Israel between 2015 and 2017.

14. See Moses, "Conceptual Blockages."

15. Quoted in Abitbol, *Jews of North Africa*, 60.

16. Hoisington, *Casablanca Connection*, 26–28; Kenbib, *Juifs et musulmans*, 551–56; Renucci, "Débat sur le statut," 12.

17. L. Joly, *Vichy dans la "solution finale,"* 85n1.

18. Peyrouton, *Du service public*, 154–55. The American consul general reported in August that some 200 ships of refugees reached Casablanca after the fall of France, but this would have been before Peyrouton's tenure as minister of the interior, which began on September 6, 1940. Report of the American consul general, Herbert S. Goold, to the Secretary of State, Casablanca, August 13, 1940, National Archives and Records Administration, RG 84, Morocco—Casablanca, Entry no. 2997, Box 36.

19. See Abitbol, *Jews of North Africa*. For an excellent comparative analysis of the anti-Semitic legislation across North Africa, see Zytnicki, "Politique antisémite." More specifically, for Algeria, see Ansky, *Juifs d'Algérie*; Cantier, *Algérie*, 130–34; and Msellati, *Juifs d'Algérie*.

20. Cantier, *Algérie*, 130–34, 315–20; Roberts, "Jews, Citizenship, and Anti-Semitism," 304–5, 324–27. Details on how the anti-Jewish measures affected the lives of Jews in Algeria can be found in Darmon, *Algérie de Pétain*, 389–415.

21. Le Cour Grandmaison, *Coloniser, exterminer*, 262–71.

22. Saada, *Empire's Children*, 249, 305n35.

23. Decroux, "Le nouveau statut des juifs," 154, quoted in Urban, *Indigène*, 472; translation mine.

24. To use the neologism adopted by Renucci, "Débat sur le statut," 12. "De-citizenized" is a more apt description than denaturalization, which would imply that Jews were being returned to their previous status, but in the case of Algeria, the Jews were born as French citizens.

25. Renucci, "Débat sur le statut," 17–19.

26. On the devastation felt by Algerian Jews as a result of the abrogation of the Crémieux Decree, see Roberts, "Jews, Citizenship, and Anti-Semitism"; and Hammerman, "Heart of the Diaspora," 33–38. Hundreds of Jewish war veterans appealed to the Vichy government to reconsider their loss of citizenship, only to be rejected.

27. In his personal narrative on the history of the Jews of Algeria, Benjamin Stora refers to the "three exiles": The first came with the Crémieux Decree, which separated the Jews from the indigenous Muslim population; the second exile was the decree's abrogation, which set the Jews apart from the French community; and the third was the mass exodus from Algeria that came with independence in 1962. Stora, *Trois exils juifs*, 12–14. Jacques Simon, a Jewish supporter of the Algerian independence movement, writes that with "the suppression of the Crémieux decree, my family plunged into the precolonial Maghreb. . . . We became indigenous, but with an inferior condition to that of the *dhimmi* since we were deprived of the protection of the Beylik" (J. Simon, *Juif berbère*, 24–25).

28. Urban, *Indigène*, 472; Cantier, *Algérie*, 332.

29. Kalman, *French Colonial Fascism*, 64–69.

30. Aouate, "Algériens musulmans." Yves-Claude Aouate assembles evidence to emphasize that Algerian Muslims approved of the abrogation of the Crémieux Decree and the anti-Jewish laws; he is critical of those who write that Muslims rejected Vichy anti-Semitism and disapproved of the anti-Jewish measures and who falsely assume that the attitude of a few enlightened leaders reflected a unanimous opinion of the population.

31. Le Foll Luciani, *Juifs algériens*, 83–101; Cantier, *Algérie*, 332–34; Zytnicki, "Politique antisémite," 167; Aouate, "Algériens musulmans."

32. This was the first time in French nationality law that "indigenous" was associated with the territory of origin. Urban, *Indigène*, 308.

33. Literature on the Crémieux Decree is extensive. Although much of the older scholarship tends to discuss the decree in terms of emancipation, recent scholarship places greater emphasis on the colonial context and implications of the decree, such as in the work of Stora, *Trois exils juifs*. For background leading to the decree, see Schreier, *Arabs of the Jewish Faith*, 143–76.

34. Blévis, "Citoyenneté française," 28–29.

35. Saada, *Empire's Children*, 101.

36. Renucci, "Débat sur le statut," 5–7; Ansky, *Juifs d'Algérie*, 43–44. Algeria serves as a kind of laboratory for defining the division between citizen and subject in French colonies, and the challenge to the Crémieux Decree with the Lambrecht Decree anticipated the hardening of the legal distinction between natives and citizens. Saada, *Empire's Children*, 99–104.

37. Urban, *Indigène*, 310–11.

38. Lewis, *Divided Rule*, 71–73; Renucci, "Débat sur le statut," 7–10.

39. The question of the Mzabi Jews is studied in depth by Stein, *Saharan Jews*. See also Shepard, *Invention of Decolonization*, 242–47.

40. Brubaker, *Citizenship and Nationhood*, 85–113; Shepard, *Invention of Decolonization*, 29–31.

41. Urban, *Indigène*, 163; Weil, *How to Be French*, 44–53.

42. Roberts, "Jews, Citizenship, and Anti-Semitism," 44–57; Lorcin, "Rome and France in Africa," 311–12.

43. Urban, *Indigène*, 300–309.

44. Roberts, "Jews, Citizenship, and Anti-Semitism," 24–31, 63–73; see also Godley, "Almost-Finished Frenchmen."

45. Ansky, *Juifs d'Algérie*, 53–62; Ageron, *Algériens musulmans*, 1: 583–608.

46. Dermenjian, "Juif est-il français."

47. Lorcin, *Imperial Identities*, 174.

48. Ansky, *Juifs d'Algérie*, 41–42.

49. Lewis, *Divided Rule*, 88–91; Marglin, *Across Legal Lines*, 175–80; Kenbib, *Juifs et musulmans*, 405–22; Laskier, *Alliance Israélite Universelle*, 153, 163–71; Wyrtzen, *Making Morocco*, 183–89.

50. Urban, *Indigène*, 291.

51. At the origins of this legislation about nationality was a dispute with the British government, which opposed the collective naturalization of British subjects from Malta. See Urban, *Indigène*, 292–94, 418–21; and Lewis, *Divided Rule*, 112–17. For a general discussion on the naturalization of Tunisian Jews, see Sebag, *Histoire*, 179–84.

52. Lewis, *Divided Rule*, 117–19.

53. Schroeter, "Philo-Sephardism."

54. Rohr, *Spanish Right*, 21; Kenbib, *Juifs et musulmans*, 453–54.

55. On the complicated question of the status of Sephardi Jews of the former Ottoman Empire, see Stein, *Extraterritorial Dreams*, 73–96.

56. Schroeter, "Philo-Sephardism"; Wyrtzen, *Making Morocco*, 208–9.

57. The first resident-general of Morocco, Hubert Lyautey, established a policy of selective and limited naturalization of Jews. See Rivet, *Lyautey*, 2: 266–67.

58. Kenbib, *Juifs et musulmans*, 422–30; Laskier, *Alliance Israélite Universelle*; Wyrtzen, *Making Morocco*, 183–89.

59. "L'application du statut des juifs et des disposition raciales à la population juive du Maroc," February 1943, Raphael Benazeraf Collection, Ben-Zvi Institute (Jerusalem), file 18. The report was written by Raphael Benazeraf, a Jewish community leader in Casablanca, with the help of collaborators. There are no precise statistics of Jews with French citizenship residing in Morocco, but the estimate seems plausible. The 1936 census breaks down Moroccans into Muslims and Jews, but not foreign nationals. Of the 135,546 French citizens, 33,047 were born in Morocco. *Résultats statistiques du recensement de la population de la zone française de l'empire chérifien effectué le 8 Mars 1936* (Rabat, 1936), v, 6.

60. Marglin, "Two Lives of Mas'ud Amoyal"; Schroeter, "Identity and Nation," 136–38.

61. Blévis, "Avatars de la citoyenneté," 568.

62. Urban, *Indigène*, 414–17; Ageron, *Algériens musulmans*, 2: 1217–27. The number of naturalized Muslim citizens based on the new procedure was limited. Between 1919 and 1923, only 202 out of 317 applications were accepted. The total number of naturalized Muslims was 7,635 in 1936, including those naturalized according to the *sénatus-consulte* of 1865 (Ageron, *Algériens musulmans*, 2: 1223).

63. Katz, "Crémieux's Children," 147.

64. Ageron, *Modern Algeria*, 96–98.

65. Katz, "Crémieux's Children," 147; Stora, *Trois exils juifs*, 63–64.

66. Schreier, *Arabs of the Jewish Faith*, 143–76.

67. Weil, *How to Be French*, 87–88.

68. Bensousan, "Juifs d'Algérie," 171–73. See also Msellati, *Juifs d'Algérie*, 88–89.

69. Schroeter, "Vichy in Morocco," 232–34; Wyrtzen, *Making Morocco*, 204–5.

70. The *dahir* was published in the *Bulletin Officiel* (November 8, 1940). The *Bulletin Officiel* has published government legislation since 1912 and is accessible online at www.sgg .gov.ma/Législation/BulletinOfficiels.aspx.

71. Schroeter, "Vichy in Morocco," 215–50.

72. The text of the *dahir* is found in *Bulletin Officiel* (August 8, 1941). On the 1941 Statut des Juifs promulgated in metropolitan France, see Marrus and Paxton, *Vichy France*, 92; and L. Joly, *Vichy dans la "solution finale,"* 183–230. I have not discovered any cases of Muslim converts or their descendants who were subjected to discrimination by the anti-Jewish *dahir*s of 1941. It seems unlikely that the protectorate authorities in Morocco would have vigorously pursued this.

73. Vallat's visit, discussed by the U.S. chargé d'affaires in the legation in Tangier, J. Rives Childs, August 23, 1941, National Archives and Records Administration, RG 84, Tangier Legation, Entry no. 2977, Box 44. The visit was reported in the heavily censored French Moroccan press. See *Le Petit Marocain* (August 20, August 21, and August 28, 1941); and *La Vigie Marocaine* (August 19 and August 20, 1941).

74. Schroeter, "Vichy in Morocco"; Wyrtzen, *Making Morocco*, 205–6.

75. Renucci, "Débat sur le statut," 13, 18; Urban, *Indigène*, 480–88.

76. On changes in the legal status of Jews during the protectorate, see Schroeter and Chetrit, "Emancipation and Its Discontents"; and Marglin, *Across Legal Lines*, 171–96.

77. Cited in Bowie, "Aspect of Muslim-Jewish Relations," 5.

78. A. Chouraqui, *Condition juridique*, 60–62; Urban, *Indigène*, 295.

79. An example of the intervention of Mohammed ben Youssef in Rabat in October 1940 is given in Bensadoun, *Juifs de la République*, 143–50.

80. The case of Léon Sultan, an Algerian-born lawyer who was disbarred in 1941 and founded the Moroccan Communist Party in 1943, is studied by Heckman, "Multivariable Casablanca," 13–14, 24. After Sultan was disbarred, he advocated for Jews who were victims of the anti-Jewish laws.

81. Numerous petitions and correspondence concerning Jews of Moroccan origin who claimed to have been naturalized in Algeria after 1870 and who were seeking to retain their status as French citizens are held in the United States Holocaust Memorial Museum (USHMM), RG 81.001M-9 (original records from the Bibliothèque Nationale du Royaume du Maroc [BNR], Rabat 9, D.317). See, for example, Fridga Benhaim to the Resident-Général du Maroc, Taza, December 19, 1940; and Isaac Ben Hamou to the Resident Général du Maroc, Taza, December 19, 1940.

82. Général François, Président de la LFC de l'Afrique du Nord, to Monsieur le Général, Président de la LFC du Maroc à Rabat, October 11, 1941, USHMM, RG 81.001M-9, Algiers (original records from BNR, D.317).

83. Noguès to le Garde des Sceaux, Ministre Secrétaire d'État et le Justice, Vichy, October 21, 1941, USHMM, RG 81.001M-9 (original records from BNR, D.317).

84. Noguès to le Garde des Sceaux, October 21, 1941.

85. Much correspondence on the revision of the law is found in the archives of the Commisariat Général aux Questions Juives (CGQJ). See, for example, Minister of the Interior to the CGQJ, June 10, 1941, USHMM, RG-43.023M (original records from the Archives Nationales, CGQJ, AJ 38).

86. For a detailed discussion of the abrogation of the Crémieux Decree in 1940 and 1942 and its legal meaning, see Urban, *Indigène*, 472–88.

87. Urban, *Indigène*, 480–87.

88. Ansky, *Juifs d'Algérie*, 92–93, 173.

89. Schroeter, "Philo-Sephardism."

90. USHMM, RG-43.154 (original records from the Ministère des affaires étrangères, Nantes, DI, 1MA/250, article 5). The archives contain reports in response to the circular from authorities in Oujda, Meknes, Taza, Rabat, Port Lyautey, Fez, Casablanca, Marrakesh, and Salé from October 9 to October 18, 1940.

91. Debono, "Difficile rétablissement," 401–12.

92. Le Foll Luciani, *Juifs algériens*, 103–8; Le Foll Luciani, "Juifs d'Algérie."

93. Arendt, "Crémieux Decree" (1943), 118–19.

94. Debono, "Difficile rétablissement," 411; Katz, "Crémieux's Children," 148–58.

95. Abitbol, *Jews of North Africa*, Ansky, *Juifs d'Algérie*, 8–9; Msellati, *Juifs d'Algérie*, 250–52, 159–65; Debono, "Difficile rétablissement," 410–11.

96. Urban, *Indigène*, 488.

97. Contrôleur Civil, Chef de l'Annexe de Martimprey du Kiss, to Contrôleur Civil, Chef de la Circonscription des Beni Snassen, Martimprey du Kiss, November 22, 1943; and Contrôleur Civil, Chef de la Région d'Oujda, to Directeur des Affaires politiques, Oujda, December 1, 1943, USHMM, RG-43.154 (original records from MAE-Nantes, DI, 1MA/250, article 5).

98. Cantier, *Algérie*, 320–27; Le Foll Luciani, "Juifs d'Algérie," 8; Schroeter, "Vichy in Morocco," 236–37.

Notes to Chapter 2

1. Bernhard, "Behind the Battle Lines," 427.

2. Bernhard, "Kolonialachse," 149. Bernhard, "Behind the Battle Lines," 427. Elsewhere, Patrick Bernhard gives the larger number of 100,000 victims of the fascist war in Libya between 1922 and 1931.

3. Bernhard, "Kolonialachse," 154–58.

4. Picciotto, "Groupe de juifs libyens," 45–56. The text is available at bookpopenedition .org/cjb/163 (accessed September 16, 2016). Paragraph 10 provides details of the 1931 census.

5. Picciotto, "Ebrei in Libia," 85.

6. Sarfatti, "Autochthoner Antisemitismus," 234–38.

7. Rodogno, "Faschistische Neue," 213; Schlemmer and Woller, "Italienische Faschismus," 176, 180.

8. Herf, *Nazi Propaganda*, 265.

9. Motadel, *Islam*, 5.

10. Mallmann and Cüppers, *Halbmond und Hakenkreuz*.

11. Commentary on a judgment of the Federal Supreme Court of January 27, 1960, by lawyer Dr. Alfred Schüler from Frankfurt am Main, in *Rechtsprechung zum Wiedergutmachungsrecht* (1960): 266.

12. OLG Frankfurt am Main, March 7, 1958, 2 (8) U 166/56 (not final and absolute), in *Rechtsprechung zum Wiedergutmachungsrecht* (1958): 308–9.

13. Bundesgerichtshof, January 27, 1960, IV ZR 201/59 (Hamm), in *Rechtsprechung zum Wiedergutmachungsrecht* (1960): 209–10.

14. Cf. *Rechtsprechung zum Wiedergutmachungsrecht* (1967): 267–69; and *Rechtsprechung zum Wiedergutmachungsrecht* (1972): 136–37, 262.

15. *Bundesentschädigungsgesetz in der Fassung des 2. Änderungsgesetzes (BEG-Schlussgesetz): Kommentar von Dr. Walter Brunn und Richard Hebenstreit unter Mitwirkung von Heinz Klee* (Berlin: Erich Schmidt Verlag, 1965), §43, Rz. 14.

16. This figure is given in *Rechtsprechung zum Wiedergutmachungsrecht* (1978): 127.

17. OLG Koblenz, March 17, 1978, 8 U (WG) 355/77, in *Rechtsprechung zum Wiedergutmachungsrecht* (1978): 127–28.

18. Schrafstetter, "British Victims," 617, 620. "Compensation for Victims of Nazi Persecution, 34 Lists with Recipients of British Payments, Among Them Numerous Jews from Libya," National Archives, Kew, Foreign Office collection, File FO 950/767. My thanks go to Susanna Schrafstetter for informing me of these lists.

19. Roumani, *Jews of Libya*, 17.

20. Sarfatti, *Jews in Mussolini's Italy*, 48.

21. Sarfatti, *Jews in Mussolini's Italy*, 49–50.

22. Roumani, *Jews of Libya*, 22.

23. De Felice, *Jews in Fascist Italy*, 191.

24. Sarfatti, *Jews in Mussolini's Italy*, 50.

25. Schlemmer and Woller, "Italienische Faschismus," 173.

26. Schlemmer and Woller, "Italienische Faschismus," 173.

27. Roumani, *Jews of Libya*, 19–20.

28. Goldberg, *Jewish Life*, 75.

29. Goldberg, *Jewish Life*, 97–98.

30. Goldberg, *Jewish Life*, 105.

31. Sarfatti, "Autochthoner Antisemitismus," 238; Sarfatti, *Jews in Mussolini's Italy*, 97.

32. Rodogno, "Faschistische Neue," 212–13.

33. Collotti, *Fascismo et gli ebrei*, 35.

34. Schlemmer and Woller, "Italienische Faschismus," 176.

35. Sarfatti, *Jews in Mussolini's Italy*, 95–139.

36. Sarfatti, *Jews in Mussolini's Italy*, 132–33.

37. Even if the person was Catholic until October 1938 but the children were members of a Jewish community, the person counted as Jewish.

38. These metrics were based on a decision by the newly established Demorazza (Direzi-

one Generale per la Demografia e la Razza) in the Ministry of the Interior that regarded all individuals with more than 50% "Jewish blood" as Jews.

39. Picciotto, "Ebrei in Libia," 90.

40. Bernhard, "Kolonialachse," 160n71.

41. Goldberg, *Jewish Life*, 103.

42. Roumani, *Jews of Libya*, 25.

43. Roumani, *Jews of Libya*, 24.

44. Roumani, *Jews of Libya*, 28.

45. "Gli ebrei vennero presto accusati di speculare e di arricchirsi grazie all guerra, di comprare e vendere di continuo le case per alzarne constantemente il valore, di nascondere scorte alimentari da vendere poi al mercato nero, di fare segnalazioni luminose per guidare i bombardamenti degli aerei alleati" (Magiar, *E venne la notte*, 43; translation mine).

46. Herf, *Nazi Propaganda*, 54, 75; Mallmann and Cüppers, *Halbmond und Hakenkreuz*, 125, 128.

47. Motadel, *Islam*, 112.

48. Herf, *Nazi Propaganda*, 54.

49. Roumani, *Jews of Libya*, 29.

50. De Felice, *Jews in an Arab Land*, 359n26.

51. My thanks go to Haim Saadoun at the Ben-Zvi Institute in Jerusalem for pointing this out. See de Felice, *Ebrei in un paese arabo*, 271–73.

52. De Felice, *Jews in an Arab Land*, 179.

53. De Felice, *Jews in an Arab Land*, 183.

54. Picciotto, "Ebrei in Libia," 91–92.

55. Abramski-Bligh, *Pinkas Hakehillot*, 68.

56. R. Simon, "It Could Have Happened There," 417.

57. This law is printed in Di Porto, *Leggi della vergogna*, 266–76.

58. De Felice, *Jews in an Arab Land*, 361n43.

59. Roumani, *Jews of Libya*, 28.

60. There is no exact record of all British Jews who were deported from Libya to Italy. Liliana Picciotto ("Ebrei in Libia," 96, 102) talks of 387–400 people who were shipped to Italy, some 370 of whom were then deported to German camps. Only 187 of the latter have been identified by name.

61. Picciotto, "Groupe de juifs libyens," online version, pars. 28–29.

62. Picciotto, "Groupe de juifs libyens," online version, pars. 34–35. De Felice states that in 1945, 140 more Libyan Jews returned from Germany and southern France (*Jews in an Arab Land*, 362n1).

63. Roumani, *Jews of Libya*, 31.

64. Roumani mentions this incident that he himself witnessed as a child in La Marsa (*Jews of Libya*, 31).

65. "Die Libyenflüchtlinge waren sehr schlecht untergebracht, litten unter Hunger und Durst. Die hygienischen Verhältnisse und die ärztliche Versorgung waren äußerst mangelhaft, so daß viele Lagerinsassen erkrankten. Auch wenn einzelne Lagerinsassen mit besonderer Genehmigung und in Begleitung das Lager zu Einkäufen ab und zu verlassen

durften, so blieb doch die Masse der Libyenflüchtlinge über Monate in dem Lager *Gabes* eingeschlossen und konnte es nicht verlassen" (Cologne Higher Regional Court, September 18, 1974, II U [decision] 6/74, in *Rechtsprechung zum Wiedergutmachungsrecht* [1975]: 29; translation mine).

66. Abramski-Bligh, *Pinkas Hakehillot*, 65–66.

67. Salerno gives for June 25, 1942, the slightly different number of 2,537 Libyan Jews and 47 Italian ("metropolitan") Jews who were imprisoned in Giado (*Uccideteli tutti*, 79).

68. Roumani, *Jews of Libya*, 34.

69. Picciotto, "Groupe de juifs libyens," online version, par. 20.

70. For example, *Enzyklopädie des Holocaust: Die Verfolgung und Ermordung der europäischen Juden*, 2: 862. Picciotto ("Ebrei in Libia," 102) named these camps summarily "piccoli campi di internamento nel Garian" (little internment camps of Garian).

71. Roumani, *Jews of Libya*, 35.

72. Roumani, *Jews of Libya*, 35.

73. The German word *Kapo* (similar to the Italian *capo*, "head") was used by concentration camp inmates for an appointed *Funktionshäftling* (prisoner functionary) who worked for the camp administration. In Giado the Italian word *capo* was used for an elected prisoner functionary, who together with other *capos* built the camp council. Therefore the same term described two different things.

74. Hoppe, "Giado."

75. Abramski-Bligh, *Pinkas Hakehillot*, 120.

76. Roumani, *Jews of Libya*, 35.

77. Hoppe, "Sidi Azaz." De Felice writes that one of the incidents with Arabs from the area ended fatally (*Jews in an Arab Land*, 361n41).

78. Roumani, *Jews of Libya*, 33.

79. Hoppe, "Buk Buk."

80. Bernhard, "Behind the Battle Lines," 431.

81. Bernhard, "Behind the Battle Lines," 431; Salerno, *Uccideteli tutti*, 116.

82. Bernhard, "Behind the Battle Lines," 427.

83. Bernhard, "Kolonialachse," 152.

84. Bernhard, "Behind the Battle Lines," 438.

85. Motadel, *Islam*, 113–14.

86. Roumani, *Jews of Libya*, 38.

87. Roumani, *Jews of Libya*, 44–45.

88. Roumani, *Jews of Libya*, 46–47.

89. Goldberg, *Jewish Life*, 114.

90. Roumani, *Jews of Libya*, 48–49.

91. Goldberg, *Jewish Life*, 112.

92. Roumani, *Jews of Libya*, 49.

93. Roumani, *Jews of Libya*, 50, 65.

94. Goldberg, *Jewish Life*, 113.

95. Roumani, *Jews of Libya*, 50. According to a 1945 British list mentioned by de Felice (*Jews in an Arab Land*, 362n1), at that time eighty-four Jews were living in Beni Ulid and the

survivors of Zanzur were the only community to emigrate together to Israel in 1949–1950 (cf. de Felice, *Jews in an Arab Land*, 379, chart 9).

96. Roumani, *Jews of Libya*, 52.

97. Roumani, *Jews of Libya*, 51.

98. Roumani, *Jews of Libya*, 56.

99. Herf, *Nazi Propaganda*, 240.

100. Goldberg, *Jewish Life*, 118, 134–35.

101. De Felice, *Jews in an Arab Land*, 168.

102. This scope of violence is characterized by the fact "daß das faschistische Italien von Beginn an Krieg führte und dabei zunächst in Libyen und dann Abessinien Mittel einsetzte, die in der Geschichte des Kolonialismus ohne Beispiel sind, ja die in vielem schon die Kriegs- und Vernichtungspraktiken vorweggenommen haben, die dann im Zweiten Weltkrieg zur vollen Entfaltung gelangt sind: Massenumsiedlungen, Repressaltötungen, Konzentrationslager, der kalkulierte Einsatz von Hungersnöten als Instrument der Kriegsführung und die gezielte Ausschaltung politisch-kultureller Eliten, vom Einsatz von Giftgas ganz zu schweigen" (Schlemmer and Woller, "Italienische Faschismus," 199; translation mine).

103. Regarding the Ferramonti camp, see Follino, *Ferramonti*; Capogreco, *Ferramonti*; and Rende, *Ferramonti di Tarsia*.

104. Sarfatti, "Autochthoner Antisemitismus," 243.

105. Minerbi, "Progetto"; Minerbi, "Project," 111–18.

106. Bernhard, "Kolonialachse."

107. In many BEG files on Libyan Jews applying for German indemnification payments, the former Jewish camp inmates mentioned control visits by Germans in their description of the persecution until 1943.

108. Bernhard, "Behind the Battle Lines," 433.

109. Abramski-Bligh, *Pinkas Hakehillot*, 66.

110. R. Simon, "It Could Have Happened There," 416–17.

111. De Felice, *Jews in an Arab Land*, 183.

112. Bernhard, "Behind the Battle Lines," 432.

113. Bernhard, "Behind the Battle Lines," 428.

114. Regarding the situation in Italy, see Wildvang, *Feind von nebenan*.

115. This translation is based on Sayyid Qutb; Herf, *Nazi Propaganda*, 258.

116. Herf, *Nazi Propaganda*, 91.

117. Motadel, *Islam*, 108.

118. Motadel, *Islam*, 108–9.

119. Schlemmer and Woller mention the scapegoat function concerning Italy, but this can be assigned to Libya ("Italienische Faschismus," 197).

120. Goldberg, *Jewish Life*, 108.

121. Magiar, *E venne la notte*, 93.

122. Herf, *Nazi Propaganda*, 263; Mallmann and Cüppers allude to the menacing potential for hatred of Jews in the region (*Halbmond und Hakenkreuz*, 256).

123. Motadel, *Islam*, 73.

124. Herf, *Nazi Propaganda*, 234, 236.

Notes to Chapter 3

1. See, for example, de Benoist, "Brazzaville Conference"; and Gifford and Louis, *Transfer of Power*.

2. Ginio, *French Colonialism Unmasked*. The recent edited volume by Byfield et al., *Africa and World War II*, includes several chapters on the war in French West Africa and in French Equatorial Africa: Catherine Bogosian Ash, "Free to Coerce: Forced Labor During and After the Vichy Years in French West Africa"; Eric T. Jennings, "Extraction and Labor in Equatorial Africa and Cameroon Under Free French Rule"; Ruth Ginio, "African Soldiers, French Women, and Colonial Fears After World War II"; Barbara M. Cooper, "American Missions in Wartime French West Africa: Travails of the Sudan Interior Mission in Niger"; and Elizabeth Schmidt, "Popular Resistance and Anticolonial Mobilization: The War Effort in French Guinea."

3. See, for example, Katz et al., *Colonialism and the Jews*.

4. For an overview of the variety of peoples and cultures in this vast region, see Conklin, *Mission to Civilize*, 25–30.

5. The métis were descendants of French men and local African women. Their relations were usually institutionalized in what was called a *mariage à la mode du pays*, meaning a marriage performed in the local way and valid only so long as the French man stayed in Senegal. Many of the métis received French education in either Senegal or France and were considered part of the local elite. French administrators mostly saw them as troublemakers. On the métis in the French empire, see Saada, *Empire's Children*. More specifically on the métis of Senegal, see Jones, *Métis of Sénégal*.

6. Jones, "Rethinking Politics."

7. W. Cohen, "Colonial Policy," 368.

8. Lydon, "Women, Children," 171.

9. Coquery-Vidrovitch, "Popular Front," 155.

10. Coquery-Vidrovitch, "Popular Front," 90–92.

11. Chafer and Sackur, *French Colonial Empire*, 12.

12. Echenberg, *Colonial Conscripts*, 88.

13. Akpo, *AOF*, 24.

14. Crowder, *Colonial West Africa*, 272.

15. Crowder, *Colonial West Africa*, 28–33.

16. Paxton, *Vichy France*, 43.

17. Hitchcock, "Pierre Boisson," 317.

18. Jennings, *France libre*, 25.

19. Suret-Canale, *Afrique Noire*, 2: 577. On the deterioration of Anglo-French relations in this period, see Thomas, "Anglo-French Divorce."

20. Jennings, *France libre*, 47–50.

21. Azéma, *Munich*, 51–52.

22. Quoted in *La Légion* (August 1940).

23. Ageron, "Vichy," 132.

24. Viard, *Empire*, 12–13.

25. Viard, *Empire*, 13.

26. Jennings, *Vichy in the Tropics*, 17–19.

27. On Vichy propaganda in FWA, see Ginio, *French Colonialism Unmasked*, 33–43; and Ginio, "Marshal Pétain."

28. Between 300,000 and 350,000 Jews lived in France at that time and 400,000 lived in North Africa.

29. Victims of Vichy, Archives Nationales du Sénégal (ANS), 2D6 (14).

30. Marrus and Paxton, *Vichy France*, 3.

31. Marrus and Paxton, *Vichy France*, 152–55.

32. Schroeter, "Vichy in Morocco," 230–31.

33. Letter from Boisson to the head of the Service of Political Affairs, November 12, 1940, ANS, 2D6 (14).

34. Memorandum from Boisson to all territory governors, August 1941, ANS, 2D (14). Boisson asks to delay the census of the Jews in FWA until he receives clearer instructions from France with regard to the way in which it should be conducted.

35. Memorandum from Boisson to all territory governors, August 1941, ANS, 2D (14).

36. "A Study About the Decree of 4 July 1942, Regarding Taking Control Over Business, Merchandise, and Assets Belonging to Jews," September 16, 1942, ANS, 2D6 (14).

37. Annet, *Aux heures troublées*, 51.

38. Annet, *Aux heures troublées*, 55

39. Part of a letter seized by postal censors, Senegal, March 5, 1941, ANS, 10N/193.

40. Letter from Hubert Dechamps, Governor of the Ivory Coast, to the bank manager, August 18, 1942; and letter from the bank manager to Dechamps, August 19, 1942, ANS, 2D6 (14).

41. "A Report on the Subject of Jews," September 1942, ANS, 2D6 (14).

42. Letter from Lucien Bloch to the general prosecutor, August 17, 1942, ANS, 2D6 (14).

43. "Report on Jewish Affairs," ANS, 2D6 (14).

44. Lawler, "Reform and Repression," 89.

45. Akpo, *AOF*, 151.

46. Paxton, *Vichy France*, 280–82.

47. Bouche, "Retour de l'AOF," 45.

48. Schroeter, "Vichy in Morocco," 231–32.

49. Akpo, *AOF*, 53–54.

Notes to Chapter 4

1. Agamben, *Means Without End*, 37.

2. Hull, *Absolute Destruction*, 123–24.

3. Arendt, *Origins of Totalitarianism*, 186.

4. In contrast, the contexts of Algeria's European settlers and colonial authorities reflecting their long-term anti-Jewish politics have received considerable attention, including important works by such English-language scholars as Samuel Kalman, Joshua Schreier, Jonathan Cole, Sophie Roberts, and Sung-Eun Choi.

5. Azan, "Général Bedeau."

6. See images of the camp in 1936 and 1938 posted on the website of Robert Lavina,

"Sidi-Bel-Abbes, juin 1843–juin 1962," www.mekerra.fr/pages/vieux-sba/bedeau/bedeau01 .html (accessed April 1, 2018).

7. Aouate, "Juifs d'Algérie," 1: 48.

8. Exceptions to Jews granted citizenship by the Crémieux Decree were Algeria's south-ern Mzabi Jews. On the complexities of when Jews did and did not attain French national-ity throughout the southern Algerian territories, see Stein, *Saharan Jews*.

9. *Journal Officiel* (October 13, 1940).

10. No exact numbers are currently available, although see secondary sources about these camps in Ansky, *Juifs d'Algérie*, 261–81; Cantier, *Algérie*, 346–54; Abitbol, *Juifs d'Afrique du Nord*, 102–4; Bel Ange, *Quand Vichy*; Oliel, *Camps de Vichy*; Bensadoun, *Juifs de la République*; Cohn, "Une page"; Levisse-Touzé, "Camps d'internement"; Aouate, "Juifs d'Algérie," 1: 47–58; and Boum, "Bedeau." Separate from camps for Algerian Jewish soldiers were camps for foreign Jews, who were mixed with others deported to Algeria. See Szajkowski, *Jews and the French Foreign Legion*; and Moine, *Déportation*.

11. "Les militaires juifs algériens récemment déchus de la nationalité françaises seront regroupés en une unité des travailleurs jusqu'à la libération de la classe à laquelle ils sont attachés" (Bel Ange, *Quand Vichy*, 23).

12. On GTEs, see Gaida, *Camps de travail*, 254–83. On Vichy's comprehensive system of internment of GTEs, see Eggers, *Unerwünschte Ausländer*; Eggers, "Internement"; and Peschanski, *La France de camps*.

13. In Chapter 7 Boum describes and analyzes the terrible living conditions in several Algerian camps. Rated among the worst camps were those exploiting forced labor for the Vichy-inspired Trans-Saharan railroad; for example, see Tartakower and Grossman, *Jewish Refugee*, 208. I thank Aomar Boum for generously encouraging my research as well as direct-ing me to additional sources.

14. Bel Ange, *Quand Vichy*, 96.

15. On the legislation and the legal and diplomatic history leading to the establish-ment of the "Remembrance, Responsibility, and the Future" Foundation, see Zumbansen, *Zwangsarbeit im Dritten Reich*. The website for the Foundation is www.stiftung-evz.de/eng/ home.html.

16. On legal peace, see Bazyler, *Holocaust Justice*, 83.

17. See Slyomovics, *German Reparations*.

18. *Bundesgesetzblatt*, 1 (1977): 1786–1852 and 46 (1982): 1571–79.

19. I thank Jens Hoppe, historian for the Claims Conference offices, who is based in Frankfurt, Germany (and a contributor to this volume), for providing me with the fol-lowing court references that demonstrate recognition of claims by individual inmates: for Djelfa camp, court decision from February 5, 1959, *Rechtsprechung zum Wiedergutmachungs-recht* (1959), *Beiheft*, 23–24; and for Ain Sefra, Boghari, Suzzoni, and Kenadsa camps, the later court decision from November 25, 1970, *Rechtsprechung zum Wiedergutmachungsrecht* (1971): 74–76.

20. Jens Hoppe, e-mail communication, November 23, 2016.

21. *Gesamtverzeichnis "anderer Haftstätten."*

22. *Gesamtverzeichnis "anderer Haftstätten,"* 3.

23. *Gesamtverzeichnis "anderer Haftstätten,"* 29th page of 640 pages of German camp lists ordered alphabetically and providing dates of recognized camp, camp classifications, and reparation decision.

24. Slyomovics, "French Restitution," 894–95, quoting written question 1527 published in France's *Journal Officiel* (July 31, 2007): 5005. The response by the ministry in charge of veterans was published in the *Journal Officiel* (September 18, 2007): 5666.

25. See the valuable testimony and bibliography by one of the network co-founders: Aboulker, "Témoignage." Also see Aboulker, *Victoire*; and Amipaz-Silber, *Maḥteret Yehudit*.

26. Bouysse, *Encyclopédie de l'ordre nouvel*. According to Algiers rabbi Maurice Eisenbeth's chronicle, the head of Bedeau camp was the former SOL section chief for Eckmuhl, Algeria. See Eisenbeth, *Pages vécues*, 27.

27. "Au point de vu politique et moral: *impression de camp de concentration*, bagarres avec les civils de Bedeau, insultes par l'encadrement et par la Légion Étrangère, avec pour thèmes: sales Youpins, sales corbeaux. *REMARQUE*.—Cette étape a marqué une empreinte indélébile sur le Camp de Bedeau; malgré toutes les notes et tous les ordres, le Camp reste encore aujourd'hui sous une espèce de sortilège de mesquinerie et d'infériorité dont ne peuvent se débarrasser ni les chefs ni les hommes" ("Le traitement infligé aux soldats français d'origine juive: Le camp de Bedeau," dated by Sidney Chouraqui as January 1943, Centre de Documentation Juive Contemporaine [CDJC], CCCLXXXV-5, p. 1; emphasis in original).

28. Mannoni, *Prospero and Caliban*.

29. See interviews in Bel Ange, *Quand Vichy*, 124.

30. Aouate, "Juifs d'Algérie," 1: 232. Sidney Chouraqui recounted that he left Bedeau with a booklet of his "native" earnings that showed a balance of 624 francs per month. See S. Chouraqui, "Camp de juifs français," 232.

31. Images appear on pp. 117, 118, 121, 122, 127, and 128 in Bel Ange, *Quand Vichy*. See caption on p. 128 refuting that the *corbeaux* attire during the GTA phase was imposed in Bedeau.

32. See André Nouschi, "Les deux parties ont sous-estimé le racisme toujours présent chez les Européens," *Les deux rives de la Méditerranée* (March 2012), ldh-toulon.net/Andre-Nouschi-les-deux-parties-ont.html (accessed April 1, 2018). Nouschi was interned in Cheragas, the second, entirely Algerian Jewish camp for soldiers from the Constantine region. On France's Ministry of Defense decision no. 02PA00247 of June 17, 2003, which denied BPI units of Bedeau "political internee" status, see also Gaida, *Camps de travail*, 583 n927.

33. "Manifeste des juifs de Bedeau," dated by Sidney Chouraqui as beginning of January 1943, CDJC, CCCLXXXV-5.

34. See 1997 testimony in S. Chouraqui, "Camp de juifs français." During the BPI period, Chouraqui estimates that 12,000 Jewish soldiers were mobilized to Bedeau camp, conscripted from each year between 1933 and 1943. Chouraqui's life story is recounted on the occasion of his receiving a medal in 2010 by the Conseil répresentatif des institutions juives de France (CRIF), which chronicles how he joined General Leclerc's outfit in Libya and embarked on a stellar military career with the Free French Forces, which included participating in the liberation of Paris: www.crif.org/fr/actualites/Sidney-Chouraqui-un-homme-d-honneur21211 (accessed April 1, 2018). Chouraqui left North Africa for France

in 1965. Related to his Bedeau internment, he was instrumental in preserving another internment site, Camp des Milles, near his adopted hometown of Aix-en-Provence.

35. Baïda, "Ayache, Germain."

36. "Nous juifs mobilisé à Bedeau, déclarons ce qui suit: Nous détestons le nazisme, nous le détestons parce qu'il torture la France meurtrie et parce qu'il persécute spécialement les juifs. Il y a deux mois est né en nous un espoir immense, celui de reprendre la lutte avec des armées modernes et de contribuer à l'écrasement définitif de l'ennemi de l'humanité. La réalisation de ce voeu nous a été refusé. Rassemblés pêle-mêle, fantassins, artilleurs, cavaliers, aviateurs, nous avons été transformés en pionniers. . . . Qu'on nous ait retirés de nos unités respectives et qu'on nous ait tous transformés en travailleurs, au mépris de l'utilisation des compétences, ce fait ne peut avoir qu'une conséquence dans le publique: nous présenter comme suspects ou incapables de combattre les armes à la main. Nous déclarons que personne n'a le droit de douter de notre valeur combative: ce serait insulter à la mémoire de nos ainés qui reposait encore par milliers en terre de France. Nous exprimons le profond regret de nous voir délibérément exclus de la lutte actuelle dont nous demeurons les champions ardents. . . . En 1940, nous nous sommes battus comme français. Depuis, on nous a exclus de la communauté nationale. . . . Qu'on nous affecte tous automatiquement dans les unités auxquelles nous étions normalement destinés, qu'on nous permette de combattre chacun selon nos compétences, mais dans la dignité comme les autres soldats. Qu'on nous le permette, et tous unis nous répondrons 'Présent'" ("Manifeste des juifs de Bedeau," CDJC, CCCLXXXV-5).

37. Arendt, "Crémieux Decree" (2007), 252–53.

38. On Victor Bahloul's multiple transfers among Algerian internment camps, I rely on the lecture by his daughter Joelle Bahloul: Bahloul, "Tragedies That Linger."

39. "Là nous avons vécu pendant deux longues années sous des tentes marabout, vêtus d'un vieil uniforme et d'un calot noir, aux ordres d'un détachement de légionnaires du 1er régiment étranger commandé par un officier français, le capitaine Orsini qui ne manquait pas de communiquer à ses subordonnés son hostilité haineuse à l'égard des juifs. Nous étions soumis aux plus pénibles corvées: l'hygiène était absente et, en guise de latrines, des fosses creusées dans la nature laissaient échapper une puanteur qui nous empoisonnait. L'alimentation était à l'avenant. Une chaleur épouvantable nous accablait dans la journée et nous étions gelés de froid la nuit. En guise d'éclairage et de chauffage nous utilisions l'huile des boîtes de sardine conservée précieusement. Nous étions privés de radio, de journaux, de tout moyen de communication avec l'exterieur" (Benhamou, "Camps d'Algérie," 15). See also Golski, *Buchenwald français*.

40. "C'est en toute bonne foi que nous avions naïvement répondu à l'appel sous les drapeaux pour mobilisation générale adressé aux Français, apposé sur les murs de toutes nos communes, pour nous apercevoir, à notre grande surprise que notre lieu de regroupement, le camp de Bedeau, était spécifique aux juifs. Tout avait donc été préparé en secret, par des officiers français ainsi que par une haute administration, pour aménager ce camp dans lequel, finalement, le cynisme de l'encadrement et notre humiliation aidant, le pire aurait pu arriver. Hypocrisie, racisme fanatique, duplicité et trahison, nous apprîmes plus tard que c'était là l'essentiel de la méthode nazie. A Bedeau, les très rares réclamations

étaient brutalement sanctionées sans commentaire. C'est l'intelligence et la discipline d'une jeunesse juive qui firent qu'aucune rébellion grave n'eut lieu: elle nous aurait été fatale car nous n'étions pas armés pour faire face à une situation et à des processus aussi barbares" (Benkemoun, "Camp de Bedeau," 5).

41. "Nous avons donc été mobilisés en tant qu'étrangers et, en particulier, dans la Légion étrangère. L'immense majorité des Juifs rassemblés dans le camp de la Légion pensait qu'il s'agissait d'une péripétie de l'Histoire et que le temps viendrait où l'on nous rendrait la citoyenneté française. J'ai été au camp de Bedeau de 1943 à 1944, puis j'ai fait la guerre dans la Coloniale, un corps de métier de l'infanterie française. Ce que j'ai vécu au cours de cette période a certainement travaillé souterrainement et, au moment où j'ai rencontré la réalité israélienne, cela s'est dénoué tout naturellement. Au fond, si j'avais dû vivre en diaspora, je me serais davantage considéré comme un Juif algérien de culture française que comme un Juif français de culture algérienne. L'Algérie est devenue par la suite un pays arabe et je ne pouvais pas me considérer comme un Arabe.

Encore aujourd'hui, je n'arrive pas à comprendre la manière dont les Juifs nord-africains en France se considèrent comme Français. Indépendamment du caractère anti-Juif ou anti-israélien des pays arabes, il ne leur vient pas à l'idée de se considérer comme des Arabes mais comme des Français. Cette attitude relève du racisme. Elle s'explique par le fait que les Juifs considèrent que l'indice culturel français est supérieur à l'indice culturel arabe. Ce qui est objectivement un non-sens parce que ces cultures ne se mesurent pas aux mêmes critères. Mais il y a une évidence pour un Juif qui a vécu en pays d'Islam: la différence entre le Juif et l'Arabe n'est pas seulement d'ordre religieux, elle est aussi d'ordre national. Cette double différence n'existe pas par rapport à l'Européen. C'est l'un des éléments qui explique la perpétuation de la diaspora en milieu européen.

A posteriori, ce fut pour moi une expérience très enrichissante de connaître ce milieu de la Légion étrangère, mais nous n'étions pas organisés en tant que Juifs pour pouvoir développer en nous la conscience nationale. Nous nous considérions comme une espèce de minorité de type diasporique. La vie religieuse dans le camp était très intense et c'est là peut-être que j'ai commencé à comprendre la condition d'exil, dont je me suis complètement débarrassé en devenant Israélien. J'ai senti que je n'étais pas chez moi et que, par conséquent, je n'avais aucun droit à réclamer. Je ne pouvais qu'essayer, par une stratégie de soumission, d'obtenir des faveurs" (Askénasi, *Histoire de ma vie*, n.p.)

42. I develop these themes more fully in my lecture " 'False Friends' Algeria, the Algerian Jewish Question, and Settler Colonial Studies" (first delivered at UCLA on March 10, 2017) (see Slyomovics, "False Friends"). One example of the identification of Algerian Jews as "Mizrahi" or "French Jew" is discussed in the biography of Roger Azoulay, an Oran-born Algerian Jew interned in Bedeau camp who left for Israel in 1948, as seen through the eyes of his daughter Ariella. Azoulay, "Mother Tongue." See also my January 28, 2006, interview with Azoulay in Netanya, Israel, in Slyomovics, "French Restitution," 886–89.

43. English translation in Bourdieu, *The Algerians*, 133–34.

44. Bourdieu, *The Algerians*, 133.

45. Bourdieu, *The Algerians*, 146.

46. Bourdieu, *The Algerians*, 120.

Notes to Chapter 5

The archival research for this work was funded by a generous Judith B. and Burton P. Resnick Postdoctoral Fellowship at the United States Holocaust Memorial Museum. We thank Daniel Schroeter, Khalid Bensrhir, Thomas Park, Susan Slyomovics, and Sarah A. Stein for their valuable comments. We also thank Joanna L. Rutter-Bent for her valuable editing. We alone are responsible for the ideas and opinions made in the final version.

1. Goldberg, "Mellahs."

2. Boum, *Memories of Absence*; Larhmaid, *Yahud mantaqat Sus.*

3. Interview by Aomar Boum with Izza, an elderly woman in her late 90s, March 2004, Anti-Atlas, Morocco.

4. This interview is part of an ethnographic project on Muslims' memories about Jews in the region of Tata. For more information, see Boum, *Memories of Absence.*

5. Maxwell, *Lords of the Atlas*; Gellner, *Saints of the Atlas*; Peyron, "Glaoui/Glaoua."

6. De Foucauld, *Reconnaissance au Maroc*; Schroeter, "Jews of Essaouira"; Laskier, "Aspects of Change."

7. See "Rapport militaire du Bureau de Foum Zguid," 3ème semestre, 1939, Service Historique de la Défense à Vincennes, 3 H 1875.

8. Ibn Khaldun, *Muqaddimah.*

9. Boum, *Memories of Absence.*

10. Wharton, *In Morocco*, 9–10.

11. Bidwell, *Morocco Under Colonial Rule*, 33. Also see Pennell, "Makhzan and Siba."

12. Ilahiane, *Ethnicities.*

13. Bénabou, *Jacob, Manahem et Mimoun*; De Nesry, *Juifs de Tanger*; Dahan, *Regard d'un juif marocain*; Sasson, *Couturiers du sultan*; Arman, *Était.*

14. Le Tourneau, *Fès avant le Protectorat*; Dunn, "Trade of Tafilalt."

15. Boum, "Schooling in the Bled."

16. Shokeid, "Jewish Existence"; Hirschberg, "Jewish Quarter."

17. See "Rapport militaire du Bureau de Foum Zguid."

18. F. Joly, "Situation économique."

19. Goldberg, "Mellahs"; Boum, *Memories of Absence.*

20. Shokeid, "Jewish Existence."

21. Bilu and Levy, "Nostalgia and Ambivalence"; Schroeter, "Jewish Farmers."

22. Boum, "Colonial Minorities."

23. Schroeter, *Merchants of Essaouira*; Boum, *Memories of Absence.*

24. See Marglin, *Across Legal Lines.*

25. Kenbib, *Juifs et musulmans*; Marglin, *Across Legal Lines.*

26. See Le Capitaine de Leyris, Chef de Bureau du Cercle de Goulmime, to Colonel De Saint Bon, Chef de Territoire de Tiznit, Goulmime, May 12, 1951, Service Historique des Armées de Terre (SHAT)/Château de Vincennes, 3H 2214.

27. See "Rapport mensuel," Septembre 15, 1935, Archives du Maroc/Rabat, Région de Marrakech.

28. Laskier, *North African Jewry*, 62.

29. Wagenhofer, "Contested Narratives."

30. L. Joly, *Vichy dans la solution finale*; Laskier, "Between Vichy Antisemitism"; Ageron, "Populations du Maghreb."

31. Laskier, *North African Jewry*, 77.

32. Boum, *Memories of Absence*.

33. Schroeter, "Dhimmis to Colonized Subjects."

34. Boum and Schilt, "Agdz."

35. De Foucauld, *Reconnaissance au Maroc*.

36. Swearingen, *Moroccan Mirages*, 26. Also see Knight, *Morocco*, 83.

37. Larhmaid, *Yahud mantaqat Sus*.

38. Sebti and Lakhsassi, *Mina as-shay ila al-atay*; Ben-Srhir, *Britain and Morocco*.

39. Baïda, *Presse marocaine*.

40. Centre des Archives Diplomatiques de Nantes, 1 MA/200/94, Propagande.

41. Arsenian, "Wartime Propaganda."

42. Park, "Essaouira," 114.

43. Flamand, *Diaspora*, 84–88.

44. See "Note au sujet des transactions immobilières du Tafilalet," July 15, 1946, SHAT/ Château de Vincennes, 3 H 1705, Transactions entre Musulmans et Israélites, 1946.

45. See Lieutenant-Colonel Bertot to La Direction de l'Intérieur, January 14, 1941, SHAT/Chateau de Vincennes, 3 H 1709.

46. Boum, *Memories of Absence*.

47. Baïda, "Maroc et la propagande."

48. See Lieutenant-Colonel Bertot to La Direction de l'Intérieur, January 14, 1941.

49. See "Note au sujet des transactions immobilières du Tafilalet."

50. See Colonel Astier de Villatte, February 22, 1942, SHAT/Château de Vincennes, 3 H 1709.

51. "Affaires juives," SHAT/Château de Vincennes, 3 H 1710.

52. Chef de Batailles Paulin to Lieutenant-Colonel Chef du Territoire de Tafilelt, objet: Remise en vigueur du décret Crémieux, November 19, 1943, SHAT/Château de Vincennes, 3 H 1705.

53. Colonel Astier de Villate, February 22, 1942.

Notes to Chapter 6

This chapter was made possible thanks to my tenure as a Ben and Zelda Cohen Fellow at the Jack, Joseph, and Morton Mandel Center for Advanced Holocaust Studies, United States Holocaust Memorial Museum. My gratitude goes to Elizabeth J. Marcus and Daniel J. Schroeter for helping me shape and hone my ideas and argument in this essay. I would also like to thank the editors of this volume, Aomar Boum and Sarah Abrevaya Stein, along with the two anonymous reviewers, for their constructive comments, which helped strengthen the chapter.

1. The census return is in the Assal Family Collection, donated to the United States Holocaust Memorial Museum (USHMM) by Ruth Assal.

2. Filippo Petrucci's excellent academic study is in the minority. See Petrucci, *Ebrei in Algeria*. For nonacademic studies, see Allali, *Juifs de Tunisie*.

3. In Israel, raising awareness has been led by Haim Saadoun and Claude Sitbon.

4. Namely, Borgel's *Étoile jaune et croix gammée*, Ghez's *Six mois sous la botte*, and Nataf's *Les juifs de Tunisie sous le joug nazi*.

5. The success of the film *Victor "Young" Perez*, concerning the Tunisian Jewish boxer Victor Perez, who was deported to Auschwitz in October 1943, offers only one example.

6. See Abitbol, *Jews of North Africa*; Laskier, "Between Vichy Antisemitism"; Zytnicki, "Politique anti-Semite"; and Nataf, "Juifs de Tunisie." An exception to this is the recent article by Terrence Peterson that examines Vichy's racial laws through the prism of France's colonial rivalry with Italy. See Peterson, "Jewish Question."

7. On Morocco, see Schroeter, "Vichy in Morocco."

8. Sabille, *Juifs de Tunisie*, 23–28.

9. See Part III of Memmi, *Pillar of Salt*, 270–322.

10. "Loi portant statut des juifs du 3 octobre 1940," *Journal Officiel de la République Française* (October 18, 1940): 5323. Esteva signed it into law in the *Journal Officiel Tunisien* on December 3, 1940.

11. Robert Levy is an example of another Tunisian Jew whose memoir begins in November 1942. See R. Levy, *180 jours de Tunis*.

12. For only one example, see the interview with Bernard Epelbeim, April 1997, University of Southern California Shoah Foundation. The interviewee appears unwilling to reflect on the period before the Germans occupied the non-occupied zone.

13. Letter from Pierre de Font-Réaulx to René de Chambrun, September 14, 1955, in De Chambrun, *France During the German Occupation*, 716.

14. Zytnicki, "Politique anti-Semite," 160.

15. L. Joly, *Vichy dans la "solution finale,"* n234.

16. In his groundbreaking work on the CGQJ, Joseph Billig did not investigate the reception of the institution in North Africa. See Billig, *Commissariat Général*.

17. See L. Joly, *Vichy dans la "solution finale,"* 233–35; and Marrus and Paxton, *Vichy France*, 278–85.

18. Laloum, "Politique d'aryanisation économique."

19. See Esteva's statements in London, *Amiral Esteva*, 53–54, 66–67.

20. Nataf, *Juifs de Tunisie*, 206–7.

21. Peterson, "Jewish Question."

22. Letter quoted in an "Enquiry into the Situation of the Jews of Tunisia" by the Renseignements Généraux, October 10, 1941, USHMM, RG-43.023M, Reel 175, AJ38 988.

23. Full details of Aryanization and spoliation appear in the monthly reports by Hayaux du Tilly to Darquier de Pellepoix. See, for example, Report of June 30, 1942, USHMM, RG-43.023M, Reel 2, AJ38 5. A list of Jewish lawyers to be expelled was drawn up on June 5, 1942, with the Jewish lawyers losing their jobs on August 6, 1942. On the expulsion of Jews from the Tunis bar in 1942, see Nataf, "Exclusion des avocats."

24. Vallat, *Nez de Cléopâtre*, 246.

25. Letter from Vallat to Pucheu, September 23, 1941, USHMM, RG-43.023M, Reel 2, AJ38 5.

26. Marrus and Paxton, *Vichy France*, 134; and L. Joly, *Vichy dans la "solution finale,"* 503.

27. "Application en Algérie de la loi sur le recensement des juifs," May 1941, USHMM, RG-43.023M, Reel 175, AJ38 988. Despite the title of the document, Vallat makes clear to include the protectorates.

28. Report from Hooker Doolittle, Tunis, July 30, 1941, National Archives and Records Administration (NARA), RG 59, General Records of the Department of State, Decimal File, 1940–44, 851S.C1/1 0–2344, Box 5219.

29. Report from Hooker Doolittle, Tunis, September 3, 1941, NARA, RG 59, General Records of the Department of State, Decimal File, 1940–44, 851S.C1/1 0–2344, Box 5219.

30. See Lee, *Pétain's Jewish Children*, 172.

31. Letter from Valentin to Vallat, September 4, 1941, USHMM, RG-43.023M, Reel 2, AJ38 5.

32. Aouate, "Place de l'Algérie," 604.

33. Letter from Darlan to Vallat in which he cites Esteva's objections, October 12, 1941, USHMM, RG-43.023M, Reel 175, AJ38 988.

34. See, for example, letter from Hayaux to the CGQJ, August 7, 1942, USHMM, RG-43.023M, Reel 2, AJ38 5.

35. I was not surprised to discover that Hayaux's grandson had no knowledge of his grandfather's role at the CGQJ; he was aware only of his work with the Red Cross under Vichy. Interview with Hayaux's grandson, Yves de Joybert, January 2, 2013.

36. List of letters run from January 1942 to the summer of that year, USHMM, RG-43.023M, Reel 176, AJ38 992.

37. List of letters, USHMM, RG-43.023M, Reel 176, AJ38 992. The subject lines of the letters show the extent of Hayaux's actions in Tunisia.

38. See, in particular, Hayaux's detailed reports from May and June 1942, USHMM, RG-43.023M, Reel 2, AJ38 5.

39. See correspondence from June 1942, in particular, the letter from Darquier to Laval, June 18, 1942, USHMM, RG-43.023M, Reel 2, AJ38 5.

40. See letter from Hayaux to the CGQJ, August 7, 1942, and letter from Darquier to Hayaux, September 5, 1942, USHMM, RG-43.023M, Reel 2, AJ38 5.

41. Letter from Darquier to Hayaux, May 26, 1942, USHMM, RG-43.023M, Reel 2, AJ38 5.

42. Lee, "Chantiers de la Jeunesse," 166.

43. Gide, *Journals*, 144.

Notes to Chapter 7

The archival research for this work was funded by a generous Judith B. and Burton P. Resnick Postdoctoral Fellowship at the United States Holocaust Memorial Museum. I thank Daniel Schroeter, Thomas Park, Susan Slyomovics, and Sarah Abrevaya Stein for their valuable comments. I also thank Joanna L. Rutter-Bent for her valuable editing. I alone am responsible for the ideas and opinions made in the final version.

1. Agamben, *Homo Sacer*, 42.

2. Agamben, "*What Is a Camp?*" 252.

3. Overy, "Concentration Camp." Also see Brecht, "Concentration Camp."

4. Kogon, *Theory and Practice*; Allen, *Business of Genocide*.

5. Drinnon, *Keeper of Concentration Camps*; Schiffrin, "Language and Public Memorial"; Walston, "History and Memory"; Cate-Arries, *Spanish Culture*; González-Ruibal, "Archaeology of Internment"; Mühlhahn, "Concentration Camp"; Jakobson, *Origins of the Gulag*; Howard, *Concentration Camps*; Mendiola, "Reeducation Through Work"; Fall, *Travail force*; Monfort, "Campos de concentración"; Peschanski, *France des camps*; Eggers, "Internement."

6. A number of international workshops and conferences have been organized around the question of North Africa and the Holocaust with the participation of many North African scholars. In July 2009 the Center for Advanced Holocaust Studies at the United States Holocaust Memorial Museum organized the workshop "North Africa and Its Jews in the Second World War." As part of the European Research Council's project "Judging Histories: Experience, Judgment, and Representation of World War II in an Age of Globalization," the international workshop "Historical Comprehension and Moral Judgement of World War II and the Holocaust: The View from North Africa—Morocco, Algeria, Tunisia, and Libya" took place in June 2015 at the Hebrew University of Jerusalem. In November 2015 another conference, "On the Margins of the Holocaust: Jews, Muslims, and Colonialism in North Africa During the Second World War," was organized by the United States Holocaust Memorial Museum, the UCLA Alan D. Leve Center for Jewish Studies, the UCLA Center for Near Eastern Studies, and the 1939 Society at UCLA.

7. Aub, *Diarios*.

8. Despite the absence of official documentation on many Vichy camps in North Africa, the French colonial archives house many administrative military reports on the camp of Djelfa. The Archives Nationales de France (Paris) has a number of reports, including André Jean-Faure's mission in North Africa (F7 15111) and two reports by Henri Martel and Antoine Demusois about their official visits to the camp in March 1943 (72AJ270). In addition, the archives of Max Aub include valuable information about his experience in camps in France and North Africa; see boxes at the Archivo Max Aub, vol. 6, "Fondos de la Diputación de Valencia" (Segorbe: Fundación Max Aub). There is also an unedited text left by Max Aub on his experience in the Djelfa camp ("Campo de Djelfa, Argelia" [Camp of Djelfa, Algeria], Biblioteca Daniel Cosío Villegas, El Colegio de México, Mexico City). See Archivo Max Aub (vol. 34, 541–47). Also see Núñez, "Max Aub."

9. Nos, "Campos de concentratión."

10. Dickey, "Campos de la Memoria," 248.

11. Boum, "Djenien-Bou-Rezg."

12. Arezki Berkani, *Mémoire*.

13. Despite the colonial censorship and prohibition regarding writings about the camps, a number of prisoners were able to write short diaries and witness accounts about their experience. They include D'Hérama, *Tournant dangereux mémoires*; Garaudy, *Mon tour du siècle*; Moine, *Déportation*; and Iancu-Agou, "Être expulse." In addition to the personal diaries that chronicle detainees' lives in Vichy camps, other biographies of prisoners under Nazi occupation of Tunisia include Nataf, *Tunisie*; Borgel, *Étoile jaune*; G. Guez, *Nos martyrs*; Boretz, *Tunis*; Ghez, *Six mois*; J. A. Guez, *Camp de Bizerte*; Attal, *Mémoires*; and Memmi, *Pillar of Salt*.

14. Kahan, "Honte du témoin."

15. Bal et al., *Acts of Memory*; Bernard-Donals and Glejzer, *Witnessing the Disaster*.

16. Blanchot, *Writing of the Disaster*.

17. Abitbol, *Jews of North Africa*.

18. Thénault, *Violence ordinaire*; Gaida, *Camps de travail*.

19. There are many studies about forced labor in the context of French colonialism. See Fall, *Travail forcé*.

20. Rosen, *Two Arabs*, 296.

21. Oliel, *Camps de Vichy*; Szajkowski, *Jews and The French Foreign Legion*; Bachoud, *Sables d'exil*; Satloff, *Among the Righteous*; Morro Casas, *Campos africanos*.

22. See United States Holocaust Memorial Museum (USHMM), Collections, RG-67.007M, Folder 41 of 95, Folder 15 of 36, and Folder 33 of 36. Also see Bauer, *American Jewry*.

23. See USHMM, Collections, RG-68.115M.

24. See USHMM, Personal Narratives. For example, see the oral history interview with Arlette Taïb (RG-50.030*0632), the oral history testimony of Josy Adida-Goldberg (RG-50.904*0002), the oral history interview with Josiane Azoulay (RG-50.030*0647), and the oral history interview with Charles Malka (RG-50.030*0610).

25. Slyomovics, *German Reparations*, 96–100.

26. Rothberg, *Multidirectional Memory*; Young, *Writing and Rewriting*; Silverman, *Palimpsestic Memory*.

27. Dickey, "Voices," 159.

28. Aub, *Diarios*, 269, quoted in Dickey, "Voices," 159.

29. Arezki Berkani, *Mémoire*.

30. Bejui et al., *Chemins*.

31. Boum, "Bou Arfa."

32. Boum, "Colomb-Béchar."

33. Boum, "Berrouaghia."

34. Bejan, "Kindia"; Bejan, "Kankan."

35. Bejan, "Koulikoro."

36. Boum, "Sebikotane."

37. Wriggins, *Picking Up the Pieces*.

38. See Susan Miller, "Passage to Casablanca: The Refugee Crisis in Morocco During WWII," talk given at the Center for Middle Eastern Studies, Berkeley, December 8, 2014, cmes.berkeley.edu/susan-gilson-miller-passage-to-casablanca-the-refugee-crisis-in-morocco-during-wwii-2/ (accessed January 2015).

39. Abitbol, *Jews of North Africa*; Aron, *Histoire de Vichy*; Ansky, *Juifs d'Algérie*.

40. Laskier and Bashan, "Morocco," 493.

41. Boum, "Partners Against Anti-Semitism."

42. Wriggins, *Picking Up the Pieces*, 65.

43. Szajkowski, *Jews and the French Foreign Legion*, 160.

44. Cantier, "Camps d'internement," 22.

45. Brower, *Desert Named Peace*, 123–38.

46. *Jewish Herald* 260 (August 1, 1867): 114.

47. Stein, *Saharan Jews*, 209.

48. Navib, *Cultures oasiennes*.

49. Quoted in Núñez, "Max Aub," 351.

50. Boum, "Partners Against Anti-Semitism."

51. See D'Hérama, *Tournant dangereux mémoires*, 119.

52. Garaudy, *Parole d'homme*, 16.

53. Aub, *Diario de Djelfa*, 7.

54. D'Hérama, *Tournant dangereux mémoires*, 92–93.

55. Wyss-Dunant report, USHMM, RG-67.008M, box 1, folder 15.

56. Quoted in Núñez, "Max Aub," 353.

57. Letter from François Darlan to the Governor-General of Algeria, March 12, 1941, Centre des Archives d'Outre-mer, 9 H 116, 117, 120, and 93/3354.

58. Wyss-Dunant report.

59. Wyss-Dunant report.

60. Oliel, *Camps de Vichy*.

61. Aub, *Diario de Djelfa*.

62. Harry Alexander oral history interview, April 4, 1991, USHMM, RG-50.030*0007; D'Hérama, *Tournant dangereux mémoires*, 116.

63. Satloff, *Among the Righteous*.

64. Aub, *Diarios*, 14.

65. Aub, *Diarios*, 14.

Notes to Chapter 8

A narrower version of this essay was initially presented under the title "Une écriture à chaud: Chronicles of the Holocaust in North Africa," at the conference "Performances and Performatives of the Holocaust: French and North African Acts of Resistance, Collaboration, and Testimony," held at UCLA on May 1, 2009. I would like to thank Andrea Loselle, Josh Lambert, and Daniel Lee for their comments on the original essay and its subsequent revisions. All translations from the French are my own.

1. Based on the same Statut des Juifs applied to Jews in France, this complex anti-Jewish legislation established parameters for defining Jews and deprived them of civil rights, including access to certain professions and universities. The application and enforcement of these laws varied greatly across France's North African territories. See Marrus and Paxton, *Vichy France*; Abitbol, *Jews of North Africa*; and Laskier, *North African Jewry*.

2. Laskier, "Between Vichy Antisemitism," 357. Claude Nataf has suggested that the relatively small number of deportations is explained by the logistical difficulty of organizing sea or air transport at a critical moment in the war when air- and seacraft were reserved for military operations. See Nataf, "Préface," 18.

3. Page numbers cited in this chapter refer to the 1943 publication of Ghez's *Six mois sous la botte*. Ghez's chronicle was reissued in 2009 in the series Témoignages de la Shoah (co-published by La Fondation pour la Mémoire de la Shoah and Le Manuscrit), with a preface and annotations by Claude Nataf. The English-language translations of the chronicles are my own.

4. Ghez subsidized the publication of his diary locally just a few months after Tunisia was liberated (likely in the summer of 1943). Although the Société africaine de publicité et d'imprimerie had offices in both Tunis and Paris, *Six mois* did not circulate in mainland France, which was still occupied at the time of its publication. It is not currently possible to ascertain whether the original version was edited for publication or whether Ghez kept the journal with an eye to future publication; Nataf's preface to the 2009 edition, however, suggests that *Six mois* is indeed a work of direct reportage, written day by day as events unfolded (Ghez, *Six mois* [2009], 28)

5. Borgel's *Étoile jaune* was first published in Tunis in 1944 by the Société africaine de publicité et d'imprimerie. The new edition has a preface and annotations by Claude Nataf. Like Ghez, Borgel subsidized the publication of the manuscript.

6. There is little information available about the genesis of Guez's *Nos martyrs sous la botte allemande* and its publication history. The book was published on July 15, 1946, presumably in Tunis, by the press of a local newspaper ("Les presses Typo-Litho du journal 'La Presse'"). Perhaps in keeping with his role in the Jewish community, Guez opted to produce a bilingual edition (in French and Judeo-Arabic) and to include prayers (in Hebrew).

7. Little is known about Eugène Boretz, whose chronicle was published in 1944 by the Office français d'édition in Algiers. The neutrality of the reportage-style chronicle and its place of publication seem to indicate that its author may be neither Jewish nor even Tunisian. The chronicle written by Trenner, an Austrian Jew thrown into Tunisian history by fate, is unique in the corpus: Traveling in Tunis on business at the moment of the German invasion, Trenner was arrested by the Nazis and pressed into service as an interpreter between the Gestapo and the Jews when German officials learned that he was fluent in French. The only available copy appears, excerpted, in Nataf's compendium *Tunisie sous le joug nazi*. One hundred pages of this sourcebook of anecdotes, oral testimonies, correspondence, and shorter chronicles are given over to Trenner's *Croix gammée* (Nataf, *Tunisie*, 225–330).

8. In the last decades of the twentieth century, a substantial corpus of literary theory emerged to grapple with questions of memory, witnessing, and trauma in the context of writing on the Holocaust. See, for example, Felman and Laub, *Crises of Witnessing*; Caruth, *Unclaimed Experience*; Young, *Writing and Rewriting*; and LaCapra, *Representing the Holocaust*.

9. See Suleiman, "Do Facts Matter"; White, *Tropics of Discourse*; and, specifically, Young, "Interpreting Literary Testimony," 407.

10. Nataf, "Préface," 19.

11. I have chosen to focus on Ghez and Borgel's chronicles in this analysis because their similar positions in the Tunisian Jewish community afforded them privileged insight into the events they recount and because of their texts' temporal proximity to the occupation itself. The other chronicles (by Guez, Boretz, and Trenner) are equally fascinating and also merit sustained scrutiny.

12. Three Jewish intellectuals of Warsaw, S. Ansky, Y. L. Peretz, and Y. Dinezon, formulated the plea to "Become Historians of Yourselves" in 1915, in the aftermath of the Kisniev pogrom. Peretz et al., "Appeal to Collect Materials," 210.

13. Ghez was something of a renaissance man and a notable figure in Tunisois society. A secular Jew, he was nonetheless an active leader in the Jewish community and a fiercely public opponent of anti-Semitism. In 1940, at the moment the anti-Jewish laws were being applied in Tunisia, Ghez was granted an official exemption in recognition of his service in both world wars. Ghez wanted to refuse special treatment in protest and out of solidarity, but the leaders of the Jewish community compelled him to accept, reasoning that his protected status could potentially serve the interests of the Jews. See Nataf, "Biographie de Paul Ghez"; and Nataf's preface to Ghez, *Six mois* (2009), 16, 25.

14. Ghez, *Six mois* (1943), 12–13.

15. Ghez, *Six mois* (1943), 17–18.

16. Ghez, *Six mois* (1943), 13.

17. Ghez, *Six mois* (1943), 19.

18. Ghez, *Six mois* (1943), 14.

19. There is ample evidence that the word *exterminer* (to exterminate) was in use in the French press during the summer and fall of 1942, before Ghez's writing. See Poznanski, *Propagandes*, 318.

20. Borgel, *Étoile jaune*, 26.

21. Although beyond the immediate scope of this essay, it is worth observing that Borgel's remark that the Jew had been abandoned by the government of the French protectorate (helmed by Admiral Jean-Pierre Esteva) is followed by conciliatory gestures of forgiveness.

22. In Nataf's prefaces, Borgel is figured as a far less fascinating character than Ghez. Also a lawyer by training, Borgel appears to have led a quiet life in Tunis and was deeply entwined with the Jewish community because of his father's leadership role and his in-laws' attachment to the community notables (Borgel's wife was the niece of Eugène Bessis, president of the community before Moïse Borgel).

23. Borgel, *Étoile jaune*, 27.

24. Borgel, *Étoile jaune*, 25.

25. Borgel, *Étoile jaune*, 26

26. Borgel, *Étoile jaune*, 78.

27. Borgel, *Étoile jaune*, 159, 184, 223, 414.

28. Set during the German occupation of Tunisia, Karin Albou's 2008 historical fiction film *Le chant des mariées* (The Wedding Song)—the story of a friendship between two teenage girls, one Jewish and one Muslim—is one of the few cultural productions to represent the sexual violence perpetrated by the Nazis against Jewish women in this context. Albou's representation of this episode is, like Borgel's, steeped in restraint; the film uses evocative shots and imagery rather than direct portrayal.

29. Borgel, *Étoile jaune*, 383.

30. Borgel, *Étoile jaune*, 383.

31. Unique in this historiographic corpus is Sabille's *Les juifs de Tunisie*, the earliest work of scholarship to take up this period and, still, the only one to focus exclusively on the experience of Tunisian Jews.

32. Serels, "Non-European Holocaust," 130.

33. "...ce silence trop peu fréquemment rompu, sur les Juifs d'Afrique du Nord, comme

s'ils n'avaient pas souffert, eux aussi, des effets de la persécution raciale, comme s'ils avaient été préservés des malheurs de la guerre, en un mot: *comme s'ils avaient survécu à l'écart de la Shoah*" (Kaspi, *Juifs pendant l'Occupation*, 175; my emphasis).

34. This is undeniably true: 2,500 Tunisian Jews (out of a population of 85,000) lost their lives during the six-month occupation, and most of these deaths were the result of the conditions in the camps: general insalubrity, malnutrition, strenuous work details, and exposure to weather. A small percentage of the deaths occurred directly at the hands of SS soldiers, usually as punishment for attempted escape or as a way of exerting authority over the Jewish workers. According to Abitbol, 17 Jews were either shot or deported during the occupation (Abitbol, *Jews of North Africa*, 217).

35. Abitbol, *Jews of North Africa*, 119.

36. "Gardons-nous malgré tout de dramatiser à l'excès. Rien de comparable ici à ce qui s'est passé en metropole. C'est une période de quelques mois seulement" (Kaspi, *Juifs pendant l'occupation*, 205).

37. Debates over whether the Final Solution was intended to include the Jews of Tunisia persist, although numerous sources suggest that the Nazi project was foiled only by time and material constraints. See Satloff, *Among the Righteous*, 18–21; Abitbol, *Jews of North Africa*, 119–25; and testimony recorded by Laskier in "Between Vichy Antisemitism," 359.

38. Memmi, *Statue de sel*, 222.

39. Memmi, *Pillar of Salt*, 271. I have substantially modified the published English translation by Edourd Roditi to bring it closer into line with the original French.

40. Polemics regarding terminology, both scholarly and anecdotal, are too numerous to catalog here. Nonetheless, it is illustrative to note that various sources have either argued or simply assumed that the term *Holocaust* applies exclusively to the fate of *European* Jews. As its title indicates, Hilberg's *Destruction of the European Jews*, considered a landmark in Holocaust historiography, refers only to Europe; the *Columbia Encyclopedia* defines *Holocaust* as "the persecution and elimination of European Jews"; and the 2008 edition of *Le Petit Larousse*, a major French dictionary, explains that the term *Holocauste* refers to the "genocide of the Jews of Europe." Nonetheless, a significant number of scholars have sought to either expand these definitions or make visible the limitations of certain terms, most notably when it comes to understanding the wide net cast by the Nazi machine and accounting for their non-Jewish victims (Roma, homosexuals, the handicapped). See, for example, Burleigh and Wippermann, *Racial State*. And yet the question of whether the Jews of Tunisia are "victim enough" (paraphrasing Memmi) to be deemed survivors of the Holocaust or the Shoah remains a murky one, crystalizing the paradox outlined by the editors of this volume: Even as the field of Holocaust studies has become "ever more detailed . . . entire geographic realms of Holocaust history remain opaque" (8).

41. Gavriel Rosenfeld defines the "politicization" of the Holocaust as "a process of appropriation and distortion that began in the late 1960s and gained momentum in the 1970s and 1980s" (Rosenfeld, "Politics of Uniqueness," 33).

42. For an exploration of the "uniqueness discourse" and other debates in Holocaust studies, see Rosenfeld, "Politics of Uniqueness"; and Michman, "Jewish Dimension," 17–28.

43. Roskies, *Literature of Destruction*.

44. Roskies, *Literature of Destruction*, 2.

45. Roskies, *Literature of Destruction*, 14.

46. "For greater convenience and affordability, the entire usable past was anthologized in the Five Books of Moses, The Five Scrolls, the Sabbath and festival prayer books, the Ein Ya'akov, and the Book of Jashar" (Roskies, *Literature of Destruction*, 1).

47. Roskies, *Literature of Destruction*, 3.

48. Rothberg, *Multidirectional Memory*; Silverman, *Palimpsestic Memory*.

Notes to Chapter 9

Parts of the "Interwar Fusions" section are taken from the first chapter of my doctoral dissertation, "Radical Nationalists."

1. El Maleh, *Parcours immobile*, 37. All translations are my own unless otherwise noted.

2. By Gallicism I mean the particular model of French Republicanism and citizenship advocated by philanthropic and educational organizations such as the Alliance Israélite Universelle. The Alliance instilled this Gallicism among its students, Jews (and a few non-Jews) in the Middle East and North Africa, through French-language instruction, French literature and history courses, and more. Indeed, the foundational goals of the Alliance Israélite Universelle included preparing Jewish students in the Middle East and North Africa for citizenship in their home counties along the lines of France's emancipation of Jews in 1790 and 1791. Interestingly, by teaching in French and instilling such French cultural hegemony in the educational program, the Alliance may have ultimately served to widen the gap between Jews in its schools and the predominant surrounding Muslim and Christian populations. See, for example, Rodrigue and Benbass, *Sephardi Jewry*; and Malino, *Teaching Freedom*.

3. Pierre Birnbaum has written extensively on what he calls "State Jews," or *les fous de la République*, entailing an utter devotion to the French Revolution principles that underpinned the French Republic—it is this vision of Gallicism, combined with what Lisa Moses Leff calls the "sacred bonds of solidarity," that foregrounds the Alliance Israélite Universelle's role in Gallicization and the politics thereof in Morocco. See Birnbaum, *Jews of the Republic*; and Leff, *Sacred Bonds*.

4. See, for example, D. Joly, *French Communist Party*; and Le Foll Luciani's masterful *Les juifs algériens*. Because of Algeria's status as an integral part of France rather than as a protectorate, like Tunisia and Morocco, the PCF's dithering and ultimate support for Algerian independence is the most dramatic case.

5. See Schroeter, *Merchants of Essaouira*; and Schroeter, *Sultan's Jew*.

6. Interview with Encarnación Lévy, January 2012, Casablanca, Morocco. Encarnación's husband, Simon Lévy, was one of the most prominent Moroccan Jewish communists from the late 1940s until his death in 2011. Simon Lévy worked alongside El Maleh at Lycée Mohammed V in Casablanca in the early 1960s.

7. El Maleh, *Parcours immobile*, 53.

8. El Maleh, *Parcours immobile*, 37.

9. El Maleh, *Parcours immobile*, 181. El Maleh leaves this deliberately vague, continually imploring the reader to "erase that date!" when referencing the year of the protagonist's birth.

10. El Maleh, *Parcours immobile*, 177.

11. El Maleh, *Parcours immobile*, 210.

12. El Maleh, *Parcours immobile*, 54.

13. Miller, *History of Modern Morocco*, 116.

14. Beevor, *Battle for Spain*, 16.

15. Beevor, *Battle for Spain*, 17.

16. Moneta, *Politique du Parti communiste*, 18.

17. Ayache, *Mouvement syndical*, 11.

18. Ayache, *Mouvement syndical*, 11.

19. Miller, *History of Modern Morocco*, 110.

20. Halstead, *Rebirth of a Nation*, 151.

21. Wohl, *French Communism*, 109.

22. Wohl, *French Communism*, 409.

23. PCF archives, 3 MI 6, 92 Séquence 598—Résolutions, projets de résolutions, manifeste (1933).

24. Notable exceptions from the past century include Abitbol, *Juifs d'Afrique du Nord*; Msellati, *Juifs d'Algérie*; and a significant section on World War II in Kenbib, *Juifs et musulmans*.

25. Susan Gilson Miller is currently at work on an account of the Joint Distribution Committee's work with the refugee crisis in Morocco; Aomar Boum and Daniel Schroeter are co-authoring a book about the popular story of Sultan Mohammed V refusing to bow to French protectorate authorities to "save" all the Jews of Morocco. See, for example, Boum, *Memories of Absence*; the September 2014 special issue of the *Journal of North African Studies* devoted to World War II (vol. 19, no. 4); Stein, *Saharan Jews*; and Achcar, *Arabs and the Holocaust*. Within the last ten years, the United States Holocaust Memorial Museum (USHMM) in Washington, D.C., has hosted numerous conferences and scholars working on Vichy North Africa and has collected copies of significant archival material from North Africa and the Middle East during the World War II period.

26. The story of Hélène Cazès Benatar is the core of Susan Gilson Miller's forthcoming book on the Joint Distribution Committee and refugees in Morocco during World War II.

27. Kenbib, "Moroccan Jews," 542.

28. Kenbib, "Moroccan Jews," 543.

29. Kenbib, "Moroccan Jews," 544.

30. Kenbib, "Moroccan Jews," 545.

31. Kenbib, "Moroccan Jews," 547.

32. Kenbib, "Moroccan Jews," 547.

33. Boum, "Partners Against Anti-Semitism," 565.

34. Boum, "Partners Against Anti-Semitism," 565.

35. Kenbib, "Moroccan Jews," 549.

36. Kenbib, "Moroccan Jews," 547.

37. By "fickle French Republicanism" I am referring to the pervasive hope among Jews in North Africa that "true France" was the France of the Revolution, universalist ideals, and French Republicanism. Pierre Birnbaum has written about the sense of betrayal of the "State Jew" in the person of Léon Blum, the first Jew and the first socialist to become prime

minister of France. See Birnbaum, *Léon Blum*. According to this belief, Vichy could be an aberration in the *longue durée*; however, because of Vichy legislation in light of antecedents such as the Dreyfus affair, French Republicanism's fragility was palpable. As demonstrated by Aron Rodrigue, Esther Benbassa, Lisa Moses Leff, and others, the Alliance Israélite Universelle school system was one mode of transmission of the French Republican ideal among Jews in North Africa and the Middle East. Indeed, one of the goals of the Alliance was to prepare Jews for citizenship in their home countries along the lines of the emancipation of French Jews in 1790 and 1791. Presumably, their home countries would themselves "evolve" over time to more closely resemble the governing norms of the French Republic.

38. El Maleh, *Mille ans*, 55.

39. El Maleh, *Mille ans*, 57.

40. El Maleh, *Mille ans*, 57.

41. El Maleh, *Mille ans*, 61.

42. El Maleh, *Mille ans*, 98

43. El Maleh, *Mille ans*, 103.

44. El Maleh, *Mille ans*, 107.

45. El Maleh, *Mille ans*, 108.

46. El Maleh, *Mille ans*, 109.

47. El Maleh, *Mille ans*, 110.

48. El Maleh, *Mille ans*, 112.

49. El Maleh, *Mille ans*, 180–81.

50. "Bulletin de Renseignements Politiques et Economiques du 21 au 27 Juillet 1940" and "Bulletin de Renseignements Politiques et Economiques du 25 au 31 Août 1940," Résidence Générale de la République Française au Maroc, Direction des Affaires Politiques, Section Politique, "A ne pas reproduire ni divulger," Archives nationales d'outre mer (ANOM), FR CAOM/COL/1AFF-POL/1424.

51. "Bulletin de Renseignements Politiques et Economiques du 28 Juillet au 3 Août 1940," Résidence Générale de la République Française au Maroc, Direction des Affaires Politiques, Section Politique, "A ne pas reproduire ni divulger," ANOM, FR CAOM/COL/1AFF-POL/1424.

52. "Bulletin de Renseignements Politiques et Economiques du 15 au 21 Septembre 1940," Résidence Générale de la République Française au Maroc, Direction des Affaires Politiques, Section Politique, "A ne pas reproduire ni divulger," ANOM, FR CAOM/COL/1AFF-POL/1424.

53. "Bulletin de Renseignements Politiques et Economiques du 27 Octobre au 2 Novembre 1940," Résidence Générale de la République Française au Maroc, Direction des Affaires Politiques, Section Politique, "A ne pas reproduire ni divulger," ANOM, FR CAOM/COL/1AFF-POL/1424.

54. "Bulletin de Renseignements Politiques et Economiques du 3 au 9 Novembre 1940," Résidence Générale de la République Française au Maroc, Direction des Affaires Politiques, Section Politique, "À ne pas reproduire ni divulger," ANOM, FR CAOM/COL/1AFF-POL/1424.

55. Benseddik, *Syndicalisme*, 281–82.

56. Benseddik, *Syndicalisme*, 282.

57. Chakib, *Contribution*, 93.

58. Chakib, *Contribution*, 94.

59. Lévy, *Essais d'histoire*, 66.

60. "*Parti Communiste Marocain: pour un Maroc prospère et démocratique, résolution politique du Premier Congrès National des 5–6–7 Avril 1946*" (booklet), PPS (Parti du Progrès et du Socialisme) Archives, Rabat, Morocco, uncatalogued material. Many thanks to the staff and activists at the PPS headquarters in Rabat for allowing me access to this material in January 2014.

61. For more on Léon Sultan's activities under Vichy in Morocco, see Heckman, "Multivariable Casablanca."

62. *Parti Communiste Marocain*.

63. By "compromised Republicanism," I mean the perceived betrayal of the universalist, emancipationist values of the Republicanism generation by the French revolution of 1789.

64. *Parti Communiste Marocain*, 1.

65. *Parti Communiste Marocain*, 1.

66. *Parti Communiste Marocain*, 3.

67. *Parti Communiste Marocain*, 3.

68. *Parti Communiste Marocain*, 4.

69. *Parti Communiste Marocain*, 7.

70. *Parti Communiste Marocain*, 22.

71. *Parti Communiste Marocain*, 25.

72. El Maleh, *Parcours immobile*, 62, 73.

73. El Maleh, *Parcours immobile*, 62.

74. El Maleh, *Parcours immobile*, 69.

75. El Maleh, *Parcours immobile*, 71.

76. El Maleh, *Parcours immobile*, 73.

77. El Maleh, *Parcours immobile*, 103.

78. In her 1944 essay "The Jew as Pariah," Arendt describes four "pariah" categories into which modern Jews fit. These are the "lord of dreams" (exemplified by Heinrich Heine), the "conscious pariah" (Bernard Lazare), the "suspect" (Charlie Chaplin), and, finally, the "man of good will" (Franz Kafka). Here I am referencing the conscious pariah, which is the Jew who acknowledges pariah status in the dominant society and consciously militates for the acceptance of Jews toward "an admission of Jews *as Jews* to the ranks of humanity, rather than a permit to ape the gentiles or an opportunity to play the *parvenu*" (Arendt, "Jew as Pariah," 100). Karl Marx's concept of alienation typically relates to the socially constructed gulf between how a person functions in the world and their inherent humanity of "species essence." The foundations for this concept can been seen in Marx's infamous 1844 essay "On the Jewish Question."

79. El Maleh, *Parcours immobile*, 104.

80. El Maleh, *Parcours immobile*, 99. The full quote is, "A game of complex margins. A word to be invented: leftism."

Notes to Chapter 10

1. See, most recently, Stone, *Liberation of the Camps*.

2. On this special treatment, see, for example, G. D. Cohen, "Between Relief and Politics"; G. D. Cohen, "Politics of Recognition"; Patt, "People Must Be Forced"; Grossmann, "Grams"; and Zahra, "Prisoners of the Postwar."

3. See, for example, Douglas, *Memory of Judgment*.

4. See Ofer, *Escaping the Holocaust*; Porat, *Blue and Yellow Stars*; and Morse, *While Six Million Died*.

5. Yablonka, *Survivors*; Yablonka, *State of Israel*; Bauer, *Out of the Ashes*.

6. Barkan, *Guilt of Nations*; Rousso, *Vichy Syndrome*.

7. Bartov, "Holocaust as Leitmotif."

8. Himka and Michlic, *Bringing the Dark Past to Light*.

9. See, for example, Rudling, "Memories"; Mick, "Incompatible Experiences"; and Mick, "War and Conflicting Memories."

10. See, for example, Novick, *Holocaust in American Life*; Chaumont, *Concurrence des victimes*; Moses, *Empire*; Bloxham and Moses, *Oxford Handbook*; and Bloxham and Kushner, *Holocaust*.

11. Stauber, *Holocaust in Israeli Public Debate*; Segev, *Seventh Million*; Segev, *1949*; Bartov, "Kitsch and Sadism."

12. Shapira, *Ben-Gurion*; Segev, *Biography*.

13. Morris, *Birth of the Palestinian Refugee*.

14. Redlich, *Life in Transit*; Grossmann, "Remapping Relief."

15. See, for example, Beker, "Forgotten Narrative"; Stillman, *Jews of Arab Lands in Modern Times*; and Stillman, *Jews of Arab Lands*.

16. See, for example, Arad, "Israel and the Shoah"; and Zerubavel, *Recovered Roots*.

17. See, for example, Roby, *Mizrahi Era*; Bashkin, *Impossible Exodus*; Shohat, "Invention of the Mizrahim"; and Shohat, "Sephardim in Israel."

18. This point is discussed further in Bartov, "Defining Enemies."

19. For North African Jews, see Gottreich and Schroeter, *Jewish Culture*; and Gottreich, "Historicizing the Concept of Arab Jews." For Middle Eastern Jews, see L. Levy, "Historicizing the Concept of Arab Jews"; and L. Levy, "Reorienting Hebrew Literary History."

20. See more in Bartov, *The "Jew" in Cinema*.

21. For thoughtful ruminations on the manner in which the traumas of the past can bring Israeli Jews and Arabs together, see, for example, Bashir and Goldberg, "Deliberating the Holocaust"; Hever and Katz, "Post-Zionist Condition"; Ghanem and Mustafa, "Coping with the Nakba"; and Khadem, "Permanence of an Ephemeral Pain."

Notes to Chapter 11

1. The *Encyclopedia*, under the general editorship of Geoffrey P. Megargee, is projected to run to 7 volumes and to list more than 20,000 sites. It will include material about camps in North Africa.

2. For microhistories, see, for example, Mariot and Zalc, *Face à la persécution*, which follows the fate of Jews in the city of Lens in France; and Browning, *Remembering Survival*,

which focuses on a single camp at Wierzbnik-Starachowice in Poland. The use of diaries and testimonies in broader histories was inaugurated by Saul Friedländer, in his magnus opus *Nazi Germany and the Jews*.

3. Rothberg, *Multidirectional Memory*, 3, 4.

4. Suleiman, "1.5 Generation"; and Suleiman, *Crises of Memory*, ch. 8.

5. Marianne Hirsch first formulated the concept of postmemory in her book *Family Frames* and theorized it further and introduced the notion of affiliative postmemory in her subsequent work, *The Generation of Postmemory*.

6. See especially Derrida, "Circonfession"; Cixous, "La venue à l'écriture"; and Cixous, *Rêveries*.

7. See, among the many works she has edited on this subject, Sebbar, *Enfance algérienne*; Sebbar, *Enfances tunisiennes*; Sebbar, *Enfance juive*; and Sebbar, *Enfance des français d'Algérie*.

Notes to Chapter 12

1. Abramson, "Double Occlusion," 285.

2. Abramson, "Double Occlusion," 285. I take the liberty of using the terms *Sephardim* and *Sephardi* in a broad sense, to mean not only Ladino-speaking Jews of Spanish and Portuguese descent but also Jews of the Mediterranean, southeastern Europe, the Middle East, North Africa, and Central Asia, who were non-Yiddish-speaking. Linguistically diverse, they spoke Arabic, Turkish, Persian, and myriad other local languages and dialects in addition to Hebrew and even, sometimes, Ladino. These groups have customarily been excluded from the category of Sephardim, even though they share Sephardi influences as an essential part of their cultural composition. Scholars have accentuated the problem by emphasizing the vast geographic spread of the non-Ashkenazi world, its physical disjuncture, and its intellectual fragmentation, building a case (either purposely or inadvertently) for its unsuitability as a single analytical unit. Here, I take a different view, one which is sensitive to continuities across time and space that are the product of centuries of Jews living harmoniously together with non-Jews under the protection of Muslim rule. Finally, the term *Mizrahi* (eastern), as applied to new immigrants and their descendants by the Israeli state, is widely regarded as politically laden. Moreover, it is rejected by many of the people to whom it has been applied, so I do not use it here.

3. Rodrigue, *Sephardim* (esp. 1–4), makes a foundational argument close to the one made here. The destruction of Ladino-speaking communities of southeastern Europe has received more attention of late, though nowhere nearly as much as it deserves. An outstanding example is Mazower, *Salonica*, ch. 22, a gripping account of the destruction of Salonica's Jewish community. For the most part, Rodrigue's critique still holds. Hayes and Roth's *Oxford Handbook of Holocaust Studies*, a hefty tome of nearly 800 pages with many articles by distinguished Holocaust scholars, mentions the word *Sephardim* only once (p. 105); North Africa also makes a single appearance, in the section "Future Study of the Holocaust in Jewish Culture." Jeffry Shandler makes the claim that "in Israel, the official public history of the Holocaust has recently been expanded to include the wartime experience of Mizrahi Jews in North Africa (as evinced by the new museum at Yad Vashem, which opened in 2005), reflecting the

state's commitment to maintain the Holocaust as a defining event for all Israelis" (Shandler, "Jewish Culture," 603). This suggests that inclusion of non-European Jews in Holocaust historiography is an Israeli problem, ignoring its meaning for Holocaust studies more generally.

4. The original article was in French: Dan Michman, "Le sort des juifs d'Afrique du Nord pendant la seconde guerre mondiale: fait-il partie de la Shoah?" unpublished manuscript, in my possession.

5. Michman, "Sort des juifs d'Afrique du Nord," 15n34, citing Longerich, *Unwritten Order*, 96.

6. Michman, "Sort des juifs d'Afrique du Nord," 17, citing Hilberg, *Destruction of the European Jews*, 411.

7. Michman, "Sort des juifs d'Afrique du Nord," 12, quoting Eichmann, who reportedly said, "I realize we made some mistakes in numbers."

8. Michman, "Sort des juifs d'Afrique du Nord," 26–27.

9. The exact title is the Ben-Zvi Institute for the Study of Jewish Communities in the East.

10. The United States Holocaust Memorial Museum (USHMM) has taken the lead in assembling a vast and well-organized documentation based on North Africa and the Holocaust. Collections can be consulted online at collections.ushmm.org/search.

11. For a good general introduction to cultural history, see Chartier, "Cultural History," 420–25.

12. Stone, "Holocaust Historiography," 2.

13. On the question of refugees in North Africa, the bibliography is thin. See Tartakower and Grossmann, *Jewish Refugee*, esp. ch. 6, which includes a section on North Africa. Also see Bauer, *Out of the Ashes*; Gleizer, *Unwelcome Exiles*; Wriggins, *Picking Up the Pieces*; Ben Ya'akov, "European Jewish Refugees"; Baïda, "Réfugiés juifs européens"; and Abitbol, "Afrique du Nord."

14. Here I mention the work of Moroccan-Israeli historian Michel Abitbol. Despite limited access to documents, a generation ago Abitbol collated and interpreted the then existing sources in his *Jews of North Africa* to produce a credible narrative. See also his "Waiting for Vichy." Also noteworthy is a recent book by well-known Israeli Holocaust scholar Hanna Yablonka, *Juifs d'Orient*, a state-of-the-art report covering topics such as Holocaust education, memorialization, and indemnification within the context of the Israeli "Oriental" experience of the Shoah.

15. I mention in regard to this issue Satloff's *Among the Righteous*, which has reverberated beyond its modest intentions, largely because of the absence of more historically factual, archive-based research.

16. Goda, "Hitler's Demand."

Notes to Chapter 13

1. Eisenbeth, *Pages vécues*.

2. Guez, *Nos martyrs*. Zuares from Libya wrote songs after the liberation of the Giado camp.

3. Sebag, *Communist de Tunisie*.

4. Saadoun, "Élaboration." Memmi's book was the second critique of the leadership

of the Jewish community to be published after the war. The first was Gaston Guez's *Nos martyrs sous la botte allemande* (Our Martyrs Under the German Boot), published in 1946. Although Memmi's criticism is direct and harsh, Guez's is indirect and focused on victims.

5. Ansky, *Juifs d'Algérie*.

6. Abitbol's *Juifs d'Afrique du Nord* was also published in Hebrew in 1986 and in English in 1989. More than a decade earlier, Dina Farella wrote a master's thesis in French on Vichy rule in Tunis, but the work was not published and hence had no academic or public impact. Similarly, Yves Claude Aouate's doctoral dissertation on Algerian Jews' experience of the war was little circulated. Farella, "Condition des juifs"; Aouate, "Juifs d'Algérie."

7. See the index in Attal, *Juifs d'Afrique du Nord*. 3

8. Yablonka, *State of Israel*.

9. The French edition was published under the title *Les juifs d'Afrique du Nord sous Vichy*; the Hebrew edition came out in 1986, and an English edition was issued in 1989.

10. *Pe'amim*, vols. 27–29.

11. Edited by Irit Abramski-Bligh and published in 1997.

12. I had the honor of being the initiator and organizer of this workshop as part of my work at the Documentation Center on North African Jewry During World War II.

13. Houri, *Journal of Clément Houri*.

Notes to Chapter 14

1. Derrida, *Monolingualism*.

2. Derrida, *Monolingualism*, 16.

3. Derrida's account of the assimilation process is not uncommon among Algerian Jews, but historians now present a more complex picture of how Algerian Jews negotiated the French "civilizing mission." See, for instance, Schreier, *Arabs of the Jewish Faith*.

4. Derrida does not appear in the essays collected here, but he does figure briefly in related work by Susan Slyomovics. See Slyomovics, *German Reparations*, 216, 221.

5. Derrida, *Monolingualism*, 7.

6. See Rothberg, *Multidirectional Memory*. The concept of multidirectionality is an attempt to capture the dynamic relation between histories—in particular, the histories of Nazi genocide and European colonialism—that are usually considered separately. Although in *Multidirectional Memory* I am primarily concerned with interactions between the *memories* of those histories, I also offer conceptual tools for thinking about the interacting histories themselves.

7. This volume thus contributes to the kind of project outlined in Katz et al., *Colonialism and the Jews*.

8. On postfascism, see Traverso, *Les nouveaux visages du fascisme*.

Notes to Chapter 15

1. The conference was held at the University of California, Los Angeles, on April 25–29, 1990, under the auspices of the UCLA Department of History and the 1939 Club of Los Angeles. It resulted in the following publication: Friedländer, *Probing the Limits of Representation*.

2. Friedländer, *Probing the Limits of Representation*, 5. For Friedländer's later reflections on the conference, see Friedländer, "Epilogue," 411–25.

3. Friedländer, *Probing the Limits of Representation*, 4.

4. White, *Figural Realism*, 25, 39.

5. For instance, in the context of this volume, Aomar Boum explores the memoirs and literary works of Max Aub, a Mexican-Spanish Jew and survivor of the Djelfa labor camp (Chapter 7); and Lia Brozgal explores the "poetics" and "strategies of representation" of Judeo-Tunisian chronicles of occupation to uncover the forgotten "microhistories" contained in them (Chapter 8).

6. For an analysis of the "warm peace" between Friedländer and White in relation to "the compatibility of . . . literary history joined to the real in history not only as supplement but as confirmation and even necessity," see Lang, "White, Friedländer," 264.

7. Friedländer, "Epilogue," 419–21.

8. Friedländer, "Epilogue," 421.

9. White, "Historical Truth," 54. Also see White, *Practical Past*, for an articulation of the Kantian framework for writing about the "practical" past.

10. This conference was held at UCLA on April 22–23, 2012, and was sponsored by the UCLA Center for Jewish Studies, the University of California Humanities Research Institute, the UCLA Department of History, and the 1939 Club. It resulted in the volume *Probing the Ethics of Holocaust Culture*, edited by Claudio Fogu, Wulf Kansteiner, and Todd Presner.

11. These debates are captured foremost in the following chapters of Fogu et al.'s *Probing the Ethics of Holocaust Culture*: A. Dirk Moses, "Anxieties in Holocaust and Genocide Studies," 332–54; Omer Bartov, "The Holocaust as Genocide: Experiential Uniqueness and Integrated History," 319–31; Michael Rothberg, "The Witness as 'World' Traveler: Multidirectional Memory and Holocaust Internationalism Before Human Rights," 355–72; Judith Butler, "Fiction and Solicitude: Ethics and the Conditions for Survival," 373–88; and Elisabeth Weber, "Catastrophes: Afterlives of the Exceptionality Paradigm in Holocaust Studies," 389–409.

12. Arendt, *Origins of Totalitarianism*.

13. Zimmerer, "Colonialism and the Holocaust," 51. For an assessment of the history of the uniqueness of the Holocaust, see Stone, *Histories of the Holocaust*, esp. ch. 5.

14. The term *colonial paradigm* comes from Kühne, "Colonialism and the Holocaust." Without presuming to be exhaustive, key works of scholarship for establishing the field of Holocaust and colonial studies include Traverso, *Origins of Nazi Violence*; Zimmerer and Zeller, *Genocide*; Mazower, *Hitler's Empire*; Zimmerer, *Von Windhuk nach Auschwitz*; and Baranowski, *Nazi Empire*.

15. Michael Rothberg's concept of multidirectional memory has given rise to comparative, entangled approaches to the study of multiple competing cultural memories and histories. See Rothberg, *Multidirectional Memory*.

16. Confino, *World Without Jews*, 11. On the issue of continuities, see Madley, "Africa to Auschwitz."

17. For an assessment of some of the lingering anxieties in the field, see Moses, "Anxieties."

18. Snyder, *Bloodlands*. This geographic definition of the "bloodlands" comes from p. 384.

19. Snyder, *Black Earth*, 324–26.

20. For a thorough assessment, see Giaccaria and Minca, *Hitler's Geographies*. Also see Fogu, "Spatial Turn."

21. See, for example, the projected seven-volume *Encyclopedia of Camps and Ghettos, 1933–1945* developed by the United States Holocaust Memorial Museum. The series will document more than 42,000 concentration camps, subcamps, forced labor camps, death camps, transit camps, detention centers, ghettos, and other sites of atrocity: www.ushmm. org/research/publications/encyclopedia-camps-ghettos/about-the-encyclopedia. For a methodological approach to Holocaust studies built on GIS and data visualization, see Knowles et al., *Geographies of the Holocaust*.

22. The conference was co-sponsored by the UCLA Alan D. Leve Center for Jewish Studies, the United States Holocaust Memorial Museum, the 1939 Society, and the UCLA Center for Near Eastern Studies. It took place on November 15–16, 2015, and was co-organized by Aomar Boum, Sarah Stein, Leah Wolfson, and Todd Presner. This book is an outgrowth of that conference.

23. Boum and Stein provide some of the key references to the state of scholarship in their introduction to this volume. However, as both Boum and Susan Slyomovics note in their contributions (Chapters 7 and 4, respectively), a significant amount of archival research still needs to be done to understand the full range of Vichy camps in North Africa, the experiences and fates of those interned, and the complex colonial bureaucracies and racial policies that governed their administration.

24. Hilberg, *Destruction of the European Jews*, 662–65.

25. Yahil, *The Holocaust*, 174–75.

26. Cesarani, *Final Solution*, 593; Longerich, *Holocaust*, 391.

27. The intention of the Nazis to murder the Jews of North Africa has been the subject of recent speculation and controversy (see the commentary by Susan Miller in Chapter 12).

28. Many of the contributors to this volume pursue such an approach, including Lia Brozgal (Chapter 8) and Alma Heckman (Chapter 9).

Bibliography

Abitbol, Michel. "L'Afrique du Nord et le sauvetage des réfugiés juifs pendant la seconde guerre mondiale: l'échec de la solution du camp de Fédala." In *Présence juive au Maghreb: Hommage à Haïm Zafrani*, ed. N. S. Serfaty and J. Tedghi, 37–49. St. Denis: Bouchene, 2004.

————. *The Jews of North Africa During the Second World War*, trans. Catherine Tihanyi Zentelis. Detroit: Wayne State University Press, 1989.

————. *Les juifs d'Afrique du Nord sous Vichy*. Paris: Maisonneuve et Larose, 1983; Riveneuve, 2008.

————. "Waiting for Vichy: Europeans and Jews in North Africa on the Eve of World War II." *Yad Vashem Studies* 14 (1981): 139–66.

Aboulker, José. "Témoignage: Alger, 8 novembre 1942." *Le monde juif* 152 (1994): 146–53.

————. *La victoire du 8 novembre 1942: la Résistance et le débarquement des Alliés à Alger*. Paris: Félin, 2012.

Abramski-Bligh, Irit. *Pinkas Hakehilot: Encyclopedia of the Jewish Communities from Their Foundation Until After the Holocaust*. Jerusalem: Yad Vashem, 1997.

Abramson, Henry. "A Double Occlusion: Sephardim and the Holocaust." In *Sephardic and Mizrahi Jewry from the Golden Age of Spain to Modern Times*, ed. Z. Zohar, 285–99. New York: New York University Press, 2005.

Achkar, Gilbert. *The Arabs and the Holocaust: The Arab-Israeli War of Narratives*. New York: Metropolitan Books, 2010.

Agamben, Giorgio. *Homo Sacer: Sovereign Power and Bare Life*. Stanford, CA: Stanford University Press, 1998.

————. *Means Without End: Notes on Politics*. Minneapolis: University of Minnesota Press, 2000.

————. "What Is a Camp?" In *The Holocaust: Theoretical Readings*, ed. Neil Levi and Michael Rothberg, 252–56. New Brunswick, NJ: Rutgers University Press, 2003.

Ageron, Charles Robert. *Les Algériens musulmans et la France (1871–1919)*, 2 vols. Paris: Presses Universitaires de France, 1968.

———. *Modern Algeria*. Trenton, NJ: African World Press, 1991.

———. "Les populations du Maghreb face à la propagande allemande." *Revue d'Histoire de la Deuxième Guerre Mondiale* 29.114 (1979): 1–39.

———. "Vichy, les français et l'empire." In *Le Régime de Vichy et les français*, ed. Jean Pierre Azéma and François Bédarida, 122–34. Paris: Fayard, 1992.

Akpo, Catherine. *L'AOF et la deuxième guerre mondiale*. Paris: L'Harmattan, 1996.

Allali, Jean-Pierre. *Les juifs de Tunisie sous la botte allemande*. Paris: Editions Glyphe, 2014.

Allen, Michael Thad. *The Business of Genocide: The SS, Slave Labor, and the Concentration Camps*. Chapel Hill: University of North Carolina Press, 2002.

Amipaz-Silber, Gitta. *Maḥteret yehudit be-Alg'eryah, 1940–1942*. Tel Aviv: Ministry of Defense, 1983.

———. *La résistance juive en Algérie, 1940–1942*. Jerusalem: R. Mass, 1986.

Annet, Armand. *Aux heures troublées de l'Afrique française, 1939–1943*. Paris: Editions du Conquistador, 1952.

Ansky, Michel. *Les juifs d'Algérie: du décret Crémieux à la libération*. Paris: Editions du Centre, 1950.

Aouate, Yves-Claude. "Les Algériens musulmans et les mesures antijuives du gouvernement de Vichy (1940–1942)." *Pardès* 16 (1992): 189–202.

———. "Les juifs d'Algérie pendant la seconde guerre mondiale (1939–1945)," 2 vols. Ph.D. dissertation, University of Nice, 1984.

———. "La place de l'Algérie dans le projet antijuif de Vichy (octobre 1940–novembre 1942)." *Revue Française d'Histoire d'Outre-Mer* 80.301 (1993): 599–613.

Arad, Gulie Ne'eman. "Israel and the Shoah: A Tale of Multifarious Taboos." *New German Critique* 90 (autumn 2003): 5–26.

Arendt, Hannah. "The Jew as Pariah: A Hidden Tradition." *Jewish Social Studies* 6.2 (1944): 99–122.

———. *The Origins of Totalitarianism*. New York: Harcourt Brace, 1979 [1966].

———. "Why the Crémieux Decree Was Abrogated." *Contemporary Jewish Record* 6.2 (1943): 115–23.

———. "Why the Crémieux Decree Was Abrogated." In Hannah Arendt, *The Jewish Writings*, ed. Jerome Kohn and Ron H. Feldman, 244–53. New York: Schocken, 2007.

Arezki Berkani, Mohamed. *Mémoire "Trois années de camp": un an de camp de concentration, deux ans de centre disciplinaire—Djenien-Bou-Rezg Sud Oranais (1940–1943 Régie Vichy)*. Koudia-Sétif: published by author, 1965.

Armand, Lévy. *Il était une fois les juifs du Maroc*. Paris: L'Harmattan, 1995.

Aron, Robert. *Histoire de Vichy, 1940–1944*. Paris: Arthème Fayard, 1954.

Arsenian, Seth. "Wartime Propaganda in the Middle East." *Middle East Institute* 2.4 (1948): 417–29.

Askénasi, Léon. "L'histoire de ma vie." La Fondation Manitou, 2001. www.manitou.org.il/ (accessed March 20, 2018).

Attal, Robert. *Les juifs d'Afrique du Nord, Bibliographie*. Jerusalem: Yad Izhak Ben-Zvi Publications, 1993.

———. *Mémoires d'un adolescent à Tunis sous l'occupation nazie*. Jerusalem: Private imprint, 1996.

Aub, Max. *El Cementerio de Djelfa: Historias de mala muerte*. Mexico City: Joaquin Mortiz, 1965.

———. *Diario de Djelfa*. Madrid: Coleccíon Visor, 2015.

———. *Diarios (1939–1972)*. Barcelona: Alba Editorial, 1998.

Ayache, Albert. *Le mouvement syndical au Maroc*, Tome 1, *1919–1942*. Paris: L'Harmattan, 1982.

Azan, Paul. "Le général Bedeau (1804–1863)." *Revue Africaine* 263.4 (1906): 317–35.

Azéma, Jean-Pierre. *De Munich à la libération, 1938–1944*. Paris: Le Seuil, 1979.

Azoulay, Ariella. "Mother Tongue, Father Tongue: Following the Death of the Father, and the Death of the Mother." *Sternthal Journal*, cargocollective.com/ariellaazoulay (accessed March 20, 2018).

Azses, Hayim, ed. *The Shoah in the Sephardic Communities: Dreams, Dilemmas, and Decisions of Sephardic Leaders*. Jerusalem: Sephardic Educational Center in Jerusalem, 2005.

Bachoud, Andrée. *Sables d'exil: les républicains espagnols dans les camps d'internement au Maghreb (1939–1945)*. Perpignan: Mare Nostrum, 2009.

Bahloul, Joelle. "Tragedies That Linger: The Aftermath of WWII on Algerian Jews Until the End of the 20th Century." Lecture given at the symposium "New Approaches to Algerian Jewish Studies," University of California, Los Angeles, October 23–24, 2011.

Baïda, Jamâa. "The American Landing in November 1942: A Turning Point in Morocco's Contemporary History." *Journal of North African Studies* 19.4 (2014): 518–23.

———. "Ayache, German." In *Encyclopedia of Jews in the Islamic World*. Leiden: Brill, 2010. referenceworks.brillonline.com/entries/encyclopedia-of-jews-in-the-islamic-world/ay ache-germain-SIM_0002640?s.num=0&s.f.s2_parent=s.f.book.encyclopedia-of-jews -in-the-islamic-world&s.q=ayache+germain (accessed March 20 2018).

———. "Le Maroc et la propagande du IIIe Reich." *Hespéris-Tamuda* 28 (1990): 91–106.

———. *La presse marocaine d'expression française des origines à 1956*. Rabat: Faculté des sciences et des lettres humaines, 1996.

———. "Les 'réfugiés' juifs européens au Maroc pendant la seconde guerre mondiale." In *La bienvenue et l'adieu: migrants juifs et musulmans au Maghreb, XVe–XXe siècles*, 2 vols., ed. K. Dirèche, R. Aouad, and F. Abécassis, 2: 57–66. Paris and Casablanca: Karthala, 2012.

Bal, Mieke, Jonathan Crewe, and Leo Spitzer, eds. *Acts of Memory: Cultural Recall in the Present*. Hanover, NH: University Press of New England, 1999.

Baranowski, Shelly. *Nazi Empire: German Colonialism and Imperialism from Bismarck to Hitler*. Cambridge, UK: Cambridge University Press, 2011.

Barkan, Elazar. *The Guilt of Nations: Restitution and Negotiating Historical Injustices*. New York: Norton, 2000.

Bartov, Omer. "Defining Enemies, Making Victims: Germans, Jews, and the Holocaust." *American Historical Review* 103.3 (1998): 771–816.

———. "The Holocaust as Genocide: Experiential Uniqueness and Integrated History." In *Probing the Ethics of Holocaust Culture*, ed. Claudio Fogu, Wulf Kansteiner, and Todd Presner, 319–31. Cambridge, MA: Harvard University Press, 2016.

———. "The Holocaust as Leitmotif of the Twentieth Century." In *Lessons and Legacies*

VII: The Holocaust in International Perspective, ed. Dagmar Herzog, 3–25. Evanston, IL: Northwestern University Press, 2006.

———. *The "Jew" in Cinema: From The Golem to Don't Touch My Holocaust*. Bloomington: Indiana University Press, 2005.

———. "Kitsch and Sadism in Ka-Tzetnik's Other Planet: Israeli Youth Imagine the Holocaust." *Jewish Social Studies* 3.2 (1997): 42–76.

Bashir, Bashir, and Amos Goldberg. "Deliberating the Holocaust and the Nakba: Disruptive Empathy and Binationalism in Israel/Palestine." *Journal of Genocide Research* 16.1 (2014): 77–99.

Bashkin, Orit. *The Impossible Exodus: Iraqi Jews in Israel*. Stanford, CA: Stanford University Press, 2017.

Bauer, Yehuda. *American Jewry and the Holocaust: The American Jewish Joint Distribution Committee, 1939–1945*. Detroit: Wayne State University Press, 1996.

———. *Out of the Ashes: The Impact of American Jews on Post-Holocaust European Jewry*. Oxford: Pergamon Press, 1989.

Bazyler, Michael. *Holocaust Justice: The Battle for Restitution in America's Courts*. New York: New York University Press, 2003.

Beevor, Antony. *The Battle for Spain: The Spanish Civil War, 1936–1939*. London: Weidenfeld & Nicolson, 2006.

Bejan, Cristina. "Kankan." In *The United States Holocaust Memorial Museum Encyclopedia of Camps and Ghettos, 1933–1945*, Vol. 3, *Camps and Ghettos Under European Regimes Aligned With Nazi Germany*, gen. ed. Geoffrey Megargee, 274–76. Bloomington: Indiana University Press, 2018.

———. "Kindia." In *The United States Holocaust Memorial Museum Encyclopedia of Camps and Ghettos, 1933–1945*, Vol. 3, *Camps and Ghettos Under European Regimes Aligned With Nazi Germany*, gen. ed. Geoffrey Megargee, 280. Bloomington: Indiana University Press, 2018.

———. "Koulikoro." In *The United States Holocaust Memorial Museum Encyclopedia of Camps and Ghettos, 1933–1945*, Vol. 3, *Camps and Ghettos Under European Regimes Aligned With Nazi Germany*, gen. ed. Geoffrey Megargee, 280–82. Bloomington: Indiana University Press, 2018.

Bejui, Pascal, Luc Raynaud, and Jean-Pierre Vergez-Larrouy. *Les chemins de fer de la France d'Outre-Mer*, Vol. 2, *L'Afrique du Nord: le Transsaharien*. Chanac: La Regordane, 1992.

Beker, Avi. "The Forgotten Narrative: Jewish Refugees from Arab Countries." *Jewish Political Studies Review* 17.3–4 (2005): 3–19.

Bel Ange, Norbert. *Quand Vichy internait ses soldats juifs d'Algérie: Bedeau, sud oranais, 1941–1943*. Paris: L'Harmattan, 2006.

Bénabou, Marcel. *Jacob, Manahem et Mimoun: une épopée familiale*. Paris: Seuil, 1996.

Benhamou, Léon. "Les camps d'Algérie." *Information Juive* 136 (May 1994): 15.

Benkemoun, Maurice. "Le camp de Bedeau." *Information juive* 138 (July 1994): 5.

Bensadoun, Roger. *Les juifs de la République en Algérie et au Maroc: chroniques et mémoires d'autres temps (de Oran, place d'Armes à Ribat-el-Fath, le camp de la Victoire)*. Paris: Publisud, 2003.

Benseddik, Fouad. *Syndicalisme et politique au Maroc*, Tome I, *1930–1956*. Paris: L'Harmattan, 1990.

Bensousan, Renée Dray. "Les juifs d'Algérie à Marseille pendant la second guerre mondiale." In *Les juifs d'Algérie: une histoire de ruptures*, ed. Joëlle Allouche-Benayoune and Geneviève Dermenjian, 167–78. Aix-en-Provence: Presses Universitaires de Provence, 2015.

Bensoussan, Georges. "Les juifs d'Orient face au nazisme et à la Shoah." *Revue d'Histoire de la Shoah* 205 (October 2016): 7–23.

Ben-Srhir, Khalid. *Britain and Morocco During the Embassy of John Drummond Hay, 1845–1886*, trans. Malcolm William and Gavin Waterson. London: Routledge/Curzon, 2005.

Ben Ya'akov, Michal. "European Jewish Refugees in Morocco During World War II." *Avotaynu* 31.2 (2015): 41–45.

Bernard-Donals, Michael, and Richard Glejzer, eds. *Witnessing the Disaster: Essays on Representation and the Holocaust*. Madison: University of Wisconsin Press, 2003.

Bernhard, Patrick. "Behind the Battle Lines: Italian Atrocities and the Persecution or Arabs, Berbers, and Jews in North Africa During World War II." *Holocaust and Genocide Studies* 26.3 (2012): 425–46.

———. "Die 'Kolonialachse': Der NS-Staat und Italienisch-Afrika 1935 bis 1943." In *Die "Achse" im Krieg: Politik, Ideologie und Kriegführung, 1939–1945*, ed. Amedeo Osti Guerrazzi, Thomas Schlemmer, and Lutz Klinkhammer, 147–75. Paderborn: Verlag Ferdinand Schöningh, 2010.

Bidwell, Robin. *Morocco Under Colonial Rule: French Administration of Tribal Areas, 1912–1926*. London: Frank Cass, 1973.

Billig, Joseph. *Le Commissariat Général aux Questions Juives: 1941–1944*, vol. 2. Paris: Éditions du Centre, 1955.

Bilu, Yoram, and André Levy. "Nostalgia and Ambivalence: The Reconstruction of Jewish-Muslim Relations in Oulad Mansour." In *Sephardi and Middle Eastern Jewries: History and Culture in the Modern Era*, ed. Harvey Goldberg, 288–311. Bloomington: Indiana University Press, 1996.

Birnbaum, Pierre. *The Jews of the Republic: A Political History of State Jews in France from Gambetta to Vichy*, trans. Jane Marie Todd. Stanford, CA: Stanford University Press, 1996.

———. *Léon Blum: Prime Minister, Socialist, Zionist*, trans. Arthur Goldhammer. New Haven, CT: Yale University Press, 2015.

Blanchot, Maurice. *The Writing of the Disaster*. Lincoln: University of Nebraska Press, 1986.

Blévis, Laure. "Les avatars de la citoyenneté en Algérie coloniale ou les paradoxes d'une categorization." *Droit et Société* 48 (2001–2002): 557–81.

———. "La citoyenneté française au miroir de la colonisation: étude des demandes de naturalisation des 'sujets français' en Algérie colonial." *Genèse* 53 (2003–2004): 25–47.

Bloxham, Donald, and Tony Kushner. *The Holocaust: Critical Historical Approaches*. New York: Palgrave, 2005.

Bloxham, Donald, and A. Dirk Moses, eds. *The Oxford Handbook of Genocide Studies*. New York: Oxford University Press, 2010.

Boretz, Eugène. *Tunis sous la croix gammée*. Alger: Office Français d'Édition, 1944.

Borgel, Robert. *Étoile jaune et croix gammée*. Paris: Le Manuscrit, 2007.

Bouche, Denise. "Le retour de l'AOF dans la lutte contre l'ennemi aux côtés des alliés." *Revue d'Histoire de la Deuxième Guerre Mondiale* 29.114 (1979): 41–68.

Boum, Aomar. "Bedeau." In *The United States Holocaust Memorial Museum Encyclopedia of Camps and Ghettos, 1933–1945*, Vol. 3, *Camps and Ghettos Under European Regimes Aligned With Nazi Germany*, gen. ed. Geoffrey Megargee, 249–50. Bloomington: Indiana University Press, 2018.

———. "Berrouaghia." In *The United States Holocaust Memorial Museum Encyclopedia of Camps and Ghettos, 1933–1945*, Vol. 3, *Camps and Ghettos Under European Regimes Aligned With Nazi Germany*, gen. ed. Geoffrey Megargee, 252. Bloomington: Indiana University Press, 2018.

———. "Bou Arfa." In *The United States Holocaust Memorial Museum Encyclopedia of Camps and Ghettos, 1933–1945*, Vol. 3, *Camps and Ghettos Under European Regimes Aligned With Nazi Germany*, gen. ed. Geoffrey Megargee, 254–55. Bloomington: Indiana University Press, 2018.

———. "Colomb-Béchar." In *The United States Holocaust Memorial Museum Encyclopedia of Camps and Ghettos, 1933–1945*, Vol. 3, *Camps and Ghettos Under European Regimes Aligned With Nazi Germany*, gen. ed. Geoffrey Megargee. Bloomington: Indiana University Press, 2018.

———. "Colonial Minorities: Jewish-Muslim Relations in Southern Morocco Re-Evaluated." *Hespéris-Tamuda* 48 (2013): 25–40.

———. "Djenien-Bou-Rezg." In *The United States Holocaust Memorial Museum Encyclopedia of Camps and Ghettos, 1933–1945*, Vol. 3, *Camps and Ghettos Under European Regimes Aligned With Nazi Germany*, gen. ed. Geoffrey Megargee, 266–67. Bloomington: Indiana University Press, 2018.

———. *Memories of Absence: How Muslims Remember Jews in Morocco*. Stanford, CA: Stanford University Press, 2013.

———. "Partners Against Anti-Semitism: Muslims and Jews Respond to Nazism in French North African Colonies, 1936–1940." *Journal of North African Studies* 19.4 (2014): 554–70.

———. "Schooling in the Bled: Jewish Education and the Alliance Israélite Universelle in Southern Rural Morocco, 1830–1962." *Journal of Jewish Identities* 3.1 (2010): 1–24.

———. "Sebikotane." In *The United States Holocaust Memorial Museum Encyclopedia of Camps and Ghettos, 1933–1945*, Vol. 3, *Camps and Ghettos Under European Regimes Aligned With Nazi Germany*, gen. ed. Geoffrey Megargee, 294–295. Bloomington: Indiana University Press, 2018.

Boum, Aomar, and Eliezer Schilt. "Agdz." In *The United States Holocaust Memorial Museum Encyclopedia of Camps and Ghettos, 1933–1945*, Vol. 3, *Camps and Ghettos Under European Regimes Aligned With Nazi Germany*, gen. ed. Geoffrey Megargee, 247–48. Bloomington: Indiana University Press, 2018.

Bourdieu, Pierre. *The Algerians*. Boston: Beacon Press, 1962.

———. *Sociologie de l'Algérie*. Paris: Presses Universitaires de France, 2006.

Bouysse, Grégory. *Encyclopédie de l'ordre nouvel: histoire de S.O.L., de la Milice Française et des mouvements de collaboration*. Raleigh, NC: Lulu, 2016.

Bowie, Leland L. "An Aspect of Muslim-Jewish Relations in Late Nineteenth-Century Morocco: A European Diplomatic View." *International Journal of Middle East Studies* 7 (1976): 3–39.

Brecht, Arnold. "The Concentration Camp." *Columbia Law Review* 50.6 (1950): 761–82.

Brower, Benjamin Claude. *A Desert Named Peace: The Violence of France's Empire in the Algerian Sahara*. New York: Columbia University Press, 2009.

Browning, Christopher. *Remembering Survival: Inside a Nazi Slave-Labor Camp*. New York: Norton, 2010.

Browning, Christopher, with Jürgen Matthäus. *The Origins of the Final Solution: The Evolution of Nazi Jewish Policy, September 1939–March 1942*. Lincoln: University of Nebraska Press; and Jerusalem: Yad Vashem, 2004.

Brubaker, Rogers. *Citizenship and Nationhood in France and Germany*. Cambridge, MA: Harvard University Press, 1992.

Burleigh, Michael, and Wolfgang Wippermann. *The Racial State: Germany, 1933–1945*. Oxford, UK: Cambridge University Press, 1991.

Butler, Judith. "Fiction and Solicitude: Ethics and the Conditions for Survival." In *Probing the Ethics of Holocaust Culture*, ed. Claudio Fogu, Wolf Kansteiner, and Todd Presner, 373–88. Cambridge, MA: Harvard University Press, 2016.

Byfield, Judith A., Carolyn A. Brown, Timothy Parsons, and Ahmad Alawad Sikainga, eds. *Africa and World War II*. Cambridge, UK: Cambridge University Press, 2015.

Cantier, Jacques. *L'Algérie sous le régime de Vichy*. Paris: Odile Jacob, 2002.

———. "Les camps d'internement dans l'Algérie de Vichy." In *Sables d'exil: les républicains espagnols dans les camps d'internement au Maghreb (1939–1945)*, ed. Andrée Bachoud and Bernard Sicot, 37–53. Perpignan: Mare Nostrum, 2009.

Capogreco, Carlo Spartaco. *Ferramonti: la vita e gli uomini del più grande campo d'internamento fascista (1940–1945)*. Florence: La Giuntina, 1987.

Caruth, Cathy. *Unclaimed Experience: Trauma, Narrative, and History*. Baltimore: Johns Hopkins University Press, 1996.

Cate-Arries, Francie. *Spanish Culture Behind Barbed Wire: Memory and Representation of the French Concentration Camps, 1939–1945*. Lewisburg, PA: Bucknell University Press, 2004.

Cesarani, David. *Final Solution: The Fate of the Jews 1933–1949*. New York: St. Martin's Press, 2016.

Chafer, Tony, and Amanda Sackur, eds. *French Colonial Empire and the Popular Front: Hope and Disillusion*. London: Macmillan, 1999.

Chakib, Arslane. "Contribution à l'étude de l'histoire du PCM durant la période coloniale." Dissertation, Université Hassan II, Faculté des Sciences Juridiques, Economiques et Socialies, Casablanca, 1985.

Chartier, Roger. "Cultural History." In *The International Encyclopedia of the Social and Behavioral Sciences*, 2nd ed., ed. James Wright, 420–25. Amsterdam: Elsevier, 2015.

Chaumont, Jean-Michel. *La concurrence des victimes: génocide, identité, reconnaissance*. Paris: La Découverte, 1997.

Cheyette, Bryan. *Diasporas of the Mind: Jewish and Postcolonial Writing and the Nightmare of History*. New Haven, CT: Yale University Press, 2014.

Chouraqui, André. *La condition juridique de l'Israélite marocain*. Paris: Presses du Livre Français, 1950.

Chouraqui, Sidney. "Le camp de juifs français de Bedeau ou Vichy après Vichy." *Revue d'Histoire de la Shoah* 161 (1997): 217–45.

Cixous, Hélène. *Les rêveries de la femme sauvage: scènes primitives*. Paris: Galilée, 2000.

———. "La venue à l'écriture." In Hélène Cixous, Madeleine Gagnon, and Annie Leclerc, *La venue à l'écriture*. Paris: Union générale d'éditions, 1977.

Cohen, G. Daniel. "Between Relief and Politics: Refugee Humanitarianism in Occupied Germany, 1945–1946." *Journal of Contemporary History* 43.3 (2008): 437–49.

———. "The Politics of Recognition: Jewish Refugees in Relief Policies and Human Rights Debates, 1945–1950." *Immigrants and Minorities* 24.2 (2006): 125–43.

Cohen, William. "The Colonial Policy of the Popular Front." *French Historical Studies* 2.3 (1972): 368–93.

Cohn, Louis. "Une page non écrite des années 1940: les camps d'internement en Algérie française." *Les Nouveaux Cahiers* 116 (1996): 27–29.

Collotti, Enzo. *Il fascismo et gli ebrei: le leggi razziali in Italia*. Rome: Editori Laterza, 2003.

Confino, Alon. *A World Without Jews: The Nazi Imagination from Persecution to Genocide*. New Haven, CT: Yale University Press, 2014 [2005].

Conklin, Alice. *A Mission to Civilize: The Republican Idea of Empire in France and West Africa, 1895–1930*. Stanford, CA: Stanford University Press, 1997.

Coquery-Vidrovitch, Catherine. "The Popular Front and the Colonial Question: French West Africa—An Example of Reformist Colonialism." In *French Colonial Empire and the Popular Front: Hope and Disillusion*, ed. Tony Chafer and Amanda Sackur, 155–69. London: Macmillan, 1999.

Crespil, Marcel. *Mogador, mon amour*. Casablanca: Eddif Maroc, 1990.

Crowder, Michael. *Colonial West Africa*. London: Frank Cass, 1978.

Dahan, Jacques. *Regard d'un juif marocain sur l'histoire contemporaine de son pays*. Paris: L'Harmattan, 1995.

Darmon, Pierre. *L'Algérie de Pétain: les populations algériennes ont la parole (septembre 1939–novembre 1942)*. Paris: Perrin, 2014.

de Benoist, Joseph Roger. "The Brazzaville Conference; or, Involuntary Decolonization." *Africana Journal* 15 (1990): 39–58.

Debono, Emanuel. "Le difficile rétablissement du décret Crémieux (novembre 1942–octobre 1943): 'L'épouvantail arabe,' une légende?" *Revue d'Histoire de la Shoah* 205 (October 2016): 401–12.

De Chambrun, René. *France During the German Occupation: A Collection of 292 Statements on the Government of Maréchal Pétain and Pierre Laval—A Bibliographic Supplement*. Stanford, CA: Hoover Institution, 1958.

de Felice, Renzo. *Ebrei in un paese arabo: gli ebrei nella Libia contemporanea tra colonialismo, nazionalismo aravo e sionismo (1835–1970)*. Bologna: Il Mulino, 1978.

———. *Jews in an Arab Land, Libya 1835–1970*. Austin: University of Texas Press, 1985.

———. *The Jews in Fascist Italy: A History*. New York: Enigma Books, 2001.

de Foucauld, Charles. *Reconnaissance au Maroc, 1883–1884*. Paris: Challamel, 1888.

De Nesry, Carlos. *Les juifs de Tanger et du Maroc.* Casablanca and Tangier: Éditions Internationales, 1956.

Dermenjian, Geneviève. "Le juif est-il français: antisémitisme et l'idée républicaine en Algérie (1830–1839)." In *L'identité des juifs d'Algérie: une experience originale de la modernité,* ed. Shmuel Trigano, 49–69. Paris: Éditions du Nadir, 2003.

Derrida, Jacques. "Circonfession." In Geoff Bennington and Jacques Derrida, *Jacques Derrida,* transl. Patrick Mensah, Paris: Seuil, 1991.

———. *Monolingualism of the Other: or, The Prosthesis of Origin,* transl. Patrick Mensah, Stanford, CA: Stanford University Press, 1998.

———. *Le monolinguisme de l'autre.* Paris: Galilée, 1996.

D'Hérama, Paul. *Tournant dangereux, mémoires d'un déporté politique en Afrique du Nord (1940–1945).* La Rochelle: Imprimerie Jean Foucher, 1957.

Dickey, Eric. "Los Campos de la Memoria: The Concentration Camp as a Site of Memory in the Narrative of Max Aub." Ph.D. dissertation, University of Minnesota, 2009.

———. "Voices from Beyond the Grave: Remembering the Civil War in the Work of Max Aub." *Hispanic Issues On Line* 11 (2012): 157–77.

Di Porto, Valerio, ed. *Le leggi della vergogna: norme contra gli ebrei in Italia e Germania.* Florence: Felice Le Monnier, 2000.

Douglas, Lawrence. *The Memory of Judgment: Making Law and History in the Trials of the Holocaust.* New Haven, CT: Yale University Press, 2001.

Dreyfus, Jean-Marc. *L'impossible réparation: déportés, biens spoliés, or nazi, comptes bloqués, criminels de guerre.* Paris: Flammarion, 2015.

Drinnon, Richard. *Keeper of Concentration Camps: Dillon S. Myer and American Racism.* Berkeley: University of California Press, 1987.

Dunn, Ross E. "The Trade of Tafilalt: Commercial Change in Southeast Morocco on the Eve of the Protectorate." *African Historical Studies* 6.2 (1971): 271–304.

Echenberg, Myron. *Colonial Conscripts: The Tirailleurs Sénégalais in French West Africa, 1857–1960.* Portsmouth, NH: Heinemann, 1991.

Eggers, Christian. "L'internement sous toutes ses formes: approche d'une vue d'ensemble du système d'internement dans la zone de Vichy." *Le Monde Juif* 51.153 (1995): 7–75.

———. *Unerwünschte Ausländer: Juden aus Deutschland und Mitteleuropa in französischen Internierungslagern 1940–1942.* Berlin: Metropol, 2002.

Eisenbeth, Maurice. *Pages vécues.* Algiers: Charras, 1945.

El Maleh, Edmond Amran. *Mille ans, un jour.* Paris: La Pensée Sauvage, 1986.

———. *Parcours immobile.* Paris: François Maspero, 1980.

Enzyklopädie des Holocaust: Die Verfolgung und Ermordung der europäischen Juden, 2nd ed., ed. Israel Gutman, with Eberhard Jäckel, Peter Longerich, and Julius H. Schoeps. Munich: Piper, 1998.

Fall, Babacar. *Le travail forcé en Afrique Occidentale Française (1900–1945).* Paris: Karthala, 1993.

Fanon, Frantz. *The Wretched of the Earth.* New York: Grove Press, 1963.

Farella, Dina. "La condition des juifs du protectorat français de Tunisie sous le gouvernement de Vichy de juin 1940 à novembre 1942." Master's thesis, University of Nice, Sophia Antipolis, France, 1972.

Felman, Shoshana, and Dori Laub. *Crises of Witnessing in Literature, Psychoanalysis, and History*. New York: Routledge, 1992.

Flamand, Pierre. *Diaspora en terre d'Islam: les communautés israélites du sud du Maroc— essai de description et d'analyse de la vie juive en milieu berbère*. Casablanca: Imprimeries Réunies, 1959.

———. "Quelques renseignements statistiques sur la population israélite du sud marocain." *Hespéris* 37 (1950): 363–97.

Fleming, Katherine Elizabeth. *Greece: A Jewish History*. Princeton, NJ: Princeton University Press, 2008.

Fogu, Claudio. "A 'Spatial Turn' in Holocaust Studies?" In *Probing the Ethics of Holocaust Culture*, ed. Claudio Fogu, Wolf Kansteiner, and Todd Presner, 218–39. Cambridge, MA: Harvard University Press, 2016.

Fogu, Claudio, Wulf Kansteiner, and Todd Presner, eds. *Probing the Ethics of Holocaust Culture*. Cambridge, MA: Harvard University Press, 2016.

Follino, Francesco. *Ferramonti, un lager di Mussolini: gli internati durante la guerra*. Cosenza: Brenner, 1985.

Friedländer, Saul. "Epilogue: Interview with Saul Friedländer." In *Probing the Ethics of Holocaust Culture*, ed. Claudio Fogu, Wolf Kansteiner, and Todd Presner, 411–25. Cambridge, MA: Harvard University Press, 2016.

———. *Nazi Germany and the Jews*, 2 vols. New York: Harper Collins, 2007 [1997].

———, ed. *Probing the Limits of Representation: Nazism and the Final Solution*. Cambridge, MA: Harvard University Press, 1992.

———. *The Years of Extermination: Nazi Germany and the Jews, 1939–1945*. New York: Harper, 2007.

Gaida, Peter. *Camps de travail sous Vichy: les "groupes de travailleurs étrangers" (GTE) en France et en Afrique du Nord 1940–44*. Raleigh, NC: Lulu Press, 2015.

Garaudy, Roger. *Mon tour du siècle en solitaire: mémoires*. Paris: Robert Laffont, 1980.

———. *Parole d'homme*. Paris: Laffont, 1975.

Garbarini, Alexandra. *Numbered Days: Diaries and the Holocaust*. New Haven, CT: Yale University Press, 2006.

Gasquet, Frédéric. *La lettre de mon père: une famille de Tunis dans l'enfer nazi*. Paris: Éditions du Félin, 2006.

Gellner, Ernest. *Saints of the Atlas*. Chicago: University of Chicago Press, 1969.

Gershoni, Israel, ed. *Arab Responses to Fascism and Nazism: Attraction and Repulsion*. Austin: Texas University Press, 2014.

Gershoni, Israel, and James Jankowski. *Confronting Fascism in Egypt: Dictatorship Versus Democracy in the 1930s*. Stanford, CA: Stanford University Press, 2009.

Gesamtverzeichnis "anderer Haftstätten" [Complete Catalog of "Other Places of Detention"], ed. Kathrin Janka, Dorothee Lüke, Ralf Possekel, Jens Schley, and Ulrike Vasel. Berlin: Stiftung "Erinnerung, Verantwortung und Zukunft," 2004.

Ghanem, As'ad, and Mohanad Mustafa. "Coping with the Nakba: The Palestinians in Israel and the 'Future Vision' as a Collective Agenda." *Israel Studies Forum* 24.2 (2009): 52–66.

Ghez, Paul. *Six mois sous la botte*. Paris: Le Manuscrit, 1943.

———. *Six mois sous la botte: les juifs de Tunis aux prises avec les SS*. Paris: Le Manuscrit and La Fondation pour la Mémoire de la Shoah, 2009.

Giaccaria, Paolo, and Claudio Minca, eds. *Hitler's Geographies: The Spatialities of the Third Reich*. Chicago: University of Chicago Press, 2016.

Gide, André. *The Journals of André Gide*, vol. 4, *1939–1949*, trans. Justin O'Brien. New York: Knopf, 1951.

Gifford, Prosser, and Roger Louis, eds. *The Transfer of Power in Africa: Decolonization, 1940–1960*. New Haven, CT: Yale University Press, 1986.

Ginio, Ruth. *French Colonialism Unmasked: The Vichy Years in French West Africa*. Lincoln: University of Nebraska Press, 2006.

———. "Marshal Pétain Spoke to Schoolchildren: Vichy Propaganda in French West Africa, 1940–1943." *International Journal of African Historical Studies* 33.2 (2000): 291–312.

Gleizer, Daniela. *Unwelcome Exiles: Mexico and Jewish Refugees from Fascism, 1933–1945*. Leiden: Brill, 2013.

Goda, Norman J. W. "Hitler's Demand for Casablanca in 1940: Incident of Policy?" *International History Review* 26.3 (1994): 441–60.

Godley, Nathan Charles. "'Almost-Finished Frenchmen': The Jews of Algeria and the Question of French National Identity, 1830–1902." Ph.D. dissertation, University of Iowa, 2006.

Goldberg, Harvey. *Jewish Life in Muslim Libya: Rivals and Relatives*. Chicago: University of Chicago Press, 1990.

———. "The Mellahs of Southern Morocco: Report of a Survey." *Maghreb Review* 8.3–4 (1983): 61–69.

Golski. *Un Buchenwald français sous le règne du Maréchal*. Périgueux: Pierre Fanlac, 1945.

González-Ruibal, Alfredo. "The Archaeology of Internment in Francoist Spain (1936–1952)." In *Archaeologies of Internment*, ed. Adrian Myers and Gabriel Moshenska, 53–73. London: Springer, 2011.

Gottreich, Emily Benichou. "Historicizing the Concept of Arab Jews in the Maghrib." *Jewish Quarterly Review* 98.4 (2008): 433–51.

Gottreich, Emily Benichou, and Daniel Schroeter, eds. *Jewish Culture and Society in North Africa*. Bloomington: Indiana University Press, 2011.

Grossmann, Atina. "Grams, Calories, and Food: Languages of Victimization, Entitlement, and Human Rights in Occupied Germany, 1945–1949." *Central European History* 44.1 (2011): 118–48.

———. "Remapping Relief and Rescue: Flight, Displacement, and International Aid for Jewish Refugees During World War II." *New German Critique* 117.3 (fall 2012): 61–79.

Guez, Gaston. *Nos martyrs sous la botte allemande: où les ex-travailleurs juifs de Tunisie racontent leurs souffrances*. Tunis: Presses Typo-Litho du Journal "La Presse," 1946.

Guez, Jacob André. *Au camp de Bizerte*. Paris: L'Harmattan, 2001.

Halstead, John P. *Rebirth of a Nation: The Origins and Rise of Moroccan Nationalism, 1912–1944*. Cambridge, MA: Harvard University Press, 1967.

Hammerman, Jessica R. "The Heart of the Diaspora: Algerian Jews During the War of Independence." Ph.D. dissertation, City University of New York, 2013.

Hayes, Peter, and John Roth. *The Oxford Handbook of Holocaust Studies*. Oxford, UK: Oxford University Press, 2010.

Heckman, Alma Rachel. "Multivariable Casablanca: Vichy Law, Jewish Diversity, and the Moroccan Communist Party." *Hespéris-Tamuda* 51.3 (2016): 13–34.

———. "Radical Nationalists: Moroccan Jewish Communists." Ph.D. dissertation, University of California, Los Angeles, 2015.

Herf, Jeffrey. *Nazi Propaganda for the Arab World*. New Haven, CT: Yale University Press, 2009.

Hever, Hannan, and Lisa Katz. "The Post-Zionist Condition." *Critical Inquiry* 38.3 (2012): 630–48.

Hilberg, Raul. *The Destruction of the European Jews*. Chicago: Quadrangle Books, 1961.

Himka, John-Paul, and Joanna B. Michlic, eds. *Bringing the Dark Past to Light: The Reception of the Holocaust in Postcommunist Europe*. Lincoln: University of Nebraska Press, 2013.

Hirsch, Marianne. *Family Frames: Photography, Narrative, and Postmemory*. Cambridge, MA: Harvard University Press, 1997.

———. *The Generation of Postmemory: Writing and Visual Culture After the Holocaust*. New York: Columbia University Press, 2012.

Hirschberg, Haim Z. "The Jewish Quarter in Muslim Cities and Berber Areas." *Judaism* 17 (1968): 405–21.

Hitchcock, William. "Pierre Boisson, French West Africa, and the Postwar *Epuration*: A Case from the Aix Files." *French Historical Studies* 24.2 (2001): 305–41.

Hoisington, William. *The Casablanca Connection: French Colonial Policy, 1936–1943*. Chapel Hill: University of North Carolina Press, 1984.

Hoppe, Jens. "Buk Buk [Buq-buq]." In *The United States Holocaust Memorial Museum Encyclopedia of Camps and Ghettos, 1933–1945*, Vol. 3, *Camps and Ghettos Under European Regimes Aligned With Nazi Germany*, gen. ed. Geoffrey Megargee, 527–28. Bloomington: Indiana University Press, 2018.

———. "Giado." In *The United States Holocaust Memorial Museum Encyclopedia of Camps and Ghettos, 1933–1945*, Vol. 3, *Camps and Ghettos Under European Regimes Aligned With Nazi Germany*, gen. ed. Geoffrey Megargee, 528–29. Bloomington: Indiana University Press, 2018.

———. "Sidi Azaz." In *The United States Holocaust Memorial Museum Encyclopedia of Camps and Ghettos, 1933–1945*, Vol. 3, *Camps and Ghettos Under European Regimes Aligned With Nazi Germany*, gen. ed. Geoffrey Megargee, 529–30. Bloomington: Indiana University Press, 2018.

Houri, Clément. *Journal of Clement Houri: The Occupation of Tunisia by the Axis Army, November 20, 1947–May 7, 1943, as Seen from Cremieuxville (Suburb of Tunis)*. Jerusalem: Yad Vashem and Ben-Zvi Institute, 2013. [Hebrew]

Howard, John. *Concentration Camps on the Home Front: Japanese Americans in the House of Jim Crow*. Chicago: University of Chicago Press, 2008.

Hull, Isabel V. *Absolute Destruction: Military Culture and the Practices of War in Imperial Germany.* Ithaca, NY: Cornell University Press, 2005.

Iancu-Agou, Danièle. "Être expulsé ou interné à Djelfa aux siècles derniers (1893–1942)." *Revue du Monde Musulman et de la Méditéranée* 115–116 (2007): 276–82.

Ibn Khaldun. *The Muqaddimah: An Introduction to History,* abridged ed., trans. Franz Rosenthal. Princeton, NJ: Princeton University Press, 2017.

Ilahiane, Hsain. *Ethnicities, Community Making, and Agrarian Change: The Political Ecology of a Moroccan Oasis.* Boulder, CO: University of America Press, 2004.

Jakobson, Michael. *Origins of the Gulag: The Soviet Prison Camp System, 1917–1934.* Lexington: University Press of Kentucky, 1993.

Jennings, Eric. *La France libre fut africaine.* Paris: Perrin, 2014.

———. *Vichy in the Tropics: Pétain's National Revolution in Madagascar, Guadeloupe, and Indochina, 1940–1944.* Stanford, CA: Stanford University Press, 2001.

Joly, Danièle. *The French Communist Party and the Algerian War.* London: Macmillan, 1991.

Joly, Fernand. "La situation économique du Maroc." *Annales de Géographie* 305 (January–March 1948): 65–70.

Joly, Laurent. *Vichy dans la "solution finale": histoire du commissariat général aux questions juives, 1941–1944.* Paris: Grasset, 2006.

Jones, Hillary. *The Métis of Sénégal: Urban Life and Politics in French West Africa.* Bloomington: Indiana University Press, 2013.

———. "Rethinking Politics in the Colony: The Métis of Senegal and Urban Politics in the Late Nineteenth and Early Twentieth Century." *Journal of African History* 53 (2012): 325–44.

Kahan, Claudine. "La honte du témoin." In *Parler des camps penser les génocides,* ed. Catherine Coquio, 493–513. Paris: Albin Michel, 1999.

Kalman, Samuel. *French Colonial Fascism: The Extreme Right in Algeria, 1919–1939.* New York: Palgrave Macmillan, 2013.

Kaspi, André. *Les juifs pendant l'occupation.* Paris: Seuil, 1991.

Katz, Ethan. *The Burdens of Brotherhood: Jews and Muslims from North Africa to France.* Cambridge, MA: Harvard University Press, 2015.

———. "Crémieux's Children: Joseph Reinach, Léon Blum, and René Cassin as Jews of French Empire." In *Colonialism and the Jews,* ed. Ethan B. Katz, Lisa Moses Leff, and Maud S. Mandel, 129–65. Bloomington: Indiana University Press, 2017.

———. "Did the Paris Mosque Save Jews? A Mystery and Its Memory." *Jewish Quarterly Review* 102.2 (2012): 256–87.

Katz, Ethan B., Lisa Moses Leff, and Maud S. Mandel, eds. *Colonialism and the Jews.* Bloomington: Indiana University Press, 2017.

Kenbib, Mohammed. *Juifs et musulmans au Maroc, 1859–1948: contribution à l'histoire des relations intercommunautaires en terre d'Islam.* Rabat: Publications de la Faculté des Lettres et des Sciences Humaines, 1994.

———. "Moroccan Jews and the Vichy Regime, 1940–42." *Journal of North African Studies* 19.4 (2014): 540–53.

Khadem, Amir. "The Permanence of an Ephemeral Pain: Dialectics of Remembrance in Two Novels of the Israel-Palestine Conflict." *The Comparatist* 39 (October 2015): 275–93.

Klarsfeld, Serge. *Memorial to the Jews Deported from France, 1942–1944: Documentation of the Deportation of the Victims of the Final Solution in France.* New York: B. Klarsfeld Foundation, 1983.

Knight, Melvin M. *Morocco as a French Economic Venture: A Study of Open Door Imperialism.* New York: D. Appleton-Century, 1937.

Knowles, Anne, Tim Cole, and Alberto Giordano, eds. *Geographies of the Holocaust.* Bloomington: Indiana University Press, 2014.

Knowles, Anne Kelly, and Paul B. Jaskot, with Benjamin Perry Blackshear, Michael De Groot, and Alexander Yule. "Mapping the SS Concentration Camps." In *Geographies of the Holocaust,* ed. Anne Kelly Knowles, Tim Cole, and Alberto Giordano, 19–52. Bloomington: Indiana University Press, 2014.

Kogon, Eugen. *The Theory and Practice of Hell: The German Concentration Camps and the System Behind Them,* trans. Heinz Norden. New York: Farrar, Straus & Giroux, 1950.

Kossler, Reinhard. *Namibia and Germany: Negotiating the Past.* Namibia: University of Namibia Press, 2015.

Kozlovsky-Golan, Yvonne. "Site of Amnesia: The Absence of North African Jewry in Visual Depictions of the Experiences of World War II." *Jewish Film and New Media: An International Journal* 2.2 (2014): 153–80.

Kühne, Thomas. "Colonialism and the Holocaust: Continuities, Causations, and Complexities." *Journal of Genocide Research* 15.3 (2013): 339–62.

LaCapra, Dominick. *Representing the Holocaust: History, Theory, Trauma.* Ithaca, NY: Cornell University Press, 1994.

Laloum, Jean. "La politique d'aryanisation économique des bien juifs, mise en oeuvre durant le régime de Vichy, en Algérie, 1941–43." Unpublished manuscript.

Laloum, Jean, and Jean-Luc Allouche. *Les juifs d'Algérie: images et textes.* Paris: Biblieurope, 2006.

Lang, Berel. "White, Friedländer, '. . . And the Rest is History': A Pax Historiana." *History and Theory* 56.2 (June 2017): 258–66.

La Porte des Vaux, Capitaine de. *Les tribus Berbères du Haut Sous.* Centre des Hautes Études sur l'Afrique et l'Asie Moderne, no. 991 (November–December 1946).

Larhmaid, Abdellah. *Yahud mantaqat Sus: dirasat fi tarikh al-maghrib al-ijtimaʻi.* Rabat: Bouregreg, 2016.

Laskier, Michael. *The Alliance Israélite Universelle and the Jewish Communities of Morocco: 1862–1962.* Albany: State University of New York Press, 1983.

———. "Aspects of Change and Modernization: The Jewish Communities of Morocco's Bled." In *Communautés juives des marges sahariennes du Maghreb,* ed. Michel Abitbol, 329–64. Jerusalem: Ben-Zvi Institute, 1982.

———. "Between Vichy Antisemitism and German Harassment: The Jews of North Africa During the Early 1940s." *Modern Judaism* 11.3 (1991): 343–69.

———. *North African Jewry in the Twentieth Century: The Jews of Morocco, Tunisia, and Algeria.* New York: New York University Press, 1994.

———. *Yehudei ha-Maghreb be-Tzel Vichy ve-Tzlav ha-Keres.* Tel Aviv: Tel Aviv University Press, 1992.

Laskier, Michael, and Eliezer Bashan. "Morocco." In *The Jews of the Middle East and North Africa in Modern Times*, ed. Reeva S. Simon, Michael Laskier, and Sara Reguer, 471–504. New York: Columbia University Press, 2003.

Lawler, Nancy. "Reform and Repression Under the Free French: Economic and Political Transformation in the Côte d'Ivoire, 1942–1945." *Africa* 60.1 (1990): 88–110.

Le Cour Grandmaison, Olivier. *Coloniser, exterminer: sur la guerre et l'état colonial.* Paris: Fayard, 2005.

Lee, Daniel. "The Chantiers de la Jeunesse, General de la Porte du Theil and the Myth of the Rescue of Jews in Vichy France." *French Historical Studies* 38.1 (2015): 139–70.

———. *Pétain's Jewish Children: French Jewish Youth and the Vichy Regime, 1940–1942.* Oxford, UK: Oxford University Press, 2014.

Leff, Lisa Moses. *Sacred Bonds of Solidarity: The Rise of Jewish Internationalism in Nineteenth-Century France.* Stanford, CA: Stanford University Press, 2006.

Le Foll Luciani, Pierre-Jean. *Les juifs algériens dans la lutte anticoloniale: trajectoires dissidentes (1934–1965).* Rennes: Presses Universitaires de Rennes, 2015.

———. "Les juifs d'Algérie face aux nationalités française et algérienne, 1940–1963." *Revue des Mondes Musulmans et de la Méditerranée* 137 (May 2015): 115–32.

Le Tourneau, Roger. *Fès avant le Protectorat: étude économique et sociale d'une ville de l'Occident musulman.* Casablanca: Publications de l'Institut des Hautes Études Marocaines, 1949.

Levisse-Touzé, Christine. *L'Afrique du Nord dans la guerre, 1939–1945.* Paris: Albin Michel, 1998.

———. "Les camps d'internement en Afrique du Nord pendant la second guerre mondiale." In *Mélanges Charles-Robert Ageron*, ed. Abdeljelil Temimi, 601–5. Zaghouan: FTERSI, 1996.

Levy, Lital. "Historicizing the Concept of Arab Jews in the 'Mashriq.'" *Jewish Quarterly Review* 98.4 (2008): 452–69.

———. "Reorienting Hebrew Literary History: The View from the East." *Prooftexts* 29.2 (2009): 127–72.

Levy, Robert. *Les 180 jours de Tunis: chronique d'un adolescent sous l'occupation, novembre 1942—mai 1943.* Paris: L'Harmattan, 2004.

Lévy, Simon. *Essais d'histoire et de civilisation judeo-marocaines.* Rabat: Centre Tarik Ibn Ziyad, 2001.

Lewis, Mary Dewhurst. *Divided Rule: Sovereignty and Empire in French Tunisia, 1881–1938.* Berkeley: University of California Press, 2008.

Lipschitz, Chaim U. *Franco, Spain, the Jews, and the Holocaust.* New York: Ktav, 1984.

Litvak, Meir, and Esther Webman. *From Empathy to Denial: Arab Responses to the Holocaust.* New York: Columbia University Press, 2009.

London, Geo. *L'Amiral Esteva et le Général Dentz devant la Haute Cour de Justice.* Lyon: Roger Bonnefon, 1945.

Longerich, Peter. *Holocaust: The Nazi Persecution and Murder of the Jews.* Oxford, UK: Oxford University Press, 2012.

————. *The Unwritten Order: Hitler's Role in the Final Solution.* Charleston, SC: Tempus, 2001.

Lorcin, Patricia M. E. *Imperial Identities: Stereotyping, Prejudice, and Race in Colonial Algeria.* London: I. B. Tauris, 1999.

————. "Rome and France in Africa: Recovering Algeria's Latin Past." *French Historical Studies* 25.2 (2002): 311–12.

Lower, Wendy. *Hitler's Furies: German Women in the Nazi Killing Field.* New York: Houghton Mifflin Harcourt, 2013.

————. *Nazi Empire Building and the Holocaust in the Ukraine.* Chapel Hill: University of North Carolina Press, 2005.

Lydon, Ghislaine. "Women, Children, and the Popular Front's Missions of Inquiry in French West Africa." In *French Colonial Empire and the Popular Front: Hope and Disillusion*, ed. Tony Chafer and Amanda Sackur, 170–89. London: Macmillan, 1999.

Madley, Benjamin. "From Africa to Auschwitz: How German South West Africa Incubated Ideas and Methods Adopted and Developed by the Nazis in Eastern Europe." *European History Quarterly* 35.3 (2005): 429–64.

Maghraoui, Driss. "The Goumiers in the Second World War: History and Colonial Representation." *Journal of North African Studies* 19.4 (2014): 475–89.

Magiar, Victor. *E venne la notte: ebrei in un paese arabo*, 2nd ed. Florence: La Giuntina, 2004.

Malino, Frances. *Teaching Freedom: Jewish Sisters in Muslim Lands.* London: Palgrave Macmillan, 2016.

Mallmann, Klaus-Michael, and Martin Cüppers. *Halbmond und Hakenkreuz: das Dritte Reich, die Araber und Palästina*, 3rd ed. Darmstadt: Wissenschaftliche Buchgesellschaft, 2011.

Mannoni, Octave. *Prospero and Caliban: The Psychology of Colonization.* New York: Praeger, 1964.

Marglin, Jessica. *Across Legal Lines: Jews and Muslims in Modern Morocco.* New Haven, CT: Yale University Press, 2014.

————. "The Two Lives of Mas'ud Amoyal: Pseudo-Algerians in Morocco, 1830–1912." *International Journal of Middle East Studies* 44 (2012): 651–70.

Mariot, Nicolas, and Claire Zalc. *Face à la persécution: Juifs dans la guerre.* Paris: Odile Jacob, 2010.

Marrus, Michael, and Robert Paxton. *Vichy France and the Jews.* New York: Basic Books, 1981.

Marx, Karl. *On the Jewish Question*, trans. Hellen Lederer. Cincinnati: Hebrew Union College–Jewish Institute of Religion, 1958 [1844].

Maxwell, Gavin. *Lords of the Atlas: The Rise and Fall of the House of Glaoua (1893–1956).* New York: Dutton, 1966.

Mazower, Mark. *Hitler's Empire: How the Nazis Ruled Europe.* New York: Penguin, 2008.

————. *Salonica, City of Ghosts: Christians, Muslims, and Jews, 1430–1950.* New York: Knopf, 2005.

Memmi, Albert. *The Pillar of Salt.* Boston: Beacon Press, 1992.

————. *La statue de sel.* Paris: Gallimard, 1966 [1953].

Mendiola, Fernando. "Reeducation Through Work? Mountain Roads in the Spanish Concentration Universe (Western Pyrenees, 1939–1942)." *Labor History* 55.1 (2014): 97–116.

Michman, Dan. "Jewish Dimension of the Holocaust in Dire Straits? Current Challenges of Interpretation and Scope." In *Jewish Histories of the Holocaust: New Transnational Approaches*, ed. Norman J. W. Goda, 17–28. New York: Berghahn, 2014.

Mick, Christoph. "Incompatible Experiences: Poles, Ukrainians, and Jews in Lviv Under Soviet and German Occupation, 1939–44." *Journal of Contemporary History* 46.2 (2011): 336–63.

———. "War and Conflicting Memories: Poles, Ukrainians, and Jews in Lvov, 1914–1939." *Jahrbuch des Simon-Dubnow-Instituts* 4 (2005): 257–78.

Miller, Susan Gilson. "Filling a Historical Parenthesis: An Introduction to 'Morocco from World War II to Independence.'" *Journal of North African Studies* 19.4 (2014): 461–74.

———. *A History of Modern Morocco.* New York: Cambridge University Press, 2013.

Minerbi, Sergio I. "Il progetto di un insediamente ebraico in Etiopia (1936–1943)." *Storia Contemporanea* 17 (1986): 1083–1137.

———. "The Project of Establishing a Jewish State in Ethiopia (1936–1943)." *World Union of Jewish Studies* 9.3 (1985): 111–18.

Moine, André. *La déportation et la résistance en Afrique du Nord (1939–44).* Paris: Éditions Sociales, 1972.

Moneta, Jacob. *La politique du Parti communiste français dans la question coloniale, 1920–1963.* Paris: François Maspero, 1971.

Monfort, Aram. "Los campos de concentración franquistas y su funcionamiento en Cataluña." *Hispania* 69.231 (2009): 147–77.

Morris, Benny. *The Birth of the Palestinian Refugee Problem Revisited,* 2nd ed. New York: Cambridge University Press, 2004.

Morro Casas, José Luis. *Campos africanos: el exilio republicano en el Norte de África.* Madrid: Memoria Viva, 2012.

Morse, Arthur D. *While Six Million Died: A Chronicle of American Apathy.* New York: Ace, 1968.

Moses, A. Dirk. "Anxieties in Holocaust and Genocide Studies." In *Probing the Ethics of Holocaust Culture*, ed. Claudio Fogu, Wolf Kansteiner, and Todd Presner, 332–54. Cambridge, MA: Harvard University Press, 2016.

———. "Conceptual Blockages and Definitional Dilemmas in the 'Racial Century': Genocides of Indigenous Peoples and the Holocaust." *Patterns of Prejudice* 36 (2002): 7–36.

———, ed. *Empire, Colony, Genocide: Conquest, Occupation, and Subaltern Resistance in World History.* New York: Berghahn, 2008.

———. "Hannah Arendt, Imperialisms, and the Holocaust." In *German Colonialism, Race, the Holocaust, and Postwar Germany*, ed. Volker Langbehn and Mohammad Salama, 72–92. New York: Columbia University Press, 2011.

———. "The Holocaust and Colonialism." In *The Oxford Handbook of Holocaust Studies*, ed. Peter Hayes and John Roth, 68–80. Oxford, UK: Oxford University Press, 2010.

Moses, [A.] Dirk, and Dan Stone, eds. *Colonialism and Genocide.* New York: Routledge, 2007.

Motadel, David. *Islam and Nazi Germany's War*. Cambridge, MA: Harvard University Press, 2014.

Msellati, Henri. *Les juifs d'Algérie sous le régime de Vichy, 10 juillet 1940–3 novembre 1943*. Paris: L'Harmattan, 1999.

Mühlhahn, Kaus. "The Concentration Camp in Global Historical Perspective." *History Compass* 8.6 (2010): 543–61.

Nahum, André. *Le roi des briks*. Paris: L'Harmattan, 1992.

Nataf, Claude. "Biographie de Paul Ghez" and "Préface de la présente édition." In *Six mois sous la botte*, by Paul Ghez. Paris: Le Manuscrit, 2009.

———. "L'exclusion des avocats juifs en Tunisie pendant la seconde guerre mondiale." *Archives Juives* 41.1 (2008): 90–107.

———. "Les juifs de Tunisie face à Vichy et aux persécutions allemandes." *Pardès* 16 (1992): 203–31.

———. *Les juifs de Tunisie sous le joug nazi (9 novembre 1942–8 mai 1943)*. Paris: Fondation pour la mémoire de la Shoah/Le Manuscrit, 2012.

———. "Préface de la présente édition." In *Étoile jaune et croix gammée*, by Robert Borgel. Paris: Le Manuscrit, 2007.

Navib, Youssef. *Cultures oasiennes: essai d'histoire sociale de l'aosis de Bou-Saâda*. Algiers: Entreprise Nationale du Livre, 1986.

Nicosia, Francis R. *Nazi Germany and the Arab World*. New York: Cambridge University Press, 2014.

Nora, Pierre, ed. *Les lieux de mémoire*, 7 vols. Paris: Gallimard, 1984–1992.

Nordbruch, Götz. "Cultural Fusion of Thought and Ambitions? Memory, Politics, and the History of Arab–Nazi German Encounters." *Middle Eastern Studies* 47.1 (2011): 183–94.

Nos, Eloísa. "Campos de concentratión." In *Max Aub en el laberinto del siglo XX*, ed. Juan María Calles, 194–203. Valencia: Biblioteca Valenciana, 2003.

Novick, Peter. *The Holocaust in American Life*. Boston: Houghton Mifflin, 1999.

Núñez, César, "Max Aub, Campo de Arjelia." In *Homenaje a Max Aub*, ed. James Valender and Gabriel Rojo, 351–55. Mexico City: El Colegio de México, 2005.

———. "Max Aub en 'el país del viento': algunos poemas del denominado Ciclo de Djelfa (1941–1942)." In *Homenaje a Max Aub*, ed. James Valender and Gabriel Rojo, 283–347. Mexico: El Colegio de México, 2005.

Ofer, Dalia. *Escaping the Holocaust: Illegal Immigration to the Land of Israel, 1939–1944*. New York: Oxford University Press, 1990.

———. "History, Memory, and Identity: Perceptions of the Holocaust in Israel." In *Jews in Israel: Contemporary Social and Cultural Patterns*, ed. Uzi Rebhun and Chaim I. Waxman, 394–417. Hanover, NH: Brandeis University Press, 2003.

Oliel, Jacob. *Les camps de Vichy, Maghreb-Sahara, 1939–1945*. Montreal: Éditions du Lys, 2005.

Olusoga, David, and Casper W. Erichsen. *The Kaiser's Holocaust: Germany's Forgotten Genocide and the Colonial Roots of Nazism*. London: Faber & Faber, 2010.

Oppenheimer, Yochai. "The Holocaust: A Mizrahi Perspective." *Hebrew Studies* 51.1 (2010): 303–28.

Overy, Richard. "The Concentration Camp: An International Perspective." *Eurozine* (2011). www.eurozine.com/articles/2011-08-25-overy-en.html (accessed September 23, 2016).

Park, Thomas K. "Essaouira: The Formation of a Native Elite, 1940–1980." *African Studies Review* 31.3 (1988): 111–32.

Patt, Avinoam. "'The People Must Be Forced to Go to Palestine': Rabbi Abraham Klausner and the *She'erit Hapletah* in Germany." *Holocaust and Genocide Studies* 28.2 (2014): 240–76.

Paxton, Robert. *Vichy France: Old Guard and New Order, 1940–1944.* New York: Norton, 1975.

Pennell, C. Richard. "Makhzan and Siba in Morocco: An Examination of Early Modern Attitudes." In *Tribe and State: Essays in Honour of David Montgomery Hart,* ed. E. G. H. Joffe and C. R. Pennell. Cambridgeshire, UK: Middle East and North African Studies Press, 1991.

Peretz, S., Jacob Dinezon, and S. Ansky. "Appeal to Collect Materials About the World War." In *Literature of Destruction: Jewish Responses to Catastrophe,* ed. David G. Roskies, 209–10. Philadelphia: Jewish Publication Society, 1989.

Peschanski, Denis. *La France des camps: l'internement, 1938–1946.* Paris: Gallimard, 2002.

Peterson, Terence. "The 'Jewish Question' and the 'Italian Peril': Vichy, Italy, and the Jews of Tunisia, 1940–42." *Journal of Contemporary History* 50.2 (2015): 234–58.

Petrucci, Filippo. *Gli ebrei in Algeria e Tunisia, 1940–1943.* Florence: Giuntina, 2011.

Peyron, Michael. "Glaoui/Glaoua." In *Encyclopédie Berbère* (1999), 21: 3151–60. Aix-en-Provence: Edisud, Editeur en ligne, and Livres de Provence et de Méditerranée. journals.openedition.org/encyclopedieberbere/1736 (accessed March 20, 2018).

Peyrouton, Marcel. *Du service public à la prison commune: souvenirs—Tunis, Rabat, Buenos Aires, Vichy, Algier, Fresnes.* Paris: Librairie Plon, 1950.

Picciotto, Liliana. "Gli ebrei in Libia sotto la dominazione italiana." In *Ebraismo e rapport con le culture del Mediterranea nei secoli XVIII–XX,* ed. Martino Contu, Nicola Melis, and Giovannino Pinna, 79–106. Villacidro: Casa Editrice Giuntina, 2003.

———. "Un groupe de juifs libyens dans la Shoah 1942–1944." In *La bienvenue et l'adieu: migrants juifs et musulmans au Maghreb (XVe–XXe siècle),* ed. Frédéric Abécassis, Karima Dirèche, and Rita Aouad, 45–56. Paris: Karthala, 2010.

Porat, Dina. *The Blue and the Yellow Stars of David: The Zionist Leadership in Palestine and the Holocaust, 1939–1945.* Cambridge, MA: Harvard University Press, 1990.

Poznanski, Renée. *Propagandes et persécutions: la Résistance et le "problème juif" (1940–1944).* Paris: Librairie Arthème Fayard, 2008.

Redlich, Shimon. *Life in Transit: Jews in Postwar Lodz, 1945–1950.* Brighton, MA: Academic Studies Press, 2010.

Rein, Arielle. "L'historiographie israélienne de la Shoah: état de la recherché." *Revue d'Histoire de la Shoah* 188.1 (2008): 39–45.

Rende, Mario. *Ferramonti di Tarsia: voci da un campo di concentramento fascista, 1940–1945.* Milan: Mursia, 2009.

Renucci, Florence. "Le débat sur le statut politique des israélites en Algérie et ses acteurs, 1870–1943." In *Contributions du séminaire sur les administrations coloniales (2009–2010).*

Paris: Institut d'Histoire du Temps Présent, 2011. halshs.archives-ouvertes.fr/halshs
-00599296/document (accessed March 20, 2018).

Rivet, Daniel. *Lyautey et l'institution du protectorat français au Maroc, 1912–1925*, 3 vols.
Paris: L'Harmattan, 1996.

Roberts, Sophie Beth. "Jews, Citizenship, and Anti-Semitism in French Colonial Algeria,
1870–1943." Ph.D. dissertation, University of Toronto, 2011.

Roby, Bryan K. *The Mizrahi Era of Rebellion: Israel's Forgotten Civil Rights Struggle, 1948–
1966.* New York: Syracuse University Press, 2016.

Rodogno, Davide. "Die faschistische Neue Ordnung und die politisch-ökonomische Umges-
taltung des Mittelmeerraums 1940 bis 1943." In *Die "Achse" im Krieg: Politik, Ideologie
und Kriegführung, 1939–1945*, ed. Amedeo Osti Guerrazzi, Thomas Schlemmer, and Lutz
Klinkhammer, 211–30. Paderborn: Ferdinand Schöningh, 2010.

Rodrigue, Aron. *Sephardim and the Holocaust.* Washington, DC: Center for Advanced
Holocaust Studies, United States Holocaust Memorial Museum, 2005.

Rodrigue, Aron, and Esther Benbass. *Sephardi Jewry: A History of the Judeo-Spanish Community, 14th–20th Centuries.* Berkeley: University of California Press, 2000.

Rohr, Isabelle. *The Spanish Right and the Jews, 1898–1945: Antisemitism and Opportunism.*
Brighton, UK: Sussex Academic Press, 2007.

Rosen, Lawrence. *Two Arabs, a Berber, and a Jew: Entangled Lives in Morocco.* Chicago:
University of Chicago Press, 2016.

Rosenfeld, Gavriel D. "The Politics of Uniqueness: Reflections on the Recent Polemical
Turn in Holocaust and Genocide Scholarship." *Holocaust and Genocide Studies* 13.1
(1999): 28–61.

Roskies, David, ed. *The Literature of Destruction: Jewish Responses to Catastrophe.* Lincoln:
University of Nebraska Press, 1989.

Rothberg, Michael. *Multidirectional Memory: Remembering the Holocaust in the Age of Decolonization.* Stanford, CA: Stanford University Press, 2009.

———. "The Witness as "World" Traveler: Multidirectional Memory and Holocaust In-
ternationalism Before Human Rights." In *Probing the Ethics of Holocaust Culture*, ed.
Claudio Fogu, Wolf Kansteiner, and Todd Presner, 355–72. Cambridge, MA: Harvard
University Press, 2016.

Roumani, Maurice M. *The Jews of Libya: Coexistence, Persecution, Resettlement.* Brighton,
UK: Sussex Academic Press, 2008.

Rousso, Henry. *Le syndrome de Vichy: de 1944 à nos jours.* Paris: Seuil, 1987.

———. *The Vichy Syndrome: History and Memory in France Since 1944*, trans. Arthur Goldhammer. Cambridge, MA: Harvard University Press, 1991.

Rudling, Per Anders. "Memories of 'Holodomor' and National Socialism in Ukrainian
Political Culture." In *Rekonstruktion des Nationalmythos?: Frankreich, Deutschland
und die Ukraine im Vergleich*, ed. Yves Bizeul, 227–58. Göttingen: V & R Unipress,
2013.

Saada, Emmanuelle. *Empire's Children: Race, Filiation, and Citizenship in the French Colonies*, trans. Arthur Goldhammer. Chicago: University of Chicago Press, 2012.

Saadoun, Haïm. "Élaboration de la mémoire historique concernant l'époque de l'occupation allemande en Tunisie: nouvelle lecture de La Statue de sel d'Albert Memmi." *Revue d'Histoire de la Shoah* 205 (October 2016): 561–70.

Sabille, Jacques. *Les juifs de Tunisie sous Vichy et l'occupation.* Paris: Éditions du Centre, 1954.

Salerno, Eric. *"Uccideteli tutti": Libya 1943—gli ebrei nel campo di concentramento fascista di Giado; una storia italiana.* Milan: Il Saggiatore, 2007.

Sansal, Boualem. *Le village de l'Allemand ou le journal des frères Schiller.* Paris: Gallimard, 2008.

Sarfatti, Michele. "Autochthoner Antisemitismus oder Übernahme des deutschen Modells? Die Judenverfolgung im faschistischen Italien." In *Die "Achse" im Krieg: Politik, Ideologie und Kriegführung, 1939–1945,* ed. Amedeo Osti Guerrazzi, Thomas Schlemmer, and Lutz Klinkhammer, 231–43. Paderborn: Ferdinand Schöningh, 2010.

———. *The Jews in Mussolini's Italy: From Equality to Persecution,* trans. John Tedeschi and Anne C. Tedeschi. Madison: University of Wisconsin Press, 2006.

Sasson, Albert. *Les couturiers du sultan: itinéraire d'une famille juive marocaine.* Rabat: Marsam, 2007.

Satloff, Robert. *Among the Righteous: Lost Stories of the Holocaust's Long Reach into Arab Lands.* New York: Public Affairs, 2006.

Schiffrin, Deborah. "Language and Public Memorial: 'America's Concentration Camps.'" *Discourse and Society* 12.4 (2001): 504–34.

Schlemmer, Thomas, and Hans Woller. "Der italienische Faschismus und die Juden 1922 bis 1945." *Vierteljahrshefte für Zeitgeschichte* 53 (2005): 165–201.

Schrafstetter, Susanna. "'What About Paying *British* Victims of Nazi Hell Camps?' Die Entschädigungsfrage in den deutsch-britischen Beziehungen." In *Grenzen der Wiedergutmachung: Die Entschädigung für NS-Verfolgte in West- und Osteuropa, 1945–2000,* ed. Hans Günter Hockerts, Claudia Moisel, and Tobias Winstel, 568–629. Göttingen: Wallstein, 2006.

Schreier, Joshua. *Arabs of the Jewish Faith: The Civilizing Mission in Colonial Algeria.* New Brunswick, NJ: Rutgers University Press, 2010.

Schroeter, Daniel. "From Dhimmis to Colonized Subjects: Moroccan Jews and the Sharifian and French Colonial State." In *Jews and the State: Dangerous Alliances and the Perils of Privilege,* ed. Ezra Mendelsohn, 104–23. Oxford, UK: Oxford University Press, 2013.

———. "Identity and Nation: Jewish Migration and Inter-Community Relations in the Colonial Maghreb." In *La bienvenue et l'adieu: migrants juifs et musulmans au Maghreb (XVe–XXe siècle),* ed. Frédéric Abécassis, Karima Dirèche, and Rita Aouad, 1: 125–39. Casablanca: La Croisée des Chemins; and Paris: Karthala, 2012.

———. "In Search of Jewish Farmers: Jews, Agriculture, and the Land in Rural Morocco." in *The Development of Judaism and Islam: Interdependence, Modernity, and Political Turmoil,* ed. Michael Laskier and Yaacov Lev, 143–59. Gainesville: University of Florida Press, 2011.

———. "The Jews of Essaouira (Mogador) and the Trade of Southern Morocco." In *Communautés juives des marges sahariennes du Maghreb,* ed. Michel Abitbol, 365–90. Jerusalem: Ben-Zvi Institute, 1982.

———. *Merchants of Essaouira: Urban Society and Imperialism in Southwestern Morocco, 1844–1886.* Cambridge, UK: Cambridge University Press, 1988.

———. "Philo-Sephardism, Anti-Semitism, and Arab Nationalism: Muslims and Jews in the Spanish Protectorate of Morocco During the Third Reich." In *Nazism, the Holocaust, and the Middle East*, ed. Francis Nicosia and Boğaç Ergene, 179–215. New York: Berghahn, 2018.

———. *The Sultan's Jew: Morocco and the Sephardi World.* Stanford, CA: Stanford University Press, 2002.

———. "Vichy in Morocco: The Residency, Mohammed V, and His Indigenous Jewish Subjects." In *Colonialism and the Jews*, ed. Ethan B. Katz, Lisa Moses Leff, and Maud S. Mandel, 215–50. Bloomington: Indiana University Press, 2017.

Schroeter, Daniel J., and Joseph Chetrit. "Emancipation and Its Discontents: Jews at the Formative Period of Colonial Rule in Morocco." *Jewish Social Studies* 13.1 (2006): 170–206.

Schwartz, Adi. "A Tragedy Shrouded in Silence: The Destruction of the Arab World's Jewry." *Azure* 45 (spring 2011): 30–55.

Sebag, Paul. *Communistes de Tunisie, 1939–1943: souvenirs et documents.* Paris: L'Harmattan, 2001.

———. *Histoire des juifs de Tunisie des origines à nos jours.* Paris: L'Harmattan, 1991.

Sebbar, Leila. *Une enfance algérienne.* Paris: Gallimard, 1997.

———. *L'enfance des français d'Algérie avant 1962.* Saint-Pourçain-sur-Sioule: Bleu Autour, 2014.

———. *Une enfance juive en Méditerranée musulmane.* Casablanca: La Croisée des Chemins, 2013.

———. *Enfances tunisiennes.* Tunis: Elyzad, 2010.

Sebti, Abdelahad, and Abderrahmane Lakhsassi. *Mina as-shay ila al-atay: al-ʿadat wa al-tarikh.* Rabat: Faculté de lettres et des sciences humaines, Université Mohammed V, 1999.

Secrétariat Général du Protectorat. *Dénombrement général de la population de la zone française de l'empire chérifien effectué le 01 Mars 1947.* Fascicule 2. Rabat: Service des Statistiques, 1947.

Segev, Tom. *The Biography of David Ben-Gurion.* New York: Farrar, Straus & Giroux, 2017.

———. *1949, The First Israelis*, ed. Arlen Neal Weinstein. New York: Free Press, 1986.

———. *The Seventh Million: The Israelis and the Holocaust*, trans. Haim Watzman. New York: Hill & Wang, 1993.

Serels, M. Mitchell. "The Non-European Holocaust: The Fate of Tunisian Jewry." In *Del Fuego: Sephardim and the Holocaust*, ed. Haham Gaon and M. Mitchell Serels, 129–52. New York: Sepher-Hermon Press, 1995.

Shandler, Jeffrey. "Jewish Culture." In *The Oxford Handbook of Holocaust Studies*, ed. Peter Hayes and J. K. Roth, 465–85. New York: Oxford University Press, 2010.

Shapira, Anita. *Ben-Gurion: Father of Modern Israel*, trans. Anthony Berris. New Haven, CT: Yale University Press, 2014.

Shepard, Todd. *The Invention of Decolonization: The Algerian War and the Remaking of France.* Ithaca: Cornell University Press, 2006.

Shohat, Ella. "The Invention of the Mizrahim." *Journal of Palestine Studies* 29.1 (1999): 5–20.

————. "Sephardim in Israel: Zionism from the Standpoint of Its Jewish Victims." *Social Text* 19–20 (autumn 1988): 1–35.

Shokeid, Moshe. "Jewish Existence in a Berber Environment." In *Jews Among Muslims: Communities in the Precolonial Middle East*, ed. Shlomo Deshen and Walter Zenner, 109–20. London: Palgrave Macmillan, 1996.

Silverman, Max. *Palimpsestic Memory: The Holocaust and Colonialism in French and Francophone Fiction and Film*. New York: Berghahn, 2013.

Simon, Jacques. *Juif berbère d'Algérie: itineraire, 1933–1963*. Paris: L'Harmattan, 2012.

Simon, Rachel. "It Could Have Happened There: The Jews of Libya During the Second World War." *Africana Journal* 16 (1994): 391–422.

Slyomovics, Susan. " 'False Friends'? Algeria, the Algerian Jewish Question, and Settler Colonial Studies." Lecture given at University of California, Los Angeles, March 10, 2017. Available as a podcast at *Jadaliyya*.

————. "French Restitution, German Compensation: Algerian Jews and Vichy's Financial Legacy." *Journal of North African Studies* 17.5 (2012): 881–901.

————. *How to Accept German Reparations*. Philadelphia: University of Pennsylvania Press, 2014.

Snyder, Timothy. *Black Earth: The Holocaust as History and Warning*. New York: Tim Duggan Books, 2015.

————. *Bloodlands: Europe Between Hitler and Stalin*. New York: Basic Books, 2010.

Stauber, Roni. *The Holocaust in Israeli Public Debate in the 1950s: Ideology and Memory*, trans. Elizabeth Yuval. London: Vallentine Mitchell, 2007.

Stein, Sarah Abrevaya. *Extraterritorial Dreams: European Citizenship, Sephardi Jews, and the Ottoman Twentieth Century*. Chicago: University of Chicago Press, 2016.

————. *Saharan Jews and the Fate of French Algeria*. Chicago: University of Chicago Press, 2014.

Stillman, Norman A. *The Jews of Arab Lands: A History and Source Book*. Philadelphia: Jewish Publication Society of America, 1979.

————. *The Jews of Arab Lands in Modern Times*. Philadelphia: Jewish Publication Society, 1991.

Stone, Dan. *Histories of the Holocaust*. Oxford, UK: Oxford University Press, 2010.

————. "Holocaust Historiography and Cultural History." In *The Holocaust and Historical Methodology*, ed. D. Stone, 44–60. New York: Berghahn, 2012.

————. *The Liberation of the Camps: The End of the Holocaust and Its Aftermath*. New Haven, CT: Yale University Press, 2015.

Stora, Benjamin. *Les trois exils juifs d'Algérie*. Paris: Stock, 2006.

Sucary, Yossi. *From Benghazi to Bergen-Belsen*. CreateSpace Independent Publishing Platform, 2016.

Suleiman, Susan. *Crises of Memory and the Second World War*. Cambridge, MA: Harvard University Press, 2006.

————. "Do Facts Matter in Holocaust Memoirs? Wilkomirski/Wiesel." In *Obliged by Memory: Literature, Religion, Ethics*, ed. Steven Katz and Alan Rosen, 21–42. Syracuse, NY: Syracuse University Press, 2005.

————. "The 1.5 Generation: Thinking About Child Survivors and the Holocaust." *American Imago* 59.3 (2002): 372–85.

Suret-Canale, Jean. *Afrique Noire*, vol. 2. Paris: Sociales, 1964.

Swearingen, Will Davis. *Moroccan Mirages: Agrarian Dreams and Deceptions, 1912–1986.* Princeton, NJ: Princeton University Press, 1987.

Szajkowski, Zosa. *Analytical Franco-Jewish Gazetteer*. New York: Ktav, 1966.

————. *Jews and the French Foreign Legion*. New York: Ktav, 1975.

Tartakower, Ariel, and Kurt R. Grossman. *The Jewish Refugee*. New York: Institute of Jewish Affairs of the American Jewish Congress and World Jewish Congress, 1994.

Thénault, Sylvie. *Violence ordinaire dans l'Algérie colonial: camps, internements, asignations à residence*. Paris: Odile Jacob, 2012.

Thomas, Martin. "The Anglo-French Divorce over West Africa and the Limitations of Strategic Planning, June–December 1940." *Diplomacy and Statecraft* 6.1 (1995): 252–78.

Traverso, Enzo. *Les nouveaux visages du fascisme: conversation avec Régis Meyran*. Paris: Éditions Textuel, 2017.

————. *The Origins of Nazi Violence*. New York: New Press, 2003.

Trenner, Maximilien. "La croix gammée s'aventure en Tunisie." In *Tunisie sous le joug nazi (9 novembre 1942–8 mai 1943)*, ed. C. Nataf, 225–330. Paris: Le Manuscrit, 2012.

The United States Holocaust Memorial Museum Encyclopedia of Camps and Ghettos, 1933–1945, Vol. 3, *Camps and Ghettos Under European Regimes Aligned With Nazi Germany*, gen. ed. Geoffrey Megargee. Bloomington: Indiana University Press, 2018.

Urban, Yerri. *L'indigène dans le droit colonial français, 1865–1955*. Paris: LGDJ, 2010.

Vallat, Xavier. *Le nez de Cléopâtre: souvenirs d'un homme de droite, 1919–1944*. Paris: Éditions "Les Quatre Fils Aymon," 1957.

Viard, René. *L'empire et nos destins*. Paris: Sorlot, 1942.

Vincent, Isabel. *Hitler's Silent Partners: Swiss Banks, Nazi Gold, and the Pursuit of Justice*. New York: William Morrow, 1997.

Wagenhofer, Sophie. "Contested Narratives: Contemporary Debates on Mohammed V and the Moroccan Jews Under the Vichy Regime." *Quest: Issues in Contemporary Jewish History* 4 (November 2012). www.quest-cdecjournal.it/focus.php?id=318 (accessed March 20, 2018).

Walston, James. "History and Memory of the Italian Concentration Camps." *Historical Journal* 40.1 (1997): 169–83.

Weber, Elisabeth. "Catastrophes: Afterlives of the Exceptionality Paradigm in Holocaust Studies." In *Probing the Ethics of Holocaust Culture*, ed. Claudio Fogu, Wolf Kansteiner, and Todd Presner, 389–410. Cambridge, MA: Harvard University Press, 2016.

Weil, Patrick. *How to Be French: Nationality in the Making Since 1789*. Durham, NC: Duke University Press, 2008.

Wharton, Edith. *In Morocco*. New York: Charles Scribner's Sons, 1920.

White, Hayden. *Figural Realism: Study in the Mimesis Effect*. Baltimore: Johns Hopkins University Press, 1999.

————. "Historical Truth, Estrangement, and Disbelief." In *Probing the Ethics of Holocaust*

Culture, ed. Claudio Fogu, Wolf Kansteiner, and Todd Presner, 53–71. Cambridge, MA: Harvard University Press, 2016.

———. *The Practical Past*. Evanston, IL: Northwestern University Press, 2014.

———. *Tropics of Discourse: Essays in Cultural Criticism*. Baltimore: Johns Hopkins University Press, 1985.

Wien, Peter. "Coming to Terms with the Past: German Academia and Historical Relations Between the Arab Lands and Nazi Germany." *International Journal of Middle Eastern Studies* 42.2 (2010): 311–21.

Wildvang, Frauke. *Der Feind von nebenan: Judenverfolgung im faschistischen Italien, 1936–1944*. Cologne: Böhlau Köln, 2008.

Wohl, Robert. *French Communism in the Making, 1914–1924*. Stanford, CA: Stanford University Press, 1966.

Wriggins, Howard. *Picking Up the Pieces from Portugal to Palestine: Quaker Refugee Relief in World War II—A Memoir*. Lanham, MD: University Press of America, 2004.

Wyrtzen, Jonathan. *Making Morocco: Colonial Intervention and the Politics of Identity*. Ithaca: Cornell University Press, 2015.

Yablonka, Hanna. *Harhek meha-mesila: ha-mizrahim veha'shoah*. Tel Aviv: Miskal-Yedioth Ahronoth Books, 2008.

———. *Les juifs d'Orient, Israël et la Shoah*. Paris: Calmann-Lévy, 2016.

———. *The State of Israel vs. Adolf Eichmann*, trans. Ora Cummings. New York: Schocken, 2004.

———. *Survivors of the Holocaust: Israel After the War*, trans. Ora Cummings. New York: New York University Press, 1999.

Yahil, Leni. *The Holocaust: The Fate of European Jewry*. Oxford, UK: Oxford University Press, 1990.

Young, James. "Interpreting Literary Testimony: A Preface to Rereading Holocaust Diaries and Memoirs." *New Literary History* 18.2 (1987): 403–23.

———. *Writing and Rewriting the Holocaust: Narrative and the Consequences of Interpretation*. Bloomington: Indiana University Press, 1988.

Zahra, Tara. " 'Prisoners of the Postwar': Expellees, Displaced Persons, and Jews in Austria After World War II." *Austrian History Yearbook* 41 (2010): 191–215.

Zerubavel, Yael. *Recovered Roots: Collective Memory and the Making of Israeli National Tradition*. Chicago: University of Chicago Press, 1995.

Zimmerer, Jürgen. "Colonialism and the Holocaust: Towards an Archaeology of Genocide." In *Genocide and Settler Society: Frontier Violence and Stolen Indigenous Children in Australian History*, ed. Dirk Moses, trans. Andrew H. Beattie, 49–76. New York: Berghahn, 2004.

———. *Von Windhuk nach Auschwitz: Beiträge zum Verhältnis von Kolonialismus und Holocaust*. Münster: Lit, 2011.

Zimmerer, Jürgen, and Joachim Zeller. *Genocide in German South-West Africa: The Colonial Ward of 1904–1908 and Its Aftermath*, trans. E. J. Neather. Pontypool, Wales: Merlin Press, 2010.

Zumbansen, Peer. *Zwangsarbeit im Dritten Reich: Erinnerung und Verantwortung—Juristische und zeithistorische Betrachtungen.* Baden-Baden: Nomos Verlagsgesellschaft, 2002.

Zytnicki, Colette. "La politique antisémite du régime de Vichy dans les colonies." In *L'empire colonial sous Vichy,* ed. Jacques Cantier and Eric Jennings, 153–76. Paris: Odile Jacob, 2004.

Index

CPSIA information can be obtained
at www.ICGtesting.com
Printed in the USA
JSHW081245190723
45043JS00002B/322

9 781503 607057